Research Methods in Education:
an introduction

The Lippincott Series in
Psychology and Research in Education
under the editorship of
Dr. Richard E. Ripple   *Cornell University*

Research Methods
an introduction

William Wiersma

University of Toledo

in Education

J. B. LIPPINCOTT COMPANY

Philadelphia / New York

To Joan and Susan and Lisa

Preface

This book is primarily designed for an introductory course in research methodology for students in education. The main purpose of such a course is to provide instruction in basic research techniques so that the student can begin the pursuit of independent research associated with the graduate program. In order to meet this purpose it is important that the student attain some technical and methodological competence through which he can pursue his research ideas. This text, along with conscientious study, should enable the student to rise above the stage of ideas and pursue his research in a meaningful and correct manner.

This book was fundamentally prepared as a text for an introductory course. However, it can be used independently as a reference. Students should find it helpful as a supplement to courses that emphasize research studies. Teachers and administrators should find it helpful in pursuing their own research and in attaining an understanding of educational research reports. Since considerable emphasis is placed upon the underlying reasoning of methodology, the book can be used as a supplement by graduate students, either independently or in connection with more advanced courses. Finally, it could be used in an inter-disciplinary context. Since education includes content from many disciplines, students in other areas, especially the behavioral sciences, should find the text beneficial.

Although this is an introductory text, it is not simplistic and was not meant to be. Research procedures are too precise and complex to be superficially dismissed as "easy." Educational research is a demanding activity, requiring interest, concentrated study, and attention to details. Research will involve frustrations and disappointments. However, the student should be willing to put forth the personal effort necessary to attain the goal of a well-done research study. The mastery of research methodology is an essential part of attaining this goal.

The procedures discussed in this text have wide applications. Procedures are illustrated with examples. The ideas presented are general enough so that they apply to many specific research problems. Although formulas occasionally appear, especially in the chapters on hypothesis testing, this is not a statistics text. Computation, when it appears, is included only for the purpose of illustration and enhancing understanding. For this purpose, a minimum of mathematical background is necessary. A course in elementary high school algebra should suffice. The student of educational research needs to be cognizant of the existence, reasoning, and significance of statistical procedures. This text provides such background but does not attempt to develop computational proficiency in the use of such procedures.

The orientation of the text is toward the quantitative procedures of dealing with the data involved in a research study. The content of the text is organized into ten chapters. Three of the early chapters deal with the underlying reasoning and procedures of hypothesis testing. These chapters, along with the introductory chapters and a chapter on the role of measurement in educational research, provide the necessary specifics of methodology. This background is followed by two chapters, one dealing with experimental designs and the other with non-experimental research. These two chapters provide a broader approach to a research study. The final two chapters deal with doing a research study and reading and writing about research.

The content of the text follows basically a sequential development. Ideas developed and discussed in early chapters are often included in later chapters. However, all users of the text need not consider the entire content in sequence. For example, an individual who has a background in hypothesis testing and is interested in experimental design could consider Chapter 7. If an overview of the research endeavor is desired before dealing with more specifics, Chapter 9 can be considered prior to earlier chapters. An individual interested in reading research and what to look for in a report can consider the early portion of Chapter 10. This final chapter also contains a discussion of preparing a research proposal which in itself could prove helpful to an individual anticipating this activity. Thus, parts of the text independently could prove useful for specific purposes.

The content of the text is not intended to be a treatment of advanced, specialized topics. Educational research procedures are extensive and sometimes complex. Excellent textbooks on advanced, specialized topics are available and occasional references to such texts are made throughout this book. This is an introductory text and should be viewed in this light. The reader who masters the ideas of this text should be well on his way to competency in the methods of educational research.

December 6, 1968   WILLIAM WIERSMA

Contents

3   Testing Hypotheses by Parametric Techniques   69

4   Testing Hypotheses by Nonparametric Techniques   110

7 Experimental Design 221

8 Non-Experimental Research 257

9   Organizing and Doing a Research Project   301

10   Reading and Writing About Research   322

Research Methods in Education:
an introduction

1 *Introduction*

Overview

The word "research" has very wide and varied meanings in our
contemporary culture. Although an attempt at a common definition may be futile, there seems to be some kind of positive value
judgment associated with the word. The sophisticated scholars
of the various disciplines engage in research. Some are found
meditating in secluded rooms; others in laboratories with equipment of various degrees of elaboration; others in the ruins of
ancient cities or on the streets of modern cities, to mention just
a few of the possible research settings. We know that large industrial concerns pour vast sums of money into research activities and great advances in all fields are attributed to research.

The beginning graduate student hardly identifies with any of these situations. He does not have the experience or knowledge of the sophisticated scholar. His financial resources are usually very limited so that he cannot entertain the approach of industry. Yet he realizes that to successfully pursue his degree he is required to produce some original research. The realization that research is necessary and repeatedly hearing the term does not provide the student with much knowledge or direction as to what he can do about it.

The plight of the average elementary or high school teacher, guidance counselor, or administrator is not much better than that of the beginning graduate student, when it comes to matters of research. In fact, a considerable proportion of the graduate student population is often made up of school personnel pursuing a graduate program on a part-time basis. A professional educator may not be called upon to produce an original piece of research, but to ignore research entirely is to do both himself and the profession an injustice. There is a great deal of change, innovation, and experimentation occurring in education today, some of it prompted and supported by federal programs but much of it initiated from within the profession itself. It is necessary for the professional educator to know and understand the research related to his area. This is essential before he can participate in a meaningful way in educational innovation and change. Much of the educational research is reported in such a way that a knowledge of methodology is invaluable. In fact, such knowledge may be essential for a meaningful implementation of research results.

The physical and behavioral sciences have long placed a premium upon research. We hear statements to the effect that the behavioral sciences are becoming more "scientific" and developing better research procedures. The graduate schools of our nation's universities attach a marked premium on the ability to carry out "original" research. Consequently, it becomes apparent to the student that knowledge of research methods will be an essential tool of his academic repertoire.

Educational research is a complex and demanding endeavor interested in understanding and improving that discipline. Many of its activities come under the general heading of research methods. These methods range from relatively simple, single procedures to complex combinations of procedures. We sometimes talk about qualitative and quantitative methods. The overview of an entire research project from the initial identification of the research problem to the completed report may reveal an extensive effort involving considerable study and activity, along with numerous interrelated procedures. Educational research is a demanding but not impossible task. There are often frustrations and errors along the way but with organized and concentrated study the aspiring educational researcher should be able to master the research methods.

Basically the only way to acquire competence in research is by doing. But before this can be accomplished, some skills must be acquired. The matter of knowing what to do in specific situations is important. How is a research problem started? What procedures apply so that the solution to a problem can be specifically pursued? How are the data to be collected and interpreted? How is a satisfactory and lucid report produced? When viewed in the context of a specific research project, these are all matters that have certain skills connected with them.

How is the individual to acquire such skills? One approach which is becoming increasingly popular at universities is to develop courses which help the student master research skills. In fact, some institutions have developed entire programs in this area. Closely related to courses are books which also serve as aids to the individual. Courses and books vary greatly in their levels of sophistication: some are abstract and theoretical while others place a great deal of emphasis on application. The approach of this text is more of the latter, although some of the underlying ideas may seem more abstract when initially presented. This is done in the interest of enhancing understanding.

A misconception sometimes develops in connection with the term "typical research project." There is no typical research project since each project has its own unique problems and conditions. Since research is a personal matter, every researcher develops unique characteristics. There may be considerable similarity between specific projects but doing a research project is not like baking a cake from a recipe. This text discusses basic concepts of research methods but the potential researcher must project these concepts into his own unique situation.

We should always aim for a respectable, competent product.

However, it is extremely unlikely that there has ever been a perfect study. The researcher should not become discouraged when the result is less than perfect. No finished project will be totally immune from criticism. There are many pitfalls, and errors are likely to occur. Criticism should be offered and accepted in a strictly constructive sense for the purpose of improving that particular project or future projects. The graduate student—or any researcher, regardless of the degree of sophistication—should seek the criticism of his professors and peers and be willing to accept their suggestions.

What Is Educational Research?

We talk about a work of research as if research is a noun or we may consider research as a verb. In addition to this, research may take on various broad and restricted meanings. In order to more succinctly develop our concept of research let us consider statements from two contemporary authors. Mouly describes the nature of research as:

> . . . simply the process of arriving at dependable solutions to problems through the planned and systematic collection, analysis and interpretation of data . . . we can define educational research as the systematic and scholarly application of the scientific method; interpreted in its broadest sense, to the solution of educational problems.[1]

Note that in the above description of research we have the idea of a systematic approach applied through the scientific method. This idea of a systematic approach is essential. Educational research, as indicated above, involves the solution of educational problems. This includes both practical and theoretical problems.

A definition of scientific research is presented by Kerlinger as:

> . . . systematic, controlled, empirical and critical investigation of hypothetical propositions about the presumed relations among natural phenomena.[2]

[1] Mouly, G. J., *The Science of Educational Research* (New York: American Book Company, 1963), p. 4.

[2] Kerlinger, F. M., *Foundations of Behavioral Research* (New York: Holt, Rinehart and Winston, Inc., 1964), p. 13.

Again we encounter the idea of a systematic approach. This, along with the idea of control, characterizes scientific research as ordered and disciplined so that the researcher can have confidence in the outcome of his endeavors. The characteristic of being empirical essentially means that in scientific research the conjectures of the researcher are put to an objective test and the outcomes are subjected to the critical scrutiny of himself and others.

With these relatively broad concepts of research considered in the context of educational research, we see the emphasis on a systematic approach, in essence a scientific approach, to the study of problems and phenomena related to education. Thus, we can consider "scientific" as an adjective summarizing those characteristics which essentially makes the method of inquiry more systematic. The scientific method is a general set of procedures or steps through which we develop the systematic approach. The scientific method is usually broken down into a series of steps beginning with the encounter of some problem to a final step of drawing conclusions and integrating them into the existing body of knowledge. The terminology for the various steps of the scientific method varies somewhat from writer to writer, as do the numbers of steps. The scientific method is a general formulation of steps and should not be viewed as a single correct method (e.g., experimentation, historical) for attacking all problems. At this point let us consider each step of the scientific method in greater detail.

The initial step of the scientific method, that of observing some phenomena, represents an insight into some experience. This insight may manifest itself as a problem or obstacle or some unexplained situation. The need to resolve the problem or situation is felt, and the individual prepares to do something about the need or difficulty.

The second step is to more precisely identify the problem. This step involves the formulation of tentative hypotheses, based on the observed phenomena. The factors involved with the problem are more closely identified, and their relationships are clarified. Observations related to the problem are made.

The third step of the scientific method is to develop and apply a design for the solution of the problem. Theories or hypotheses may be used as tentative explanations of the facts being observed. Hypotheses are tested and either retained, modified, or discarded.

The next step usually identified is a continuation of the previous step, the continued testing and refinement of theories and hypotheses. Results from initial tests are subjected to further analyses and tests.

The final step is that of drawing conclusions based on data and tests and integrating these conclusions with the existing body of knowledge. In connection with the observed facts and the procedures conducted earlier, the individual arrives at what is to him the most reliable solution to the problem or explanation of the situation.

The method by which the steps of the scientific method are presented, that is, the one, two, . . . , etc. fashion, may give the impression that the steps will necessarily follow a definite order and time sequence. This may, in fact, be true, but the use of the scientific method is not rigid and the researcher rarely follows the pattern in such an orderly fashion. The steps are not isolated. The researcher may be involved with two or more steps simultaneously, he may take them out of order, or he may fluctuate back and forth among the steps. The steps are not an end in themselves but a means to an end, namely the systematic solution of a research problem.

The use of the scientific method rests upon certain fundamental assumptions. Van Dalen [1] has identified these assumptions as the uniformity of nature and those dealing with the psychological process. With these assumptions are six postulates, that is, basic principles that are assumed to be true without proof.

The assumption of the uniformity of nature is exactly what the name implies, that what has been found to be true will continue to be true; that similarity of circumstances will produce consistently similar results; in essence, that nature is orderly. The postulates related to this assumption are those of natural kinds, constancy and determinism. The postulate of natural kinds is the principle that natural phenomena can be classified according to common characteristics. We can classify objects

[1] Van Dalen, D. B., *Understanding Educational Research* (New York: Mc-Graw-Hill Book Co., 1966), pp. 34–40.

according to physical characteristics such as shape or color. We may classify student behavior or performance. There are countless taxonomies and classification schemes in continuous use in education. The grading system employed in most schools is a classification system of student performance. By using classification schemes the researcher attempts to increase and organize his knowledge.

The postulate of constancy assumes that nature has a certain amount of consistency. Certainly all phenomena do not have the same amount of consistency, but related to specific phenomena relatively constant conditions exist and these can be discovered. We are quite aware of many physical changes that take place and we can predict such changes with relative certainty. A rate of change may be one of the factors that is quite stable or constant. The performances of students given certain conditions are expected to be quite the same as before, given the same conditions.

The postulate of determinism assumes that within the orderliness of nature, the occurrence of a phenomenon is preceded by certain antecedent events or phenomena. Events are not random or accidental occurrences. If a student has a severely hostile attitude toward school, we assume that this is the result of antecedent factors or events.

The assumption dealing with the psychological process is basically that the researcher can acquire knowledge through the processes of perceiving, remembering, and reasoning. The three postulates, one related to each of these psychological processes, are very similar, namely the postulates of reliability for each (e.g., the postulate of reliability of perceiving). In each case we do not assume absolute reliability; we are all aware of the fact that errors can occur in connection with perception, remembering, and reasoning. Despite the possibility of error, the researcher assumes that these psychological processes can aid him in acquiring knowledge and securing solutions to his problems.

Thus far in our discussion of educational research the emphasis has been primarily directed toward the systematic approach as exemplified by the scientific method. In essence, this discussion assumes that educational research does involve a scientific approach if, in fact, it is to be considered a legitimate part of the research endeavor. As such, the general goals of educational research coincide with those of all scientific research, namely explanation, prediction, understanding, and control. In order to enhance the understanding of what we mean by educational research, we often classify specific educational research endeavors on the basis of the goals to be attained. In order to do this we use alternate classifying schemes, not necessarily that of the goals specified above. A discussion of two such arbitrary classification schemes now follows.

We have heard the terms "basic" and "applied" research as well as the misconceptions that may develop with their use. One such misconception is that basic research is complex and applied research is simple in its methodology. Related to this is the misconception that applied research is carried on by an unsophisticated practitioner and basic research is performed by an abstract but impractical thinker. Another misconception is that applied research is often sloppy and haphazard but of great practical value, while basic research is precise and exacting but of little or no value in a real situation. Basic and applied research are not differentiated by complexity or value but by their goal orientation, that is, the goals which they pursue. The aim of applied research is to solve an immediate, practical problem. It is oriented to a specific problem. Basic research has a more general orientation — addition to the existing body of knowledge in the discipline. Basic research does not necessarily provide results of immediate, practical use, although such a possibility is not ruled out. If this does occur, it is supplemental and not the result of the primary goal. It should also be noted that applied research in its solution of a specific problem may contribute to the general knowledge of the field. Both basic and applied research are important and should not be differentiated by a hierarchy of value judgments.

An example of basic research would be to conduct experiments concerning learning in a laboratory setting. The purpose of such an experiment would be to contribute to the knowledge about how learning takes place. The experiment might be focused on one or a very limited number of factors associated with learning such as the difference between presenting the learning materials in a figural or verbal manner.

Suppose a biology department proposes that a team-teaching

approach would be more challenging and effectual than individual teachers. The members of the department then set about to conduct a research study which will help them decide between the feasibility and effectiveness of the two approaches in their specific situation. This is an example of applied research.

The distinction between basic and applied research may not be an extremely useful one, primarily because of the considerable overlap between the two. The major purpose of introducing the terms at this point is to clear up any misconceptions the reader may have concerning this terminology.

Another method of classifying research which may be more definitive than simply basic or applied is a three-category system: problem-solving, theory-developing and theory-testing.[1] Again, this method of classifying research is based on the goal orientation of the research and often there is an overlap between these major goals. Nevertheless, most educational research projects can be viewed in terms of the major goal orientation. There is no hierarchy of value judgments, either a priori or empirically based, that label one type of research superior to the others. Educational research involves all three types, and the types not only have some overlap but often support each other.

Problem-solving research is directed toward an applied goal, usually the solution of a specific problem. It is not performed for the purpose of developing or testing theories, although the actual problem may be more or less related to some theoretical constructs. Research associated with the instructional programs of specific schools is often of this type. For example, suppose the teachers in a school are concerned about whether to use additional group work involving overhead projection or an individual programmed text as a supplement to the regular textbook and classroom instruction for teaching elementary science. The teachers are concerned about the relative effectiveness of the two methods in their particular situation. They want to make a decision that they can apply. They have little concern, if any, for theory-development and -testing.

[1] Scott, W. A., and Wertheimer, M., *Introduction to Psychological Research* (New York: John Wiley and Sons, Inc., 1962), pp. 4–8.

Theory-developing research is oriented toward clarifying a tentative guess. As such, theory-developing research is exploratory in nature. The research is conducted in order to formulate the theory and to further refine it. Very basic aspects of the theory may be under consideration; for example, not only the type of effect a certain stimulus may have but whether or not it has an effect at all. Suppose an educational psychologist has an idea that the frequency of encountering instructional materials (e.g., word lists, mathematics problem solutions) has an effect upon the retention of the concepts involved with the materials. Note that he conjectures some effect, not that increased use would either decrease or increase retention. The theory to be developed relative to this idea may be part of a larger theory of learning. Nevertheless, the educational psychologist is developing theory at this point, he is not formally testing any part of the theory.

The greatest amount of overlap is between theory-developing and theory-testing research. Theory-testing research in essence requires some formulation of the theory, usually through hypotheses which can be either supported or discounted. The support (or lack thereof) of initial hypotheses may lead to additional theory-developing which, if necessary, would include revision. In theory-testing research, the researcher may be making a decision among several alternative hypotheses.

Suppose that in our educational psychology example the researcher had formulated the hypothesis that increased use enhances retention. Along with this idea, there might be formulated several conditions relating to factors such as complexity of the materials and level at which continued use would no longer affect retention. (Actually there would likely be hypothesized some relationships among factors as well.) Theory-testing research would enable the researcher to test his theory with its major and related hypotheses. Presumably his research would either confirm or refute his theory.

Role of Theory

Thus far we have discussed theory-developing and theory-testing research but little has been said about the meaning of a theory and the role that theory has in educational research. Kerlinger has defined theory as:

> . . . a set of interrelated constructs (concepts), definitions, and propositions that presents a systematic view of phenomena by specifying relations among variables, with the purpose of explaining and predicting the phenomena.[1]

Brodbeck[2] includes many of the same ideas in her discussion of theory, adding that a theory is a deductively connected set of laws and that all statements in a theory both explained and explaining, are generalizations; the laws doing the explaining being the axioms and those explained the theorems.

A *theory*, then, is a generalization or series of generalizations by which we attempt to explain some phenomena in a systematic manner. Theories can range from a single, simple generalization to a complex formulation of laws. The definition of theory also allows for flexibility in the stage of development or formulation. Most theories in education require a process of refinement through revision and extension.

We have already mentioned the goal orientation of theory-developing and theory-testing research, but what of the role and purpose of theory in research? Basically, theory helps to provide a framework for research by serving as the point of departure for the pursuit of a research problem. The theory identifies the crucial factors. It provides a guide for systematizing and interrelating the various facets of the research. However, it not only provides the systematic view of the factors under study but may very well identify gaps, weak points, and inconsistencies which then alert the researcher to the need for additional research. Also, the development of the theory may well light the way for continued research of the phenomena under study. Thus, it serves as a tool of science in the research context. Let us consider the functions that a theory can serve in educational research.

---

[1] Kerlinger, F. N., *Foundations of Behavioral Research* (New York: Holt, Rinehart and Winston, Inc., 1964), p. 11.

[2] Brodbeck, M., "Logic and Scientific Method in Research on Teaching," in Gage, ed., *Handbook of Research on Teaching* (Chicago: Rand McNally & Company, 1963), p. 68.

Theory serves a synthesizing function in educational research, synthesizing ideas and individual bits of empirical information into a set of constructs which, when combined, provide for deeper understanding, broader meaning, and wider applicability.* In a sense, a theory attaches meaning to facts and places them in proper perspective. Through this process the theory aids in defining the research problem. That is, it serves as an aid in identifying the proper questions to be asked in the context of the specific research project.

As indicated in the above definition, a theory also serves the purposes of explaining and predicting. It provides an explanation of observed phenomena. A theory may also predict as yet unobserved or undiscovered factors by indicating their presence if the theory is consistent. The researcher is then "tipped off" in terms of what to look for.

Theories provide the researcher with one or more generalizations that he can test and either refute or retain. These generalizations can then be used through application and further research. This development of generalizations is based on the assumption that generalizations do exist in education or any area under study, and that individual observations are special cases of such generalizations.

The various conditions of a research project and the bits of information collected in conducting research must be incorporated into a meaningful, interrelated set of constructs. The interrelationship of theory and research is well summarized by Mouly:

> Research and theory go hand in hand: theory guides and stimulates research while research tests and stimulates theory development, resulting in more adequate theories and better and clearer facts. . . . Facts derive their significance from the theoretical framework into which they fit, just as theories derive their acceptability from the extent to which they bring facts into clearer focus.[1]

We note that the purposes and functions of theory are certainly not independent of the goals of scientific research. The cri-

[1] Mouly, G. J., *The Science of Educational Research* (New York: American Book Company, 1963), p. 52.

terion by which we judge a theory is not by its truth or falsity, but rather by its usefulness. Theories sometimes decrease in usefulness in the light of new knowledge. Theories are combined, replaced and refined as more knowledge is made available.

Let us briefly consider some of the characteristics of what we might call a "good" theory. When theories are developed they must be developed in such a way that the generalizations can be tested. When observations are made relative to the theory, the theory must be compatible with the observations and already existing knowledge. The theory must adequately explain the events or phenomena under study. The greater the generalizability of the theory, the more useful it will be because of its wider applicability.

Another characteristic of a good theory is reflected in the *law of parsimony*. This means that theories should be stated in the simplest form, but one that adequately explains the phenomena. This does not mean that all theories are simple statements; they should be stated succinctly and precisely, avoiding ambiguities and confusing complexity. Important factors must not be overlooked and the comprehensiveness of the theory must be adequate for its purpose.

Definition and Operational Definition

As we have discussed the meaning of educational research, we have thus far related it to scientific research and theory and have discussed classifying educational research relative to goal orientation. Another matter of considerable importance in educational research is that of definition. We know that words mean different things to different people, and the problem of ambiguity, confusing semantics, and misinterpretation are very real and must be considered.

The research problems, hypotheses, and related theories are stated in words and sentences. The words and sentences convey meanings and concepts, but semanticists point out that the definition of words is not in the words but in ourselves.[1] We put meaning into words by the use we make of them. (It does not take extensive reading or conversation to realize that educational research, for example, means different things to different people.) Yet, when we are dealing with specific research projects, it is important that we maintain adequate definition, that the words and sentences mean to our audience what we intended them to mean.

We usually ascribe to the researcher the right of definition within the context of existing use and knowledge. What this means is that the researcher can assign to the words his intended meaning. The right of definition also carries with it the responsibility of adequately communicating this meaning to the audience. Every area of study contains a great many defined terms. However, the definitions of all objects, concepts, etc. are not equally easy or difficult. It may be relatively easy to transmit what is meant by the color yellow to a group of individuals who can be shown visual examples of physical objects that have as one of their characteristics the color yellow. It may be considerably more difficult to transmit a meaning of anxiety. This is a characteristic that an organism might take on under certain conditions and is manifest more by behavior than physical characteristics.

Some things in the natural world are essentially defined for us through repeated use and common experience. Many objects from direct experience need no definition because the mere association with the name transmits a precise meaning. Other objects and concepts need qualifying terms. A physical object can be defined by providing its observable characteristics. Suppose a science student is asked to define a rattlesnake. Observable characteristics, such as rattles and their position on the tail, color patterns of the skin, etc. can be listed until the individual has adequate information to recognize an instance of a rattlesnake.

All objects that require definition do not possess observable characteristics that can be identified and listed. What about abstract concepts such as cognition? We can say that cognition

[1] Hayakawa, S. I., *Language in Thought and Action* (New York: Harcourt, Brace and World, Inc., 1949), p. 292.

is a process that involves immediate discovery, awareness, rediscovery, or recognition of information that has been discriminated.[1] We could provide synonyms for cognition. What we are doing in attempting to secure a definition is replacing certain words with other words. In our definition of cognition, what does immediate discovery, awareness, etc. mean? When do we stop the word replacement process? It stops when there is no longer any ambiguity about the referents of the original term being defined. This essentially sets up a chain of definition. The more abstract the concept being defined, the longer is the chain of definition before it terminates.

How do we know when we have an adequate definition? Brodbeck summarizes the conditions for an adequate definition:

> An adequate definition permits us always to tell when a sentence containing the defined term is true and when it is false. An adequately defined concept is also called "reliable." If a concept is reliable, then different people or the same person at different times always agree about whether or not there is an instance of the concept.[2]

The educational researcher often deals with objects that do not readily manifest themselves. If we are interested in the weights of the pupils in a first-grade class, we can measure these using a common weight scale. But what if we wanted to measure ability to learn or reading comprehension? If we are going to measure and quantify these variables, we must have something to do it with. Perhaps we could set up the chain of definition for ability to learn and meet the criterion of an adequate definition. But in order to achieve empirical measurement we need something more in the definition. We must include in the definition the processes or operations that are going to be used to measure or quantify the objects under study. Such a definition is called an *operational definition*. In the example dealing with ability to learn we might "measure" this as the pupil's score on an I.Q. inventory, specifically the score attained on the LM Form of the Stanford Binet. The use of an operational definition not only

[1] Klausmeier, H. J., and Goodwin, W., *Learning and Human Abilities*, 2nd ed. (New York: Harper and Row, Publishers, 1966), p. 39.

[2] Brodbeck, M., "Logic and Scientific Method in Research on Teaching," in Gage, ed., *Handbook of Research on Teaching* (Chicago: Rand McNally & Company, 1963), p. 48.

indicates the means used to measure the objects under study, but by adequately describing the operations used in measurement the researcher enhances clarity.

Selection of a Research Topic

The selection of an appropriate research topic is in part a matter of asking good questions. Our discussion of the research process thus far has dealt primarily with how good answers, that is, solutions to research problems, are secured. But educational research also involves initially asking good questions as well. Without a workable research topic, the most carefully designed procedures for securing answers are to no avail.

There is no standardized set of procedures that can be prescribed for selecting a research topic. However, certain factors can be considered which will aid in the selection of a topic.

The research topic should be of interest, not only to the individual researcher, but to at least some recognized segment of the educational community. The topic should have a place in the educational context. The matter of originality should be considered, especially if the research topic is being selected for a thesis. However, a completely original research idea is rare. It depends upon the specific area of research as to what comprises undesirable duplication and what can be tolerated in terms of replication of previous research studies.

Closely related to the matter of interest is the question of the significance of the topic. What significance does the research topic have for education, either from a practical or theoretical viewpoint? Trivial problems can and do appear. For example, the proportions of elementary students wearing low-cut and high-cut shoes and the relationship of this to achievement is a problem that could be procedurally researched. But such a problem has no theoretical framework and no significance, regardless of what the resulting proportions happen to be. The research problem should add to the existing knowledge or contribute to education in a meaningful way.

Not all problems in education are researchable. Some topics are philosophical in nature and can be discussed but not researched. For example, should the required English courses in the first year of college include one semester of English literature? Without any additional conditions, this question can only be discussed.

Some problems may be researchable but doing the research is not feasible. The necessary data for the study may be excessive or too difficult to obtain. Ethical considerations may be involved. For example, it is not feasible to require a selected group of nine-year-olds to stay home for one year to determine the effects of fourth-grade instruction.

Research topics are not selected in a vacuum of information and experience. The aspiring researcher should familiarize himself with the area in which he plans to do research. He should know the relevant theories and his research question should be framed in the context of such theories. We do put a premium on original and creative thinking, but the possibility of such thinking is very remote if the individual has no knowledge with which to work.

A study of the related research and a familiarization with practical and/or theoretical problems in the area will aid the researcher in formulating appropriate questions in connection with his research topic. Suppose an individual is interested in doing research related to learning and specifically to transfer. Let us say that the identical elements theory of transfer is the basis for considering transfer. This theory assumes that elements present in the original learning are also present in the new learning. But what actually comprises identical elements? Suppose it was desirable to test the theory relative to a unique learning task and the visual stimuli involved in that task. Would an identical element of color be adequate for transfer? Would shapes or sizes by themselves be adequate? Are some combinations of the possible elements conducive to transfer? What implications would the results have for a practical learning situation? How could the results be used for testing the theory in a practical learning situation? In terms of these visual stimuli, what would it mean to confirm the theory? To refute the theory? These are examples of questions related to the theory and the specific area of research. In any research study it is not adequate to simply accumulate empirical results. The theory, questions, and research problem provide meaning for the empirical results.

Statement of the Research Problem

Let us consider some general characteristics and specific examples of the statement of the research problem. The statement of the research problem should be well defined and specific. If the problem is vague or too broad it is difficult to pin down. Considerable difficulty will result in applying the research procedures since it is unclear as to what is actually under investigation. The tendency may be for the beginning researcher to state his problems too broadly at the outset. This is not undesirable *if* the problem is systematically restricted through the review of the literature and initial stages of organizing the project. It is better to work in this direction than to start with a problem that is too narrow and then attach pieces to it in order to expand the problem.

There is an extensive discussion of the identification of a problem in a later chapter. However, at this point it is well to illustrate some unsatisfactory and satisfactory statements of research problems. A problem stated as "the elementary curriculum" is far too broad. A more satisfactory statement would be: The effects of elementary curriculum practices upon the reading achievement of fourth-grade students of City A. Following are several examples of original statements and their subsequent restatement into a more manageable statement of the problem.

Original: Creativity of elementary school students.

Restatement: A study of the relationship between divergent thinking scores and selected factors of fifth-, sixth-, and seventh-grade students.

Original: Achievement and teaching techniques.

Restatement: The effect of three teaching techniques upon science achievement of junior high school students.

Original: The elementary primary school.

Restatement: A study of the effects of the ungraded primary school organization upon the personality scores of the students.

Original: The role of the guidance counselor in the high school.

Restatement: A survey of the practices of the guidance counselors in the high schools of City B.

A good statement of the problem should provide the researcher with considerable direction in pursuing the project. The statement identifies certain key factors in the research project. For example, the word "relationship" in the first statement above implies certain procedures. The grade level limits and defines the population under study. "Divergent thinking score" is certainly more specific than "creativity," as presented in the original statement. Divergent thinking requires an operational definition. It should be noted that in the restatements of the above problems, considerable definition of terms would be necessary. Along with divergent thinking, the selected factors in the first example would require identification and any necessary definition. The three teaching techniques of the second example would require definition for the specific situation. Such definition should accompany the statement of the problem. It is usually not included in the statement because it would make the statement excessively long, cumbersome, and awkward. Assuming that adequate definition accompanies the statement of the problem, there should be no ambiguity about what is to be investigated.

The statement of the problem itself usually provides only general direction for research procedures. Hypotheses associated with the problem may provide more specific direction for research procedures by tying-in the statement of the problem to related theory or theories. Actually, the form for stating the problem is relatively unimportant. The problem may be stated, for example, in the form of hypotheses or questions. What is important is that the statement of the problem be precise and definitive enough so that there is no confusion as to what is under study.

Role of Hypotheses

A hypothesis in the context of a research project may be considered a conjecture or a tentative statement of the situation.

It can be considered a hunch or a guess of what the existing situation is truly like. In this general sense, a hypothesis takes on the characteristics of a theory. Usually we consider a theory as some larger set of generalizations about a certain phenomenon. Thus, a theory might include several hypotheses. Logically, the approach is to proceed so that a decision can be made about whether or not the hypotheses are tenable. This is called *testing the hypotheses*. The test of a hypothesis does not prove or disprove the hypothesis, it merely sustains or rejects the hypothesis.

The purpose of stating hypotheses, as well as that of theories that may be involved, is to provide a framework for the research endeavor. The hypotheses, either directly or indirectly, formulate the statement of the problem. They may also imply research procedures and necessary data. Finally, the conclusions may be stated in the context of the initial hypotheses.

A research project need not proceed from a statement of hypotheses. Such hypotheses are not ends in themselves but rather aids to the research process. Objections have been raised against stating hypotheses. One such objection is that hypotheses bias the researcher in favor of certain conclusions and hence threaten his objectivity. Closely allied to this is the objection that in his pursuit of the stated hypothesis the researcher overlooks other possibly worthwhile hypotheses. The statement of hypotheses in some situations may appear premature. A research situation might develop about which there is very little background information. Perhaps considerable theory-development is necessary. The researcher may decide to defer any hypotheses or theories until he has some empirical evidence upon which to base a hypothesis.

Nonetheless, the overall consensus is in favor of stating hypotheses *whenever they are feasible*. However, it should be emphasized that hypotheses are not stated in a vacuum. Hypotheses should not be formed on the basis of sporadic or irrelevant bits of information or data. Hypotheses should be stated on the basis of the available body of organized information and the related theory, if such a theory exists. Certainly hypotheses should relate to and reflect the research problem.

Different forms may be used for stating hypotheses. It is not necessary to develop elaborate categorizing systems for hypotheses. However, since this text does contain considerable emphasis upon hypothesis testing using inferential techniques, we introduce two forms: one which implies a direction of results and the other a nondirectional form.

Suppose we have a research situation in which we are experimenting with a new technique of teaching third-grade spelling. We hypothesize that the spelling achievement of third-grade pupils being taught with the new technique exceeds that of students being taught with traditional methods. This is a directional hypothesis since a direction of results is implied, namely that the pupils taught by the new technique will attain the greater achievement. Other examples of directional statements of hypotheses are as follows:

1. The mathematics achievement of high-ability students exceeds that of average-ability students.
2. The reading level of first-grade girls is higher than that of first-grade boys.
3. There is a positive relationship between academic aptitude scores and scores on a social adjustment inventory.
4. As a teacher's salary scale increases he has a more favorable opinion of school administrative personnel.

A second form of stating hypotheses is the nondirectional form. The statement in such a form hypothesizes no difference or no relationship. The nondirectional form is also referred to as the *"null" form* or *null hypothesis*, especially when used in a statistical context. The null hypothesis is often used when statistical procedures are employed to test the hypothesis.[1] Null hypotheses corresponding to those stated above would be as follows:

1. The mathematics achievement of high-ability students equals that of average-ability students, or, there is no difference between the mathematics achievement of average- and high-ability students.

[1] It should be noted that if the null hypothesis is used in a statistical context, specific statistics such as means would be identified. This point will be discussed in later chapters. The purpose here is to generally illustrate the directional and nondirectional forms.

2. The reading level of first-grade girls is the same as that of first-grade boys.
3. There is no relationship between academic aptitude scores and scores on a social adjustment inventory.
4. A teacher's salary scale is independent of his opinion of school administrative personnel.

A specific research problem may have several hypotheses associated with it. Hypotheses may be more specific than those stated above. When statistical procedures are anticipated, the hypotheses often refer to the specific statistics that will be involved. In the context of statistical tests of hypotheses, the definition of a hypothesis becomes more restrictive. This will be discussed later when the necessary terminology has been introduced.

The researcher should not hesitate to be specific in his statement of the hypothesis. A weakness of many hypotheses is that they are too broad to pin-point the specific problem under investigation. The elaborateness or complexity should be that which is necessary to adequately state the hypothesis. It is generally not good policy to run several hypotheses together into a single general one. They will most likely require separation during the course of the research study.

Role and Nature of Research Methodology

Perceptive observation and the identification of research problems are very important but not sufficient in the overall picture of educational research. The methods of research are the tools by which we attack the problem. Methodology consists of the systematic procedures by which we travel from the initial identification of the problem to the final conclusions. The role of the methodology is to complete the research job in a scientific, applicable, and valid manner. A host of procedures and techniques, both simple and complex, come under the methods of research.

We generally do not attempt to tighten a bolt with a hammer or drive a nail with a screwdriver. By the same token, the research methods must fit the requirements of the specific problem. The hypotheses, data gathering techniques, analyses, and interpretations must be appropriate for the specific research study. This seems like a common sense requirement and on the surface may not seem to bear pointing out, but the use of improper methods, unfortunately, does appear in educational research.

The tools in themselves will not get the job done. All the available hammers and nails placed side by side will not get the nails driven. Research procedures are of little value unless they are used, and, as indicated above, used properly. The proper use of research methods is something to be learned. Our analogy between the nail driving and educational research methods begins to break down at this point. It is enough for a passerby to realize that the nail has been driven without understanding how to drive the nail. However, the understanding of the results and conclusions of a research study is a more demanding situation. The reason why many teachers and other educators say that they have difficulty understanding the research in an area is because they do not understand the methodology behind the research. For the same reason, graduate students often encounter unnecessary difficulties when they identify problems and immediately want to inspect some data and press to conclusions without proper regard for the research methodology along the way. Thus, the mastery of the methodology will enhance the understanding of the research.

Research methodology involves data collection, measurement, review of the literature, identifying problems, formulating hypotheses, procedures for testing hypotheses, analyses, interpreting analyses, and drawing conclusions (not necessarily in that order), to mention some of the more general activities. For a specific research study the procedures within each of the more general activities should be identified. The researcher, in pursuing a study, will bring many procedures to bear. Some of the procedures may involve the specific measurement necessary to acquire the desired data. Others may involve the manipulation of the data in order to make decisions about the hypotheses. Another procedure involves the review of the literature in order to pull together the existing information about the problem under investigation. And so it goes, until the various procedures piece together the various facets of the research study and bring it to a conclusion.

At this point it may be well to summarize general activities of conducting a research study. This will appear to emphasize the sequential nature of the research process. To a certain extent this is fine, but the reader should not be left with the impression that the research process is rigid and completely structured. Activities have some overlap and certainly at times two or more activities can be in process simultaneously. There may be some fluctuation in the sequence of certain activities. For example, preliminary analysis may begin while data collection is still in process. Nevertheless, it is helpful to impose some order on the various activities and consider a sequential pattern even if such a pattern is not rigid.

Figure 1.1 presents a sequential pattern of activities in a flow chart form and should provide the reader with an overview of the research activities. These are general activities, and within each of these, more specific activities could be listed. For example, the review of related literature would be an activity aiding in the identification of the research problem. The top line of boxes in Figure 1.1 represents the general activities. (The size of the boxes in no way reflects the relative amount of effort, activities, or resources devoted to each activity.) The lower boxes with the corresponding arrows reflect the relationship between the activities and existing knowledge, related theory, etc. Related theory is considered to be a part, but not necessarily all, of the body of knowledge relative to the research problem. Expanded, revised, and new theory, if forthcoming from the research project, then becomes part of the existing body of knowledge, as does new information not considered to be theory. Obviously, all general activities draw on existing knowledge, but for the purposes of this figure we consider the major impact of the body of knowledge relative to the research problem.

The naïve researcher may at times attempt to begin the research study by breaking into the pattern at a point such as data collection. This results in working backwards (or possible seesawing) in the pattern. Sometimes hypotheses are formulated on the basis of available data or the analysis of existing data. An attempt is then made to extract a research problem from the hypotheses. Breaking the sequential pattern in this manner re-

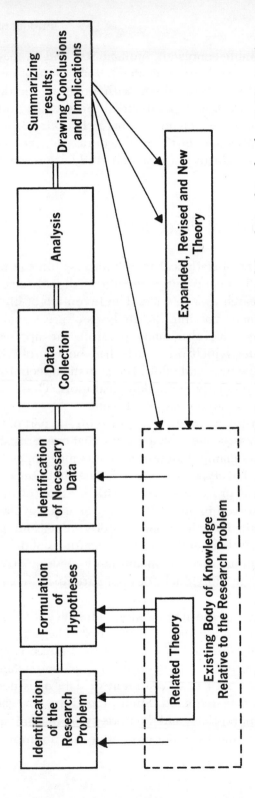

Figure 1.1 A sequential pattern of general activities in conducting a research study and the relationship of such activities to existing knowledge.

sults in considerable confusion, inefficiency, and an inadequate research study. As has been indicated before, there often is some fluctuation in the pattern, along with possible reordering of activities. However, this depends upon the specific project and where in the sequence a change is made. Breaking in at a point such as data collection is to be discouraged. The details of organizing and conducting a research study are discussed in a later chapter.

Role of Statistical Procedures

The development of statistical techniques within the past four or five decades has contributed greatly to the advancement of educational research as a science. The invention of high-speed computers has made possible the analyses of great quantities of data. Computers have also made possible the application of certain techniques which previously had been prohibitive because of excessive time and effort. But statistical techniques and computers are again only methodological tools. They should be applied when they can do the job at hand.

There is often considerable reluctance on the part of students and educators to associate with anything that concerns statistics. Formulas and the manipulation of numbers may appear difficult and foreboding. This type of an attitude does both the educators and the statistical procedures an injustice. Some of the actual computation involved in an analysis may be extensive and complex. However, the basic ideas and underlying reasoning should be mastered by students and educators regardless of the teaching level. It is essential for the meaningful reading of research articles, even if the individual does not participate in a research study.

The basic ideas of the methodology of educational research are discussed in the remainder of this text. The early chapters may seem heavily directed toward statistical ideas. However, a statistical background is not essential for an understanding of these basic ideas. Statistical treatment of data does not necessarily make the research good. Such procedures are good only when they are appropriate, and the underlying reasoning of their application determines whether or not they are appropriate. The reader should pay particular attention to the underlying reasoning. Formulas are introduced only for illustration. It is not necessary that the reader memorize any formulas or perform any computation.

The chapters on hypothesis testing are directed to the underlying reasoning and application of techniques on which to base a decision concerning the hypotheses. The ideas about experimental design and non-experimental research in the later chapters are basic and quite general. The final chapters deal with organizing and conducting a research project and reading and writing about research. With the background of the earlier chapters these final chapters should enable the reader to pull together the methodology of a research project.

Role of Educational Research

At the conclusion of this first chapter it is well to consider the role of educational research in a general sense. The question might be raised by an already overloaded teacher: Why bother with educational research at all? What type of a role or function does educational research have in the overall enterprise of education and its specific facets? We know that the federal government and various foundations have allotted considerable funds for the pursuit of educational research. School systems and universities are increasing their activities relative to educational research. It would seem reasonable to assume that the purpose of such expenditures in money and effort is not simply to keep educational researchers off the rolls of the unemployed.

We might say that the overall function of educational research is to improve educational procedures through the refinement and extension of knowledge. The refinement of existing knowledge or the acquisition of new knowledge is essentially an intermediate step toward the improvement of the educational process. However, this intermediate step is extremely important and may occupy a considerable proportion of the time allotted to the project. The refinement of existing knowledge should not be taken lightly, since in many situations the initial ideas and procedures of a research study may be relatively crude and remain adequate for only a short time.

Within the broad framework of improvement, the specific roles of educational research are viewed differently by the people associated with various aspects of education. Consider two examples. The researcher concerned with a learning experiment may be attempting to reinforce or refute his theory of how learning takes place. The function of research here is to aid in making a decision concerning the refinement or extension of knowledge in this particular area. The classroom teacher, on the other hand, grappling with the problem of coming up with a more effective technique for teaching slow learners how to read, looks to research for tangible evidence by which to solve this immediate problem. For research to meet its function, it should satisfy both requirements. That is, it should aid the theorist in making a decision about his theory and it should provide the teacher with information that will lead to the solution of the non-theoretical classroom problem. The long-range goal of both theorist and teacher is to improve the educational process; the teacher in a much more immediate situation and the theorist on the assumption that knowing more about learning would increase the effectiveness of the learning process.

The demands of contemporary culture upon the educational systems of today are many and intense. The various areas of education are being exposed to objective examination. The problems associated with the development, operation, and improvement of the educational systems must be met by extensive and systematic applications of knowledge. Educational research provides the impetus, background, and vehicle by which systematic examination, development, and improvement take place. The teacher, the administrator, the specialist of any kind in the schools, the college professor, the researcher—all of these are taking part. All concerned should be consumers of research findings. Almost everyone should at some stage or another be an active participant in research studies. The practitioner, such as a teacher, will use research primarily for shedding light on some immediate problem. It is likely that the practitioner will become a better educator because of his research involvement. Teachers, administrators, and the like should engage in on the job research as a normal part of the professional activity and growth. To be sure, there will be different types of research and different amounts of involvement. Educational research should have the image of a helpful mechanism which can be used by all educators in one way or another, for the improvement of the educational process.

Suggested Study Exercises

1.1 Select three or four research articles from publications such as the *Journal of Educational Psychology* or the *Journal of Educational Research*. Identify the statement of the problem and decide whether or not it is clear to the reader what research problem is under investigation.

1.2 Suppose someone decides to do research on elementary curriculum or secondary curriculum. This is not a satisfactory way of stating a research topic. Choose an aspect of one of the curriculums, identify a research problem, and write a one-paragraph statement of the problem.

1.3 What is the essential characteristic of the statement of a hypothesis in null hypothesis form?

1.4 Consider the following *inadequate* statements of a research problem. Restate each problem, being specific enough so that it becomes a satisfactory statement of a research problem.
   (a) The modern mathematics curriculum of the senior high school.
   (b) Personality and academic achievement.
   (c) Orientation sessions for junior high students.
   (d) An attitude study in a low socio-economic area.
   (e) The learning of arithmetic concepts.

1.5 For each of your restatements of Exercise 1.4 give two hypotheses that might be associated with the research problem. State one of each of the pairs of hypotheses in null hypothesis form. Select one of the pairs of hypotheses and discuss any related theory and how this theory might be useful in formulating revised or additional hypotheses.

1.6 Assuming that you are associated with education, what do you see as the role of research in education; specifically in your own situation? How do you use research findings in your own situation?

2 Basic Concepts

Observations

The educator pursuing a research problem soon arrives at the point where he must secure information about the phenomena under study. If he has stated explicit hypotheses, he must then gather data that will enable him to test these hypotheses. Suppose, for example, a researcher is interested in the aspect of discipline infractions in a team-teaching versus a self-contained classroom. He must then secure information about the discipline in these two teaching situations. We say that "observations" are taken and the classrooms observed become the observable units. Suppose further that the researcher is interested only in the number of discipline infractions. An observation is then the number of such infractions that occurred in a single classroom during a specified period. We are assuming that such infractions could be accurately identified.

Consider a second example. A research study is being conducted in a learning laboratory. High school seniors are individually required to perform a learning task which consists of solving a problem. The researcher records the time required to arrive at a correct solution. The time of an individual senior is an observation or score. The observable units are individual seniors in contrast to the example above in which the observable units were classrooms. If each senior solved one problem, the researcher would secure as many observations as there are seniors participating in the learning task. In this example the seniors might be referred to as the *subjects* (Ss) of the research study. This use of the term "subject" is common in the context of conducting experiments and refers to the individual participants of the research study.

A researcher doing a study of fifth-grade arithmetic achievement would secure such achievement scores as his observations. It is unlikely that he would draw a conclusion about the arithmetic achievement on the basis of one such score from a single fifth grader. Rather, he would observe a considerable number of fifth graders. This would result in as many observations or scores. The data for his study would consist of the observations on arithmetic achievement.

Constants, Variables, and Measurement Scales

A *constant* is a characteristic that is the same for all observable units or Ss. A *variable*, on the other hand, is a characteristic that takes on different values for different observable units. In the arithmetic achievement example discussed above, the grade level, that is, the fifth grade, is a constant. Arithmetic achievement is a variable. Suppose the researchers were doing a more comprehensive achievement study. It might have been possible to observe the same group on reading achievement and spelling achievement as well. These achievement scores would also be variables. The achievement scores are variables not because there are two or more measures of achievement but because for any one type of achievement the fifth-grade students do not all attain the same score. We can now assign the term "data" a more general definition, that is, observations on one or more variables.

A distinction is made between independent and dependent variables. For some research purposes, an independent variable may be considered as a classifying variable. It classifies the observable units. In the discipline example discussed earlier, type of classroom organization would be an independent variable. A classroom would be either team-taught or self-contained, the two classifications or "levels" of this variable. (Two is the minimum number of levels for a variable.) In experimental research, the independent variables are those deliberately manipulated by the researcher.

A dependent variable is the consequent (at least presumed to be) of the independent variable. It is the variable we are attempting to explain in the light of the independent variable. Referring again to the discipline example, the number of infractions would be the dependent variable. The terminology of dependent and independent variable comes to us from mathematics. In a general sense we say that the values of the dependent variable are dependent upon the independent variables. However, a word of caution. Simply assigning names does not establish a cause and effect relationship between variables. Pursuing such relationships and effects is often the purpose of conducting the research.

To further illustrate the use of variable and constant, an example follows. Suppose a study is conducted to determine the effect of three different teaching methods upon achievement in elementary algebra. Three ninth-grade algebra sections in the same school, taught by the same teacher, are each taught using one of the methods. Both boys and girls are included.

The recognized constants in the study are grade level, school, and teacher. (This is assuming the teacher can hold constant teaching effectiveness, except for the method.) The independent variables in the study are teaching method and sex of the student. Teaching method has three levels which we can arbitrarily designate as methods A, B, and C, and the sex of the student has, of course, two levels. Achievement in algebra, as objectively measured at the end of the instructional period, is the dependent variable. The reader should not interpret this example as a complete research design but only as an illustration of the terms variable and constant.

It soon becomes apparent that not all measurement is the same. If we had a zoo full of animals we could go out and decide what each animal happens to be. We can tell that zebras are different than bears, and so on. The measurement here is only to say that animals are different. Now suppose we talk about measuring attitudes. If one S says that he is highly favorable toward something and another S says that he is neutral, we not only say that they are different but we can also order the Ss on degree of favorableness which is being measured. Thus, in addition to having difference we also have order. However, there is no concept of equidistance between points on this particular type of measurement scale.

Now, consider the measurement of something like I.Q. If three Ss have scores of 105, 110, and 115 respectively, we say that the difference between S_1 and S_2 is five points, as is the difference between S_2 and S_3. This gives us not only difference and order but also a unit of equal differences established in the measurement. Finally, consider the weight of different quantities of apples. If we have an empty bag, one of 50 pounds, and one of 100 pounds, we say that the one of 100 pounds is twice that of the 50 pound bag. An empty bag contains zero pounds of apples. Thus we not only have difference, rank, and a unit, but also a comparison in terms of the ratio of one observation to another. We can say that a 100 pound bag of apples weighs twice as much as one of 50 pounds, but we cannot say that a S with an I.Q. of 140 has twice whatever I.Q. measures as one with an I.Q. of 70. Thus, we have a hierarchy of four types of measurement scales.

The measurement scales are defined and summarized below. The four types are as follows:

1. *Nominal:* categorizes without order, simply indicates that the two or more categories are different. *Example:* color of eyes.
2. *Ordinal:* categorizes with order, indicates that the categories are different and can be rank-ordered. *Example:* the letter grading system.

3. *Equal Unit:* all of the characteristics of an ordinal scale plus the establishment of numerically equal distances on the scale. *Example:* performance on an I.Q. test. (This type of scale is also called an equal-interval or interval scale.)

4. *Ratio:* contains an absolute or true zero point in addition to equal units. *Example:* height.

This classification of types of scales may be considered a hierarchy with the ratio scale being the highest level.

Variables whose measurement scales are ordinal or higher may be divided into those which are numerically scaled and those which are not. For example, observations for variables such as weight in pounds are on a numerical scale. However, if we used more general categories such as light weight, medium weight, and heavy weight, then the variable weight would still be ordered but no longer numerically scaled. A variable measured as poor, fair, good, and excellent is another example of one ordered but not numerically scaled.

Numerically scaled variables are considered as discrete or continuous in their measurement. A variable is said to be *discrete* if it can assume only certain or "discrete" values in the range of measurement. The number of discipline infractions in the example discussed earlier would be a discrete variable. That is, only whole numbers of infractions would occur and the scores would be integers with no values in between. A *continuous* variable, in contrast, can take on any values in the range of measurement. The height of individuals, for example, is considered continuous because the possible scores include fractions of an inch as well as whole numbers of inches. If an accurate measuring stick were available, a person could be measured to a thousandth or ten-thousandth of an inch. Even with this precision, it would still be possible for the variable to assume only a finite number of values. The precision of measurement is never absolute and the researcher must round off at some point. For our purposes the practical distinction between discrete and continuous variables is not a difference in reality of a finite or infinite number of possible values. The important distinction lies in the theoretical continuity of the variable.

Distributions

We have seen that the data of a study consist of the observations on one or more variables. When we consider the set of observations or the data of a single variable we have a *distribution*. Suppose we have a set of scores on an achievement measure and we simply record these in some order, say the order by which the answer sheets were turned in. Such a set of scores is usually not easily interpreted. By inspection we could determine the extreme scores, but by and large we would find some reordering of the scores necessary. One common way of reordering is to arrange the scores from the smallest to the largest and tabulate the frequency of occurrence for each score. Such a reordering is called a *frequency distribution*.

As an example, let us consider the set of scores in Table 2.1.

TABLE 2.1

Set of Hypothetical Scores on an Arithmetic Test

82	79	72	85	99
72	72	80	83	61
89	93	76	84	66
72	92	87	82	66
89	94	69	90	80
98	86	82	81	77
84	86	83	75	81
75	67	74	93	97
75	98	78	66	74
91	95	78	60	95

These scores could represent the achievement scores on an arithmetic test. There are 50 scores and we assume that measurement was on at least an interval scale. We can tabulate the frequency of each score. The extreme scores are 99 and 60. A tabulation of the frequencies of the scores between the values 99 and 60 inclusive gives the frequency distribution which appears in Table 2.2. Note that including all possible integer val-

TABLE 2.2

Frequency Distribution of Arithmetic Test Scores

Score	f	Score	f	Score	f	Score	f
60	1	70	0	80	2	90	1
61	1	71	0	81	2	91	1
62	0	72	4	82	3	92	1
63	0	73	0	83	2	93 .	2
64	0	74	2	84	2	94	1
65	0	75	3	85	1	95	2
66	3	76	1	86	2	96	0
67	1	77	1	87	1	97	1
68	0	78	2	88	0	98	2
69	1	79	1	89	2	99	1

ues between 99 and 60 inclusive requires 40 values, even though some of these values have frequencies of zero. The distribution of Table 2.2 has the observed scores tabulated and ordered. This is the only change from the original set of scores. Sometimes the original set of scores is referred to as the *raw scores* and Table 2.2 is then a frequency distribution of raw scores.

The distribution presented in Table 2.2 is in tabular form. We can also present the distribution in graphic form by indicating the frequency on the vertical axis and the values of the possible scores on the horizontal axis. Such a representation is called a *histogram*. The histogram for our example is quite flat and spread out due to relatively small frequencies and a wide range of scores. Figure 2.1 presents the histogram. The raw score frequency distribution may be cumbersome to deal with, especially when the number of scores is small relative to the range of the scores. It may be difficult to determine the pattern of the data. A more efficient procedure is to group the scores into class inter-

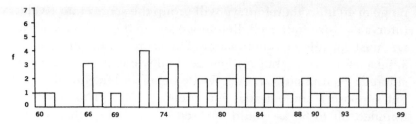

Figure 2.1 Histogram for the frequency distribution of the raw scores on an arithmetic test.

vals. When scores are tabulated according to class intervals we say that we have *grouped data*. That is, all of the scores in a specified interval are "grouped" together. Prior to being grouped, the raw scores are sometimes called *ungrouped scores* or *ungrouped data*.

The grouping of data raises the question of what class interval size to use. The raw data of our example was essentially grouped in class intervals of size one. The other extreme would be to group all scores in one class interval of size 40. Neither one of these extremes is satisfactory for the purpose of extracting information: the original scores are too spread out; the other extreme would essentially obscure all information. The selection of the class interval is an arbitrary matter. As we increase the size of the class interval, the distribution becomes increasingly smoother in form. However, increasing the class interval size has the disadvantage of possibly distorting some of the scores. The scores in a class interval will be represented (in any computation) by the mid-point of the class interval. As the class interval size increases, the possibility of greater discrepancies between observed scores and class interval mid-point also increases. Therefore, if the class interval size is large, resulting in too few class intervals, excessive errors due to grouping may be introduced. Also, the graph of the entire distribution may be distorted by having too few class intervals. An intuitive inspection of the raw scores will give some indication of the appropriate number of class intervals, but usually somewhere between 10 and 20 inclusive will be most effective.

Consider again the scores of our example. The scores cover a range of 40 units therefore we will group the scores into 10 class intervals of size four each. Before we set up these class intervals we must consider another matter. The scores of the distribution appear as integers, but arithmetic achievement could be considered a continuous variable. We do not record fractional scores, but suppose a student attained a score of 59.7. This would be rounded off to 60 as would any score that is less than 60 but exceeds 59.5. Now suppose another student had received a score of 63.2. Such a score would be rounded off to 63 as would any score greater than 63 and up to 63.5. (Possibly we would include 63.5 so that the score that hits right on the .5 could be rounded off consistently.) Thus, if we designate all scores of 60 to 63 inclusive as falling in our first class interval we are really including all scores of 59.5 to 63.5, which covers a class interval size of four. These new points, 59.5 and 63.5, are called the *true* or *real limits* of the class *interval*. The frequency distribution for the scores of Table 2.1, grouped into class intervals of size 4, appears in Table 2.3. The histogram for the frequency distribution of Table 2.3 follows immediately in Figure 2.2.

TABLE 2.3

Frequency Distribution For Grouped Data of Arithmetic Test

Interval	f
59.5–63.5	2
63.5–67.5	4
67.5–71.5	1
71.5–75.5	9
75.5–79.5	5
79.5–83.5	9
83.5–87.5	6
87.5–91.5	4
91.5–95.5	6
95.5–99.5	4

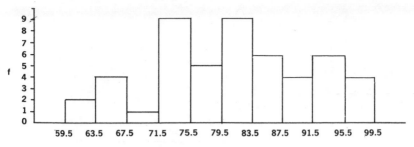

Figure 2.2   Histogram for the grouped data of the arithmetic test.

An inspection of Figures 2.1 and 2.2 reveals that the grouping of the scores has markedly pulled the frequency distribution together. It should be noted that in constructing the histogram, the equal class intervals are represented by equal spaces on the horizontal axis. The initial selection of the unit length on the vertical scale is arbitrary as long as it remains consistent throughout the histogram. With the data grouped and class intervals constructed we see that the histogram is a series of rectangles, with the area of a rectangle directly proportional to the frequency of the class interval.

Distributions may take on an unlimited number of shapes. The shape of the histogram in Figure 2.2 has no specific name. It has a considerable up and down effect, although the heavy concentration of frequencies is around the center. There are many distributions whose shapes are given specific names. A distribution which, at least theoretically, occurs frequently in educational research is the "normal" distribution. The *normal distribution* is not a single distribution which always has specific numerical class intervals but rather a smooth, symmetrical distribution which follows the general shape of the distributions in Figure 2.3. The general shape is sometimes referred to as *bell shaped.* In education there is considerable evidence that variables such as achievement in many areas and intelligence are normally distributed.

Another distribution is the *uniform distribution,* so-called because it is a symmetrical distribution which assumes the shape of a rectangle. Other distributions, especially theoretical ones, will be discussed later in this text.

Figure 2.3 Examples of "normal distributions."

Distributions are not always symmetrical in shape. When frequencies are concentrated toward one end of the distribution we say that the distribution is *skewed.* The ends of a distribution are often called the *tails.* Technically, skewness is a departure from symmetry. If the heavy concentration of scores is toward the right part of the distribution, we say that the distribution is *negatively skewed.* A *positively skewed* distribution has the heavy concentration of scores in the left part of the distribution with the longer, lower tail extending to the right. Figure 2.4 presents examples of skewed distributions.

The identification of the shape of a distribution is a beginning but it hardly exhausts the available information of a set of scores. We need additional measures of a distribution in order to describe and interpret the distribution adequately. Basically we use two types of descriptive measures, measures of central tendency and measures of variability or dispersion.

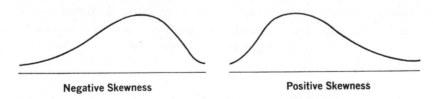

Negative Skewness   **Positive Skewness**

Figure 2.4 Examples of skewed distributions.

Measures of Central Tendency

Measures of central tendency are what we commonly refer to as *averages*. In this sense they give an indication of what a "typical" observation in the distribution is like. The measures of central tendency are *locators* of the distribution; that is, they locate the distribution on the scale of measurement. They are points in the distribution and derive their name from the tendency to be centrally located in symmetrical distributions. However, in skewed and unusually shaped distributions the measures of central tendency are neither centrally located nor necessarily located at the scores with the greatest numbers of frequencies.

The mean, median, and mode are the most commonly used measures of central tendency. *Mean,* used in this context, refers to the arithmetic mean. To determine the mean we simply add the scores in a distribution and divide by the number of scores in the distribution. The *median* by definition is the point on the scale of measurement below which one-half of the scores of the distribution lie. The *mode,* which is the least frequently used of these three measures of central tendency, is simply the score with the greatest frequency. There exist other measures of central tendency but their infrequent use in educational research does not warrant their consideration in this text.

To illustrate the idea of a locator, suppose we have two distributions of weights: one for adult men and the other for adult women. Suppose that the mean weight of the distribution for men is 170 pounds and that for the women's distribution 132 pounds. Both distributions have the same measurement scale, that of pounds, and can be located on the measurement scale by their means. If we set the distributions on the measurement scale, the distribution for the men would be located to the right, that is, further up the scale than the distribution of the women.

An example is now introduced in which the mean for a distribution is determined. The primary purpose of this example is not to introduce statistical computation, but to introduce and define some elementary notation which will facilitate the presentation of ideas and enhance understanding.

Suppose we have the following distribution of ten scores: 9, 7, 8, 6, 7, 5, 4, 7, 7, 6. We could arrange them in order from lowest to highest which would give 4, 5, 6, 6, 7, 7, 7, 7, 8, 9. An inspection of the data quickly reveals that the mode is 7. The sum of the ten scores is 66. In terms of notation this sum could be noted by $\sum_{i=1}^{10} X_i = 66$. The symbol Σ is a summation sign and is simply an indication to add the numbers represented by the letter symbol which follows. The letter symbol X_i stands for a particular number in our distribution. The i is a subscript and is used as a substitute for the values 1 to 10 inclusive, since we have ten scores in our distribution. The $i = 1$ immediately below the summation sign tells us to begin adding with the first X, that is, score in our distribution, and the 10 above the summation sign tells us to stop with the tenth X. The mean of the distribution is defined as the sum of the scores divided by the number of scores. Thus, our mean would be 66 divided by 10 or 6.6.

The determination of the mean of a distribution of grouped scores requires that the scores in a specific class interval be represented by the mid-point of that class interval. If class intervals are large this introduces the possibility of substantial grouping errors between the raw scores and the class interval mid-points. This is an example of the possible distortion introduced by grouping discussed earlier. We will not compute the median of our distribution. The computation of the median can appear complicated due to finding the proportionate amount of an interval necessary to locate the median. For the purposes of this discussion, it is adequate that the reader know the definition of the median, that is, the point below which one-half or 50 per cent of the observations lie.

Measures of Variability

We have introduced the ideas of shape and central tendency or location in describing a distribution, but this description is still not comprehensive enough. The variability or dispersion of a distribution also should be considered. *Variability* refers to the spread or scatter of the distribution scores; thus, the measures of variability give an indication of the spread in a distribution. In contrast to measures of central tendency which are points, measures of variability are intervals. That is, they occupy or are designated by a number of units on the measurement scale.

There are several measures of variability which can be used in describing a distribution. Probably the crudest of these is the *range*, defined as one plus the difference between the two extreme scores. When determining the range we want to include both extreme scores in the interval and hence the one plus. It is very easy to calculate since it can usually be determined by a quick inspection of the scores. However, the range has serious limitations. Since it considers only two scores, it does not reveal the pattern of variation between the scores. Two distributions could have identical ranges but have different dispersion throughout the distributions.

The measures of variability most commonly used are the variance and the standard deviation. Before these measures are defined, we must consider the meaning of a deviation in this context. *Deviation* means the difference between an observed score and the mean of the distribution. In our example in connection with measures of central tendency, an observed score of 8 would have a deviation of +1.4 from the mean of 6.6. There are as many deviations as there are scores in the distribution, although some of the deviations might be zero. If an observed score corresponds exactly with the mean, the deviation is zero.

Suppose we use the summation notation and notation for the scores introduced earlier. We will let n be the number of scores in the distribution and $\bar{X}$ (read X-bar) represent the mean of the distribution. Then the variance of a distribution is given by:

$$\text{Variance}^{1} = \frac{\sum_{i=1}^{n} (X_i - \bar{X})^2}{n}$$

That is, the deviation of each score from the mean is squared. The squares of these deviations are then summed and this sum is divided by the number of observations in the distributions.

[1] The denominator of the variance formula is given here as n since we are not considering sampling and inferential statistics at this point, only the matter of describing a distribution. A discussion of the use of $n-1$ as the denominator of the variance formula appears later.

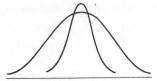 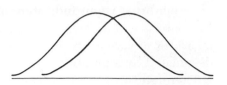

Figure 2.5 Distributions with like central tendency but different variability.

Figure 2.6 Distributions with like variability but different central tendency.

The *standard deviation* is defined as the positive square root of the variance. The variance and standard deviation are undoubtedly the most important measures of variability in terms of theoretical and practical usefulness.

Up to this point we have discussed shape, measures of central tendency, and measures of variability in providing a description of the distribution of observations. It is intuitively clear that, in addition to knowing something about the shape, both types of measures are necessary. When we talk about distributions being alike it is important to specify in what way they are alike. Figures 2.5 and 2.6 illustrate distributions alike in one respect, yet very different in the other.

The importance of adequate descriptions of the distributions under study should not be overlooked or dismissed lightly. Sometimes providing descriptions is looked down upon as too simple and for many research studies descriptions are not adequate for the purposes of the study; but providing descriptions is often an essential preliminary task and can certainly be a valuable contribution to the research study. The possibility of a descriptive study of this nature is often overlooked, especially in areas where the information about the distributions is incomplete or inconclusive. The measures (and procedures for determining them) discussed in connection with describing a distribution are referred to as *descriptive statistics*. In this sense, descriptive statistics are the measures by which we pull together the facts in order to describe the phenomenon under study. Statistics, however, has a broader and actual multiple meaning in the context of educational research. Other uses will be introduced and toward the close of this chapter a summary of the meaning of statistics will be presented.

Making Inferences from Samples to Populations

In many situations we are interested in studying a specific group with the expectation that we will be able to generalize to some larger group. For example, a research director for a large city system might set up five third grades and expose them to some experimental treatment, with the purpose of generalizing to all third-grade students of the system. In a more ambitious vein it might be attempted to generalize to third-grade students in all school systems. In any event, an attempt is being made to infer about a relatively large group by the investigation of a segment of that larger group. The smaller group under investigation is a sample of the larger group called a *population*. A *sample* is, then, a subgroup or subset of the population, the group that is measured. The distribution of observations that is acquired is the *distribution of the sample*. A descriptive measure of the sample distribution is a *statistic*. For example, if the mean of the sample is determined this mean is a statistic.

A descriptive measure of a population is called a *parameter*. Typically, the entire population is not measured but we want to make inferences and draw conclusions about parameters from the statistics of the sample. Had the mean been determined for a set of population observations, we would have a parameter. The distinction between a statistic and a parameter is very important in the logic of making inferences from samples to populations. Further emphasis will be placed on this distinction in the chapters on hypothesis testing.

The notation used for parameters is indicated by Greek letters and the notation for statistics by letters of the English alphabet. As examples, consider means and variances. The population mean is indicated by μ (Mu) and $\bar{X}$ is the sample mean. (The symbol $\bar{X}$ has been introduced earlier in connection with descriptive measures of a distribution.) The variances of the population and sample are given by σ^2 and s^2 respectively. The standard deviations are the correspondingly positive square roots.

The basic idea of making inferences from statistics to parameters is that of observing the sample distribution and then employing accepted and scientific techniques to make the inference. We conduct the research by determining statistics (sample measures) on the basis of which we generalize to the parameters (population measures). The theory and methodology underlying this procedure is known as *inferential statistics*. The following sections discuss the basic ideas of this theory and methodology.

The Concept of Underlying Distributions

In order to construct the chain of reasoning from statistics to parameters, it is necessary to consider some basic ideas about probability. Everyone at some time or other encounters probability notions. We talk about odds on the outcomes of various sports events. Sweepstakes are entered but intuitively we feel (and rightly so) that the probability of winning is very small. Certain combinations of winners at the race track pay many times the initial investment because their occurrence is a rare event. The same is true for the appearance of certain combinations on a slot machine.

Probability of an event is often referred to as small, large, or some other descriptive word implying magnitude. For the sake of consistency, computation, and mathematical tradition, the probability of an event can take on values from zero to plus one inclusive. A probability of zero indicates no possible chance of occurrence and a plus one indicates certainty of occurrence. *Probability* can be considered as a ratio: it is the ratio of the number of possible favorable ways an event can occur to the number of all possible ways of occurrence, both favorable and unfavorable.

Consider the toss of an unbiased coin. Suppose we define the appearance of a head as favorable. There is only one head on a coin and hence only one way for a head to appear. However, there are two sides to the coin, thus the probability of a head appearing is 1/2. This is sometimes referred to as a 50–50 chance.

The tossing of a pair of dice poses some interesting probability problems. We know that there are six faces on each die. In a single throw of both dice there are 36 possible different ways the dice may appear. This can be quickly established by considering that each face of one die may appear with the six faces of the other. Suppose that the appearance of a sum of 7 on the two faces is considered a favorable event. How many ways can a sum of 7 appear? Combinations of 6 and 1, 2 and 5, and 3 and 4 are three favorable events. But the above combinations could appear on the opposite dice. Thus, combinations of 1 and 6, 5 and 2, and 4 and 3 are also favorable. This gives a total of six possible favorable events. The probability of a sum of 7 appearing in a single throw of a pair of unbiased dice is 6/36 or 1/6.

Most of the probability associated with sampling and statistics is not as simple an enumeration as in the dice example. What we must consider are underlying distributions. Given an underlying distribution of the number of ways an event can occur, we can designate the area under this distribution curve to be 1. This corresponds to the total number of all possible ways of occurrence and hence the probability 1. If we designate certain events to be favorable, we can determine the proportion of the area their numbers occupy. This, then, is the probability of the favorable event.

Let us consider again our example of the throw of the two dice. We can illustrate the concept of underlying distribution by considering all possible ways the two dice can roll as the underlying distribution. The possible sums that can appear in a single roll of two dice are 2 (double one) to 12 (double six) inclusive. But we know that there are 36 different combinations of faces. There is only one way that a double 1 can appear, namely a 1 on each die for a sum of 2. A sum of 3 may appear in two ways, a sum of 4 in three ways and so on through the 11 possible values until we arrive at a sum of 12 which can appear in only one way or combination of faces, that of a 6 on each die.

The distribution of possible sums should contain 36 equal areas, each representing one combination of faces. The areas are equal because, assuming unbiased dice, each combination has equal probability of occurrence. Suppose we put each of the corresponding areas with the sum that it represents which gives us the distribution of all possible outcomes of a single throw of two

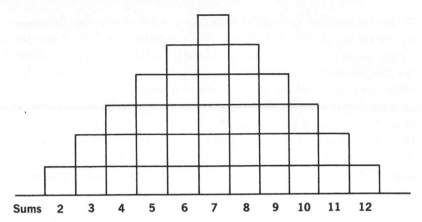

Sums 2   3   4   5   6   7   8   9   10   11   12

Figure 2.7 The distribution of possible outcomes of a single roll of two dice.

dice. The distribution appears in Figure 2.7. The sums are designated on the horizontal scale.

The distribution of Figure 2.7 can be considered the underlying sampling distribution of the outcomes of a single roll of two dice. The area of the distribution is designated as 1.0 since if we throw the dice some outcome of the 11 possible will appear. Thus, each area represents 1/36 and the probability of the outcome which it represents is 1/36. It can be seen by inspection that the probability of a 7 appearing is 6/36 or 1/6. What would be the probability of getting a 5 or less? It would be the proportion of the area occupied by the sums 5, 4, 3, and 2. This area is 10/36 or 5/18. We could take the area between any two points that divide specific sums. Consider the probability of getting a sum greater than 5 but less than 11. This probability is 23/36. In this case, the favorable event is rolling a sum greater than 5 but less than 11. The area occupied by the favorable event is 23/36.

The dice-throwing example provides an illustration of an underlying distribution, in that there is a distribution of possible outcomes of a single throw of two dice. The outcome in our example was defined as the sum on the two dice. Since we know the underlying distribution we can determine the probability of any of the possible outcomes. As a specific sum is an outcome in the dice-throwing example, so a statistic such as a mean may also be considered an outcome. A specific sum appears from the throw of the dice, so a statistic appears from the sample of observations. Thus, statistics may be considered events in the probability sense. Just as a specified sum on two dice has a probability of appearing if we know the underlying distribution of these sums (Figure 2.7), so a specified mean (or other statistic) has a probability of appearing if we know its underlying distribution. This requires a distribution of the possible values of the statistic. To know a distribution is to know its shape, location, and dispersion. These underlying distributions of statistics are called *sampling distributions*. They are theoretical distributions and are commonly arrived at through mathematical proofs. For the purposes of this text we are not concerned with the proofs and development of these distributions, but with the ideas underlying their use.

The theoretical underlying distributions are based on certain conditions. Recall that we are working with a sample from which we get statistics, and are attempting to make inferences to parameters. One of the conditions is that the sample be a random sample. A *simple random sample* by definition is one drawn in such a manner that every member of the population has an equal probability of inclusion.[1] A simple random sample also requires the selection to be made in such a way that the inclusion of any member in the sample in no way affects the probability of the selection of any other population member. With a small population a random sample is not difficult to obtain. A table of random numbers may be used to draw the sample. When sampling from large populations, the sampling procedure may become quite complex. In any event, random sampling is not haphazard or careless sampling.

Let us consider the sampling distribution or underlying distribution of the mean. This is the distribution of the values of the means of all possible random samples of a given size, say n, drawn from the population. From each possible sample one

---

[1] Samples other than simple random samples are discussed in a later chapter. If we sample from a finite population without replacement, a slight adjustment in the definition is necessary. A sample is then considered to be random if drawn in such a way that every possible sample of a given size has an equal probability of being selected.

and only one value is contributed to this distribution of means. As a distribution, this distribution of means has its own shape, mean, and variability. Since the mean is a statistic we now have a distribution of a statistic. This is analogous to the distribution of outcomes in the dice-throwing example, except that we now have means that come from samples, rather than sums observed on two dice.

We want to know about the shape, location (central tendency), and dispersion of our distribution of means. Eventually we want to make our inferences from the statistic to the parameter, in this case from the sample mean to the population mean. To locate the distribution of means we consider its mean in terms of the location of the population mean. It can be mathematically shown that the mean of this distribution of means of all samples of a given size, n, randomly drawn from the population, is equal to the mean of the population. The reader should not interpret this as indicating that if we select a sample and determine its mean, that this one sample mean will exactly equal the population mean. This one sample mean is only one of the scores in the distribution of sample means.

Next, we consider the shape of the distribution of means. We have already mentioned the general shape of the normal curve. If the population of observations is normally distributed, the distribution of means will also be distributed as a normal distribution. If sample size is large — 30 or greater — the distribution of the means will approximate a normal distribution regardless of the shape of the population distribution.

Now that we have the shape and location of the distribution of means, this brings us to its dispersion or variability. The specific measure of dispersion which we will consider is the variance, which was defined earlier, and let σ^2 represent the variance of the population. The variance of the distribution of means is generally less in magnitude than σ^2, in fact it can be mathematically shown that this variance is equal to the population variance divided by the sample size, that is, σ^2/n. (The reader is reminded that throughout this discussion of the distribution of the means the sample size remains constant. The variability of the underlying distribution of means, as indicated above, depends on the sample size. As sample size is increased, variability decreases.)

The positive square root of this variance, $(\sigma/\sqrt{n})$, is the standard deviation of the distribution of means. This standard deviation is called the *standard error of the mean*. The term standard error is often used in connection with the distribution of a statistic. The standard error of a statistic is simply the standard deviation of the distribution of the statistic.

At this point we have the shape, location, and variance of our distribution of means. All of this can be summarized by one of the most important theorems of statistics, namely the *central limit theorem*, given as follows:

> Given any population with mean μ and finite variance σ^2, as the sample size increases without limit the distribution of the sample means approaches a normal distribution with mean μ and variance σ^2/n.[1]

The question might arise as to how large the sample size must be in order for the distribution of means to be normally distributed. The answer depends upon the extent that the specific population under study deviates from normality. However, as indicated earlier, if sample size is 30 or greater the distribution of the mean will approximate a normal distribution even if the population distribution is not normal in shape. The central limit theorem provides an important theoretical base for our making inference from statistics to parameters through the underlying distributions of the statistics.

Let us consider a very small distribution of six scores and the underlying distribution of the mean of samples of size two. We must consider all possible combinations of the observations in pairs and compute the mean of each pair. There are 15 such possible pairs or samples of size two so there will be 15 means in the underlying distribution of the mean. (We are sampling without replacement and the order of the numbers in the sample is irrelevant since we are only interested in the combination.) The original observations are 10, 9, 8, 8, 7, and 6 that is, these six values make up the original distribution. The 15 samples of size two and their means appear in Table 2.4. Note that there are two 8's in the original distribution. Hence, there are two samples of, say, 9, 8, but they include different 8's.

[1] Huntsberger, D. V., *Elements of Statistical Inference* (Boston: Allyn and Bacon, Inc., 1961), p. 125.

TABLE 2.4

Sample Observations and Means of All Samples of Size Two From a Distribution of Six Observations

Sample	Sample Mean
10, 9	9.5
10, 8	9
10, 8	9
10, 7	8.5
10, 6	8
9, 8	8.5
9, 8	8.5
9, 7	8
9, 6	7.5
8, 8	8
8, 7	7.5
8, 6	7
8, 7	7.5
8, 6	7
7, 6	6.5

The 15 sample means make up the underlying distribution of the mean. It should be noted that if we changed the sample size the distribution would change. If, for example, we had selected samples of size three, there would have been twenty possible samples.

Let us inspect more closely the distribution of means in relation to the original distribution. The distribution of means contains more scores.[1] However, the scores are not spread out as much since they go from 6.5 to 9.5. We will not compute the standard deviation but let us consider the means. The mean of the original distribution is 48/6 or 8. To find the mean of the distribution of means we add the fifteen values and divide by

[1] Generally the distribution of means contains more values than the original population distribution. The exceptions are: if sample size is the same as population size when there is only one sample and if sample size is one or one less than the population size, the number of means is the same as the number of observations in the population distribution.

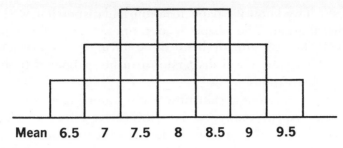

Figure 2.8 The distribution of the means of all samples of size two drawn from six observations.

15. This gives 120/15, or again, 8. Thus, we see an example of the fact that the mean of the distribution of means is equal to the mean of the original distribution. The underlying distribution of the mean is pictured in Figure 2.8.

Let us consider a probability question about a sample mean. Suppose we draw a random sample of size two from the original six observations. What is the probability that we would draw a sample with a mean of 8? We go to the underlying distribution (Figure 2.8) of the mean and see that three of the 15 equal areas are occupied by 8. In the probability sense we consider the area under the entire distribution as one. Therefore, the probability of drawing a sample with a mean of 8 is 3/15 or 1/5. In like manner, the probability of drawing a sample with a mean of 7.5 to 9 inclusive is 11/15.

The above example illustrates a specific underlying distribution. We developed the underlying distribution of a specific statistic, the mean, of all possible samples of a given size, namely two. The original distribution contained only six observations. In practice, we would rarely develop an underlying distribution in such a manner. As has been previously mentioned, the underlying distributions are theoretical distributions developed through mathematical proofs. The mean of a sample is a statistic and we have discussed the underlying distribution of this statistic. The reader can intuitively feel that there is a multitude of statistics and consequently a multitude of underlying distributions. Fortunately, the underlying distributions of many statistics behave in a similar manner, that is, they have common shapes. Thus, when working with the underlying distribution of a statistic if we know its shape, location, and dispersion, we know the distribution. The shape is determined from the type of statistic. This has already been done for us by the mathematicians. The location and dispersion can be estimated from the sample observations.

The use of inferential statistics, that is, inferring from statistics to parameters, invariably involves the use of tables which contain the values of common underlying distributions. Just as Figure 2.8 represents the underlying distribution of our example, so tables at the back of the text represent underlying distributions of various statistics. However, Figure 2.8 was specifically constructed for our example and can be used directly. The tables at the back of the text are designed for more general use and hence their use involves applying additional techniques to the sample observations. The use of these tables involves selecting the correct one (knowing the shape of our underlying distribution) and converting our observations to coincide with the same scale as that of the table. These procedures are discussed and illustrated in following sections. The idea introduced here is that underlying distributions are provided and it is not necessary to develop the distribution for each specific situation.

Let us briefly summarize the comments about underlying distributions. An underlying distribution is simply a theoretical distribution. Usually it is the theoretical distribution of a statistic. If we consider the area contained by the underlying distribution as 1.00, in a probability sense, this corresponds to the total number of all possible occurrences of the statistic. If we know the specific underlying distribution, that is, its shape, measures of central tendency, and variability, we can compute the probabilities associated with the appearance of specific values of the statistics. A very important and common underlying distribution is the normal distribution. In following sections we discuss this distribution and other important underlying distributions. In the discussion of the normal distribution, the the matter of converting observed scores to coincide with the table distribution is also discussed. This is commonly called a procedure for converting to standard scores. The procedure is introduced in the context of a specific distribution so that it can be illustrated.

The Normal Distribution

The normal distribution has been very briefly introduced earlier in this chapter in connection with shapes of distributions. Figure 2.3 presents some shapes of normal distributions. Normal distributions may be flat or peaked, spread out or close together, but they all have in common the general bell shape. The normal distribution is symmetrical around a vertical line which divides the area of the distribution into two equal parts.

A specific normal distribution, whether a distribution of observations on Ss, a distribution of means or some other statistic that is normally distributed, depends on its mean for location and standard deviation for dispersion. It would be impossible to construct tables which would cover all possible combinations. Also recall that for the probability concept we define the total area under the curve of an underlying distribution to be one.

The technique used to arrive at a common base is to convert an existing normal distribution of observations to the standard normal distribution. (This may also be called the standard normal curve.) This distribution by definition has a mean of zero, a standard deviation of 1, and the area under the curve is designated as 1. As a normal curve it is symmetrical. Approximately 68 per cent of the area is contained within one standard deviation of the mean. Within two standard deviations of the mean, about 95.5 per cent of the area is contained; within three standard deviations of the mean, approximately 99.7 per cent of the area is included. Theoretically, the standard normal distribution extends from $-\infty$ to $+\infty$ on the scale of measurement. This defines and describes the standard normal distribution.

The conversion of observed distribution scores to the corresponding values in the standard normal distribution is accomplished by the following formula:

$$z_i = \frac{X_i - \bar{X}}{\sigma}$$

Where z_i is the score in the standard distribution or the standard score of the ith S, $\bar{X}$ is the observed mean, X_i the observed score of the ith S, and σ the standard deviation of the observed distribution. Descriptively, all this formula indicates is to subtract an observed score from its mean and divide this difference by the standard deviation which gives us the corresponding score in the standard normal distribution. By inspection it can intuitively be seen that this conversion relocates the distribution around zero and the scores (z_i's) are now given in terms of standard deviation units. Since the mean is zero and in a symmetric distribution one-half of the scores are below the mean, one-half (or approximately one-half) of the standard scores will be negative. The algebraic sign of the standard score should be carefully retained.

The development thus far gives us a distribution with an area of one (sometimes called a unit curve) and a procedure for converting any normal distribution of observations to this curve. At this point it may be well to illustrate the construction and use of the standard normal table. This is Table A of the Appendix. Suppose we have a normal distribution whose mean and standard deviation are 65 and 8 respectively. Consider the question: What proportion of the scores are greater than 77? The standard score corresponding to 77 is $z_{77} = 1.50$. We find the z value of 1.50 in the table and note that the corresponding area is .433. However, the table is constructed to give the area from the mean to the z value. The curve is symmetric, thus the area from the mean to $z = 1.50$ (our z_{77}) is .433, hence the area above (to the right) is $.500 - .433$ or .067. Graphically this is illustrated by Figure 2.9.

This example may be considered in terms of probability. Suppose we had the above distribution of scores and we were to randomly select one score. What is the probability that this score would be greater than 77? The probability of this event is .067 or about seven chances out of one hundred. Another way of looking at this: suppose the number of observations in the population distribution is 100 or greater and we draw a sample of 100. How many scores would be expected to exceed 77? Clearly the answer is 6.7 or approximately 7. Note that this is what we would expect before the sample is drawn. In any one specific sample the result may deviate considerably from this expected result.

An additional illustration involving area on both sides of the

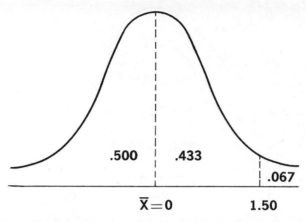

Figure 2.9 The area in a standard normal distribution relative to a standard score of 1.50.

mean follows. Referring back to the previous distribution example, suppose we want to determine the proportion of scores between the values of 55 and 71. We convert to the appropriate standard scores and find $z_{55} = -1.25$ and $z_{71} = +.75$. The corresponding area values (from the table) are .394 and .301 respectively. These are those between the mean and the values and since the values lie on opposite sides of the mean we add the values and obtain the result .695. Thus we would expect 69.5 per cent of the scores to be included between 55 and 71. The curve is symmetrical so negative z-values are not given in the table. The solution in terms of area is pictorially given by the illustration of Figure 2.10. If the values had both been on the same side of the mean a subtraction operation would be necessary to determine the proportion of scores between the two values since the proportions are given from the mean to the standard score.

We have established that the standard deviation of a distribution of means of random samples of size n is given by $\sigma/\sqrt{n}$. If the samples had been drawn from a normal population with a known mean and standard deviation, we could determine the probability of obtaining a sample mean between two specified values. The underlying probability distribution is the normal curve, that is, the normal distribution is the underlying distribution for the mean.

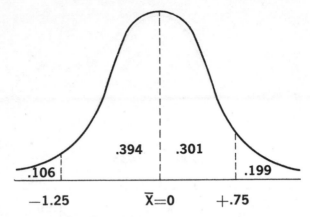

.394 .301

.106 .199

−1.25   X̄=0   +.75

Figure 2.10 The area in a standard normal distribution relative to standard scores of −1.25 and +.75.

Consider such an example. Suppose, for the purpose of illustration, the two parameters, population mean (μ) and standard deviation, are known to be 50 and 12 respectively. The size (n) of the random sample to be drawn is 64. What is the probability that this sample mean will exceed 53? We know that the distribution of means is normally distributed, that this theoretical distribution has a mean of μ and a standard deviation of $\sigma/\sqrt{n}$. To locate 53 in this distribution we consider the expression $\dfrac{\bar{X} - \mu}{\sigma/\sqrt{n}}$ which will convert us to the standard normal. Note that we let $\bar{X}$ be a score in our distribution of means, subtract the mean of the distribution of means from it, and divide by the standard deviation of the distribution of means. Substituting and solving for the z_{53} value, we get 2.00. In checking the table, we find the probability of a mean of 53 or greater appearing is .023.

The value of the expression $\sigma/\sqrt{n}$ is clearly dependent upon sample size. If σ is held constant, the variability of the mean decreases as sample size increases. We see that the maximum value for variability is when $n = 1$, in which case the variance of the mean would be the same as the variance of the original distribution of observations. This is immediately apparent because for sample size of 1 the means coincide with the original observations.

As sample size is increased (with σ held constant) the means of repeated samples would tend to cluster closer together. We say that the increase of sample size makes the mean more stable. This can be illustrated by the example above. We know that $\mu = 50$ so in sampling we would expect to get a sample mean close to 50. The sample size of 64 may be considered a substantial sample. In this case, the appearance of a mean of 53 or greater is a relatively rare event. Suppose sample size had been 16. The corresponding value of the expression $\dfrac{\bar{X} - \mu}{\sigma/\sqrt{n}}$ would be 1, i.e., $z_{53} = 1$. Under these conditions, the probability of a mean of 53 or greater appearing is about .16. Note that everything was held constant except sample size.

Parameters, being measures of the population, are rarely known and therefore it is necessary to estimate them from sample measures which are statistics. When estimating parameters from statistics these estimates may be biased or unbiased. A statistic is said to be *unbiased* if the mean of its underlying distribution is the parameter being estimated. We see that the sample mean is an unbiased estimate of the population mean since the mean of the distribution of all sample means, selected from a sample of a given size, is the population mean. An estimate is said to be *biased* if the mean of its underlying distribution does not equal the parameter being estimated.

The example discussed on the preceding page had the parameter σ known. In actual practice this parameter (and hence the parameter σ^2) is seldom known. Thus, it is usually necessary to estimate σ^2 from the sample observations. In order to get an unbiased estimate, we compute the variance of the sample by $\dfrac{\sum\limits_{i=1}^{n} (X_i - \bar{X})^2}{n - 1}$, where n is the sample size. Note that this differs slightly from the previous formula given on page 43. Then n of the denominator is replaced by $n - 1$. The positive square root is used as an estimate of σ and is commonly denoted by s.

The next logical question would be, what about the expression $\dfrac{\bar{X} - \mu}{\sigma/\sqrt{n}}$ if σ is replaced by an estimate, s? Is the underlying distribution in fact the normal? Since research often involves estimating σ, these are questions of considerable importance. Answering these questions brings us to another important underlying distribution.

Student's t-Distribution

The underlying distribution for the expression $\dfrac{\bar{X} - \mu}{s/\sqrt{n}}$ is not normally distributed, at least not for a small sample size. In fact, there is not a single underlying distribution, but rather an entire family of distributions, the specific distribution depending upon the size of n. This family of distributions was invented by a statistician who wrote under the name of Student. The distributions are called the Student's t-distributions or more commonly, simply the t-distributions.

The t-distributions are symmetric and upon casual inspection closely resemble the normal distribution. There is a t-distribution for each value of the number of *degrees of freedom*. Degrees of freedom is the number of ways the data are free to vary. Suppose that we know that the sum of two numbers must be 75. As soon as one number is given (arbitrarily assigned), the second number is fixed. Thus, there is only one degree of freedom—the assignment of the first number. If the mean is computed for n values having a fixed sum, the first $n-1$ values can be arbitrarily assigned, but once they have been assigned, the nth value is uniquely determined. Let us consider an example. Suppose we have four numbers whose sum is 23, for example, 8, 6, 7, and 2. How many of these numbers could be simultaneously altered and still have the sum equal 23? It can be seen that if three are arbitrarily changed the fourth is fixed. Suppose the first three numbers are changed to 9, 5 and 3. Then the fourth is fixed at 6 in order to meet the condition that the sum be 23. Thus, only three of the scores are, in a sense, free to vary.

Often, degrees of freedom is defined as the number of observations minus the number of parameters estimated. Suppose we were estimating a mean from a set of sample scores. One requirement of a mean is that the sum of the deviations of the scores from the mean equals zero. Therefore, if we have n scores there would be n deviations, but if $n-1$ of these deviations were altered the nth would be fixed in order to meet the condition that the sum of the deviations be zero. We had n observations, estimated one parameter, and have $n - 1$ degrees of freedom. In our example of the standard error of the mean $(\sigma/\sqrt{n})$, σ is estimated by s and the correct degrees of freedom would be $n - 1$.

The table of *t*-distributions is found in Table B of the Appendix. This table differs in certain ways from the normal distribution table. Each row of the table represents a different distribution since the values of each row are associated with a unique degrees of freedom value. The proportions [1] of area are given across the top of the table as .10, .05 down to .0005. These proportions indicate the amount of area remaining in the tails of the distributions corresponding to the points in the columns. It would require a vast number of pages to give all possible values for the entire family of distributions, therefore only the values at certain points in the distributions are given. There are six points that appear for each distribution. However, the distributions are symmetric and table values are given in standard form, that is, with a mean of zero and a standard deviation of one. Therefore, actually twelve points are known for each distribution since each positive point has a corresponding negative point on the other side of the mean. The area underneath the curve of any one distribution is again defined as one. The *t*-distributions also extend from $-\infty$ to $+\infty$.

To illustrate the area in a specific *t*-distribution, consider the *t*-distribution with nine degrees of freedom presented in Figure 2.11. Two points were selected, one on each side of the mean. The points were determined from the table values. As indicated earlier, we can actually find twelve points in the distribution since there are six tabled values for the positive half of the standard distribution. Note that the proportion of area indicated is that remaining in the tail of the distribution beyond the designated point.

Consider an illustration involving the *t*-distribution. Suppose

[1] Table B gives the proportions in terms of significance levels for one- and two-tailed tests. Such tests are discussed in greater detail in Chapter 3. For the purposes of the discussion in this chapter consider the proportions in the top row, that is, those under one-tailed tests.

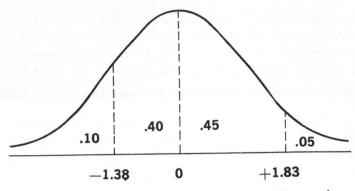

Figure 2.11 Area in the Student's t-distribution with nine degrees of freedom.

we have twenty degrees of freedom and we are selecting a single score from a distribution which we know has a mean of zero and a standard deviation of one. We also know that the distribution is distributed as the appropriate *t*-distribution. What is the probability that a random selection of one score would result in a score of 1.50 or greater? The first thing to do is to be certain that we are in the correct *t*-distribution. We go down the degrees of freedom column until we come to twenty. Moving horizontally, we find that the probability of a score of 1.50 appearing by chance is between .1 and .05. We cannot determine it exactly as in the case with the normal distribution. However, our value is closer to the .1 value than that for .05. Let us estimate the probability as .08. In terms of area, the scores of 1.50 and greater occupy .08 of the area of the standard *t*-distribution with twenty degrees of freedom. The basic idea of using the *t*-distribution is the same as for the standard normal distribution. When dealing with a specific observed distribution of scores, we must convert to standard form as when using the standard normal. The procedure involves an additional step in that we must select the appropriate *t*-distribution for our degrees of freedom.

The *F*-Distribution

A second family of distributions which has assumed considerable importance in statistical analysis is the family of *F*-distributions. This family of distributions was named in honor of Sir Ronald Fisher, the noted British statistician. Like the *t*-distributions, the *F*-distributions make up a family of distributions dependent upon degrees of freedom. The *F*-distributions require two degrees of freedom values to identify the appropriate distribution. The *F*-distributions will not be discussed in detail at this point but will be illustrated in a subsequent chapter on hypothesis testing.

There exist other underlying distributions which are frequently used in inferential statistics. However, it is not necessary to introduce them at this point. The emphasis at this point is upon the concept of underlying distribution. This concept remains the same, that of determining the underlying distribution of a statistic and considering its area in terms of probability.

There has been considerable emphasis upon the concept of underlying distribution. This concept is essential in constructing the chain of reasoning from statistics to parameters. Just as a set of scores on an algebra test, for example, has a distribution, so a statistic which is computed from a sample also has a distribution. For the most part, these are theoretical distributions and the values are provided for us in tables. Once we have determined the underlying distribution of the statistic under study, we make our inferences from the statistic to the parameter and make decisions about hypotheses. The basic ideas and specific procedures are elaborated and illustrated in subsequent chapters on hypothesis testing.

The Meaning of Statistics

The term *statistics* has multiple meanings in educational research. Probably its simplest meaning is a bit of information. If we say that 1,231 students are enrolled in a specific school, this is sometimes referred to as a statistic. The salary schedule and the number of teachers at each salary for a specific school system are sometimes called salary statistics.

Statistics has a much broader meaning than simply bits of information. It also refers to the theory, procedures, and methodology by which we analyze and study quantitative data. A common classification scheme is to divide statistics into descriptive and inferential statistics. (These two uses of statistics have been introduced earlier in this chapter.) When working with descriptive statistics we are essentially describing a distribution. The descriptive statistics that we deal with are commonly measures of central tendency and measures of variability, although these are not the only measures by which we could describe a distribution.

Inferential statistics are used when we have an observed sample, and, on the basis of the sample, we make inferences to the population from which the sample was drawn. The theory and procedures which enable us to make the inferences are statistics in a broad sense. However, in a specific situation, the statistics are the sample facts. In this sense they are the sample means, standard deviations, and the like. Although the word statistics does have multiple meanings, the specific meaning can usually be recognized by the context of its usage.

Inference from Statistics to Parameters: A Review

Let us review the basic ideas of inference from statistics to parameters which have been discussed thus far. These ideas play an extremely important role in educational research. The basic ideas, of which the concept of underlying distribution is a part, comprise the foundation for the forthcoming discussions about hypothesis testing.

The chain of reasoning from statistics to parameters is a part of what we call inferential statistics. The inference is from the statistics to the parameters. The chain is linked as follows. We

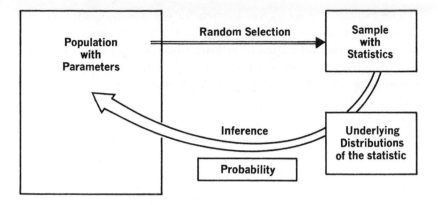

(a) We have a population and we want to make decisions about measures of the population, namely parameters.

(b) We select a random sample and compute measures of the sample which are statistics.

(c) The statistics reflect the corresponding parameters and sampling fluctuation.

(d) We observe the statistics, which are the facts that we have, and infer back to the parameters in the light of the underlying distributions and probability.

Figure 2.12   Chain of reasoning for inferential statistics.

have a population and we want to know something about the descriptive measures of this population, namely the parameters. It is undesirable or impossible to measure the entire population so a random sample is drawn. The descriptive measures of the sample are statistics, and the statistics can be determined. Since the sample is a random sample, we know that the statistics reflect the parameters within fluctuations due to sampling. At this point the underlying distributions of the statistics come in. If we know the underlying distribution, we know how the statistic behaves. The appropriate underlying distribution for a specific statistic is determined for us by mathematical theory and presented for us in tables. Underlying distributions are commonly theoretical distributions. It would be impractical, and in many cases impossible, to draw all possible samples of a specific size and tabulate the distribution of, say, the mean of all these samples. From the information of the statistic and its underlying distribution we reason back to the parameter.

The parameters are never known for certain unless the entire population is measured and then there is no inference. We look at the statistics and their underlying distributions and from here we reason to tenable conclusions about the parameters. The chain of reasoning is summarized in Figure 2.12.

The reader is reminded that it is not necessary to know or do the statistical computations to successfully study the content of this text. It is the reasoning that is important. The content of the next four chapters provides the reasoning tools which undergird research methodology. Then, in the remaining chapters, the more general topics discussed should be more meaningful in the light of this very essential methodological background.

Suggested Study Exercises

2.1 Classify each of the following variables in terms of the type of measurement scale (nominal, ordinal, equal unit, or ratio).
   (a) type of residential dwelling: duplex, single family residence, multiple apartments.
   (b) amount of calcium deposits in the organs of rats that have been subjected to different experimental treatments. (Assume the organs are removed.)
   (c) performance on the essay section of an American history test.
   (d) ratings assigned to the performance of student teachers.
   (e) strength of junior high boys on a physical task as measured in pounds of force by an electronic device.

2.2 A study is conducted to determine the effects of three sets of instructional materials upon fourth-grade reading achievement. Three random samples of fourth-grade boys are selected within the same school. These three groups are then taught by three different teachers, each using one set of instructional materials and at the end of ten weeks of instruction the students are tested on reading achievement. Identify the constant(s), independent variable(s) and dependent variable(s) of this study.

2.3 The following 80 scores represent the distribution of scores on a variable. The scores are listed from low to high. Tabulate the frequency distribution for these scores and plot the histogram for the frequency distribution.

20	29	32	34	36	38	41	45
23	29	32	34	36	39	42	45
24	29	32	35	37	39	42	46
24	30	32	35	37	39	42	46
25	30	33	35	37	40	43	47
27	30	33	35	37	40	43	47
27	30	33	35	37	40	44	48
27	30	33	35	38	41	44	49
28	31	33	36	38	41	44	51
28	31	34	36	38	41	45	52

2.4 Group the scores of the distribution of Exercise 2.3 into eleven intervals beginning with the interval 19.5–22.5 and concluding with the interval 49.5–52.5. Then plot the corresponding histogram for the grouped data and compare it to the histogram of the previous exercise.

2.5 Discuss the difference between measures of central tendency and measures of variability. Why are both types of measures necessary in describing a distribution? Present some examples of variables from the educational setting that are alike in measures of central tendency but different in variability; alike in dispersion but different in location.

2.6 What is the probability of getting a sum less than 5 or greater than 8 in a single roll of two dice? Getting either a sum of 6 or an 8? Use the distribution of Figure 2.7 of this chapter.

2.7 Suppose we have a distribution which has a mean of 50 and a standard deviation of 5. We know that the distribution is normally distributed. What is the probability of randomly selecting a score from this distribution of 57 or greater? between 55 and 65? less than 40 or greater than 60? between 40 and 55?

2.8 A researcher wants to know the end of the year reading level of approximately 1,000 first-grade students of a city school system. The entire population cannot be tested. Discuss how sampling and inferring from statistics to parameters would be used. Identify the statistic and parameter involved in this situation. Reconstruct the chain of reasoning used to arrive at some conclusion about the reading level of the entire first-grade population.

2.9 Distinguish between a statistic and a parameter in the context of inferential statistics. Discuss the role of the underlying distribution. Specifically, of what is it the underlying distribution?

2.10 Identify an article in an educational research journal such as the *Journal of Educational Research* that deals with a study in which inferences were made from a sample to a population. Read the article carefully and identify the statistics and parameters involved. Does the author discuss random sampling for his study?

3 *Testing Hypotheses by Parametric Techniques*

Basic Ideas of Hypothesis Testing

The discussion of this and the following two chapters centers around the methodology of testing hypotheses by statistical techniques. Examples of research problems and situations are discussed in order to illustrate the reasoning and procedures involved. Statistical computations appear sparingly and are only used to help illustrate a point. Such computations are at a minimum and should not discourage the non-statistically oriented reader. Recall that in using statistical tests we infer from the measures of samples, that is, statistics, to the parameters, which are measures of populations.

In the previous chapter the associated terminology was defined and discussed in order to avoid any ambiguity about what is under consideration. The various characteristics of distributions were also discussed in order to give the reader an idea of how the information about a distribution was collected and organized. The distribution itself consists of scores which, as a set of data, have certain characteristics. The characteristics are statistics or parameters, depending upon whether the distribution is of a sample or population. Generally the distribution under consideration is a sample distribution, and we want to generalize about a population.

A hypothesis will be defined in the context of this chapter as a statement about a parameter. This is a more restricted definition than was used in a previous chapter. We do not hypothesize about statistics. The statistics in fact exist and we can inspect them to determine their values. The parameters, on the other hand, will never be known for certain. This being the case, we do not set out to absolutely prove or disprove a hypothesis. We either reject or fail to reject hypotheses. To fail to reject does not necessarily mean acceptance of the hypothesis. It simply means that, in the light of the observed data for this statistical test, there is not enough evidence to reject the hypothesis. The decisions about hypotheses, and hence parameters, are made on the basis of the statistics. Since the parameters are never known for certain, there is always the possibility that an error has been made in the decision. Possible errors in hypothesis testing are discussed later in this chapter.

The Meaning of Significance Level

The reasoning in hypothesis testing associates the probability with the statistic. This may initially seem like a contradiction since the statistic is known. However, the parameter has a value (although the researcher will never know its value for certain) and has no probability associated with it. The probability is associated with the value of the statistic appearing by chance if, in fact, the value of the parameter is as stated in the hypothesis. If this probability of the statistic appearing when the hypothesis is true becomes less than a pre-determined level (usually .05 or .01) we reject the hypothesis. We cannot reject the statistic since it is a fact. If the statistical test indicates that the probability is less than the pre-determined level, we say that the test is "significant" at that level. It is at this probability or less that the hypothesis being tested will be rejected. The term *alpha level* is also used to mean significance level, and the alpha symbol, α, often appears in tables to designate the probability level. Alpha level, therefore, is the level of probability at which we reject the hypothesis being tested.

Thus, when we talk about significance level we are talking about a probability. This probability is related to the area of the underlying distribution of the statistic. It is the dividing line between rejecting and accepting the hypothesis. Suppose we have the underlying distribution of a statistic and we designate the area as one. Then, if we can locate this distribution by the hypothesis and we know its shape and dispersion, we can determine where our observed statistic would be in the distribution.

Consider an example involving a mean. A large sample, say 200 or greater, is drawn from a normally distributed population. With such a large sample size, the underlying distribution of the statistic is the normal distribution, and the standard error, that is, standard deviation, of this distribution could be estimated from the sample data. Suppose we hypothesize that the population mean is a specified value and the significance level is set at .05. The illustration of the underlying distribution in terms of area is given in Figure 3.1.

Note that the 5 per cent of the area designated by the significance level is divided equally between the two tails of the distribution. This is because extreme values of the sample mean on either side of the hypothesized mean would result in rejecting the hypothesis. Now the sample mean is computed. Suppose the sample mean falls in the 2.5 per cent of the area in the right tail. The probability that our statistic would appear by chance is less than .05, if the hypothesis of the population mean is true. The occurrence of a random sample with a mean located in the extreme right (or left) tail is a rare event, one that has a probability of occurrence that is less than the significance level. We do

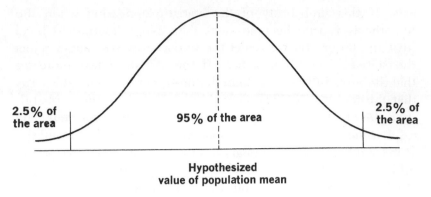

2.5% of the area

95% of the area

2.5% of the area

Hypothesized value of population mean

Figure 3.1 The area of the underlying distribution of a statistic with a significance level of .05.

not entertain the rare event as a tenable explanation of the situation. We cannot reject the statistic since that has been computed and is therefore a result that has appeared. We must then reject the hypothesis and essentially conclude that our underlying distribution is not correctly located, that it should be shifted to the right. The mean is, of course, a locator of the distribution. The hypothesis concerns the mean of the underlying distribution and rejecting the hypothesis is rejecting the hypothesized location of the underlying distribution. Note that the probability rests on statistic but the conclusion rests on hypothesis. In this example, the statistical test is said to be "significant" since the statistic fell in the rejection region as determined by the significance level.

The significance level enables us to make a decision about our hypothesis. We are comparing a statistic with a hypothesized value of a parameter. Usually there is a difference between these two values, and the task is to decide whether or not the difference is so large that we should reject the hypothesis. In order to make the decision we consider the probability that this large a difference would have occurred due to chance, that is, random sampling fluctuation. If this probability is less than the significance level, we are not willing to entertain random fluctuation as an explanation and hence we reject the hypothesis. A difference that is considered too large to be attributed to random sampling fluctuation is said to be a statistically significant difference.

Selection of the Significance Level

The choice of the significance level is, to a certain extent, an arbitrary choice of the researcher. However, it is not completely arbitrary. The levels commonly used are .05 and .01. These two levels correspond closely to two and two and one-half standard deviations from the mean in a normal distribution. The .05 level is widely used in educational research most likely because it is considered an adequately good risk. The risk is 5 chances in 100 that such an extreme statistic would occur by chance if the hypothesis is true. The .01 level may be used by a researcher if he wants to be practically certain (99 out of 100) of making a correct decision about the hypothesis. Occasionally the level is set at .10, but this generally is considered quite a high probability of chance occurrence. Decreasing the significance level, that is, going from .05 to .01, is going in what is called a conservative direction. Doing this will require more extreme (from the hypothesized values) values of the statistic to reach significance. The .001 level, which appears occasionally in the research literature, is very conservative.

The selection of a significance level depends upon what risk the researcher is willing to take in terms of making an error when making a decision about the hypothesis. This risk is related to the consequences of rejecting a true hypothesis or failing to reject a false hypothesis. Suppose he wants to be very certain that he is right if he rejects the hypothesis. Then he will set the significance level very small, possibly .01 or .001. For example, suppose a decision must be made on whether or not a new sixth-grade mathematics text should be adopted because it will result in greater mathematics achievement. However, the old texts are still adequate and a new adoption will result in a large expenditure. If we hypothesize that the mathematics achievement will be the same using both texts we want to be certain about rejecting this hypothesis before the expenditure is authorized.

A relatively large significance level (.10 or greater) would be selected if rejecting a true hypothesis is of little importance. Suppose a teacher is trying to decide which of two sets of toys is most appealing to the kindergarten children. The two sets are of equal cost. The teacher hypothesizes that the two sets are equally appealing. A large significance level provides a good chance of detecting a preference if there is one. If no preference exists nothing is lost, regardless of which set of toys is purchased.

We have discussed the significance level as a pre-determined probability. Pre-determined means that the significance level is set prior to performing the statistical test. The question might be raised whether or not the significance level should be set prior to performing the statistical test. An alternate and actually newer trend of thinking is that the significance levels should be reported as they occur in the light of the completed statistical test. That is, if we reach the .08 level in the test, this is reported. The same for the .14 or .013 or any level that might occur as a result of the statistical test. It might be difficult to determine the precise level since it is not common for the tables of the values of underlying distributions to report these intermediate values. The actual procedures are not affected by this thinking, only the manner in which a conclusion is reported. For the discussion in this text we will consider the significance level as pre-determined. However, the reader should be aware that actual significance levels, observed after the statistical test, could be reported if adequate tables are available.

Parametric Assumptions

Before investigating the parametric techniques, we must consider the assumptions underlying such techniques. These assumptions, called the parametric assumptions, must be met before the application of a parametric technique is appropriate. The assumptions arise from the mathematical derivations of the procedures and formulas that underlie the parametric techniques. If the data do not meet the assumptions, the use of parametric techniques will produce invalid results.

One of the parametric assumptions is that the observations are independent; that is, the observation or score of any one S on the dependent variable does not in any way influence the observation of any other S. Suppose in an animal laboratory we are taking observations on 30 rats running a maze. If the 30 scores, one for each rat, are to be independent, then the score of any rat, as indicated by his performance, in no way influences the score of any other rat.

A second parametric assumption is the assumption of normality. This assumption requires that the observations have been drawn from normally distributed populations. However, this assumption is not crucial when sample size increases above 30. It can be mathematically shown that as sample size increases above 30 and the samples are drawn from a population not normally distributed, the statistics which would be computed from repeated random samples would tend to have a normal distribution. It is really the statistic and its underlying distribution that we are testing in the statistical test.

A third parametric assumption is that the populations being studied have homogeneous variance. If the populations have equal standard deviations, the population variances must also be equal. What this assumption means, then, is that the populations under investigation have about the same dispersion in their distributions. The populations are not actually measured, but we can estimate their variances through the sample. The variances need not be exactly equal. In fact, there can be quite a marked departure from equality before this assumption is no longer tenable. The homogeneity of variance assumption can be checked by statistical procedures if the researcher has any reason to believe that it is not met.

A fourth parametric assumption is that the observations to be analyzed (scores on the dependent variable) are measured on at least an interval scale [1] and these observations are continu-

[1] There is some division of opinion among writers in educational research as to this assumption. Educational variables which are in fact ordinal are sometimes treated as if the measurement was on an interval scale. What occurs is that the ordinal data are assigned numerical values and to some extent when this is done information is inserted into the data that was not secured through the measurement. Once we have numerical values assigned, parametric analyses can be computed in terms of actually performing the statistical manipulations. The pertinent question is whether or not such analyses make any sense and can be interpreted in a meaningful way. The researcher should know clearly what he is doing and have enough information about his variables so that he can make a decision about the appropriateness of techniques. This is the view taken by such writers as

ous in their measurement. Recall the definition of the measurement scales from the previous chapter. An interval scale requires that an equal unit be established in the measurement. Data which consist of ranks or simple classifications do not meet this assumption. Data measured on a ratio scale would, of course, meet this assumption since a ratio scale does include equal units.

The four assumptions listed above might be summarized as:

1. independence of the observations.
2. observations selected from normally distributed populations.
3. homogeneity of variance in the population distributions.
4. interval scale measurement of the variable to be analyzed.

It should be noted that the assumptions numbered 2 and 3, dealing with distributions, are assumptions about the population distributions, not the distributions of sample observations. More complex parametric procedures may require additional assumptions. An example of this occurs with covariance, a technique discussed later in the chapter.

Estimation of a Mean

The meaning and interpretation of the various tests of hypotheses are discussed with the help of examples. Consider an imaginary study in which it is desirable to estimate the mean in geometry achievement of a large population of high school sophomores. We will assume that geometry achievement can be measured on a satisfactory equal interval scale and that such achievement is normally distributed in our population. A random sample is drawn and the members of the sample take the geometry test. A mean is computed for the geometry achievement of the sample and that mean is 82. (It is not necessary that total possible points

Ferguson, *Statistical Analysis in Psychology and Education,* 2nd ed. (New York: McGraw-Hill Book Co., Inc., 1966), and Popham, *Educational Statistics* (New York: Harper and Row, Publishers, 1967). For the purposes of consistency, we will include the assumption of interval scale measurement for parametric techniques; however, the reader should interpret this assumption in light of the above remarks.

be 100, although this may be the case.) Suppose someone hypothesizes that the mean of the population is 84, someone else that it is 81. We might intuitively say that these seem to be reasonable hypotheses. A third individual hypothesizes that the population mean is 50. Our reaction to this would be that this hypothesis is untenable. Why do we entertain the 84 and 81 and not the 50? Intuitively, again, the mean of 50 seems too distant from the sample mean.

It is hardly satisfactory to make judgments on an intuitive basis alone. It may seem reasonable for the three means of 84, 81, and 50, but where are the points of departure between entertaining and rejecting a hypothesis? The problem, then, is to find two points, one on either side of 82, which represent these points of division. All the values between these two points we will entertain as possible values of the population mean.

Suppose we set our significance level at .05. That is, we will reject the hypothesis if the probability of our mean (82) appearing, if, in fact, the hypothesis is true, is less than .05. We are dealing here with a mean and hence we must consider the underlying distribution of the mean. Based on this underlying distribution, we determine the values on either side of the mean, which include the middle 95 per cent of the area. We are leaving 2.5 per cent of the area in each tail. This is done for two reasons. The significance level is .05, hence 5 per cent of the area is left for the rejection region. Since we entertain hypotheses on both sides of the sample mean, the 5 per cent is distributed evenly for each tail.

The interval is constructed symmetrically about the sample mean. In order to decide how far out from this mean we will go, it is necessary to have a standard deviation of the distribution of means. Since it is unlikely that the population standard deviation would be known, we estimate the standard deviation of the distribution of means from the sample standard deviation. The underlying distribution would be the appropriate Student's t-distribution, or, if sample size is large enough (for example, exceeding 100), the normal distribution would suffice. We now know where to locate the interval in its appropriate underlying distribution and how to determine its width. Hence, we have the necessary ingredients for the construction of the interval.

An interval so constructed is a *confidence interval.* The term confidence comes from the fact that we are 95 per cent confident that the interval spans the population mean. Note that the probability here is on the interval (based on the statistics of the sample) and not on the parameter. It is incorrect reasoning to infer that the probability is .95 that the population mean falls in the interval. The population mean is something, it is not going to change, and has no probability associated with it. The correct probability statement is that the probability of the interval spanning the population mean is .95.

In the example it is a 95 per cent confidence interval since the significance level was set at .05. Had the significance level been set at .01, the corresponding interval would be a 99 per cent confidence interval. For the same data, a 99 per cent confidence interval would be wider than the 95 per cent confidence interval. The 99 per cent interval leaves only 0.5 per cent of the area in each tail of the underlying distribution. Thus, going in a conservative direction (.05 to .01 significance level) tends to widen the confidence interval.

The initial purpose in the geometry achievement example was to estimate the population mean. If one and only one value was demanded, the best estimate would be the sample mean of 82. This would be a point estimate. Although this is the best single point estimate, it would be rather risky to argue that the population mean is exactly 82. Thus, the estimate provided by the confidence interval gives an interval of estimates which have a 95 per cent probability of including the population mean.

Suppose that in our geometry example we computed a 95 per cent confidence interval and found this interval to lie between 78.5 and 85.5. Note that this interval is symmetrically located around the sample mean of 82 with 3.5 units on each side of 82 to reach the two points 78.5 and 85.5. The probability is .95 that this interval spans the population mean. We are 95 per cent confident that the population mean is a value between 78.5 and 85.5. Note that we do not put the probability on the population mean. The probability is on the interval which was determined from the sample information, that is, from statistics.

The confidence interval is a test of an infinite number of hypotheses. Any hypothesized value which is included in the interval will be considered tenable; those that fall outside the interval will be rejected. The confidence interval is a most useful device in estimating a parameter. It gives a basis for deciding on possible values for a parameter on probability and statistical reasoning.

Hypothesis About the Difference of Two Means

Consider an example concerning the difference of two means. We have a large group of first-grade students about to embark upon reading instruction. Suppose there are two acceptable but quite distinct ways of teaching reading. We shall call these Method 1 and Method 2, designated by M_1 and M_2 respectively. A pertinent question would be: Is there any difference in the effectiveness of the two methods? There might be some discussion as to what constitutes effectiveness, but suppose that we define achievement on some acceptable reading test as the measure of effectiveness.

The first step would be to randomly pick two samples from the population of first-grade students being studied. The two sample sizes need not be the same. Then we would use M_1 with one sample and M_2 with the other sample, attempting to hold all other relevant factors constant. Upon the completion of the period of instruction, both samples are tested by the same reading achievement tests and the mean achievement for both samples determined. We will designate these means by $\bar{X}_1$ and $\bar{X}_2$. We may compute the difference between the means by subtracting the smaller from the larger. What about this difference and what kind of a decision can we make concerning the effectiveness of the methods?

The hypothesis under consideration goes back to the populations. Here we have two populations, although the samples were randomly chosen from a single population. The reason for two populations is that at the time of measuring reading achievement, that is, after the samples have been instructed by their respective methods, the samples represent two populations. The one sample represents the population of our type of first-grader taught by M_1 and the other sample that population taught by

M_2. We assume that this is the only respect in which our populations differ.

We know that the hypothesis must deal with one or more parameters and that the parameters under consideration in this example are population means. How are we to formulate the statement of the hypothesis? Recall that in Chapter 1 the null hypothesis was introduced. To state a hypothesis in null form is to hypothesize no difference. In this example, to hypothesize no difference would be to state the hypothesis as: There is no difference in the population reading achievement means of first-graders taught by M_1 and M_2. The null hypothesis may be represented in symbol form by $\mu_1 = \mu_2$ or $\mu_1 - \mu_2 = 0$. This is the hypothesis to be tested by the statistical procedure.

Each hypothesis has a corresponding alternate hypothesis. The alternate hypothesis of our example would be that the reading achievement means of first-grade populations taught by M_1 and M_2 are not equal. That is, we are hypothesizing that there is a difference between these two populations means. Note that in this case the alternate hypothesis does not indicate which of the population means is the greater. In the null hypothesis we are essentially conjecturing that the two methods do not have different effects upon the reading achievement mean. The conjecture in the alternate hypothesis is that there does exist a difference in the effectiveness of the two methods with respect to the mean.

Assume that the reading achievement test has a substantial number of items and is adequately sensitive to reading achievement. We compute the difference between the sample means and say it turns out to be 1.75 points in favor of M_2. This doesn't seem like much of a difference and our intuitive reaction would be to accept the null hypothesis and conclude that there is no difference between the population means. Now suppose the difference in sample means had been 18.9 points in favor of M_2. This is a markedly different result and we would be inclined to reject the null hypothesis. This brings us to the question of what magnitude of difference in sample means we will tolerate to entertain the null hypothesis. We turn to our statistics and probability.

The statistic that we are dealing with is a difference of two means. If we had the underlying distribution of this statistic, we could investigate it to see where our observed difference would fall in light of the hypothesis. In order to determine the standard error (that is, the standard deviation of the underlying distribution) of this statistic, we need to work through the standard deviations of the populations. Since it is unlikely that we would know the standard deviations of the population, we must use an estimate of the population standard deviations, namely the standard deviations of the samples. With these estimates, the underlying distribution of the difference of two means is distributed as Student's t-distribution, with $N_1 + N_2 - 2$ degrees of freedom, where N_1 and N_2 are the respective sample sizes. The total number of observations is $N_1 + N_2$ and we estimate two parameters, namely the standard deviations of the samples, hence the $N_1 + N_2 - 2$ degrees of freedom. Since we now have the observed statistic, its underlying distribution, and the standard error of that distribution, we can test our hypothesis. The procedure is known as the *t-test for the difference between two means*. We determine the probability of our observed difference appearing, if, in fact, the null hypothesis of no difference is true. If this probability is less than our pre-determined level (say .05) we reject the null hypothesis. Note that the statistic has the probability associated with it, but it has been observed and cannot be rejected. The parameters of the hypothesis have no probability connected with them. If the statistical test is significant, the conclusion is that we hypothesized incorrectly. In this example we would then conclude that there is a difference in population means of reading achievement of first-graders taught by M_1 and M_2. If the statistical test is not significant, we conclude that on the basis of this information we cannot reject the hypothesis of no difference.

In light of the hypothesis, we need not determine the exact probability of the statistic. Our only concern is to which side of our significance level the probability falls. Suppose the probability is less than this level. Then we say that the difference between means is significant.

An additional comment about the reasoning is in order. Recall that the samples were randomly selected from a common population. The comment was also made that the attempt was made to hold constant all relevant factors except the teaching method. Assume this to have taken place. Thus, the only things operating on the difference in mean achievement are differences due to random sampling error and teaching method. We can check on the probability of the observed difference being due to random sampling. If this probability is less than our pre-determined level, we reject this as the source of difference, leaving the teaching method as the only remaining source. To decide upon the more effective teaching method we inspect the sample means.

A specific example follows. Two samples of size 32 and 30 are randomly selected from a population of first-graders. The samples receive reading instruction by M_1 and M_2 respectively. After the instructional period (probably several weeks in duration) all 62 are given a common reading achievement test. The results are: $\bar{X}_1 = 90.00$, $\bar{X}_2 = 81.75$, and the standard error of the difference is 3.5. The null hypothesis is: $\mu_1 - \mu_2 = 0$, that is, the means of the populations from which the samples were drawn are equal. We will set the significance level at .05.

The computation of the t-value actually is the ratio of the difference between the observed statistic and hypothesized value of the corresponding parameter, to the standard error of the statistic. In symbols this is given by:

$$\frac{(\bar{X}_1 - \bar{X}_2) - (\mu_1 - \mu_2)}{S_{\bar{X}_1 - \bar{X}_2}}$$

and substituting in our sample values we have: $\bar{X}_1 - \bar{X}_2 = 90.00 - 81.75 = 8.25$; $\mu_1 - \mu_2 = 0$ (from our hypothesis), and $S_{\bar{X}_1 - \bar{X}_2} = 3.5$. Thus, the t-value becomes $\frac{8.25 - 0}{3.5} = 2.36$, with $32 + 30 - 2 = 60$ as the associated degrees of freedom. Our null hypothesis was $\mu_1 = \mu_2$ and therefore we hypothesized no direction, and the rejection region appears in both tails of the underlying distribution. We consult Table B and find that for 60 degrees of freedom a value of 2.00 is required for significance at the .05 level. Our statistical test is significant. The probability that the observed difference between sample means of 8.25 would appear by chance, if, in fact, the population means are equal, is less than .05. Therefore we reject the null hypothesis and conclude that the population means are not equal. By inspection we can see that the difference in sample means favored M_1.

One- and Two-Tailed Statistical Tests

The hypothesis of the preceding example did not hypothesize a direction. That is, $\mu_1 - \mu_2$ could, in fact, be on either side of zero. Another way of saying this is that μ_1 may be greater than μ_2 or vice versa, μ_2 greater than μ_1. Hence we had what is called a *two-tailed test*, designating one-half of the rejection area for each tail of the distribution. The name "two-tailed" comes from the condition that the rejection region is contained in both ends or tails of the distribution. Therefore, in the preceding example when we consulted the table to determine the value necessary for significance, we came down the column for two-tailed tests at the .05 level of significance and found the value 2.00 corresponding to 60 degrees of freedom. The right part of Figure 3.2 illustrates the location of the rejection region for a two-tailed test.

Consider a slightly different situation. Suppose the two teaching methods are of such a nature that M_2 utilizes the existing textbooks and materials and M_1 involves a major change in materials. In order to justify this changeover, the evidence would have to significantly favor M_1. Thus, in this case we would hypothesize a direction, namely $\mu_1 > \mu_2$. The alternate hypothesis is that μ_2 is not greater than μ_1. In determining the rejection region we must consider our underlying distribution and its location. Recall that in our two-tailed test the null hypothesis located the underlying distribution. However, a directional hypotheses such as $\mu_1 > \mu_2$ does not locate a distribution since an infinite number of hypothesized values would satisfy $\mu_1 > \mu_2$. Therefore, we continue to use the null hypothesis for locating our underlying distribution even with a directional hypothesis. But, instead of having the rejection region located in both tails as with a two-tailed test, under the circumstances of a directional hypothesis, the rejection region would be located in one tail of the underlying distribution. Since the rejection region is located entirely in one tail, we refer to this as the one-tailed test.

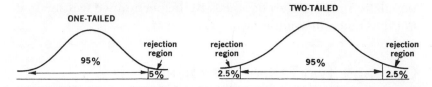

Figure 3.2   The rejection regions for one- and two-tailed tests with $\alpha = .05$.

The specific tail would be the right tail if we consider $\bar{X}_1 - \bar{X}_2$ which goes with the direction of the hypothesis. The negative values would not concern us because we are not interested in showing M_2 superior to M_1. In this case, the rejection region would be located entirely in the one tail. Suppose the significance level was again set at .05 and we have 60 degrees of freedom. The t-value now required for significance is 1.67. It can be seen that this would not be as great as the corresponding value for a two-tailed test. We do not need to go out as far from the mean in standard deviation units to have 5 per cent of the tail remaining as we do for 2.5 per cent. Figure 3.2 illustrates the rejection regions in terms of area for one- and two-tailed tests with the significance level set at .05.

Let us return to our example $\bar{X}_i - \bar{X}_2 = 8.25$ which gave a t-value of 2.36. This value exceeds the 1.67 required for significance and therefore our statistical test is significant and we reject the hypothesis that μ_1 is not greater than μ_2. Our conclusion is that μ_1 is greater than μ_2 and that M_1 is a superior method of teaching. It should be noted that had $\bar{X}_1 - \bar{X}_2$ been negative, that is, $\bar{X}_2$ greater than $\bar{X}_1$, it would not have been necessary to perform any computation since in this particular example there is no rejection region in the negative tail of the underlying distribution.

A word of caution about the conclusion when using a one-tailed test. Suppose a one-tailed test is computed and found to be significant, that is, our value is in the rejection region. What are we going to reject? The rejection region refers to the hypothesis that μ_1 is not greater than μ_2. Therefore we do not reject our initial hypothesis of μ_1 greater than μ_2. We would conclude that μ_1 is greater than μ_2 and, as noted above, that M_1 is more effective than M_2. The matter of the alternate hypothesis is relative. The rejection region refers to the hypothesis of no difference (two-tailed) or not greater than (one-tailed) (could also be formulated as not less than if the situation warranted this direction). Caution should be exercised not to become confused in reasoning from the result of the statistical test to the correct conclusion regarding the hypothesis, whether or not it is stated in null form.

The comment might be made that we do not want to make a change from M_2 to M_1 unless we are almost completely certain that M_1 shows a significantly greater mean achievement. If the t-test is found to be significant at the .05 level, our conclusion is that the probability is less than .05 (less than 1 in 20) that the observed difference occurred by chance. This probability may still be too great for some skeptics. If this is the case, it might have been preferable to go to a more conservative significance level, say .01. In extreme cases the .001 level might be used, but it is generally not used in educational research. Going in this direction actually lowers the likelihood of rejecting the hypothesis of no difference.

The preceding examples illustrate a specific use of the t-test for comparing the means of two independent samples. The t-distribution has many applications in hypothesis testing. The computation is a technical matter and not of importance for the purposes of this text. Whenever a researcher uses computational formulas, they should be checked with a statistics text to be certain of appropriateness and correct application.

Analysis of Variance: One-Way

The next question someone might ask is: What if we had three teaching methods and consequently three means to test for significant differences? One approach would be to consider the means in combinations of two and apply three separate t-tests. But it soon becomes apparent that this procedure would be inefficient. For five means it would require ten separate t-tests; for six means fifteen such tests would be necessary. More important than the inefficiency when using many multiple t-tests in the same analysis, we would expect some to be statistically significant just by chance. In order to apply multiple t-tests appropriately in the same analysis, the significance level would have to be adjusted and a separate level used for each possible number of such t-tests to be computed.

A more desirable and efficient technique is the *analysis of variance*. The analysis of variance is one of the most powerful and widely used procedures. The basic ideas were developed by Sir Ronald Fisher during the first half of the twentieth century. The discussion in this text is limited to the ideas relative to application and hypothesis testing. There are many variations of the analysis of variance and the procedures are extensively involved with the design of experiments. Computational procedures may become quite involved and complex. However, the basic ideas relative to hypothesis testing remain the same and these ideas are what we are concerned with in this discussion.

The analysis of variance may be summarized as a technique for partitioning the variation in the observed data into parts, each part assignable to different causes or combinations of causes. Analysis of variance is appropriate when it can be assumed that the several groups of observations can be treated as random samples from the populations. It is further assumed that if the populations differ, they differ only in their means.

What does it mean to partition the variance? Suppose that we had three teaching methods with thirty students taught by each method. The students are measured on an achievement test. This would give us ninety observations or scores on the dependent variable. If all ninety scores were exactly the same there would be no variance. This is extremely unlikely. Why are the scores different? One possible source of difference is the three different teaching methods. But now consider the students within a teaching method. They have been taught by the same methods, presumably the same teacher, spent the same amount of time in class and in general have been treated the same. Why don't the thirty students within a teaching method all have identical scores? The reason they don't is because there exists what we might term a "natural" variation among the students that received the same treatment. This variance is more commonly called the *error* variance, *within* variance, or *expected* variance. To partition the variance in this example means to consider the variation of all ninety scores and decide what part is attributable to teaching method and what part is due to the difference within the three groups. In this example there were only two sources of variation. In more complex analyses there might be several sources and the variance would be partitioned among the sources.

Consider a research situation. A mathematics teacher is to have four sections of elementary algebra during the upcoming school year. Prior to the scheduling he arranges with the administration to randomly assign twenty-five incoming freshmen to each of his four classes. (This is an unlikely freedom in most practical situations.) From the opening of the school year the teacher proceeds to teach each class using different experimental materials. These materials are designated as M_1, M_2, M_3, and M_4. The question under investigation is: Do the experimental materials have different effects upon algebra achievement? The independent variable in this study is type of material, or simply, material. It has four levels. The dependent variable is algebra achievement. There are several constants including school, teacher, and grade level. Note that only incoming freshmen are involved in the study.

A word might be said here about the dependent variable. We are assuming that algebra achievement is continuously distributed and can be measured on an equal unit scale. Achievement would probably be measured after a considerable instructional period, say one semester. The test may be teacher-made but caution should be exercised to avoid slanting the questions to any specific type of material. If a standardized test of algebraic achievement is available, this might be used as the measure of achievement. The test would require careful inspection to see if it covers the objectives of algebra instruction and adequately applies to the situation.

The actual data collected are the scores of the one hundred or remaining students who take the algebra test. If a student moves away or for some reason cannot participate to completion, this is not serious. The analysis of variance in this case does not require equal numbers in the four groups. We assume that no systematic dropout is occurring in the groups and any dropouts should be randomly distributed among the four groups. The scores on the tests are the data that go into the analysis of variance.

The null hypothesis of our hypothetical study is that the population means of the four groups taught using M_1, M_2, M_3, and M_4 are equal. Initially it may seem that we do not have four populations, only four samples. However, underlying these samples are four populations to which we hope to generalize our results. The four populations are considered to be alike in all characteristics except the materials used in instruction. The null hypothesis may be written symbolically as: H_0: $\mu_1 = \mu_2 = \mu_3 = \mu_4$. Note that the hypothesis is a statement about parameters, not statistics. No difference between population means is being hypothesized.

At this point we introduce the term *sums of squares*. Sums of squares means that the difference between an observation and a mean is squared, then these differences squared are summed over the number of observations. For example, in our hypothetical situation of one hundred students the total sum of squares would be given by $\sum_{i=1}^{100} (X_i - \bar{X})^2$, where $\bar{X}$ is the grand mean of all one hundred observations. This looks very much like the numerator of the formula for variance. The value of the degrees of freedom corresponds to the denominator of the formula for variance. In the analysis of variance, sums of squares are divided by the appropriate degrees of freedom for an estimate of the variance.

An estimate of the error variance (within or natural variance) is the *pooled variance* within the four groups of our study. What is a pooled variance? Suppose we compute the sum of squares individually for each of the four groups. That is, we would subtract each observation from its group mean instead of from the grand mean, square and sum these squares. Within each group, the degrees of freedom would be one less than the number in the group. Then we would add the four sums of squares and divide by the sum of the four degrees of freedom values for the estimate of error variance. This addition process is called pooling and hence the name pooled variance. The term error variance means the estimate of the existing natural or random variance. We assume that the four groups have about equal variance so we pool these variances. In the actual process, to obtain the estimate the sums of squares are pooled and this is divided by the pooled degrees of freedom. We will designate this estimate of the error variance by S_W^2.

Under the assumption that the population means are equal, the variance between the sample means should be a second estimate of the error variance. Even if the population means are equal, we would expect some variation in sample means due to sampling fluctuations. When the sum of squares between means is computed and divided by the appropriate degrees of freedom, this estimate would contain only random or error variance. There would be no variance due to differences in population means. This second estimate we will denote by S_B^2. The subscript B denotes the estimate from the difference between sample means. Now, under the assumption of equal means, we have two estimates of the same error variance. The only difference between them is the difference due to chance.

In the work with the Student's t-test we considered the difference of two means. Here we have two variances. We do not consider their difference but their ratio. The ratio S_B^2/S_W^2 is distributed as the corresponding F-distribution. Here, corresponding refers to the correct degrees of freedom. Recall from the discussion in Chapter 2 that the F-distribution requires two values of degrees of freedom. These values are the degrees of freedom associated with S_B^2 and S_W^2 in the analysis of variance. The F-distribution is the appropriate underlying distribution for the ratio of two variances and the specific distribution of this family of distributions is determined by the degrees of freedom associated with the variances that go into the ratio.

Under the null hypothesis we would expect the ratio of S_B^2/S_W^2 to be around one since S_B^2 and S_W^2 estimate the same variance. The F-distributions as given in Table D give us the values for the probability of .05 and .01. That is, the values of the ratio have probabilities of .05 and .01 of appearing by chance. If values of the ratio (F-values) are greater than the indicated table values, the probabilities of their appearing by chance are less than .05 and .01.

Suppose that the null hypothesis is not true, i.e., there are real differences between the group means. That means that S_B^2 not only contains error variance but also variation due to differences in the means. Thus S_B^2 will tend to be inflated. Since it is the numerator of our ratio, the ratio will tend to increase. As the ratio increases, its probability of appearing by chance decreases. When we reach the pre-determined level of .05 or .01, we will no longer entertain the idea that the value of this ratio occurred by chance.

At this point let us inspect the reasoning carefully. Suppose for our algebra study the analysis of variance produced a significant F-ratio. Here, significant means that its probability of occurrence by chance is less than our pre-determined probability (significance) level, say .05. There are now two possible explanations for this F-ratio:

1. There are no real differences between the population means from which the sample was drawn, and the F-ratio occurred only by chance (random sampling errors), that is, we contend that a rare event has occurred since its probability of occurrence is less than .05.
2. We reject the null hypothesis and conclude that the F-ratio did not occur by chance but due to real differences in the population means of the group.

It is the second of these explanations that we will entertain. Since our significance level is .05, we are running the risk of being wrong about one in twenty times.

A word about the degrees of freedom values of the F-ratio. In Chapter 2 it was pointed out that we lose a degree of freedom for each restriction that we place on the data. The S_B^2 is determined by squaring the deviations of the group means from the grand mean. Referring back to our example, there are four group means, but since the grand mean is known, if three of the group means are known, the fourth is also determined. Therefore, the degrees of freedom associated with S_B^2 is $4 - 1 = 3$. In general, if we let k be the number of group means, the degrees of freedom associated with S_B^2 is $k - 1$.

The S_W^2 is a pooled estimate of variance. The deviation of each observation within a group from the group mean is squared. Since a mean is necessary for each group, one degree of freedom is lost in each group. In our example, since each group contains twenty-five observations, we would have twenty-four degrees of freedom within each group. But we pool the degrees of freedom, therefore the degrees of freedom associated with S_W^2 is ninety-six. In general, we know that the sum of the observations across all groups is the total sample size, say n. We lose a degree of freedom for each group mean and if we have k groups, the degrees of freedom associated with S_W^2 is $n - k$. This value for our example is $100 - 4$ or, again, 96.

The correct degrees of freedom for the F-ratio of our example are three and ninety-six. By inspection of Table D we see that approximately 2.70 is needed for significance at the .05 level. In using the table, we take the degrees of freedom of S_B^2 across the top of the table.

If the F-ratio had not been significant, we would conclude that on the basis of these results no one of the materials will produce higher mean achievement than any of the others. That is, we fail to reject the null hypothesis of equal population means. The associated probability statement after the statistical test would be: The probability that the sample means, $\bar{X}_1$, $\bar{X}_2$, $\bar{X}_3$, and $\bar{X}_4$ would have appeared by chance if, in fact, $\mu_1 = \mu_2 = \mu_3 = \mu_4$ is greater than .05. Note the "greater than" since the test was not significant. Suppose the F-ratio is significant. Then the associated probability statement would be: The probability that the sample means, $\bar{X}_1$, $\bar{X}_2$, $\bar{X}_3$, and $\bar{X}_4$ would have occurred by chance if, in fact, $\mu_1 = \mu_2 = \mu_3 = \mu_4$ is less than .05. However, we still do not know where the significance lies. The first thing we would do is inspect the means and arrange them in descending or ascending order. But it has been pointed out that inspection is not an adequate technique in deciding about the differences in means.

At this point some post-mortem test is necessary to locate the source of the significance. Student's t-tests could be computed for difference of the means in combinations of two. However, this is an inefficient procedure since several such tests would be required. The number of t-tests would rapidly increase with the number of groups. For example, four groups would require six tests; five groups, ten tests; and six groups, fifteen such tests. Also, if a large number of means are involved, a certain number of these tests would be expected to turn up significant by chance. There are other more efficient procedures. Although the computation procedures are beyond the scope of this text, discussions relevant to this topic are treated in more advanced statistics and research design texts.[1]

Let us assume that in our example the mean of the group taught by M_3 was significantly higher than the remaining three means. We would then conclude that students taught by M_3 attain a higher mean achievement in algebra and on this basis M_3 is superior to the other three experimental materials. Note that the conclusion here refers to populations of students taught by the use of the four types of materials.

The algebra example involved a one-way analysis of variance. One-way means that only one independent variable was under investigation. The total variance was partitioned into two parts: one part due to differences between group means and a second part due to differences within groups.

Analysis of Variance: Two-Way

An important characteristic of the analysis of variance is the possibility of testing more than two group means in a single analysis. However, the analysis of variance has other important advantages over less sophisticated techniques. One of these advantages is that two or more independent variables can be investigated simultaneously in the same analysis. When two independent variables are included in the same analysis of variance, we have what is called a *two-way analysis of variance*. There may be any number of groups or levels within an independent variable.

Many research situations involve more than one independent variable. It may be of interest to check not only how the various independent variables affect the dependent variable, but also

[1] For an excellent discussion of multiple comparisons of means, the reader is referred to Edwards, A. L., *Experimental Design in Psychological Research* (New York: Holt, Rinehart and Winston, Inc., 1960), pp. 136–157.

how combinations of their levels affect the dependent variable. Independent variables in combinations may have an effect which neither one would have singly. Sometimes we say that independent variables influence or affect each other relative to the dependent variable. The effect of one independent variable upon another is referred to as *interaction*. Sometimes interaction is referred to as the lack of the effect of one independent variable to remain constant over the levels of another. The analysis of variance can be used to test (statistically) for the existence of interaction. (Interaction is discussed more fully in connection with the following example.)

Consider an example. Suppose we have three methods of teaching history and we decide to teach at two different times, say morning and afternoon. We now have two independent variables: teaching method and time of day. The teaching methods will be denoted by M_1, M_2, and M_3; the times by T_1 and T_2. To get all of the levels of the independent variables in all possible combinations with each other we need 3×2 or 6 groups. These are designated as M_1T_1, M_1T_2, M_2T_1, M_2T_2, M_3T_1, and M_3T_2.

Let us suppose that the dependent variable is achievement in history which can be objectively and adequately measured on an interval scale. Before the instructional period begins we would randomly assign equal numbers of students to each of the six groups. If this is a sophomore history class we would assign only sophomores. After an adequate instructional period, the dependent variable would be measured. The analysis of variance will be performed on the scores of the dependent variable.

There are three questions posed in this hypothetical example. Generally they are stated as follows:

1. Does teaching method affect achievement in history?
2. Does the time of day for teaching affect achievement in history?
3. Do teaching method and time have an interaction effect upon history achievement?

We must now consider the corresponding hypotheses. If there is an effect of any of these independent variables (or their combination) we expect it to show up in the mean achievement of the groups. The null hypotheses are statements about population means. The populations are the populations taught by the different methods and at the different times, of which we assume our samples to be representative. The null hypothesis for method is: H_o: $\mu_{M_1} = \mu_{M_2} = \mu_{M_3}$. The μ's represent the respective population means of the populations taught by the three teaching methods, M_1, M_2, M_3. The null hypothesis for time is H_o $\mu_{T_1} = \mu_{T_2}$.

Recall that the numbers in each of the six groups were equal and let us assume that they remained equal through the completion of the data collection. Note that the independent variables are balanced with respect to each other. Consider T_1. It contains equal numbers of students taught by M_1, M_2, and M_3. The same is true for T_2, and T_2 contains the same number of each as T_1. In looking at the methods we find that they are balanced in the same manner relative to the two times.

We shall set our significance level at .05. The workings of the analysis of variance are the same in the two-way as the one-way except that the computations are more extensive and there are additional sources of variance. In the one-way analysis of variance, we partition the total variance into two parts: one part due to differences between groups and the other due to differences within groups. In the two-way analysis of variance we partition the total variance into four parts, that is, instead of having only two sources of variance we have four sources. There is one part for each of the independent variables. In our example these would correspond to differences between the methods and differences between the times. There is also one component of variance for interaction and one component for differences within the groups.

The purpose in the two-way analysis of variance is still to get ratios of error variance under the null hypothesis. In the one-way analysis of variance there was only one ratio, the ratio of the between component to the within component. When going to the two-way analysis of variance there are three such ratios: one for each of the independent variables and one for their interaction. We want to get ratios that are distributed as the F-distributions, with the corresponding degrees of freedom.

When dealing with the one-way analysis of variance, there is no question about how to set up an F-ratio because there is only one such ratio—the between estimate of variance over the within. However, in going to the two-way analysis of variance there are other possible ways of setting up the F-ratios since there are four estimates of variance. For the purposes of this discussion and in the context of our example, we will assume that we have a fixed effects model.[1] A *fixed-effects model* is one for which the levels of the independent variables have been "fixed" by the researcher and these levels have not been randomly selected from a larger population of possible levels. In our example, the fact that method is a fixed effect means that the researcher designated and defined the three different methods and that he is attempting to generalize only to these three methods. He did not select the three methods from a larger population of methods. When the independent variables in a two-way analysis of variance are fixed, the denominator of each F-ratio for testing the effects of the independent variables and their interaction would be the within estimate of variance. In our example this estimate would be the pooled within variance of the six groups.[2]

The probability statement associated with the method means is: What is the probability that our observed means would have occurred by chance, if, in fact, there is no difference in popula-

[1] The nature of the independent variables in terms of how their levels have been selected and put into the analysis determines the components of variance that are in the respective estimates of variance. This will, of course, influence how we set up our F-ratios. In general, we want the numerator of the F-ratio to contain one and only one additional component of variance than the denominator, that being the component of the effect being tested. Under the null hypothesis this component is no more than error variance. A detailed discussion of different models is beyond the scope of this book. Allen Edwards, *Experimental Design in Psychological Research,* rev. ed. (New York: Holt, Rinehart and Winston, Inc., 1960) has an excellent treatment of this topic and the reader who anticipates computing analyses of variance with multiple independent variables should consult the Edwards reference.

[2] In the case of no replication (only one observation) in each cell, the interaction estimate can be used as the denominator of the F-ratios for testing the effects of the independent variables *if* the assumption can be made that there is no interaction effect and hence this component contains only error variance. With no replication there is no way to statistically test for an interaction effect in a two-way analysis of variance.

tions means? The analysis of variance involves, of course, the F-ratio. An equivalent way of considering our probability statement is: What is the probability of the observed F-ratio occurring by chance if there are no real differences in the population means? The second statement is more specific to what is tested in the analysis of variance. The former statement may seem more specific to the null hypothesis.

It is not necessary that we determine the exact probability. Rather, we are interested only in whether or not it is less than or greater than .05, our significance level. Knowing this will enable us to make a decision about the null hypothesis. The table of F-ratios is used for making this decision. However, before a decision can be made we must have an F-ratio. In the two-way analysis of variance, a different F-ratio is computed for each of the two main [1] effects and their interaction effect. The basic procedure is the same as that for a one-way analysis of variance. For example, to determine the F-ratio associated with the effect of teaching method we would obtain an estimate of the variance between the three method means and an estimate of error variance. The ratio of these two estimates would make up one of our F-ratios. This F-ratio would test the null hypothesis for teaching method. An analogous procedure would be used to test the null hypothesis for time of instruction and test for an interaction effect.

If a significant F-ratio appears when testing method, we say there is a significant method effect. The same would be true for the time variable. A third effect exists in this analysis and that is the interaction between the two independent variables. Interaction has been described as an effect of combinations of the independent variables. To have a significant interaction effect, the effect of one independent variable does not remain constant over the levels of the other independent variable. That is, the effect varies as we have different combinations of levels of the two independent variables. Significant interaction effects may take on several different patterns of means.

In the context of our example, a significant interaction would indicate that one (or more) method shows a greater increase in effectiveness in going from one time to the other than one (or more) of the other methods. For a specific analysis it is well to

---

[1] The effect of an independent variable singly is called a *main effect*.

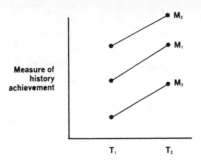

Figure 3.3   A possible plot of means indicating no significant interaction between time and method.

plot the dependent variable means for all the combinations of the independent variables on a graph. The units on the vertical axis represent the dependent variable scale of measurement while those arbitrarily spaced on the horizontal axis represent the levels of one of the independent variables. These means are sometimes referred to as *cell means*. In our example there would be six such means, one for each of the combinations (or cells), M_1T_1, M_1T_2, M_2T_1, M_2T_2, M_3T_1, and M_3T_2. Figure 3.3 shows a possible pattern of means which would indicate no interaction. Figure 3.4 shows four possible patterns which might yield a significant interaction effect. The points on the graphs represent the six cell means. To be certain of such an effect, the mathematical computations and tests of the interaction F-ratio would be necessary.

There could be many more possible plots of the six means, but if an actual analysis were done only one specific pattern would exist. A significant interaction may appear in the absence of significant main effects. An example of such a situation would be the lower left plot of Figure 3.4.

The degrees of freedom associated with the interaction is the product of the degrees of freedom associated with the independent variables in the interaction. Suppose we let k and j represent the number of levels of the independent variables. Then the degrees of freedom associated with the interaction is the product of $(k - 1)(j - 1)$. In our example the degrees of freedom would be $(3 - 1)(2 - 1) = 2$. The degrees of freedom for the main effects are determined in the same manner as for the one-way analysis of variance.

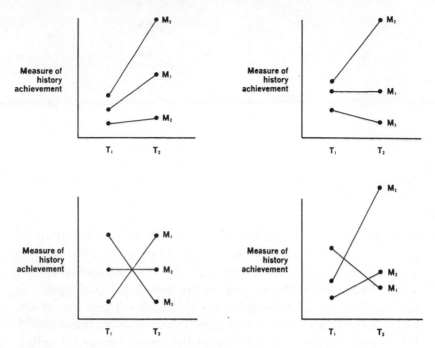

Figure 3.4 Four possible plots of means indicating significant inter-action between time and method.

The data for a two-way analysis of variance are sometimes arranged in a row- and column-array. This is done only for the purpose of structural convenience. In such an array, one variable is placed on the rows and another on the columns. The product of the numbers of rows and columns is then the number of cells in the analysis. The column by row array for our time and method example appear in Figure 3.5. Method is in the columns and time is in the rows. The row and column means are usually indicated but they are not considered a part of the k by j, in this case 3 by 2, array. We see that each row and column sum has one restriction since the dependent variable means of the levels of the independent variables are computed. Thus, by inspecting the array of our example we see that there are $(3 - 1)(2 - 1) = 2$ cells free to vary. In general, there are $(k - 1)(j - 1)$ cells free to vary and this product is the number of degrees of freedom associated with the interaction term.

Earlier in this chapter it was noted that two advantages of the

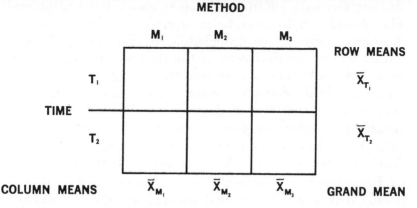

Figure 3.5   The row and column array for a two-way analysis of variance involving time and method.

analysis of variance are (1) possibility of checking on more than one independent variable simultaneously and (2) checking whether or not there exists an interaction effect. These advantages can be realized in a two-way analysis of variance, and the preceding example is an illustration of both advantages. Additional independent variables could be introduced which would extend the design and computation. As additional independent variables are included, higher order interactions may be computed. By higher order is meant a greater number of independent variables included in the interaction. If four independent variables were included in the analysis there would be four interaction terms of three variables and one of four variables, in addition to the six involving two variables. The computation of these interactions does not guarantee their interpretations. It may be difficult to interpret interactions which involve more than two variables. If there is empirical evidence or if the assumption can be made that the higher order interactions are not significant, their sums of squares along with the degrees of freedom may be pooled with the within-error estimate. This is a decision for the researcher to make in the light of his knowledge about the particular variables under study.

The assumptions underlying the analysis of variance are, of course, the parametric assumptions. The analysis of variance is a robust technique; that is, for large sample sizes the underlying distributions can depart quite markedly from normality without seriously affecting the application of the technique. This should not, however, be interpreted as an indication that the assumptions may be disregarded. An equal unit scale is required for the measurement of the dependent variable. The parametric analysis of variance is not to be applied to data measured on ordinal or nominal scales. The assumption of homogeneity of variance, that is, that the samples are from equally variable populations, is often not checked. If there is reason to believe that the assumption may have been violated, it should be checked statistically. A common procedure is the Bartlett test for homogeneity of variance. The computational procedure is discussed in detail in selected research design and statistics texts.[1]

Analysis of Covariance

A statistical technique for testing hypotheses, closely related to the analysis of variance, is the analysis of covariance. The *analysis of covariance* is a method of statistical control. It is especially useful for situations in which experimental control over an extraneous or mediating variable is impossible or undesirable. A researcher, especially one who works in a school setting, often must take "intact" groups such as classes for his research studies. For practical reasons, he cannot equate the groups through random assignment. The analysis of covariance can often be used effectively in such situations. Many investigations in educational research are or could be strengthened by the use of analysis of covariance.

Consider a research situation. A researcher is interested in determining the effects of team-teaching versus self-contained classroom instruction upon sixth-grade achievement in mathematics. The research situation is set up in a single school. It is unlikely that the administrative procedures of the school would allow for random assignment of students to the two techniques. The classes would likely have to be taken as they have been set up. Assume that somehow the teachers for the two groups can be equated and that teachers are favorable toward the method

[1] For example, see Edwards, A. L., *Experimental Design in Psychological Research* (New York: Holt, Rinehart and Winston, Inc., 1960), pp. 125–128.

they teach. The materials used, instructional time, etc. are held constant for both groups.

What is the question being investigated? The question may be stated as: Do sixth-grade students show higher mathematics achievement when taught in a self-contained classroom or a team-teaching situation? We will define the more effective method as that which indicates the higher mean achievement for the group. Since we want to generalize this to some population of sixth graders, we will consider the means on our two groups as statistics and test for a statistically significant difference. Thus, the null hypothesis is that there is no difference in the mean achievement in mathematics of sixth graders, as defined by our population, taught in a self-contained or team-teaching situation.

The instruction proceeds. Near the end of the academic year the students are objectively tested by some appropriate test of mathematical achievement. The data are assembled and analyzed. The researcher can use a Student's t-test or an analysis of variance. Suppose that he has decided to control one or more additional variables as independent variables, so the analysis technique used is the analysis of variance. Examples of such variables might be the time of day for the arithmetic instruction and the sex of the students. The statistical test is computed and the difference between the observed means is statistically significant. For illustration purposes, let us assume that the mean of the group taught by team-teaching is the greater of the two. Hence, we reject the null hypothesis and conclude that team-teaching is the more effective method.

On the surface, the procedure and conclusion may seem appropriate. But someone would be quick to point out that there is no guarantee that two groups were equal in learning ability. How do we know that the team-taught group which attained a significantly higher mean was not a more able group? Another way of saying this is that maybe the greater achievement was not due to the teaching method but due to more able students. Recall that there was no random sampling of students for the two groups, so there is no basis for the argument that learning ability was randomly distributed among the two groups.

A better procedure would be to use the analysis of covariance. What is needed is a measure of learning ability and for the purposes of this example, let us assume that a recent I.Q. score is an adequate measure of learning ability. Preferably the students' I.Q. would be measured prior to the instructional period. The I.Q. score would then become the *covariate* or, as it is sometimes called, the *pretest*. The arithmetic achievement score at the end of the year is still the dependent variable and may be referred to as the *posttest*. In the analysis of covariance, the dependent variable scores are analyzed for significant differences but the scores are adjusted for initial covariate differences between the groups. Analysis of covariance is a technique which adjusts for initial differences on some supposedly relevant variable.

The suggestion was made in our example that the I.Q. scores (covariate) be obtained prior to the instructional period. This would not be absolutely necessary, although it would guard against the possibility of the instruction affecting the I.Q. score. For some situations it is necessary to obtain the covariate data prior to conducting the research. How do we know the team-taught group did not know more arithmetic before they started sixth grade? This suggests that the groups should be pretested on arithmetic achievement and this would, of course, have to take place prior to conducting the research. Under these conditions, the pretest arithmetic achievement score would become the covariate. An analysis of covariance is not limited to a single covariate. In our example both I.Q. and pretest arithmetic achievement could be included as covariates. The posttest arithmetic achievement scores would then be adjusted on the basis of a composite of the two covariates.

The analysis of covariance is a parametric technique. As such, the parametric assumptions are to be met. The covariate also requires interval scale measurement. Like the analysis of variance, the analysis of covariance involves the F-ratio. In this case, the F-ratio does not test for difference in observed means but rather for differences in adjusted means, the means being adjusted on the basis of the covariate. The hypotheses being tested relate to the adjusted means.

The analysis of covariance is a technique by which we can gain statistical control over an extraneous but relevant variable that would otherwise be confounded with the independent variable(s). However, the purpose of doing an analysis of covariance is to serve research ends, not statistical ends. We want to be able to make a decision about the effects of our independent variable. In the arithmetic achievement example we want to make a decision about the relative effectiveness of the two instructional organizations.

The example discussed used I.Q. as the covariate. Intelligence measures are quite commonly used as covariates in educational research, especially in research concerned with academic achievement. Pretest achievement in the same academic area can also be effectively used as a covariate. Actually, any variable measured on at least an equal unit scale could serve as a covariate, although we would generally choose a variable relevant to the dependent variable.

The actual computation of an analysis of covariance is quite involved and beyond the scope of this text.[1] With the invention and availability of high speed electronic computers, the human effort has been substantially reduced. Computer programs exist for including two or more covariates in a single analysis.

Even though the computers have greatly reduced human effort, the interpretation of the computer output still remains the responsibility of the researcher. Caution should be taken to avoid confusion between observed and adjusted means. The analysis of covariance statistically tests for differences between adjusted means and the researcher must be careful not to interpret this as a test for differences between observed means. More complex designs, those involving more than one independent variable, may be analyzed by the analysis of covariance. Interaction effects may also be determined. Again, the hypotheses tested relate to adjusted means. The comments relative to interpretation of interaction made in the discussion of analysis of variance apply in the analysis of covariance.

A word might be said here about doing a research study of the magnitude as the team-teaching versus self-contained classroom study suggested in the example. Such a study would require considerable effort and time to set up and carry out. The researcher would undoubtedly be interested in all areas of sixth-

[1] For the basic formulas of an analysis of covariance the reader is referred to Lindquist, E. F., *Design and Analysis of Experiments in Psychology and Education* (Boston: Houghton Mifflin Company, 1953), pp. 319–327.

grade achievement. However, what has been said relative to arithmetic achievement would also apply to other areas as far as the research methodology is concerned. The number of dependent variables would be increased and each analyzed separately.

The preceding techniques are the most common parametric procedures used for hypothesis testing in educational research. Results based on these techniques appear frequently in research literature. Quite often F-ratios appear in tables. The F-ratio may have an asterisk and the reference immediately below the table will indicate, for example, p. $< .05$. This means that the probability of the observed F-ratio appearing by chance is less than .05. Hence the conclusion is that the corresponding independent variable (or interaction) has a significant effect upon the dependent variable.

Errors in Hypothesis Testing

Recall that in hypothesis testing we hypothesize about parameters and through the statistical test reach a conclusion about the hypothesis. This hypothesis about the parameters is either true or false, but we will never be certain about it unless we measure the entire population. Thus, in the testing of hypotheses there exists the possibility that a decision error has been made. The element of risk is ever present in hypothesis testing.

The test of a specific hypothesis will conclude in one of four possible results. These may be diagrammed in a 2 by 2 table on the basis of the actual situation in the population and the decision of the researcher. This fourfold table appears in Figure 3.6. The columns in this figure represent the situation in the population which will never be known for certain. The rows indicate the researcher's decision relative to the hypothesis. The statements in the box indicate whether the researcher's decision is correct or in error. If a true hypothesis is accepted or a false hypothesis rejected, there is no error. The other two alternatives result in errors, namely, a true hypothesis is rejected or a false hypothesis is accepted. The error of rejecting a true hypothesis is referred to as a Type I or *alpha* (α) *error*. The error of accepting a false hypothesis is a Type II or *beta* (β) *error*. In any one

**ACTUAL SITUATION
RELATIVE TO HYPOTHESIS**

		True	False
RESEARCHER'S DECISION	**Accept**	Correct	Error
	Reject	Error	Correct

Figure 3.6   The four possible outcomes in hypothesis testing.

particular test of a hypothesis, the researcher has the possibility of making only one error since he must either accept or reject the hypothesis. If the researcher rejects, he may be making a Type I error; if he accepts, he may be making a Type II error.

The problems of reducing and controlling the probabilities of these two types of errors are not simple. For a constant sample size, reducing the risk of a Type I error increases the risk of a Type II error. The probability of making a Type I error is the same as the level of significance. Thus, the significance level could be reduced, to .001 for example, and under this condition there is only a one in a thousand chance of rejecting a true hypothesis. However, since not rejecting is likely to result in accepting the hypothesis, reducing the significance level is inevitably accompanied by an increase in the risk of accepting a false hypothesis. This can be intuitively seen by considering our underlying distribution. As the significance level is reduced, the rejection region decreases in area. Since the total area is constant, this results in an increase of the acceptance region. This means that greater discrepancies between observed and hypothesized values will be tolerated before a hypothesis is rejected. Figure 3.7 illustrates this point. Note that the rejection area is decreased when the significance level goes from .05 to .01. Consider the right tail of each distribution. The distribution for the .05 level of significance contains 2.5 per cent of the area; that for the .01 level only .5 per cent of the area. Hence, there are values in the rejection area of the .05 distribution which would not fall in the rejection region of the .01 distribution. Therefore, we have decreased the probability of rejecting a true hypothesis.

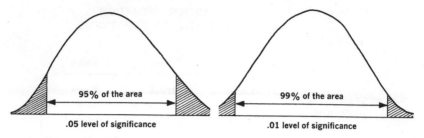

Figure 3.7 A comparison of rejection regions (shaded areas) for two significance levels with all other factors held constant.

The probability of making a Type II error is not arrived at in a simple manner. It involves the relation of the actual value of the parameter to the hypothesized value. Since we do not know the true value of the parameter, this involves a second or alternative hypothesis. If, in testing a specific hypothesis, we fail to reject it, we may pose the question: What is the probability of making a Type II error if the parameter is not the hypothesized value but some alternative value? Statistical procedures relative to this problem are commonly discussed in educational statistics texts.[1] For the purposes of this discussion it is sufficient for the reader to be aware of the existence and definition of the two possible types of errors in hypothesis testing.

Summary

Let us summarize the procedure for hypothesis testing by parametric techniques. Initially we have a statement (the hypothesis) about a parameter. A measure of the corresponding statistic is then obtained from a random sample of observations. A measure of the difference between the observed value and the hypothesized value is studied and this measure is then considered in terms of what the underlying sampling distribution would be if the hypothesis were true.

At this point the researcher should decide upon the risk he is willing to take, the risk of rejecting a true hypothesis. That is, the

[1] For example, see Walker, H., and Lev, J., *Elementary Statistical Methods*, rev. ed. (New York: Holt, Rinehart and Winston, Inc., 1958), pp. 236–243.

significance level determines the regions of acceptance and rejection in the underlying sampling distribution. Determination of these regions is generally accomplished through the use of the appropriate distribution table. On the basis of these regions we either reject or retain the hypothesis.

In rejecting the hypothesis we are in fact saying that the probability of the statistic appearing by chance is too small (less than the significance level) and hence we cannot entertain the hypothesis. Under this condition we say that the statistical test is significant. Thus, statistically significant means that the observed statistic departs from what we would expect by chance. In a nonsignificant test we conclude that this chance expectation is great enough to entertain the hypothesis.

This chapter has dealt specifically with hypothesis testing and related examples. The examples are not to be interpreted as designs for research. In actually carrying out the research, considerable attention may be necessary relative to the manipulation of the variables. Also, extraneous factors must usually be considered in educational research, especially when research is conducted in the actual classroom setting. The discussion of research design is considered in later chapters of this text.

Suggested Study Exercises

3.1 One of the parametric assumptions is that the observations are independent. Suppose that you selected a sample of 150 American history students from a college population and proposed to measure their knowledge of history by an objective test. What does the assumption of independent observations mean in this context and how would you assure that this assumption is met?

3.2 We have two teaching methods, each used with a randomly-drawn sample of students. (The samples are drawn from a common population.) After a period of instruction, we compute the mean achievement for each sample and we want to decide whether or not teaching method affects achievement. We use a Student's t-test for the difference between two means and get a significant value at the .05 level. What is the null hypothesis tested? Give the associated probability statement.

3.3 Suppose a research study is done to determine the effects of materials, age, and class size upon reading achievement. We use three types of materials, two age groups, and two class sizes. All students are girls taught by the same teacher. Identify the independent variable(s), dependent variable(s), and constant(s) of this study.

3.4 Two samples are randomly drawn from a population. The samples are then subjected to different experimental treatments, say T_1 and T_2. The members of the samples are then measured on a dependent variable which has measurement on an interval scale. A difference between the two sample means is then tested to determine if experimental treatment has had an effect. The difference is found to be significant at the .01 level. What would be an appropriate technique to test this difference in means? State the null hypothesis being tested. What is the associated probability statement? What is the conclusion relative to the null hypothesis? What type of error (state in words) in hypothesis testing may be made here? What is the probability of making such an error? Is the difference in means significant at the .05 level?

3.5 Suppose we have a study involving sixth-grade arithmetic achievement. We want to check if there is a difference between the mean achievement of boys and girls. A Student's t-test is used and found not to be significant at the .05 level. State the null hypothesis, the associated probability statement, and your conclusion based on the results of the test. Is the test significant at the .01 level? Why, why not, or don't you have enough information to make a decision?

3.6 The mean science achievement on an objective test of a ninth-grade student population is hypothesized to be 85. A sample of twenty students is randomly selected from the population and given the science test. A Student's t-test is then computed using the sample data and the t-value is found to be 3.12. Using the .05 level of significance, find the appropriate t-distribution and decide whether or not you would reject the hypothesis. What t-value is necessary for rejecting the hypothesis at the .05 level? Was the sample mean larger or smaller than the hypothesized mean?

3.7 A one-way analysis of variance is computed on the scores of a suitable dependent variable. The independent variable has six levels and there are 8 Ss in each level. The F-ratio is computed to test for a significant difference between the means. What are the degrees of freedom values that designate the correct underlying F-distribution? Suppose the computed F-ratio is 3.06. Is this value significant at the .05 level? the .01 level? What is your conclusion relative to the null hypothesis? Give the associated probability statement.

3.8 A study of efficiency on a learning task is conducted in a learning laboratory. The Ss are students enrolled in an introductory psychology course at the university. The learning task involves nonsense symbols and meaningful material, both separately arranged on random and ordered displays. Thus, we have two independent variables which we will call stimulus and display. Each independent variable has two levels: stimulus has nonsense symbols and learning materials, and display has random and ordered. The dependent variable is time to solution. Discuss an appropriate parametric technique that would test the effects of the independent variables and their possible interaction. There are really three null hypotheses in this research situation. State these hypotheses. Suppose a total of 80 Ss are equally distributed among the levels of the independent variables. What are the appropriate underlying distributions and what values are necessary for the test to be significant at the .05 level of significance?

3.9 Discuss the concept of an interaction between two independent variables. From your own experience in education select two variables that are likely to interact. Discuss your choice of variables.

3.10 Discuss under what conditions you would use an analysis of covariance in preference to an analysis of variance; an analysis of variance in preference to an analysis of covariance.

3.11 A researcher is interested in the effect of three sets of instructional materials upon reading achievement in the fourth grade. He selects three random samples of fourth graders and each is taught by a different teacher using one of the sets. The Ss are pretested and posttested and an analysis of covariance done of the data with pretest as the covariate. What is the null hypothesis? What measures are actually tested by the statistical test? Suppose the statistical test turned out to be significant. What would be your conclusion relative to the instructional materials?

3.12 Define the two possible types of errors in hypothesis testing. Why do we say that hypotheses are not proved or disproved, only accepted or rejected?

4 *Testing Hypotheses by Nonparametric Techniques*

Meaning of Nonparametric

The preceding chapter discussed hypothesis testing under conditions for which the parametric assumptions are tenable. The validity of the assumptions relate directly to the meaningfulness of the interpretation of the results. The satisfaction of the assumptions will not guarantee a valid interpretation, but lack of such satisfaction when a parametric test is used will be certain to yield meaningless results.

The parametric assumptions require homogeneity of variance, populations that are normally distributed if sample size is small, independent observations, and at least interval scale measurement of the dependent variable. There are many situations in educational research which do not meet the parametric assumptions. A case in point would be data which are measured on an ordinal or nominal scale. This would not meet the assumption of data measured on at least an equal unit scale. An example would be data consisting of responses to a preference scale with the three choices — agree, undecided, and disagree. These would consist of ordinal data.

The procedures for analyzing data and testing hypotheses under these conditions are referred to as *nonparametric techniques*. The name is derived from the fact that these statistical tests do not specify conditions about the parameters. Non parametric tests at times go by the name of *distribution free tests*. This term is derived from the fact that no assumptions are necessary about the shape of the population from which the sample is drawn.

Nonparametric Assumptions

This is not to say that there are no assumptions whatsoever associated with the use of nonparametric techniques. The individual observations are assumed to be independent. That is, the score which is assigned to any S must not influence the score of any other S. For many of the nonparametric tests the variable being investigated is assumed to have underlying continuity, even though it cannot be so measured. In generalizing to populations, the sample is assumed to be a random sample.

Independent and Related Samples

A word might be said here concerning samples. We can make a distinction between related and independent samples. If two measures on a dependent variable are taken on the same sample of Ss, we say that these two samples of observations are related samples. This might occur in a before- and after-experimental treatment situation. Another situation of related samples would be in the case of matching each S of one sample with his counterpart in the other sample. The matching procedure is based on the researcher's judgment of relevant variables on which to match. If two samples of distinct Ss are drawn and the selection of one sample in no way influences that of the other, the samples are independent samples. In either case the random selection is still a requirement for generalizing to populations.

The discussion of this chapter occasionally distinguishes between techniques as they apply to related or independent samples. This distinction was not made in the chapter on parametric techniques where samples were considered to be independent samples. There are parametric techniques which apply to related samples, however they are not discussed in this text.

The Chi-Square Distribution

In the preceding chapter on parametric techniques, the Student's t-distribution and the F-distribution received considerable emphasis as underlying distributions. When dealing with nonparametric techniques we need another underlying distribution. The basic reasoning of underlying distributions still applies. The underlying distribution for many of the nonparametric statistical tests is the chi-square (χ^2) distribution. Like the Student's t-distribution and the F-distributions, the χ^2-distribution makes up a family of distributions. The appropriate, specific χ^2-distribution is determined by a single degree of freedom value. In this respect it is similar to the t-distributions. A tabulation of χ^2-values appears in Table E of this text. Selected probabilities are given horizontally in the table. Any specific value in the table is the χ^2-value which has the corresponding probability of appearing by chance.

The table of χ^2-values actually gives the critical values for two-tailed or non-directional tests of significance. The values of the table are based on one tail only, namely the right tail of the sampling distribution of chi-square. Thus, only one tail is used, but the critical values given are for two-tailed tests. A one-tailed test is not commonly used in a chi-square test of significance. However, if such a test is required, there is a procedure [1] for de-

[1] For a discussion of this procedure see Ferguson, G., *Statistical Analysis in Psychology and Education*, 2nd ed. (New York: McGraw-Hill Book Co., 1966), pp. 210–211.

termining the critical values by relating the normal and chi-square distributions.

The reader should view the χ^2-distribution as another underlying distribution, just as the normal or Student's t-distributions. Recall that in hypothesis testing it is very important, in fact crucial, that the correct underlying distribution be used. As the normal distribution is the correct distribution under certain conditions, so the appropriate χ^2-distribution is the underlying distribution of many of the statistics used with nonparametric techniques.

Comparison of Observed and Theoretical Distributions

A research situation in which the χ^2-distribution would be used is one involving a comparison of observed and theoretical frequencies. *Observed frequencies* are those of the sample or group under study. *Theoretical frequencies* are those expected on the basis of some hypothesis. For this reason they are often referred to in literature as expected frequencies. The null hypothesis is that there are no differences between the observed and theoretical frequencies. This is really to say that no difference is hypothesized between these two distributions, the observed and the expected, whatever they may be.

Consider an example involving frequencies. The assertion is made that in a certain school the I.Q. scores of the students are heterogeneous but uniformly distributed within the 80 to 129 range. In considering the I.Q. range from 80 to 129 inclusive, there are five 10-point intervals. To be uniformly distributed means that we would expect equal numbers in the five intervals. The intervals would be defined as 80–89, 90–99, etc. to make them mutually exclusive, that is, the intervals have no overlap. Assume that I.Q. is measured by some generally acceptable intelligence test.

The hypothesis is that the distribution of I.Q. is a uniform (rectangular) distribution. If we wanted to state it in the null hypothesis form we could hypothesize no difference between this distribution and the uniform distribution. We would draw a random sample of students and test them. Let us say this sample size is n. In the light of our hypothesis we would expect one-fifth of the scores in each interval. Thus, the expected frequencies for all intervals would be the same, namely $n/5$. The observed frequencies are the sample results.

The computation of the chi-square value for this statistical test is relatively simple. The formula is given by:

$$\chi^2 = \sum_{i=1}^{k} \frac{(fo_i - fe_i)^2}{fe_i}$$

where fo_i is the observed frequency of the ith interval; [1] fe_i is the expected frequency of the ith interval under the hypothesis. The number of intervals is denoted by k. For our example k is five and the fe_i's are all equal to $n/5$, since we hypothesized the uniform distribution. The formula indicates to determine the difference between the observed and expected frequencies for each interval, square the difference, divide by the expected frequency, and sum the k quotients.

A decision is necessary relative to the significance level which we will set at .05. Recall that the significance level is a probability. In terms of distributions of our example we are asking what the probability is that our observed sample distribution would appear by chance, if, in fact, the population distribution is the uniform distribution. However, the χ^2-value is the statistic that we actually compute. Since we have set the significance level at .05, this means that we will reject the hypothesis if the probability of our χ^2-value appearing by chance is less than .05. The χ^2-value is computed and we make a decision about the hypothesis.

Before this decision can be made, we must determine the specific chi-square distribution appropriate for our situation. There are five intervals, but since n is specified the frequency of the fifth interval is determined when the frequencies of the other four are known. Thus, four degrees of freedom remain in our example. The necessary value for significance at the .05 level as indicated in Table E is 9.49. If our computed χ^2-value exceeds 9.49, we have a significant statistical test and we would reject the hypothesis.

---

[1] The terms category, group, or cell are also commonly used. Interval is used here primarily because of the context of the example.

Suppose we illustrate the preceding example by some actual data. Recall that the data being analyzed are frequencies. A sample of fifty I.Q. scores are distributed according to the distribution in Table 4.1. Since for our example the hypothesized distribution is the uniform distribution, we would expect ten scores in each interval. The computation of the χ^2-value is presented here solely for the purpose of illustration. The formula

TABLE 4.1

Sample Distribution of Fifty I.Q. Scores

	Interval				
	80–89	90–99	100–109	110–119	120–129
Observed Frequency	8	12	15	9	6
Theoretical Frequency	10	10	10	10	10

presented earlier indicates to determine the difference between observed and theoretical frequency for each interval, square this difference and divide by the theoretical frequency and then sum these quotients, one for each interval. In our example we have five intervals and the χ^2-value is given by:

$$\chi^2 = \frac{(-2)^2}{10} + \frac{(+2)^2}{10} + \frac{(+5)^2}{10} + \frac{(-1)^2}{10} + \frac{(-4)^2}{10}$$

Since we square the difference it is not necessary to retain the algebraic sign. The signs are included above to enable the reader to readily identify the difference.

The computation of the χ^2-value gives a value of 5.00. This is less than the critical value of 9.49 necessary for a significant test. Thus, the probability of this sample appearing by chance, if, in fact, the population is uniformly distributed, is greater than .05. The conclusion is that we cannot reject the hypothesis that the population is distributed as the uniform distribution.

The probability is relative to the observed distribution appearing in the light of the hypothesized distribution. In our example the probability question is: What is the probability of our observed sample frequencies appearing by chance, if, in fact, the population distribution is the uniform distribution? We need not determine the exact probability but only the probability in terms of the significance level. If the probability is less than the significance level we reject the hypothesis.

If the statistical test is non-significant, the hypothesized distribution is tenable. If the test is significant, this does not specify the population. We know, then, that it is quite unlikely that the sample distribution will appear by chance if the population distribution is as hypothesized. Neither does the χ^2-value indicate which intervals had the greatest discrepancies between observed and expected frequencies. There may be one or more intervals with large discrepancies or the discrepancies may be uniform throughout the intervals. An inspection of the interval frequencies will give an indication of the situation. This inspection will also reveal which intervals have high and low observed frequencies relative to the expected frequencies.

The above example was somewhat simplified in that all the theoretical frequencies were equal. This was due to the theoretical distribution being the uniform distribution. To be sure, the theoretical frequencies of the intervals are in general not equal. They are determined by the specific shape of the theoretical distribution of a specific research problem. For example, if the normal distribution is the theoretical distribution, the theoretical frequencies of the intervals, would not all be the same. However, the underlying reasoning and the procedures would remain the same when comparing observed and theoretical distributions.

Goodness of Fit Test

A problem closely related to the preceding example is a goodness of fit problem. Suppose a random sample is drawn from a population. How well does this sample distribution fit a known theoretical distribution? For the purpose of illustration, let us use the normal distribution as the theoretical distribution. The null hypothesis is that there is no significant difference between the population distribution and the normal distribution, in terms of the variable being investigated. The associated probability statement is: What is the probability of the sample distribution appearing, if, in fact, the population is normally distributed? If this probability drops below our pre-determined significance level we will reject the hypothesis that the population is normally distributed.

The variable under investigation would have a mean and standard deviation and would be measured on an equal unit or ratio scale. This seems to be data of a parametric nature. However, in the goodness of fit test it is not the actual scores that are being analyzed but rather the frequencies of scores in the intervals. The observed sample distribution is divided into a specified number of intervals. The corresponding normal distribution is determined by computing the expected frequencies in the various intervals if the distribution were normal. In order to do this we need the sample size, say n, and the mean and standard deviation of the scores. The area under the normal curve as given in Table A is 1.00. The points which divide the intervals must be determined in terms of standard deviation units. These will give the proportions of the area expected within the various intervals. The proportions multiplied times n will determine the expected frequencies.

Let us consider a brief example of how the expected frequency for an interval would be determined if we were computing a goodness of fit test using the normal distribution. Suppose we have a sample of 150 observations and one of the intervals spans 90–95 on the measurement scale. Also assume that by the procedures discussed in Chapter 2, the end points of this interval correspond to standard scores of +1.20 and +1.47. By using Table A we determine that .0443 of the total area in the normal curve lies between these two points. (Both points lie on the same side of the mean and recall that the area in the table is given from the mean to the point. To determine the area between the points we subtract the smaller area from the larger as given in the Table.) Therefore we would expect 150 times .0443 or 6.645 frequencies in this particular interval. The observed frequency of the interval would be known directly from the sample data. This procedure would be repeated until expected frequencies were determined for all the intervals.

Now we have a set of observed frequencies from the sample and a set of theoretical frequencies. The total frequency for the theoretical distribution should be n, within rounding errors. The situation is now ready for a chi-square test. The number of degrees of freedom associated with the test is the number of intervals minus 3. This is due to the fact that not only do we have a frequency n, but a mean and standard deviation are also needed for the theoretical normal distribution. These are estimated from the sample mean and standard deviation. Thus, the appropriate χ^2-distribution is the one with $n - 3$ degrees of freedom.

The condition of a random sample is essential in the above example. Is this a random sample of a normally distributed population? Suppose the sample were not a random sample but a sample with some sampling bias. Then no decision could be legitimately made relative to the population. If the χ^2-value were significant we would reject the hypothesis of a normally distributed population and conclude that the population is not normally distributed. But now the alternative conclusion exists — that it is the sampling bias which has produced the nonnormality in the sample. Alternatively, if the χ^2-value is nonsignificant, the bias may be operating in an opposite direction.

Assuming the sample to be random and the computation correct, a significant χ^2-value indicates that the probability of this sample appearing from a normally distributed population is too small to entertain the hypothesis of such a population. Note that the probability is on the sample but the conclusion is relative to the hypothesis which deals with the population. A non-significant χ^2-value, in the context of this example, indicates that there is no evidence on the basis of this statistical test to reject the hypothesis of a normally distributed population.

The researcher should be on the lookout for small expected frequencies. The reason for this is that if the expected frequencies become too small the χ^2-distribution is no longer the appropriate underlying distribution. This is due to the fact that with small frequencies the appropriate underlying distribution may have considerable discontinuity and the continuous chi-square distribution is a poor approximation for the appropriate underlying distribution. What is considered too small for expected frequencies? If we have a situation in which there are only two categories, the generally accepted rule is that each expected frequency should be five or greater. In situations in which the number of intervals or categories exceeds two, it is generally required that at least 4/5 of the expected frequencies are five or greater and no expected frequency is less than one. If such intervals or categories appear, they should be combined with adjacent categories. At times it may be necessary to combine several categories in the tails of the distribution. Whenever the combining of categories is done, the combinations should be meaningful and, of course, at least two categories must remain.

There are other goodness of fit tests, some of which involve special underlying distributions. In order to use the tests it is necessary to have tables of these underlying distributions available. These other tests are not discussed in this text. However, the reader should not get the impression that there exists only one goodness of fit test. In any case, the idea is the same, that of testing to see how well a sample distribution fits a theoretical distribution.

Comparison of Two Independent Sample Distributions

The preceding example dealt with a single sample distribution compared with some theoretical distribution. The expected frequencies are based on information about the theoretical distribution, external to the sample information. Research situations arise in education in which it is desirable to involve two independent samples. The data again consist of frequencies in mutually exclusive categories. The measurement may be nominal or ordinal. A distribution is determined for each of the two samples. The expected frequencies are determined from the information of the samples.

The null hypothesis of this situation is that the populations from which the samples are drawn do not differ with respect to the variable, represented by the frequencies in the categories. If, in fact, the populations are the same we would expect the respective category frequencies of the two samples to differ only due to random sampling error. Note that we are not hypothesizing a specific distribution for the populations but only that the population distributions are the same in terms of the frequencies of the categories.

If the populations are the same and the sizes of the two samples equal, we would expect the same number in each sample for a specific category. This is not to say that we would expect the same frequencies in the different categories, which would be hypothesizing a uniform distribution. Suppose in the samples the total number of frequencies in the kth category is m. Then under the null hypothesis we would expect $m/2$ frequency in this category for each sample. This is the method for determining the expected frequencies for this specific condition, determined by the arithmetic average of the total frequency for that category. In like manner, the expected frequencies of all the categories could be determined and the total of the expected frequencies would be, within rounding errors, the original sample size.

This procedure does not require equal size for the two samples. In the case of unequal sample size, the expected frequencies in a category are directly proportional to the ratio of the size of the specific sample to the total size for both samples. For example, the expected frequency for sample 1 in the kth category is the product of this ratio times m (m is the total frequency in category k). If the sample sizes are represented by n_1 and n_2 respectively, this expected frequency is given by m times $\frac{n_1}{n_1 + n_2}$. A commonly used way of viewing this is by tabulating the observed frequencies in a table, with the two samples in rows and the categories in columns. An example of such an arrangement is presented in Table 4.2. The expected frequency for a specific category is then determined by multiplying row total times column total and dividing this product by n (total for both samples). The specific row and column totals are those in which the specific category appears. The process of determining expected frequencies is the same whether or not sample sizes are equal. Let us consider a two sample example.

A researcher is interested in the problem of overweight and underweight among high school freshmen. He can classify freshmen into three categories: overweight, correct weight, and underweight. He wants to make a decision about the populations of girls and boys relative to this variable. In terms of this category classification, do the population distributions of boys and girls differ? The null hypothesis is that these population distributions are not different. It should be noted that the measurement here is at most ordinal. Nowhere is it specified that being overweight for a girl requires the same weight as that for a boy. Nor is the shape of the distribution specified. The significance level is designated as .05.

The random samples of size 40 each are drawn from the populations. The observed data appear in Table 4.2. Such a table is commonly called a *contingency table*. This is a hypothetical example for illustration purposes and does not reflect any real situation.

TABLE 4.2

Observed Weight Distributions for Freshmen Boys and Girls

	Category			
	Overweight	Correct Weight	Underweight	Total
Boys	8	29	3	40
Girls	2	31	7	40
Total	10	60	10	80

We need the theoretical frequencies under the null hypothesis of no difference between the population distributions of boys and girls in order to complete our statistical test. Since we have equal sample size (40 of each sex), we would expect the same number of boys as girls in a specific category. The theoretical frequency for underweight boys is given by multiplying the row and column totals and dividing by the total of both samples. This turns out to be 10 times 40, divided by 80, or 5. The theoretical frequency for underweight girls is also 5. In like manner we could compute the remaining theoretical frequencies and they would be 30 and 5 respectively, for correct weight and overweight for both boys and girls.

The χ^2-value can be computed by applying the formula involving observed and theoretical frequencies that was introduced earlier. The computation will not be shown here but the χ^2-value for these data is 5.27, rounded off to hundredths. We must decide on the degrees of freedom so we can locate the appropriate χ^2-distribution. In the computation there is a restriction on the category totals. For example, the overweight category contains ten and when we know that eight are boys, the remainder are girls. A specific sample, such as boys, has one restriction: that when two of the categories are assigned, the third is uniquely determined. Therefore, we have two degrees of freedom in our example. An inspection of Table E reveals a χ^2-value of 5.99 is required for significance at the .05 level. Therefore, our value does not reach significance and we do not reject the null hypothesis. The probability is greater than .05 that the sample distributions would have appeared by chance, if, in fact, the population distributions are the same. The conclusion is that the populations of freshmen boys and girls do not differ on this variable. Note carefully that we have not specified the shapes of the population distributions nor have we said that the distributions would be the same if measurement was on an interval scale. We have only considered classification on the three category variable.

Extension to More Than Two Independent Sample Distributions

The above procedure may be extended to more than two independent samples. Again, the sample sizes need not be equal. Suppose we have j samples and k possible categories. When this analysis technique is used, the data are usually tabulated in rows and columns, with the possible categories in the columns and the samples in the rows. In this kind of an array there are j times k cells, all of which need an expected frequency. The rows and columns have marginal totals. The totals of the rows are the sample sizes and column totals are the total responses to the individual categories. The totals of the row marginal totals and column marginal totals are equal. Call this grand total n_t. The expected value for a specific cell is the product of its marginal totals divided by n_t. This is the same procedure as that for the two sample case.

The χ^2-value is computed by the usual procedure summing over all cells. The degrees of freedom associated with this test is $(j-1)$ times $(k-1)$ or $(r-1)$ times $(c-1)$ if we think of r and c as the numbers of rows and columns in the array. Since the marginal totals exist, this puts one restriction on each row and one restriction on each column. Hence, the correct number of degrees of freedom is as specified.

An example follows. Since the situation with two samples is a special case of the more general case, we will consider an example involving four samples. Suppose at a liberal arts college a researcher is interested in student attitude toward compulsory attendance at college convocations. A student may respond by agree, undecided, or disagree. Thus, there are three possible response categories in this very brief measuring instrument.

A random sample is drawn from each of the four undergraduate classes at the college. The sample sizes need not be equal. For some reason the investigator may choose to draw unequal numbers for the samples. For example, he may determine sample size proportional to the class enrollment of the college population.

The null hypothesis is that the four class populations do not differ relative to the attitude toward compulsory attendance at convocations. This does not hypothesize how many in the class populations agree, disagree, or are undecided. It only hypothesizes that the population distributions do not differ. The associated probability statement is: What is the probability that the four samples would appear, if, in fact, the populations are the same? If this probability is less than our pre-determined significance level, we reject the hypothesis that the populations are the same.

The responses to the attitude item are tabulated and expected values computed. In this case there would be twelve cells and twelve expected values are necessary. The significance level is specified and the χ^2-value computed. The degrees of freedom associated with this statistical test is $(4 - 1)$ times $(3 - 1)$ or 6. This determines the appropriate chi-square underlying distribution associated with the null hypothesis. The χ^2-value necessary for significance at the .05 level is 12.59. If the significance level had been set at .01, a χ^2-value of 16.81 would be necessary for significance.

Consider some hypothetical data that might result from such a study. We will specify the significance level as .05. The sample sizes drawn from the class populations are 80, 60, 60, and 40 respectively, from freshmen through seniors. The observed sample frequencies on this variable appear in Table 4.3. This is an example of a 4×3 contingency table.

TABLE 4.3

Observed Sample Distributions for Response to Compulsory Attendance at College Convocations

| Class | Category | | | |
	Agree	Undecided	Disagree	Total
Freshmen	12	48	20	80
Sophomore	7	20	33	60
Junior	6	19	35	60
Senior	5	3	32	40
Total	30	90	120	240

Since we have twelve observed frequencies, we need twelve theoretical frequencies. We follow the procedure discussed previously for determining the theoretical frequencies. For example, the frequency for freshmen agree is 30 times 80 divided by 240, which is equal to 10. In like manner, we compute the remaining theoretical frequencies under the null hypothesis. These frequencies appear in Table 4.4. The observed frequencies appear in parentheses to indicate the contrast between observed and theoretical frequencies.

TABLE 4.4

Theoretical Distribution for Response to Compulsory
Attendance at College Convocations

Class	Agree		Undecided		Disagree		Total
		Category					
Freshmen	(12)	10	(48)	30	(20)	40	80
Sophomore	(7)	7.5	(20)	22.5	(33)	30	60
Junior	(6)	7.5	(19)	22.5	(35)	30	60
Senior	(5)	5	(3)	15	(32)	20	40
Total		30		90		120	240

The computation of the χ^2-value by the usual procedure results in a value of 33.588. With six degrees of freedom this is significant at the .05 level (also at the .01 level). Thus, the probability that the sample distributions would occur by chance, if, in fact, the population distributions are the same, is less than .05. Therefore we cannot entertain the null hypothesis and we conclude that freshmen, sophomore, junior, and senior populations differ with regard to this variable.

The statistical test was significant, therefore we conclude that the hypothesis of the populations being the same is not tenable. However, this does not tell us the source of difference between the four populations. The cells of one class sample (in this case a row) may differ markedly from the other class samples. An inspection of the differences between observed and expected cell frequencies should give an indication of the situation. A cursory inspection of the sample distributions reveals that the upperclassmen, especially seniors, seem much more decided about compulsory attendance and they tend to disagree. The freshmen have a high proportion of undecided responses.

The sample distributions may be compared in combinations of two. This would require six chi-square tests, each with two degrees of freedom. The hypothesis tested in each case would concern only the two specific populations from which the samples in the test were drawn. In any event, the question of the actual student attitude, i.e., agree, disagree, undecided, has not been tested statistically. If some theoretical distribution of attitude responses is hypothesized, the observed distributions could be tested against the theoretical distribution. The problem would then be reduced to the type discussed in an earlier example involving the comparison of an observed and a theoretical distribution. In an actual research situation, consideration would undoubtedly be given to both questions.

Test of Independence

A common use of the chi-square test is as a test of independence of two variables. Pairs of observations on two variables are necessary for this situation. The preceding example of attitude toward compulsory attendance at convocations will illustrate this use of the chi-square test. Although the actual computation would be the same as was illustrated, the reasoning undergoes a slight modification.

Year in college and attitude toward compulsory attendance are now both considered to be variables. To be sure, they are not variables measured on an equal unit scale. They may be considered nominal variables or possibly ordinal variables. The question being asked is: Are these variables independent or are they associated? The null hypothesis refers to the variables in the college population from which the sample was drawn. Note that now the four classes are considered as one population and the students in the study as a single sample. Year in college is a variable within the population and sample. The null hypothesis is that the two variables are independent in the population.

The data would again be set up in a table. The expected cell frequencies are computed from the row and column totals and are the frequencies expected if the two variables are independent. The χ^2-value is computed in the usual way and the appropriate degrees of freedom is $(r - 1)$ times $(c - 1)$.

Since the expected frequencies are what we would expect in the case of independence, a non-significant χ^2-value indicates that there is no basis to reject the hypothesis of independence of the two variables. If the chi-square test is significant we conclude that the variables are associated. However, the chi-square test does not indicate the direction of association. To get measures of magnitude of association and direction of association we would use a correlational technique. Correlation is discussed in Chapter 5.

The chi-square test of our college example was significant. Therefore, we reject the hypothesis of independence between the two variables in the population. We conclude that the variables — year in college and attitude toward compulsory convocation attendance — are associated.

The Sign Test

A nonparametric technique which applies to the situation of two related samples is the *sign test*. The variable under consideration is measured on an ordinal scale. It is assumed that this variable has an underlying continuous distribution. The samples are related in the sense that observations are taken on matched Ss or two observations on each S. The two observations on each S are usually a before and after experimental treatment situation. If matching is used, the pairs are to be matched on relevant variables.

We define Y_a and Y_b as the two scores for the matched pair or the same S. The Y_a represents the score under one condition or the "before" score and the Y_b represents the score under the other condition or the "after" score. In the sign test we direct our attention to the direction of the difference between each pair of scores. We define the direction as plus or minus. If Y_b is greater than Y_a we assign a plus sign; if Y_a is greater than Y_b we assign a negative sign. Hence the name sign test. This gives us one dichotomous distribution of plus and minus signs.

The comparison of the Y_a and Y_b scores is open to the possibility of ties. A *tie* occurs when the difference between the two scores for a S is zero, or zero in terms of the measurement. The tied cases are dropped from the analysis and the total number in the sample is reduced by the number of ties. Thus, for the purpose of analysis, we define N as the number of paired scores with a non-zero difference.

Suppose we have a random sample of Ss and two observations are taken for each S, one before and one after an experimental treatment. The distribution of plus and minus signs is determined by the above described procedure. The null hypothesis relates to the population from which the sample was drawn and concerns the effect of the experimental treatment. If there is no effect of experimental treatment, we would expect as many plus signs as negative signs in our distribution of signs. Another way of stating this is that the median difference of the Y_a and Y_b scores in the population is zero. Recall that the median is a measure of central tendency. A rough median can be computed for ordinal data, whereas it is not possible to compute a mean for ordinal data since in order to compute an arithmetic mean we need an equal unit. The associated probability statement is: What is the probability of our distribution of signs appearing, if, in fact, the distribution in the population has equal numbers of plus and minus signs? To check this probability and hence test the null hypothesis, we need an underlying sampling distribution.

The theoretical distribution that applies in this case is the binomial distribution. Since under the null hypothesis we expect the same number of plus and minus signs, this is analogous to the tossing of an unbiased coin. Suppose that we would go through repeated sessions of one hundred tosses of an unbiased coin. The number of times heads (or tails) appeared would average around 50. The appearance of say 95 heads and 5 tails would be a relatively rare event and it would be located in the tail of the distribution. Table C in the Appendix gives the associated probabilities for the binomial distribution. The vertical axis gives the total number and the horizontal axis the number of one characteristic, such as heads or plus signs. Note that the table is for a one-tailed test and gives probabilities of values as small as observed values. For samples larger than 25 the normal curve is an adequate approximation to the binomial distribution.

In order to use the normal distribution we must convert to a z-score which was discussed in an earlier chapter. To determine the z-score associated with the specific split of our dichotomy we use the formula:

$$z = \frac{(n_1 - .5) - (\frac{1}{2}) \cdot N}{(\frac{1}{2}) \sqrt{N}}$$

where N = total number of non-zero differences in the sample.

n_1 = number with the characteristic such that n_1 is greater than $(\frac{1}{2})N$.

If the z-score computed by the above procedure falls in the rejection area determined by our significance level, we reject the null hypothesis.

As with the parametric Student's t-test for the difference between two means, the sign test may be two-tailed or one-tailed. In a two-tailed test it is not hypothesized which sign, plus or minus, will occur with greatest frequency. In a one-tailed test this is hypothesized. The rejection region is located entirely in one tail of the distribution when a one-tailed test is used.

Now we have a hypothesis to test, a procedure for getting a measure from a random sample, and an underlying sampling distribution. These ingredients along with a significance level give us the necessary elements for a statistical test of a hypothesis. Let us consider an example involving the use of the sign test.

A teacher is interested in the effect of teaching a certain instructional unit in science upon insight in problem solving. Assume that insight in problem solving can be measured on an ordinal scale and that two equivalent forms of an insight measuring instrument are available. The teacher has at his disposal a class of twenty students which make up a random sample of, say, an eighth-grade population.

The students are tested before and after the instruction of the unit. These correspond to the Y_a and Y_b scores. Each student has a pair of observations. The variable under consideration is insight in problem solving which we will assume to be continuously distributed. The experimental treatment is the teaching of the instructional unit.

The teacher does not anticipate that the instruction will inhibit insight in problem solving. In fact, he is not interested in retaining the unit unless its instruction shows a significant positive effect. Thus we have the situation for a one-tailed test. The null hypothesis is that in the population there would be as many students who gain as regress on the insight measure, that is, the number of plus signs would equal the number of minus signs. However, by using a one-tailed test we can consider the alternate hypothesis that there will be a greater number of gain frequencies than regress frequencies. A significant statistical test would result in rejecting the null hypothesis and accepting the alternate hypothesis.

The twenty pairs of scores are compared and the results indicate 13 plus signs, 5 negative signs and 2 ties. We will set the significance level at .05 and Table C is consulted for the specific probability. The probability that we are concerned with is the probability of 13 plus and 5 negative signs appearing in a sample of 18 if in the population there are equal numbers of plus and negative signs.

We find the appropriate probability by going down to 18 on the vertical scale and over to 5 on the horizontal scale. The indicated probability is .048. This is less than the significance level and hence we reject the null hypothesis. The conclusion here is that the instructional unit in science does have an effect of increasing insight in problem solving. Presumably, the teacher would retain the instruction of the unit.

Consider an example involving a large sample size. The administration of a large university is concerned with the faculty opinion relative to the role of athletics, specifically football. The institutional research director is interested in whether a series of two lectures accompanied by team films will change the opinions of faculty members about the extent of participation in interscholastic football.

A random sample of 150 members is drawn from the university faculty. These members are asked whether more or less participation than present is desirable. Then the members are exposed to the two lectures, after which they are again asked the same question. This is again a situation in which two observations are taken on each S, rather than observations on matched Ss.

The null hypothesis is: The series of lectures would have no effect on the opinions of the faculty members of the university.

The population of faculty members is under consideration here. Note that it was not implied that the lectures would tend to make faculty members more or less favorable toward participation. Let us say that the lectures and films were merely statements of facts and that opinions could be influenced either way. Thus, this hypothesis requires a two-tailed statistical test.

The distribution of plus and minus signs is determined. The results show 70 plus signs, 60 negative, and 20 ties. The significance level is set at .05. The associated probability statement is: What is the probability that the sample distribution of plus and minus signs would appear, if, in fact, there would be the same number of each sign in the university faculty population?

The normal distribution is used as the underlying distribution since sample size exceeds 25. The computation of the z-score according to the procedure discussed earlier gives a z-score of 0.79. Since this is a two-tailed test we include .025 of the area in each tail of the distribution as the rejection region. The normal distribution as given in Table A indicates that a z-score of 1.96 or greater is required for the rejection region. Since our z-score was only 0.79 it does not fall in the rejection region. Therefore the probability of the sample distribution appearing under the null hypothesis is greater than the significance level. Hence there is no basis for rejecting the null hypothesis, and the conclusion is that the two lectures have no systematic effect upon the faculty opinions toward interscholastic participation in football.

The Median Test—Two Samples

The sign test, discussed in the preceding section, applies to two related samples. An analogous test for two independent samples is the *median test*. The median test requires that the scores on the dependent variable be measured on at least an ordinal scale and that the samples be randomly selected from the populations under study.

The null hypothesis for the median test is that there is no difference between the medians of the two populations from which the samples are drawn. This hypothesis calls for a two-tailed test. As in the sign test, an alternative hypothesis may be posed, namely that the median of one population is greater than that of the other. Under such an alternate hypothesis a one-tailed test is appropriate.

The median test does not require that both samples be of the same size. Let us designate N_1 and N_2 as the sample sizes and the sum of N_1 and N_2 as N. The procedure requires that we determine the common median of both samples, that is, the median of all N scores. Then the scores for each sample are dichotomized relative to this common median. Some of the scores may fall directly on the median. These scores may be removed from the analysis. However, this often is undesirable since it reduces the total number of scores in the analysis. Therefore, rather than define the dichotomy as above and below median, we can define the dichotomy as scores which exceed the median and those that do not exceed the median. With this definition, scores on the median are placed in the "do not exceed the median" category of the dichotomy. Every score falls into one and only one category and no scores are deleted. For the remainder of this discussion we will define the dichotomy in this manner.

Dichotomizing the scores for each sample gives a two by two table of the form indicated in Table 4.5. The actual numbers that appear in this array are frequencies. In order to identify a frequency, we must know which sample it came from, 1 or 2, and whether it represents the frequency that exceeds the median or that which does not. Therefore we use two subscripts on the f. The first indicates sample 1 or 2; the second subscript indicates "exceed median" (a) or "does not exceed median" (b). As an example, f_{1b} means the number of scores in sample 1 that do not exceed the median.

TABLE 4.5

The Fourfold Table for the Median Test Involving Two Samples

	Sample 1	Sample 2
Number of scores that exceed the median	f_{1a}	f_{2a}
Number of scores that do not exceed the median	f_{1b}	f_{2b}

Under the null hypothesis, that is, the population medians are the same, we would expect within each sample about one-half of the scores to exceed the median and one-half not to exceed the median of the combined samples. That is, we would expect f_{1a} to equal approximately (within sampling fluctuation) f_{1b} and f_{2a} to approximately equal to f_{2b}. These in turn would be expected to equal approximately one-half of their respective sample sizes.

At this point we have a fourfold table of frequencies. We need some combination of these frequencies which will give a statistic for which we can determine a sampling distribution under the null hypothesis. When the total number of the two samples exceeds 20 and no individual sample size is less than 10, the chi-square distribution may be used to test the null hypothesis. If the sample size does not meet this requirement, a special sampling distribution is necessary. This special distribution is not discussed in this text, therefore the remarks are relevant to the situation for which the χ^2-distribution is applicable.

The determination of the χ^2-value is accomplished by a computational formula involving only observed frequencies from the fourfold table and the total sample size. This computational formula contains a *correction for continuity*. The correction for continuity is a correction for applying the continuous χ^2-distribution to our discrete dichotomy. This correction is applied in the case of one degree of freedom which is the appropriate distribution in this situation. The formula is given by:

$$\chi^2 = \frac{N\left(\left|f_{1a} \cdot f_{2b} - f_{2a} \cdot f_{1b}\right| - \frac{N}{2}\right)^2}{(f_{1a} + f_{2a})(f_{1b} + f_{2b})(f_{1a} + f_{1b})(f_{2a} + f_{2b})}$$

This is distributed with one degree of freedom. If this χ^2-value exceeds the critical value of the table we say the test is statistically significant. In terms of probability we say that a significant χ^2-value indicates that the probability of this large a χ^2-value appearing by chance is less than our pre-determined significance level. The associated probability statement with the null hypothesis is: What is the probability that the sample frequencies relative to the median would appear, if, in fact, the samples are drawn from populations with the same median? If this probability is

TABLE 4.6

Sample Frequencies of Responses to Salary Negotiation Attitude Scale

	Sample	
	Teachers	Board Members
Frequency for exceed median	25	10
Frequency for do not exceed median	15	20
Total frequency	40	30

less than our significance level we reject the null hypothesis and conclude that the population medians are not equal. An example follows. A researcher is interested in attitudes of board members and teachers toward salary negotiations. An attitude scale is constructed in such a manner that it is possible to identify a direction from unfavorable to favorable toward the salary-negotiations concept. Thus, the measurement of this attitude variable is ordinal scale measurement.

The researcher defines his populations and randomly selects samples of 30 board members and 40 teachers. Note that the researcher is dealing with two populations, and for the purposes of this example we are simply using the sample sizes of 30 and 40. The 70 Ss are given the attitude scale, the overall median is determined, and the frequencies are tabulated in the four-fold table.

The null hypothesis of this investigation is that there is no difference between the median scores of the board member and teacher populations. No direction is hypothesized so a two-tailed test is appropriate. The significance level is set at .05. The results of the frequency tabulation of those which do and do not exceed the common median is as follows: 10 board members and 25 teachers exceed the median; 20 board members and 15 teachers do not exceed the median. These results are summarized in Table 4.6.

The computation of the χ^2-value is done by substituting the frequencies into the formula discussed earlier. This substitution gives:

$$\chi^2 = \frac{70(|(25)(20) - (10)(15)| - 35)^2}{(25 + 10)(15 + 20)(25 + 15)(10 + 20)}$$

The χ^2-value so computed is 4.725. We consult Table E and note that the critical value for the .05 significance level and one degree of freedom is 3.84. Hence, the probability of the observed χ^2-value appearing by chance is less than .05.

The conclusion relative to the null hypothesis is that on the basis of this statistical test, the null hypothesis is rejected. The probability that the sample distributions relative to the common median would appear if, in fact, the population medians are equal is less than .05. Hence, the conclusion is drawn that board members and teachers differ as to their median scores on attitudes toward salary negotiations. It should be noted that at this point nothing has been said about how they differ. If the ordinal scale of the attitude inventory is so set up that exceeding the median indicates a more favorable attitude, it could be noted that teachers have a higher observed than expected frequency in this cell. The opposite situation is true for board members. If a direction had been hypothesized, as may be done in attitude studies, a one-tailed statistical test would apply. However, there was no direction hypothesized in the example.

Extension of the Median Test to More Than Two Samples

The median test may be extended to more than two independent samples. The conditions and the procedure exactly parallel those of the median test for two independent samples. The samples need not be of equal size but the variable being investigated must be measured on at least an ordinal scale.

Let us say that we have j independent samples with j equal to or greater than three. The procedure for the extension of the median test requires that we determine the common median of all the observations in the j samples. The individual observations of each sample are then assigned plus or minus signs, depending on whether or not they exceed the common median. (The definition of above or below the median may be used instead of exceed or not exceed the median.) This procedure yields two frequencies for each sample. The frequencies may be tabulated in a $2 \times j$ table similar to the one illustrated for the two sample case. The table will contain j columns, one for each sample.

The null hypothesis is that the populations from which the j samples have been selected have the same medians, that is, they have a common median. Under the null hypothesis we would expect one-half of the observations in each sample to be above and one-half to be below the common median in the j samples. Thus, we have expected frequencies for each of the cells in our $2 \times j$ table. (If the sample sizes are equal the expected frequencies for all cells would be the same.)

The null hypothesis is tested by the computation of a χ^2-value according to the usual procedure involving observed and expected frequencies (see page 114). The difference between observed and expected frequencies of each cell is squared and divided by the expected frequency. Then we sum these quotients over the $2j$ cells. This χ^2-value is distributed as the chi-square distribution with $j - 1$ degrees of freedom.

The probability statement associated with the null hypothesis is: What is the probability that the observed sample distributions would appear, if, in fact, they come from populations with the same median? Again, this probability need not be determined exactly but only in terms of whether or not it is less than the predetermined significance level. The actual statistical test involves the probability of the χ^2-value appearing under the null hypothesis. On the basis of this probability, the decision is made relative to the hypothesis.

Let us consider an example involving the extension of the median test. A researcher at a university is interested in the extent of extra-curricular participation of the students enrolled in four of the colleges. The four colleges are Arts and Science, Education, Engineering, and Pharmacy. It is decided that only junior year students will be sampled. Four random samples are drawn from the enrolled juniors of each of the four colleges. Suppose a one in ten sample to population sampling ratio is used. Since the colleges do not have equal numbers enrolled, the sample sizes will be unequal. The records of the students are examined and the numbers of extra-curricular activities tabulated for the students. An extensive list of possible activities is used in assigning the extra-curricular scores to the students.

The null hypothesis is that there is no difference in number of extra-curricular activities of the junior year student populations of the four colleges in the study. The significance level is set at .05. That is, the null hypothesis will be rejected if the probability of the sample distributions appearing, if, in fact, the population medians are equal, is less than .05.

The four sample sizes appear in Table 4.7 below. The common median is computed and the plus or minus sign of each student in each sample is determined. To avoid throwing out data, the definition of exceed or not exceed the median is used for the dichotomy. The frequencies of this dichotomy also appear in Table 4.7.

TABLE 4.7

Example Data for the Median Test with Four Samples

	A & S	Educ.	Engi-neering	Phar-macy
Number that exceed median	92	62	41	8
Number that do not exceed median	72	58	57	16
Total in Sample	164	120	98	24

The χ^2-value for these data is 6.52 and the underlying chi-square distribution has three degrees of freedom. In consulting Table E of the Appendix we find that the probability of this size χ^2-value appearing by chance is between .10 and .05. Hence we have a probability greater than the significance level. On this statistical test there is no basis to reject the null hypothesis.

The researcher now concludes (on the basis of the statistical test) that there is no difference in the median number of extra-curricular activities of the juniors in the four colleges of the study. Note that the generalization is to the populations. Further, it regards only frequency of participation, not anything about the character of the participation. Let us look at the reasoning. The samples are randomly drawn and the observations taken and tabulated to acquire the frequencies for the extension of the median test. The differences that exist between the observed and hypothesized distributions can be due to two sources: (1) random sampling fluctuations or (2) the population distributions are not as hypothesized, that is, they do not have the same median. The probability of the first source is checked and found to be too great to discard. Hence, the conclusion is that the differences may have occurred due to chance and on this basis the researcher cannot reject the hypothesis that the populations have the same median.

The situation of this example may appear to meet the assumptions for a parametric technique. This may be so. The frequency of extra-curricular activities has ratio scale measurement if we consider a zero as no involvement at all. However, simple counting is a rather crude measure of extra-curricular activities. Also, one or more of the parametric assumptions dealing with the shapes and variances of the population distributions may not be tenable. Therefore, this example is discussed in connection with a nonparametric technique.

Kruskal-Wallis One-Way Analysis of Variance by Ranks

Nonparametric techniques may be used in doing an analysis of variance of data in ranks. One of these techniques is the *Kruskal-Wallis one-way analysis of variance by ranks*. This statistical test is applicable to two or more independent samples. It is used for deciding whether or not the samples are from a common population. The null hypothesis of the test is that the samples are drawn from a common population or from populations with identical averages. Since the data must be in ranks, the dependent variable under study must have measurement on at least an ordinal scale. This variable is also assumed to have an underlying continuous distribution.

Let us say that we have j, with j greater than or equal to two independent samples, with an equal number of observations, n_i, in each sample. Let n_i times $j = N$, the total number of observations. The computational procedure for the Kruskal-Wallis test requires that the N observations be ranked from 1 to N inclusive. The smallest score is assigned rank $1, \ldots ,$ etc. to the highest score which is assigned rank N. The data now consist of ranks instead of original scores on the dependent variable.

The statistic of the Kruskal-Wallis analysis of variance is denoted by "H." The computational form is given below. This is the identical form as given by Siegel.[1]

$$H = \frac{12}{N(N+1)} \sum_{i=1}^{j} \frac{R_i^2}{n_i} - 3(N+1)$$

where R_i = sum of the ranks in the ith sample
$\quad n_i$ = number in the ith sample
$\quad j$ = number of samples

It should be noted that the number of observations need not be the same for each sample. If the n_i's are equal, this constant may be moved out in front of the summation sign.

At this point we need an underlying distribution for our statistic H. The statistic H under the null hypothesis is approximately distributed as the chi-square distribution with $j - 1$ degrees of freedom. This approximation is adequate if all the j sample sizes exceed five. If sample size is less than or equal to five, a special table of probabilities associated with H must be consulted. Such a table does not appear in this text but does appear in statistics texts[2] dealing with specialized topics.

At this point we have a hypothesis to test and a statistic which relates to that hypothesis. The underlying distribution of that statistic is known. With the selection of a significance level we have the necessary ingredients for a statistical test of a hypothesis. An example follows using the Kruskal-Wallis test. This example is taken from an actual research situation.[3]

[1] Siegel, S., *Nonparametric Statistics* (New York: McGraw-Hill Book Co., 1956), p. 185.

[2] See for example, Siegel, S., *Nonparametric Statistics* (New York: McGraw-Hill Book Co., 1956), pp. 282–283.

[3] The entire research project is reported in Cooperative Research Project Report No. 1391 of the Office of Education, U.S. Department of Health, Education and Welfare. The title of the report is "Classroom Interaction, Pupil Achievement and Adjustment in Team Teaching as Compared with the Self-Contained Classroom" by Lambert, *et al.* The research was conducted at the University of Wisconsin.

The purpose of this research was to investigate the frequency of discipline problems between team-teaching and self-contained classroom instructional organizations. The study involved several analyses and only the analysis dealing with a Kruskal-Wallis application is discussed here. Three levels of grade, 4, 5, and 6, were observed by trained observers who recorded the number of relatively minor infractions of discipline. An intermediate team-teaching unit was used and two self-contained classroom units of the three grade levels were also included in the study. The second self-contained unit was included for reasons of experimental design. Thus there were three samples and twelve observations taken on each sample. An observation consisted of the number of discipline infractions during the first thirty minutes of the class period. The samples were considered to be random samples of the respective populations. Students had been randomly assigned to the instructional units.

The null hypothesis was that there existed no differences between the average numbers of minor discipline infractions of the populations from which the three samples were drawn. The significance level was set at .05.

The thirty-six observations were ranked in the prescribed manner and the H statistic computed. The value of the H statistic was 2.64. This statistic under the null hypothesis was approximately distributed as the chi-square distribution, with two degrees of freedom. This value does not attain the critical value of 5.99 necessary for rejecting the null hypothesis at the .05 level. Hence, there was no basis to reject the null hypothesis. It was concluded that there was no difference in the average number of minor discipline infractions in the two self-contained populations and the team-teaching population. This example concerned only grades 4, 5, and 6.

Whenever data in ranks are analyzed there is always the possibility of tied ranks. In the use of the Kruskal-Wallis one-way analysis of variance, a correction for ties may be applied in the computation of H. This correction is less than one and it is divided into the original value of H. The correction is given by:

$$1 - \sum_{i=1}^{t} \frac{(T_i^3 - T_i)}{N^3 - N}$$

where T_i = the number of tied scores in a tied group
t = the number of tied groups

The corrected H value will be larger than the initial H value since the divisor of the fraction is less than one. As a χ^2-value increases, the probability of it appearing decreases if degrees of freedom is unchanged. In the Kruskal-Wallis test, the H value is distributed as a chi-square distribution, and hence the corrected H will have associated with it a smaller probability than the original H. Thus, if the original H value is significant, there is no need to compute the corrected value since it too will be significant. Actually in most cases the correction is negligible. If the original value is close to significance, the corrected value may attain significance. The degrees of freedom value is unchanged when a corrected H value is computed.

We might make some comparisons between the Kruskal-Wallis analysis of variance and its parametric counterpart, the one-way analysis of variance. The Kruskal-Wallis analysis requires at least ordinal measurement and the parametric technique requires at least interval measurement. So the parametric technique is more demanding of the measurement.

The parametric analysis of variance analyzes the actual observed scores on the dependent variable whereas the Kruskal-Wallis technique analyzes ranks. The original scores as observed are changed to ranks and it is the actual ranks that go into the analysis. Both analyses assume that the variable measured has an underlying continuous distribution. With small sample size the parametric technique would require the assumption of a normally distributed population. The parametric analysis deals specifically with means. The Kruskal-Wallis technique deals more generally with averages or measures of central tendency. With ranked data the best that can be computed is a rough median. Therefore, the parametric analysis tests for differences between means, and the Kruskal-Wallis technique for differences between rough medians as indicated by ranks.

As long as we limit the parametric counterpart to a one-way analysis of variance, both techniques involve one independent variable. The parametric analysis has the extensions to include two or more independent variables. This opens the door to simultaneously including independent variables and investigating their interactions. There is no comparable extension to the Kruskal-Wallis analysis. There is a Friedman two-way analysis of variance by ranks but this does not have the partitioning of variance of the parametric technique.

The above comparison was not made for a "better or worse" judgment. Each type of analysis has its place and application. The correct analysis depends on the hypotheses under study and the tenable assumptions.

The Kruskal-Wallis analysis was discussed as an illustration of a nonparametric analysis of variance by ranks. Other similar nonparametric techniques exist which may be applicable under certain conditions. The Friedman two-way analysis of variance by ranks alluded to earlier is a technique which applies in the case of two or more related samples. The procedure will not be discussed in this text.

Comparison of Parametric and Nonparametric Techniques

The discussion of this and the preceding chapter has dealt with the testing of hypothesis by parametric and nonparametric techniques. Several procedures of both types were discussed and illustrated. When to use what is a logical question at this point, as far as a parametric or nonparametric technique is concerned. This is a question of extreme importance from a research point of view. This chapter concludes with a comparison of parametric and nonparametric techniques.

The type of scale on which the dependent variable is measured should be one of the researcher's primary considerations. If the measurement is on a nominal or ordinal scale, nonparametric techniques are appropriate. There are certain assumptions about the underlying population distributions which are essential for parametric techniques. If these assumptions cannot be met, the researcher should apply nonparametric techniques. If assumptions are not satisfactorily met and a parametric analysis applied, the results are actually uninterpretable.

It is often stated in research design texts that the parametric techniques are more powerful. The *power* of a statistical test is defined as the probability of rejecting the null hypothesis when in fact it is false. Recall that one of the possible errors in hypothesis testing is failing to reject a false hypothesis. This has been called a Type II or beta error. The power of a test, in mathematical terms, is one minus the probability of making a beta error. It is generally true that for a fixed sample size the parametric technique is more powerful than a corresponding nonparametric procedure. In general, the power of a statistical test is increased with increased sample size. It may be possible to achieve equivalent power between a parametric and nonparametric technique by increasing the sample size for the nonparametric technique. This is not always a desirable alternative.

When observed data, measured on an interval scale are converted to ranks, some of the information in the data is lost. However, applying parametric techniques when the data are not measured on an interval scale builds in information which does not exist. This has the end result of manufacturing distortions which is less desirable than the loss of information if a nonparametric technique had been used. If the assumptions can be met, parametric techniques are less wasteful of information.

The testing of interactions between independent variables by nonparametric techniques has not been as extensively developed as by parametric methods. The parametric analyses are much more sensitive to this type of effect. From a design standpoint the parametric techniques are often more sensitive to differences and to effects of more independent variables and their combinations.

Nonparametric techniques may be used with smaller sample size if the population distribution is not precisely known. The computation of nonparametric methods is generally easier, especially if desk calculators are to be used in the analysis. However, ease of statistical computation is only a technical matter and if computers are readily available, ease and length of computational procedures are of little concern.

The research hypothesis to be tested is, of course, an important factor in the selection of a statistical test. If the hypothesis deals with differences between means, a parametric technique is implied. When the hypothesis deals with differences in ranks or between rough medians for ordinal data, a nonparametric approach would be feasible. These are just two examples. The statistical test must test the hypothesis. It would be an error to state hypotheses which involve differences between means and then apply, say, the sign test. The researcher should carefully consider the procedures which apply to the hypothesis. The relevant aspects of assumptions and power should be given careful consideration. The researcher should have clearly in mind the information that he wants from the data and the subsequent analysis. These things should be considered before samples are drawn and data are collected. In the final analysis, only the researcher can make these decisions in the context of his specific investigation.

Suggested Study Exercises

4.1 Discuss the differences between the parametric and nonparametric assumptions. What assumptions are common to both types of techniques?

4.2 Describe in considerable detail a research situation for which you would use a nonparametric technique. Identify the type of data that you would collect. State the hypothesis.

4.3 Suppose that we have a distribution of frequencies within several categories and we test this against some expected distribution, using a chi-square test. The test is significant at the .01 level of significance. State the null hypothesis, the associated probability statement, and your conclusion. Can you conclude anything about the .05 level of significance? Why or why not?

4.4 Someone contends that blue eyes and brown eyes occur with equal frequency in a university student population. What is the null hypothesis and what technique would you use to test this hypothesis?

4.5 The median test is computed on two samples of observations. The sample sizes are 15 and 18. The significance level is designated as .05 and the χ^2-value computed. This χ^2-value is 4.81. Is this value significant? State the null hypothesis and your conclusion relative to the null hypothesis.

4.6 Suppose we have a variable measured on an ordinal scale with five categories. Four independent samples are measured on this variable. The hypothesis is that these four samples were drawn from a common population. A χ^2-test is computed. What is the necessary χ^2-value for significance at the .05 level? Suppose the χ^2-value is 23.81; what would you conclude? Give the associated probability statement.

4.7 Contrast the parametric analysis of variance and the Kruskal-Wallis one-way analysis of variance by ranks. What is the null hypothesis for the Kruskal-Wallis technique with five samples?

4.8 The sign test is used with two related samples of size 55. Consider the two samples as the before and after observations on a single group of Ss. The significance level is designated as .01. What is the appropriate underlying distribution and what value is necessary in this distribution to attain a significant test if this is a two-tailed test? Suppose the value is 3.21; what would you conclude?

4.9 Two samples of entering college freshmen are drawn; one from athletes and one from non-athletes. Two dependent variables are investigated, namely, handedness (right, left, both) and achievement on an entrance mathematics test (interval scale measurement). The question under study is whether or not the populations of athletes and non-athletes differ on these dependent variables. Why would it be undesirable to use the same type of analysis for the two dependent variables? What measures would be tested statistically in the handedness data? In the mathematics test data? What would be an appropriate technique for testing the handedness data? the mathematics test data? Suppose the technique used for the handedness data reached significance at the .05 level. What would be concluded about handedness? After this conclusion, what type of error may have been made?

4.10 A researcher tests the performance of two random samples of Ss on a task. The performance of each S is then scored as poor, fair, good, or excellent. A Student's t-test is then computed on the sample data. The investigator interprets his results as being significant at the .01 but not at .05 level. However, he decides to reject the null hypothesis and concludes that the two sample measures are in fact different. He then is concerned about his probability of having made a Type II or beta error. There are several errors in reasoning and procedure in this example. Point out these errors.

5 Testing Hypotheses by Correlational Techniques

The Meaning of Correlation and Correlation Coefficient

The discussion of earlier chapters has been primarily concerned with describing or analyzing the scores of a single variable. Frequently, however, the educational researcher is interested in examining the extent of relationship that exists between two variables. This extent of relationship is approached through the distributions of scores that represent the two variables. The two distributions are commonly made up of paired scores from a single group of Ss. In any event, the distributions make up sets of ordered pairs of scores. We are interested in how the scores in the distributions co-relate or covary. *Covary* means vary together — high scores with high, low with low, high with medium, whatever the case may be. The relationship between the two distributions, and hence the variables represented by the distributions, is based on how the pairs of scores vary together. We are concerned about changes (variation) in one variable compared with changes in the other variable. The degree of relationship or association between two variables is referred to as *correlation*. Thus, in correlational studies we are not concerned with a single distribution but with two distributions of observations.

The measure of correlation is called the *correlation coefficient* or the *coefficient of correlation*. The correlation coefficient is an index of the extent of relationship between two variables. It can take on values from −1.00 through zero to +1.00 inclusive. The end points of the interval indicate a perfect correlation between the two variables. What is a perfect correlation? Let us consider an example. Suppose an individual is earning $500 per month and we correlate the number of months worked with total amount of money earned. At the end of one month the total amount of money earned would be $500, at the end of two months $1,000, three months $1,500, and so on. Note the relationship between these two variables. Each increase of one month corresponds to an increase of exactly $500. If we look at a difference of two months we have an increase of $1,000. The correspondence between one month and $500 is uniform throughout. The unit change on one variable corresponds to a designated uniform change in the other. We have a perfect +1.00 correlation between these two variables. The algebraic sign on a correlation coefficient simply indicates the direction of the relationship, that is, if high scores on one variable go with high scores on the second variable we have positive correlation. Conversely, if high scores on one variable go with low scores on the other variable we have a negative correlation. A correlation coefficient of zero indicates no relationship.

Suppose we have a single group of Ss measured on two variables and we are interested in the relationship between the variables. Each S has two scores, one on each variable. To illustrate the concept of correlation, let us consider the plot of the scores in a two-dimensional space or plane. Such a space is sometimes referred to as the *Cartesian plane* and any point in this plane can be located by two values, one for the horizontal axis and one for the vertical axis. In order to plot the scores, we assign the scale of one variable on the horizontal axis and the other on the vertical axis. Thus each S's pair of scores may be plotted in the usual manner, by being represented as a point in the plane. Such a plot is called a *scattergram*. There will be as many points in the scattergram as Ss measured on both variables. Figures 5.1 and 5.2 below illustrate two possible scattergrams. The two variables are designated by X and Y. The horizontal scale increases to the right and the vertical scale up. By locating any specific S (point) we can determine his score on the Y variable by going to the left to the Y scale, and his score on the X variable by going down to the X scale.

By an inspection of the scattergram we can get some idea of the relationship between the variables, although we will not gain a quantified measure of the strength of the relationship. The correlation coefficient provides such a measure or numerical index. It is an index and although the greater the absolute value of the coefficient, the stronger the relationship, it is not measured on an equal unit scale. Nor can the correlation coefficient be interpreted as some kind of direct percentage.

Figure 5.1 illustrates a positive relationship between variables and hence a positive correlation coefficient. The high values of variable X are associated with high values of variable Y. The opposite situation is true for a negative correlation, i.e., high values

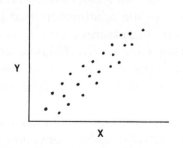

Figure 5.1 A scattergram indicating a positive correlation coefficient.

Figure 5.2 A scattergram indicating a negative correlation coefficient.

of variable X go with low values of variable Y and vice versa. In order to have a perfect correlation ($+1.00$ or -1.00) the points of the scattergram must fall on a straight line. (The example presented earlier of months worked and total money earned would, if plotted, have all points fall on a straight line.) The direction of the line would indicate the algebraic sign. It is extremely rare in educational research to discover two variables which have a perfect correlation.

An example of two variables which seem to be positively correlated are intelligence and achievement in science. That is, students who score high on I.Q. tests tend to be the highest scorers on science tests. Of course, for any one correlation coefficient the scores of only one I.Q. test and one science test would be correlated. An example of a negative correlation coefficient might be the relationship between intelligence scores and time to perform a learning task. That is, the more intelligent Ss should tend to perform the task in less time if correlation exists. Two variables which probably have zero correlation are amount of loose change in pocket and intelligence.

The correlation coefficient does not necessarily indicate a cause and effect situation between the two variables. This is to say that it does not necessarily follow that one variable is causing the scores on the other variable to be whatever they are. For example, there usually exists a positive correlation between the salaries paid teachers and the percentage of graduating seniors going on to college in a particular school or system. That is, schools with higher teachers' salaries tend to have greater percentages of graduating seniors going on to college. However, it would be difficult to argue that paying higher teachers' salaries is causing greater percentages of seniors to go on to college, or vice versa, that sending seniors to college increases teachers' salaries. A third factor or a combination of external but common factors may be influencing the scores on both variables. Multiple causation is not uncommon when dealing with educational variables.

The "scatter" or dispersion of the points in the scattergram gives an indication of the extent of relationship. As the positions of points tend to deviate from a straight line, the correlation tends to decrease. If a relationship exists but is not $+1.00$ or -1.00, the points generally fall in an elliptical ring. As the ring becomes

narrower, that is, approaches a straight line, the relationship becomes stronger and the absolute value of the correlation coefficient increases. The direction of the ring indicates whether the
relationship is positive or negative; lower left to upper right
being positive and upper left to lower right, negative. When the
points of the scattergram fall within a circle we have a correlation of zero. Figure 5.3 presents some examples of scattergrams
with the corresponding magnitude of the correlation coefficient
given by r.

The examples and the scattergrams illustrate situations in
which both variables are assumed to have continuous distributions. This is not always the case with variables in educational
research. There are different types of correlation coefficients
which apply under varied circumstances, depending upon the
variables and the assumptions which can be met. In a sense, we
have a situation analogous to parametric and nonparametric
techniques. For the use of certain correlation coefficients, more
stringent assumptions about the population distributions are
necessary. If these cannot be met we turn to other coefficients

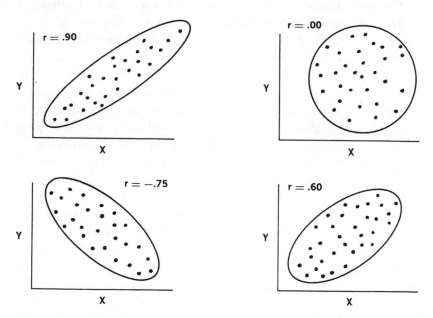

Figure 5.3   Examples of scattergrams and corresponding correlation coefficients.

not as demanding in assumptions. In any case the basic idea is still the same, that of the extent of relationship between the variables. The discussion of this chapter is devoted to different types of correlation coefficients and their applications.

We can test hypotheses about the relationship in the population from the data of the sample. The basic idea is the same as testing hypotheses with parametric or nonparametric techniques. However, difficulties may arise with the sampling distribution of the correlation coefficient. In some cases, this distribution or some of its characteristics are not known.

Pearson-Product Moment Correlation Coefficient

Probably the most frequently used correlation coefficient in educational research is the *Pearson-product moment coefficient*. This coefficient is the most sensitive measure of correlation for situations in which it applies. However, in addition to other assumptions, this correlational technique requires that both variables be measured on at least an interval scale. In many educational research situations this assumption cannot be met. The misapplication of the procedure renders the results uninterpretable.

A second assumption for the Pearson-product moment coefficient is that the distributions of the two variables are continuous and somewhat symmetrical. The distributions need not be normal; however, they should be unimodal. Unimodal means that there is only one mode in a distribution. If one of the distributions is skewed, it will tend to lower the correlation coefficient, and the researcher should be aware of this fact. Otherwise, the failure to meet this assumption will not put additional limitations on the procedure.

A linear [1] relationship between the two variables is also assumed. *Linear relationship* means that the plot of the scattergram approximates a straight-line fit. A true linear relationship would

---

[1] A more precise term would be rectilinear which means forming a straight line. However, linear refers to a straight line, while a departure from a straight line is referred to as curvilinear.

mean that the graph of the relationship between the two variables falls exactly on a straight line.

The final assumption for the use of the Pearson-product
moment coefficient is *homogeneity of variance* or *homoscedasticity*. This means that the dispersions in the rows (and columns)
of the scattergram array are about equal. If we consider the individual values of, say, the variable represented on the vertical
scale, for each such value there is a little distribution of values
on the other variable. These distributions should have about the
same variability in order to meet the homoscedastic assumption.
The same is true for the values of the other variable which would
then concern the distributions in the columns of the scattergram.
Figures 5.4 and 5.5 illustrate the shapes of scattergrams which
do not meet certain assumptions. Note that in both figures the Y
distributions are much less variable for the X_1 values than the X_2
values. A straight line would be a poor fit for the data of Figure
5.5. Thus, we say the relationship between the two variables is
nonlinear and the assumption of a linear relationship is not
tenable.

A possible set of data which would fit the scattergram of
Figure 5.4 appears in Table 5.1. These are strictly hypothetical
data and include only eighteen pairs of scores. The two variables
are denoted by X and Y. Note that the Y distribution associated
with the X score of 89 is much more variable than the Y distribution associated with the X score of 82. These two X scores

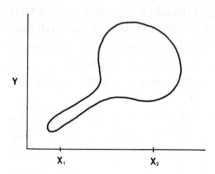

Figure 5.4 A scattergram lacking
homogeneity of variance.

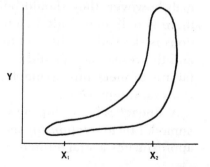

Figure 5.5 A scattergram lacking
a linear relationship and also lacking homogeneity of variance.

correspond to our X_1 and X_2 of the scattergram in the figure. This is a limited set of data with only eighteen scores and it is used only to illustrate the point.

TABLE 5.1

Hypothetical Data on Two Variables which Lack Homogeneity of Variance

Subject Number	Variables	
	X	Y
1	82	17
2	83	16
3	84	19
4	85	19
5	86	21
6	86	25
7	86	24
8	86	27
9	86	25
10	89	21
11	89	20
12	89	23
13	89	25
14	89	29
15	89	25
16	89	31
17	89	30
18	89	31

Table 5.2 contains a set of twenty pairs of observations which makes a possible fit to the scattergram of Figure 5.5. The scores of 47 and 55 correspond to the X_1 and X_2 values of the figure. The distribution of Y scores for the X value of 55 is much more variable than the Y distribution for the X value of 47. Thus, the assumption of homogeneity of variance is not tenable. The relationship is clearly nonlinear by an inspection of the scattergram.

TABLE 5.2

Hypothetical Data on Two Variables which Lack Homogeneity of Variance and a Linear Relationship

	Variables	
Subject Number	X	Y
1	46	3
2	47	3
3	48	3
4	50	3
5	53	4
6	53	3
7	54	3
8	54	4
9	54	5
10	54	5
11	55	3
12	55	3
13	55	4
14	55	5
15	55	6
16	55	6
17	55	7
18	55	8
19	55	9
20	55	10

Suppose we have two variables which meet the assumptions for a Pearson-product moment correlation coefficient. A random sample of Ss is drawn from some defined population and observations taken on both variables. The correlation coefficient for the sample is then computed and designated by "r." In keeping with our basic procedures in hypothesis testing we hypothesize about the correlation coefficient in the population. This coefficient is called "rho" and symbolized by the Greek letter ρ. A hypothesis which can be statistically tested is the hypothesis that $\rho = 0$. If we are simply concerned whether or not a relationship exists between the variables, this hypothesis takes on the characteristics of a null hypothesis, namely no relationship between the variables in the population.

The sampling distribution for r under the hypothesis of $\rho = 0$ is known. This distribution is sometimes called the *normal correlation distribution*. It is symmetrical around zero and is dependent upon sample size. Thus, with sample size held constant and as r values become increasingly larger in absolute value, their probability of being selected in random sampling decreases. The associated probability statement is: What is the probability of the observed sample r appearing by chance, if, in fact, the population correlation is zero? If this probability is less than our preassigned significance level we will reject the hypothesis that the population correlation is zero. Note that the rejection of the null hypothesis does not specify a value for ρ. The rejection simply leads to the conclusion that the population correlation is not zero.

The fact that the sampling distribution of r under the null hypothesis is dependent on sample size immediately implies a family of distributions. It is not necessary for us to compute additional statistics to test the hypothesis of $\rho = 0$. The critical values for the Pearson-product moment correlation coefficient appear in Table F[1] of the Appendix. As is the usual case with families of distributions, only specific probabilities appear in the table. The column of degrees of freedom is used to find the proper distribution. The degrees of freedom[2] associated with the proper distribution is given by $N - 2$, where N is the sample size. The correlation values of the table have the indicated probability of appearing by chance, if, in fact, the correlation between the two variables in the population is zero.

[1] The statistic underlying this table is $\dfrac{r\sqrt{N-2}}{\sqrt{1-r^2}}$ which is distributed as the corresponding t-distribution with $N - 2$ degrees of freedom. If a table of critical values of the Pearson-product moment correlation coefficient is not available, we can solve for this statistic and use a t-distribution table for testing the null hypothesis.

[2] The reason for $N - 2$ degrees of freedom is that when we are computing a statistical test for r we are testing the significance of regression, a concept discussed later in this chapter. A linear regression line involves two constants and hence two degrees of freedom are lost in fitting the line.

It should be noted that Table F contains level of significance for both one-tailed and two-tailed tests. The reasoning here is the same as for other one-tailed and two-tailed statistical tests. If we would use an alternative hypothesis of $\rho > 0$ or $\rho < 0$, a one-tailed test would be appropriate since a direction is being hypothesized. In that case, all of the area of the rejection region would be located in one tail of the distribution.

Consider an example involving the use of Table F. Suppose for the general situation discussed earlier we had a sample size of 30 and the computed correlation coefficient for the same was .42. Recall that the question being posed is whether there is a correlation between the two variables in the population from which the sample was drawn? Note that no direction is hypothesized. The null hypothesis is $\rho = 0$ and hence a two-tailed test is appropriate. The significance level is set at .05. We turn to Table F and find the critical values for degrees of freedom equal 30 minus 2 or 28. We note in the table that a correlation coefficient of .361 has a probability of .05 (our significance level) of appearing by chance if the correlation in the population is zero. Since the distribution is centered around zero and our sample r is greater than .361, it has a probability of less than .05 of appearing by chance under the null hypothesis. Hence we reject the null hypothesis and conclude that a correlation does exist in the population between the two variables.

Confidence Interval for the Pearson-Product Moment Correlation Coefficient

The question of whether or not any correlation between two variables exists in a population may be trivial under certain conditions. The researcher may have prior evidence that a relationship exists and what he is really concerned about is some information about the magnitude of the correlation in the population. The confidence interval for the correlation coefficient is a procedure for considering this problem. As in the case of the confidence interval for the mean, the confidence interval for the correlation coefficient is an interval estimate for a parameter.

That is, the researcher is attempting to answer the question: What interval of values will I entertain as tenable values for the correlation coefficient in the population under study?

The procedure is not as straightforward in this situation as it was, say, for constructing a confidence interval for the mean. The sampling distribution becomes markedly skewed as we depart from $\rho = 0$. This can be intuitively seen by considering the restrictions on the possible values the correlation coefficient can take. Consider a situation in which sampling was done from a population with $\rho = .90$. Since the upper bound on the value of r is $+1.00$, the sampling distribution is now very skewed. It will be centered around .90 and the left tail can take on values from .90 to -1.00 while the right tail can only go from .90 to $+1.00$. In addition, there is little exact knowledge about the sampling distribution except when centered on zero.

Although the computational procedures are more involved than in the case of the confidence interval for the mean, the principle is the same. Suppose that we are interested in a 95 per cent confidence interval. Two values are determined that define the interval. The probability is then .95 that this interval spans the population correlation. Our conclusion is that the values of the correlation coefficient within this interval are tenable values for the correlation in the population.

A situation in which the confidence interval might be a useful procedure would be one in which I.Q. scores are correlated separately with three different achievement measures. The question under investigation has to do with the tenable values of these correlation coefficients in the population under investigation. Note that in this situation three confidence intervals would be constructed, one for each correlation coefficient of the achievement measure with I.Q. There would undoubtedly be prior evidence that a correlation exists between I.Q. and any one of the achievement measures. The magnitude of such correlation coefficients would be of primary interest. The confidence interval would provide the interval estimate of the population correlation. Confidence intervals for correlation coefficients are not common in educational research but can be used as an effective technique. The confidence interval can provide useful information and can be considered a test of an infinite number of hypotheses in that the values within the interval are tenable values for the population correlation. Those values outside the interval would be rejected as hypothesized values.

Difference Between Two Correlation Coefficients; Independent Samples

The next question we want to consider is: What about the difference between two correlations of independent samples? That is, what magnitude of difference is required so that we no longer entertain the hypothesis that in the populations the two correlations are equal? The null hypothesis is $\rho_1 = \rho_2$ or $\rho_1 - \rho_2 = 0$. Note that it is not implied that either or both of the ρ values are zero. In order to complete the statistical computation to test this hypothesis, we would need a special transformation. The reasoning underlying the statistical test is analogous to that underlying the situation for the difference between two means. In this case we are trying to decide whether or not the correlations of the two populations are the same. A significant statistical test would result in rejecting the null hypothesis, that is, the hypothesis of no difference between the population correlations.

Consider an example. Suppose someone asks whether the correlation coefficients between I.Q. and science achievement differ significantly for seventh-grade boys and girls? Random samples of seventh-grade boys and girls are drawn from the populations. The sample of boys is considered to be independent of the sample of girls. The correlation coefficients are computed separately for each sample. The null hypothesis states that there is no difference between the correlation coefficients in the populations of boys and girls. In order to entertain the null hypothesis it must be acceptable to attribute the observed difference to chance. If this chance probability is less than the significance level, the explanation of chance is no longer acceptable. The alternative conclusion is that there is a real difference in the population correlations, and hence the null hypothesis is rejected.

Suppose the significance level is designated as .05 and the

statistical test[1] for the difference between the two correlation coefficients is significant. Then the probability that the observed difference would occur by chance, if, in fact, there is no difference in the populations, is less than .05. The conclusion is that the correlation between I.Q. scores and science achievement is not the same for boys and girls. Note that the statistical test does not indicate which correlation coefficient is largest in magnitude. An inspection of the sample coefficients will aid in drawing this conclusion.

Difference Between Two Correlation Coefficients; Related Samples

A hypothesis about the difference between two correlation coefficients of related samples may also be tested statistically. Related samples are sometimes referred to as *correlated samples.* In this situation three observations are taken on the same sample of Ss. Three correlation coefficients result and they may be compared in all combinations of two. Any combination is, of course, a single comparison.

The null hypothesis is again that of no difference between the correlation coefficients in the population. Suppose we have three variables on which the sample is measured, designated by 1, 2, and 3. The subscripts on r denote the two variables being correlated. To compare the difference between r_{12} and r_{13} we compute the statistic:

$$\frac{(r_{12} - r_{13}) \sqrt{(N - 3)(1 + r_{23})}}{\sqrt{2(1 - r_{12}^2 - r_{13}^2 - r_{23}^2 + 2r_{12} \cdot r_{13} \cdot r_{23})}}$$

which is distributed as the Student's t-distribution with $N - 3$ degrees of freedom.

Consider the question: Is there a difference between the correlations of I.Q. and science achievement and I.Q. and mathe-

[1] The computation of the statistical test involves a logarithmic transformation. For computational details the reader is referred to a statistics text such as Clark, R. B., Coladarci, A. P., and Caffrey, J., *Statistical Reasoning and Procedures* (Columbus, Ohio: Charles E. Merrill Books, Inc., 1965), pp. 292–294.

matics achievement? A random sample of Ss is drawn from a defined population and the Ss measured on the three variables. In addition to the two correlation coefficients mentioned in the question, the correlation between science and mathematics achievement is determined. Let us designate the three computed correlation coefficients as:

r_{12} = correlation between I.Q. and science achievement

r_{13} = correlation between I.Q. and mathematics achievement

and

r_{23} = correlation between science achievement and mathematics achievement

The null hypothesis is: $\rho_{12} = \rho_{13}$ or $\rho_{12} - \rho_{13} = 0$. That is, we hypothesize no difference between these respective correlation coefficients of the population. A significance level is set and the computation carried out as designated by the above formula. If the value of t is significant, the null hypothesis is rejected; if it is not significant, we fail to reject the null hypothesis.

The discussion to this point in the chapter has been concerned primarily with the Pearson-product moment coefficient of correlation. It might be well to summarize the hypotheses that can be tested by this technique. Recall that hypotheses are statements about population characteristics. We can test the hypothesis that the population correlation is zero. Then we can build a confidence interval for a specific correlation coefficient. This is actually an infinite number of tests of hypotheses since we decide which values will be considered tenable and which will be rejected. Finally, the hypotheses of no difference between two population correlations may be tested. This may be done for independent or related samples.

Spearman Rank Correlation Coefficient

Measurement of many variables is not quantitative enough to use an interval scale, yet the relationship between the variables

may be of interest. The Pearson-product moment correlation coefficient does not apply in such situations since the assumption
of interval scale measurement is not met. Thus, we must turn to
other correlational procedures.

Probably the best known correlational procedure for two variables measured on an ordinal scale is the *Spearman rank correlation coefficient*. This coefficient is often referred to as the
"Spearman rho" or simply *rho*. This may appear confusing since
we have reserved "rho" for the population coefficient. For consistency and to avoid confusion we will use r_s and ρ_s to designate the Spearman rank coefficients of the sample and the population.

Measurement on an ordinal scale allows us to rank observations. As with any correlation coefficient, measurement on two
variables is required. However, in the Spearman rank coefficient the actual observations are not correlated but rather the
ranks representing the observations. Let N be the number of Ss
in the sample. The Ss are ranked from one through N inclusive,
first on one variable and then on the other. Ss with the same
score, that is, tied ranks, are assigned the mean rank of the
ranks that they occupy. The next step is to determine the difference between the two ranks of each S. It is actually these
differences in ranks that go into the statistical computation.
The differences are squared and hence it is not necessary to
retain the algebraic sign but only the absolute values of the
differences.

The correlation coefficient of the observations is given by:[1]

$$r_s = 1 - \frac{6\Sigma d_i^2}{N(N^2 - 1)}$$

where the d_i's are the differences in ranks, d_i is the difference
for the ith S, N represents the number of Ss in the sample.
In keeping with our ideas of hypothesis testing we want to make
statements about the population correlation and test these statements.

[1] If we use the ranks of the two variables as the scores and apply the Pearson-
product moment formula we get the same result. However, this should not be
interpreted to mean that a Spearman ρ computed on interval scale data converted to ranks will equal the Pearson-product moment computed for the same
data. The Pearson-product moment takes into account the relative distances
between scores as well as their order.

The testing of hypotheses is somewhat limited for two reasons. If N is small, say less than 10, the standard deviation of the underlying distribution for r_s cannot be estimated, regardless of the hypothesized values of the population coefficient. For any hypothesized value other than $\rho_s = 0$, there is no accepted method for estimating the standard deviation of the underlying sampling distribution for r_s, no matter how large the sample size. Note that we are concerned about the standard deviation of the underlying sampling distribution, not that of the sample data. Since the sample data are converted to ranks, we cannot compute a standard deviation for these ordinal data. Hence, we cannot build confidence intervals.

The null hypothesis, $\rho_s = 0$, can be statistically tested with N greater than or equal to 10. If N is less than 25 we may compute the statistic $r_s \sqrt{\dfrac{N-2}{1-r_s^2}}$ which is distributed as the Student's t-distribution with $N-2$ degrees of freedom. A significant t-value would result in the rejection of the null hypothesis. The probability that the observed r_s would appear by chance, if, in fact, $\rho_s = 0$ is less than the significance level. If N is 25 or greater, the normal distribution may be used as the underlying distribution. Under this condition, the standard deviation of the sampling distribution of r_s, is given by

$$\frac{1}{\sqrt{N-1}}$$

Suppose a researcher is interested in the relationship between attitudes toward school and socio-economic background. Assume that these two variables are measured on ordinal scales and thus the Ss could be ranked on the variables. The author recognizes that attitudes toward school and socio-economic background are variables that may be difficult to measure. We will assume, however, that satisfactory ordinal measurement is possible. In order to limit the study somewhat, suppose that only the junior high school population of a defined and geographically limited school district is under study. The question may be stated as: Is there a relationship between these two variables in the defined junior high school population?

A random sample of Ss is drawn from the population. The Ss are administered the attitudes-toward-school inventory and scored on socio-economic background. Each S is then ranked on each variable and differences between ranks determined. Using these differences, the r_s is computed. The null hypotheses is that the correlation between attitude toward school and socio-economic background in the junior high population is zero, i.e., $\rho_s = 0$. Since no direction is hypothesized, the hypothesis implies a two-tailed test. A significance level is specified, say .05.

The appropriate underlying distribution is used to test the null hypothesis. Suppose the statistical test turns out to be significant, which results in the rejection of the null hypothesis. Then the probability that the observed sample correlation coefficient would appear by chance, if, in fact, the population correlation is zero, is less than .05. On this basis we conclude that there is a relationship between attitude toward school and socio-economic background. Note that no statement is made as to the exact magnitude of the correlation coefficient.

Point Biserial Correlation Coefficient

It is not always possible to acquire measurement of the same type on both variables. The situation arises in educational research in which one variable is continuous and measured on an interval scale and the second variable is discrete and dichotomous. For example, sex is a two-category variable and achievement in mathematics is generally considered continuous and may be measured on an interval scale. A correlation coefficient which measures the relationship between two such variables is the *point biserial correlation coefficient.* The dichotomous variable is assumed to be discrete, that is, a genuine dichotomy. The continuous variable essentially requires the assumptions of a somewhat symmetrical, unimodal distribution with interval scale measurement. The point biserial correlations of the sample and population will be designated by r_{pb} and ρ_{pb} respectively.

The point biserial correlation is actually a product moment type of correlation coefficient. If we artificially assign numerical weights, say zero and one, to the two categories of the dichotomous variable and apply the calculation of a Pearson-product moment coefficient, we would get a point biserial coefficient.

The computation of a point biserial involves the proportions of observations in the two categories of the dichotomous variable. These two proportions we will designate as p and q and, of course, $p + q = 1$. Since the continuous variable is measured on an interval scale, means and standard deviations may be computed for this variable. The computational formula for the point biserial coefficient is given by:

$$\frac{\bar{Y}_p - \bar{Y}_q}{s_y} \cdot \sqrt{p \cdot q}$$

where $\bar{Y}_p$ and $\bar{Y}_q$ are the means on the continuous variable for those Ss belonging to the respective categories of the dichotomy, and s_y is the standard deviation of all scores on the continuous variable.

The testing of hypotheses when using a point biserial coefficient is again somewhat limited. It is possible to test the hypothesis of zero correlation in the population. This may actually be done in two ways. From an inspection of the computational formula, it is immediately apparent that the value of r_{pb} is directly dependent upon the difference of two means. Thus, a Student's t-test for the difference between two means may be applied. If this statistical test is significant, we reject the hypothesis of zero correlation in the population.

A direct test of the null hypothesis, $\rho_{pb} = 0$ may be made as in the Spearman rank correlation coefficient. Note that the hypothesis deals with the population correlation. The expression:

$$r_{pb} \cdot \sqrt{\frac{N - 2}{1 - r_{pb}^2}}$$

is distributed as the Student's t-distribution with $N - 2$ degrees of freedom, where N is the total sample size. A significant t-value again leads to the rejection of the null hypothesis.

Theoretically, correlation coefficients may take on values between plus and minus one inclusively. However, with the point biserial coefficient the values of r_{pb} are dependent upon the proportional split of the dichotomous variable, i.e., the values of p and q. The maximum and minimum values of r_{pb} do not reach plus one and minus one under any proportional division.

An example for which the point biserial coefficient would apply would be the study of the relationship between type of high school attended—rural or urban—and achievement on a college entrance examination in mathematics. Type of high school attended is a variable that can be dichotomously defined and the scores on the mathematics examination are assumed to be continuously distributed. A random sample is drawn from entering college freshmen who are then given the mathematics test. Each freshman in the sample is then categorized as to whether he attended a rural or urban high school. The r_{pb} is computed for the sample.

The null hypothesis is that there is no correlation between high school attended and achievement on this entrance mathematics exam. A significance level is designated. Suppose a direct test of the hypothesis is made and the corresponding t-value is found not to be significant. Thus, we fail to reject the null hypothesis. The probability that the r_{pb} (sample correlation coefficient) would appear by chance, if, in fact, ρ_{pb} is zero, is greater than the significance level. The conclusion is that on the basis of this statistical test we cannot infer that a relationship exists between type of high school attended and achievement on this particular mathematics examination.

Biserial Correlation Coefficient

A correlation coefficient closely related to the point biserial is the *biserial coefficient*. It is applicable when the dichotomous variable is an artificial dichotomy and actually has an underlying continuous distribution. A common example of such a variable is the case for which performance on an examination is simply reduced to pass or fail. The second variable is again continuous and measured on at least an interval scale.

The computational formula for the biserial correlation coefficient is similar to the point biserial coefficient. The formula is given by:

$$r_b = \frac{\bar{Y}_p - \bar{Y}_q}{s_y} \cdot \frac{p \cdot q}{y^1}$$

The symbols have the same definitions as in the formula for r_{pb} and the one new symbol is y^1. The symbol y^1 is the ordinate of the standard normal distribution at the point of division for the proportions p and q. Since the normal curve is symmetrical, the division may be made on either side of the mean. The value of y^1 may be determined directly from an area table of the standard normal distribution as appears in Table A in the Appendix. The area under the curve is designated as 1.00 or unity. Suppose that $p = .60$ and $q = .40$. This means that for p we have all the area in one-half of the distribution plus an additional 10 per cent located between the mean and the split in the dichotomy. Coming down the area column until we come to .10 we find the corresponding ordinate or y^1 value to be .386.

The hypothesis of zero correlation in the population, i.e., $\rho_b = 0$ may be statistically tested if the sample size is quite large, say 25 or greater. Under these conditions the standard deviation of the biserial coefficient is approximated by:

$$s_{r_b} = \frac{\frac{\sqrt{p \cdot q}}{y^1}}{\sqrt{N}}$$

and the normal distribution may be used as an adequate approximation for the underlying distribution. The null hypothesis states that there is no correlation between the two variables in the population. The test of the hypothesis gives us the probability of the sample correlation coefficient appearing, if, in fact, the variables are uncorrelated in the population. If this probability is less than the pre-determined significance level, we reject the null hypothesis and conclude that the two variables are correlated in the population. Note that the statistical test does not specify the direction or the magnitude of the correlation coefficient.

Two variables whose relationship might be studied using the biserial coefficient are pass or fail performance on a physical education task and achievement on a science examination. Suppose that the performance on the physical education task is continuous, but for some reason measurement is such that the researcher chooses to dichotomize the scores on this variable. A random sample is drawn from a defined population and the r_b computed. The null hypothesis is $H_0: \rho_b = 0$, i.e., the population correlation between the two variables is zero. A significance level is specified and the null hypothesis tested. If the probability of the r_b appearing by chance under the null hypothesis is less than the significance level, the null hypothesis is rejected. If this probability is greater than the significance level, we fail to reject the null hypothesis.

The above example is a case in which the statistical test could be strengthened if it were possible to measure the performance on the physical education task on an interval scale. Under that condition an applicable correlation coefficient would be the Pearson-product moment. An interval scale takes into account differences between Ss in terms of a common or equal unit. Chances are that two Ss, one of which is slightly above and the other slightly below the pass-fail cutoff, are actually quite close in score; closer than a "just pass" and a high scorer. Going to the dichotomy loses this type of information and makes the statistical test less sensitive to an existing correlation between the variables. However, if measurement is not precise enough for an interval scale, such a scale should not be artificially forced upon the data. Measurement of attitudes is often not precise enough for interval scale measurement.

The question may arise in a specific situation whether to use the point biserial correlation coefficient or the biserial coefficient. The crucial point is whether or not the dichotomous variable is a genuine dichotomy or has an underlying continuous distribution. If there is little doubt about the underlying distribution being continuous, the biserial coefficient should be used. In doubtful situations use the point biserial coefficient. The point biserial will yield a markedly smaller coefficient if applied to a situation in which the use of the biserial is justified. A conversion formula may be applied to convert from one to the other, if afterward it becomes apparent that the other coefficient should have been applied in a specific situation.

Tetrachoric Correlation Coefficient

The *tetrachoric correlation coefficient* applies to the situation in which both variables have been artificially reduced to dichotomies. The underlying assumptions for the use of this coefficient are threefold: (1) both variables have underlying, continuous distributions, (2) both variables are normally distributed, and (3) the variables are linearly related. If these assumptions are met, the tetrachoric coefficient is an estimate of the Pearson-product moment coefficient. As such, it is useful in situations where interval scale measurement is not attainable. Since both variables are dichotomized, the data may be presented in a fourfold table. The computation of a tetrachoric coefficient is a laborious process. However, since it is a relatively crude technique due to the reduction in the measurement to dichotomies, the researcher is often not so much interested in the actual coefficient as in whether or not a relationship exists between the two variables. A test for independence, that is, the null hypothesis of no relationship, may be applied quite easily and without determining the coefficient.

A test for independence can be made by applying a chi-square test to the data in the fourfold table. The appropriate distribution is the chi-square distribution with one degree of freedom. A significant χ^2-value indicates the existence of a relationship between the two variables. Although this procedure tests the hypothesis of independence, it does not specify the magnitude of the relationship nor are interval estimates made for the correlation in the population.

The tetrachoric correlation coefficient is generally not a widely used technique, principally because it does not provide a great deal of information. Also, the use of the tetrachoric coefficient is a tenuous procedure if the variables are not split close to their medians when dichotomized. If variables measured on a multicategorized ordinal scale are arbitrarily dichotomized, there is a considerable loss of information. Under such conditions it is preferable to use another correlation coefficient.

Coefficient of Contingency

The situation may arise in which there are two or more categories for one or both of two variables measured on nominal scales. A measure of the relationship between the two variables may be computed using the *coefficient of contingency*. This coefficient involves the χ^2-value based on the $k \times j$ table, where k and j are the numbers of categories associated with the two variables under study. The coefficient is generally designated by the capital letter C and the formula is given by:

$$C = \sqrt{\frac{\chi^2}{N + \chi^2}}$$

where N is sample size and the χ^2-value is as determined from the $k \times j$ table.

The contingency coefficient is restricted in size. Its minimum value is zero, that is, it does not take on negative values. Since the concept of direction requires order, it would be without meaning when applied to strictly nominal variables. In a practical situation a researcher might attach a positive or negative sign to indicate a certain type of association in the data, such as left-handedness going with left-footedness. Since N is an integer, an inspection of the formula reveals that the denominator will always exceed the numerator and therefore the coefficient cannot attain the maximum value of plus one. The maximum value depends upon the number of categories of the two variables—as the number of categories increases, the maximal possible value of the coefficient also increases.

The null hypothesis of no correlation in the population can be tested. The standard error of the contingency coefficient can be estimated but this is not necessary since another procedure can be used. A simpler procedure for testing the null hypothesis is by using the χ^2-value from which C is computed. Under the null hypothesis this χ^2-value is distributed with $(k - 1) \times (j - 1)$ degrees of freedom. A significant χ^2-value would result in the rejection of the null hypothesis. The conclusion would be that a relationship does exist in the population between the two variables under study.

The reader of educational research literature may note that correlation coefficients such as the tetrachoric and coefficiency of contingency and even the biserials do not appear frequently in correlational studies. Yet a considerable number of correlational studies appear in the research literature. Many times the coefficient used is not specified. However, if possible, the investigator tries to apply the Pearson-product moment coefficient. It is the preferable technique if the necessary conditions can be met. The Pearson-product moment does not waste information and is more sensitive to an existing relationship under the appropriate conditions.

The Choice of a Correlation Coefficient

The researcher should be very careful in considering the assumptions necessary for the use of a specific technique in testing a hypothesis. The use of a technique when the underlying assumptions are not met yields uninterpretable results. But since almost all results are interpreted, such a procedure usually leads to erroneous conclusions. The use of one technique when a more sensitive procedure would be applicable is wasteful of information and is not considered to be good research.

At this point it might be well to summarize the correlation coefficients discussed in this chapter. Table 5.3 contains a sum-

TABLE 5.3

Correlation Coefficients and Corresponding
Measurement of the Variables

Correlation Coefficient	Variable Measurement
1. Pearson-product moment	1. Both variables on interval scales.
2. Spearman rank	2. Both variables on ordinal scales.
3. Point biserial	3. One variable on interval scale; the other a genuine dichotomy on a nominal or ordinal scale.
4. Biserial	4. One variable on interval scale; the other an artificial dichotomy on an ordinal scale. The dichotomy is artificial because there is an underlying continuous distribution.
5. Tetrachoric	5. Both variables artificial dichotomy on ordinal scales.
6. Coefficient of contingency	6. Both variables on nominal scales.

mary of the coefficients and necessary measurement conditions of the variables. The reader is reminded that other assumptions may be necessary concerning the distributions and relationship of the variables. The variable measurement of Table 5.3 indicates the minimum scale necessary. For example, the Pearson-product moment may be used with ratio scale measurement. If both variables were measured on interval scales, the scores could be reduced to ranks, that is, ordinal scale measurement. However, if the other assumptions were tenable, going in this direction would be a waste of information.

Correlation and Regression

A term which invariably appears with a discussion of correlation is "regression." Actually the idea of regression preceded the correlational methods. The origin of the idea is credited to Sir Francis Galton in connection with his studies of the relationship between the heights of parents and offspring. The details of his studies are many but one important observation was that the means of offspring for fixed parent height deviated less from their common means than the corresponding means of parents from the common parent mean. This indicates a sort of "falling back" or regression in the succeeding generation. In the case of a perfect positive correlation, the data would fall on a straight line. If the standard deviations of the two distributions are equal, the line would have a slope of plus one, the *slope* of the line being the ratio of the change in the variable on the vertical scale to the change in the variable on the horizontal scale.

When the data of two variables are plotted on a scattergram, the points make up some kind of configuration. If this configuration is such that a straight line is an adequate fit and is actually fitted, we say the regression between the two variables is linear. The use of correlation coefficients such as the Pearson-product moment assumes a linear relationship or linear regression between the two variables.

There are many variables in educational research that are not linearly related. That is, if the plot of points in the scattergram does not follow the general pattern of a straight line, the regression is nonlinear.[1] Examples of such variables might be efficiency on a learning task and the passage of time. A marked increase in efficiency would be expected early in time and then a plateau would be reached, resulting in a curved rather than a straight line. If the task is continued for a considerable time, efficiency might decrease due to a factor such as fatigue. The relationship between performance on a motor skill and chronological age may be nonlinear if the chronological age range is large. Under such conditions the application of a correlation coefficient that assumes linear regression is clearly inappropriate and will give meaningless results.

Prediction and Regression

One use of the concept of regression is in connection with prediction studies. Prediction in education has a wide range of procedural meaning, extending from subjective prediction based on casual observation to the development of multiple-term mathematical equations, connecting two or more variables. *Prediction* is the estimation of one variable from the information of one or more other variables. The variable from which we are predicting is called the *predictor* variable and the variable predicted is called the *criterion* variable. Two basic questions must be considered in the execution of a prediction study: one, what variables are related to the variable to be predicted? and two, what is the connecting expression or equation which will make for the most accurate prediction? The regression between the predictor and criterion variables is involved with this second question.

The reader should note that these remarks do not imply that it is desirable to involve a complex mathematical equation. The type of data and the conditions of the study dictate the specific procedure. We may predict using nominal variables or variables which can be quantitatively measured. The variable being predicted may be measured on a nominal, ordinal, or interval scale. Types of variables between predictors and predicted may be

[1] There exist procedures by which nonlinear regression can be handled. See for example, Ferguson, G. A., *Statistical Analysis in Psychology and Education*, 2nd ed. (New York: McGraw-Hill Book Co., 1966), pp. 246–249.

used in various combinations. The computational procedure is determined by the specific combination used in a study.

A common example of prediction in education is predicting achievement from an intelligence measure. Suppose that we define Y to be the predicted variable and X to be the predictor. An equation is developed, called the *regression equation* [1] of the form $Y = a + bX$. An equation in this general form is the equation of a straight line. This is the regression line for estimating Y from X, called the prediction equation for predicting Y from X. The coefficients a and b are the constants of the regression equation. The equation is uniquely determined with the specification of a and b. After the constants or coefficients of the prediction equation are determined, the value of Y for any one S can be predicted by substituting into the equation the S's score on X. Thus, the equation is predicting Y from a knowledge of X.

The question might be raised as to what advantage there is in using this fitted line for predicting. The answer to that question depends upon the strength or magnitude of the correlation between the predictor and criterion variables. The greater the correlation the more precisely the line will fit the points in the scattergram. Earlier in this chapter we discussed an example involving the correlation between number of months worked and amount of money earned. In this example the correlation was plus one. If we were predicting the amount of money earned from number of months worked, our prediction would be exact. All the points in the scattergram fell on the line and there would be no difference between an observed and predicted score. We would make no errors in predicting the amount of money earned. If the correlation between two variables is around zero, very little can be gained by using the regression line for prediction. The differences between observed and predicted scores would be great and there would be considerable error in prediction. Thus, when predicting one variable from another, we attempt

---

[1] An infinite number of straight lines could be fitted to the points in a scattergram. The line that we fit, which we might call the "best fitting" straight line, is the one determined by the least squares requirement. The *least squares requirement* means that the line is fitted in such a manner that the sum determined by taking all differences between the observed and predicted scores for all Ss, squaring these differences and then summing, is a minimum. In symbol form this is given by: $\sum_{i=1}^{N} (Y_i - \hat{Y}_i)^2$ is a minimum, where $\hat{Y}_i$ is a predicted score.

to select a predictor variable that has a high correlation with the criterion variable.

It may be desirable to predict a criterion variable from more than one predictor variable. This involves multiple correlation where two or more predictor variables act as a team of predictors. Again, equations are developed with a coefficient associated with each predictor variable. The idea is essentially the same, that is, developing a prediction equation; however, instead of having only one predictor in the equation, two or more will be included and each will have its own coefficient.

Interpretations of the Correlation Coefficient

One interpretation of the correlation coefficient is in terms of the variation in one variable associated with the variation in the other variable. The square of the correlation coefficient gives the proportion of the variance in Y associated with the variation in X, or the proportion of the variance in Y predictable from X. This interpretation assumes an association between the two variables, and if the correlation coefficient is significantly different from zero we conclude that there is an association. If there exists no association or relationship, the correlation is zero and hence none of the variance in Y would be associated with the variation in X. On the other extreme, if correlation is perfect, that is, plus or minus one, prediction is exact and all of the variation in Y would be associated with the variation in X.

What is a good correlation? Here "good" essentially means a coefficient of such magnitude as to be noteworthy. This question does not have a simple answer. Questions regarding the size of the correlation coefficient cannot be answered without considering the uses to be made of the coefficient. One use for the correlation coefficient is in connection with the reliability and validity of measurement, concepts discussed in the following chapter. Depending on the types of tests and procedures, we may expect relatively large correlation coefficients, say in the .70 to .95 range, when dealing with test reliability.

Suppose a researcher is working on a theoretical problem. In this case, any correlation coefficient significantly different from zero is likely to be noteworthy. Such a coefficient may be indicative of a generalization being sought. The reasons for the coefficient's small magnitude may be due to uncontrolled factors such as inadequate measurement, rather than an inadequate theory. It may be very difficult to achieve isolation for the two variables being correlated, and the contamination of other factors may be suppressing the relationship. Any number of factors may be operating in a specific situation.

The conclusion from these remarks is that the size of the correlation coefficient must always be interpreted in the light of its use in the specific situation. Size of a correlation coefficient is always relative to the conditions under which it was obtained. The researcher must specify his variables, measuring instruments, populations, and the like before interpreting the size of his correlation coefficient.

General Comments on Conducting Correlational Studies

The emphasis of this chapter has been upon the use of correlational techniques in inferential statistics. Some writers place correlation with descriptive statistics. When so considered, the primary function of the correlation coefficient is to describe the extent of relationship between two sets of scores. To be sure, many correlational studies are descriptive in nature and the findings are directed only to the observed data and the variables represented by these data. However, in many situations, the researcher is attempting to make inferences about relationships to a population. When this is done, correlational techniques are being used in an inferential context. In any event, the objectives of the specific study dictate whether descriptive or inferential techniques are appropriate.

The initial problem facing a researcher about to embark on a correlational study is the choice of variables. A review of the literature and an adequate knowledge of the educational area should alleviate much of this problem. The procedure of correlating a large number of variables in order to see what kind of coefficients turn up, sometimes referred to as the shotgun approach, is not recommended. It lacks a rationale for the relationships between variables. This is not to say that any study which correlates a considerable number of variables is a shotgun study; it is the thinking behind the study that makes the difference. The good researcher in an educational area is generally one who does not rely on guesses, but rather someone who is sensitive to the variables in the area.

In the previous section we mentioned possible factors which may have an effect upon the size of the correlation coefficient. One of these was inadequate measurement, another was the lack of isolation of the variables being correlated. The researcher should have some knowledge about his particular variables and how they are operating in the light of the measurement and specific circumstances of his study. Suppose a Pearson-product moment coefficient is anticipated. The size of the coefficient depends upon the amount of variance in the distributions of the variables being correlated. If one variable is practically reduced to a constant we can expect a very small correlation coefficient. This awareness relates not only to the variable but also the methods by which measurement for the variable is conducted. For example, suppose we have a defined population, heterogeneous in intelligence, and an adequate intelligence test for the measurement. We want to correlate intelligence with performance on a mathematics test. We would expect a relatively high correlation coefficient. Now suppose we have another population of high-ability students, those within the 130 to 150 I.Q. range, and we correlated their intelligence scores with mathematics performance. We would likely get a relatively small correlation coefficient. What is the conclusion — that for high-ability students intelligence is not related to mathematics performance? Obviously not. What has happened is that the variable of intelligence scores is much more homogeneous in the later situation than it was when it covered an entire range of ability. This reduction in variability limits the size of the correlation coefficient. The same type of outcome would occur if measurement were inadequate; for example, a large proportion of the students attained the maximum possible score on the mathematics test. This would limit the variability and the test would fail to differentiate students with different intelligence scores on mathematics performance. The instrument would not be discriminating between the students, and the size of the correlation coefficient would be relatively small. The range of the scores on one or both variables influences the size of the correlation coefficient, with the limited range giving the smaller coefficient, assuming other factors to be the same.

After the variables are identified the researcher should carefully consider his assumptions and select an appropriate correlational technique. A review of the literature should not only contribute valuable information about the variables but may give indications as to the type of correlation coefficient which is applicable. Generally, the researcher should attempt to use the most sensitive coefficient for which the assumptions are tenable. When the correlation coefficients are computed they must be interpreted in the light of existing knowledge and the circumstances of the situation. The fact that a non-zero correlation coefficient exists does not necessarily mean a causal relationship between the variables. Causal relationships may exist, but they cannot be imputed on the basis of the correlation coefficient alone.

Overview of Hypothesis Testing

This concludes the discussion on testing hypotheses by correlational techniques and at this point it might be well to briefly review hypothesis testing in general. For the inexperienced researcher, the formulation of hypotheses is often a difficult task. In fact, one frequent difficulty of the naïve researcher is that the hypotheses are never precisely and clearly stated and hence the procedure becomes muddled and confused.

The hypothesis in the context of hypothesis testing is a statement about a parameter or a characteristic of the population under study. A sample is drawn and observations taken on the members of the sample. The characteristics of the sample are statistics, and from these we make inferences about the parameters. The particular hypothesis to be tested dictates the statistics and procedures to be used in the statistical test. This is again a point for extra caution — to be certain that the procedure applies to the hypothesis.

The statistic is observed and the underlying distribution of the statistic is presumably known. Then the probability of the statistic appearing under the null hypothesis is determined and in the light of this probability the hypothesis is retained or rejected. Note that the probability applies to the statistic. In the discussion of this text, the hypothesis has generally been stated as the null hypothesis. This is not essential; hypotheses may be stated in alternate forms which means that a direction of results is hypothesized. However, if hypotheses are stated in alternate form the researcher must be careful on the rejection or acceptance of the hypothesis in light of the results of the statistical test.

The formulation and testing of hypotheses is not the whole of educational research. The most sophisticated procedures are essentially meaningless if performed with inadequate data and in a research vacuum. Subsequent chapters deal with data collection and measurement and general design of the research study.

Suggested Study Exercises

5.1 Discuss what is meant by a correlation coefficient. What are the possible values the coefficient can take? Interpret the meaning of the end points of the possible values of the coefficient.

5.2 A Pearson-product moment coefficient is computed between two variables on a sample of size 40. The correlation coefficient is .413. Is this coefficient significantly different from zero at the .05 level? State the null hypothesis and the associated probability statement. What is your conclusion about the population correlation?

5.3 Give an example of two educational variables that are likely not to be linearly related. Sketch a possible scattergram for your example.

5.4 Two random samples are drawn from their respective populations. The Ss of the samples are then measured on variables A and B and the correlations between the two variables computed. Both variables have interval scale measurement. A statistical test for the difference between the two correlation coefficients is computed and found to be significant at the .05 level. Give the null hypothesis and the associated probability statement. What is your conclusion? What type of error in hypothesis testing could be made here? Can you conclude anything about the .01 level of significance relative to this hypothesis?

5.5 Contrast the Pearson-product moment and Spearman rank co-efficients in terms of required assumptions and type of data correlated. What are the scores that actually go into the compu-tation of a Spearman rank coefficient?

5.6 Give an example of two educational variables whose correla-tion would be determined by using a Spearman rank coefficient. Using your example, state a hypothesis that you could test sta-tistically. Assume random sampling.

5.7 The performances of a sample of 25 student orations are rated as excellent, good, fair, and poor. The same sample is also tested on an English mastery test which has measurement on an inter-val scale. The problem under study is whether or not there exists a relationship between oration performance and English mastery. Would you use a point biserial or biserial coefficient? Discuss your choice of coefficient. State the null hypothesis. Suppose that your statistical test is significant at the .05 level. What is your conclusion?

5.8 Select a correlation coefficient for correlating each of the fol-lowing pairs of variables. Discuss your choice of coefficient.
(a) color of eyes and mathematics achievement.
(b) science achievement and history achievement as measured by an objective factual test.
(c) attitude toward the library and rank on an essay writing task.
(d) "pass or fail" on a speech test and performance on an !.Q. test.

5.9 A correlation coefficient of .62 is computed on a sample of 120 Ss. This correlation is between performance on an objective punctuation test and the scores on a "reading for comprehen-sion" test. The sample consisted of four classes of students enrolled in sophomore English at a specific high school. What are some interpretations of this correlation coefficient? Sug-gest one or more hypotheses that might be involved here. What population might possibly be under study? Suggest some dif-ficulty that might arise in deciding about the population due to the method of sampling.

5.10 Select an article involving correlation from an educational research journal. Read the article carefully and consider the following questions:
   (a) does the author clearly identify the variables and the type of coefficient used?
   (b) are hypotheses identified and if so, what are they?
   (c) how is the observed coefficient interpreted?
   (d) what are the conclusions in terms of correlation?

5.11 Briefly review the chain of reasoning in hypothesis testing. Consider such points as the meanings of statistic and parameter, the probability, and the inference to the population.

6 *Measurement and Data Collection*

The Meaning of Measurement

The educational researcher of any degree of sophistication will soon realize that if his data are inadequate or incomplete, the entire study is destined for failure. No matter how carefully the hypotheses are stated or how precise the analysis, adequate measurement is an essential part of good research. The attainment of such measurement is not always an easy matter in the research study.

The four general types or levels of measurement scales—nominal, ordinal, interval, and ratio—have already been defined in a previous chapter. Measurement may be defined as "the assignment of numerals to objects or events according to rules." [1] A numeral is a symbol of the type 1, 2, 3, . . . , devoid of either quantitative or qualitative meaning, unless such meaning is assigned by a rule. The rule or rules of a particular measurement situation are the guides by which the assignment of numerals proceeds. It is with the rules that most difficulties arise, resulting in sloppy and inadequate measurement. Adequate rules are necessary elements for adequate measurement. Suppose that we want to weigh a group of adult males for some research study. Determining the weight to the nearest pound may be adequate for the purpose of the study. However, for a chemist experimenting with rare compounds, measurement to the nearest pound is entirely unsatisfactory from an experimental point of view. In the case of the chemist, a modified rule is necessary and if he can empirically define his requirements, then measurement is at least theoretically possible.

Educators have been and are at present involved in a great deal of measurement. Before entering the public schools, a child has several measurements taken, including age, sex, etc. It might be noted that generally these are variables for which the measurement rules are well defined and present no difficulty. Entire texts are written about measurement procedures, whether in research situations or not. Many complicated and unresolved measurement problems arise in certain specific situations.

The problem of measurement can essentially be resolved with adequate answers to the following two questions of what to measure and how to measure it. The first of these questions may seem somewhat superficial. In fact it is not. Naïve researchers have been known to assemble a considerable quantity of data and tabulate the numerals in an orderly fashion on sheets of paper. Upon being asked what the data represent, they seem at a loss for an adequate answer. However, the primary question in their minds is what to do with the data. This is putting the cart before the horse. In measurement, it is good policy to know what you want to measure before the measurement is attempted. The first step in measurement, then, is an attempt to operationally define what is to be measured. Note the emphasis on an operational definition. For example, a researcher might be interested in

[1] Kerlinger, F. N., *Foundations of Behavioral Research* (New York: Holt, Rinehart and Winston, 1964), p. 413.

measuring the ability of his Ss to solve problems using the deductive method. A commonly accepted definition of deduction is reasoning from a premise to a logical conclusion. Thus, to measure performance using the deductive process in problem solving, it would be necessary to provide items posing problems to be solved by reasoning from a premise to a logical conclusion. The researcher must also consider the level of his Ss. It is necessary that items be so constructed that the Ss can understand the item. As a sample, the following item presents a problem in deduction:

From the statements reason to the logical conclusion:

> All dogs are animals.
> Rover is a dog.

Therefore the logical and correct conclusion would be:

> Rover is an animal.

Responding to items such as the above operationally provides evidence of the S's mastery of the deductive process. Assuming an operational definition, the researcher may consider the rules by which he can accomplish the measurement.

The data that are analyzed in many research studies consist of the performance scores on one or more tests. A single performance score is a sampling of one S's behavior. The test itself is really a procedure for comparing the behavior (or samples of behavior) of two or more Ss. In research, we are usually interested in groups of Ss rather than individual Ss. The word "test" is used in this discussion to mean a data gathering device for research purposes. A single test may serve several purposes in the educational setting. The same test, in fact the same score or set of scores on the test, may be used for grading, diagnostic, or research purposes, to mention just three possible purposes.

Quantitative Concepts of Test Scores

After the researcher has operationally defined what is to be measured and completed the assignment of numerals according to his rules, he is confronted with a distribution of scores, each representing the performance of one S. What does any one score represent quantitatively with respect to the S? Suppose a certain S has attained a score of 82 on an achievement test. Can this score and others in the distribution be partitioned into meaningful parts?

It is generally recognized that few, if any, tests are perfect. Hence, the scores obtained on tests are fallible and not free from error. Thus, a single observed score contains what we shall call an *error component*. The error component may be due to any of a number of factors, usually unknown, associated with a specific administration of the test to the S. The remainder of the observed score may then be considered a non-error or *true component*.

The true component may be viewed as the S's score if we had a perfect measuring device. Suppose the test had been independently administered a large number of times to a single S and we assume that the error components are randomly distributed around zero. That is, both positive and negative error scores would appear and tend to cancel each other over a large number of scores. Under these circumstances, the true component may be defined as the mean of this large number of scores. This is a theoretical concept of the true component since a large number of independent administrations to the same S is physically impossible.

Suppose that we let Y_o represent the observed score, Y_t the true component, and Y_e the error component. We can then express the observed score as the sum of the two components. In equation form, this expression would consist of $Y_o = Y_t + Y_e$. This then represents a partitioning of the observed score of a single S into the two independent parts.

The researcher has not one score to consider, but a distribution of scores. If we think of the observed scores in terms of the two components, we have three distributions, two of which are theoretical. We can assume that in a large distribution of scores the error components are uncorrelated with the true components. That is, the size of the true component does not influence the size of the error component. Also, error components are assumed to be both positive and negative, and in a large distribution of scores, the mean of the error scores would be zero. If in any one of the three distributions we summed all scores and divided this sum by the number of scores, we would have the mean of the distribution. (This is operationally possible only for the observed distribution.) Since the true and error components are independent, the relationship between the means may be expressed as $\bar{Y}_o = \bar{Y}_t + \bar{Y}_e$. However, we have assumed that for a large number of scores the mean of the distribution of error components $(\bar{Y}_e)$ is zero. Therefore, the observed mean is equal to the mean of the true components.

At this point let us consider the variances of our three distributions. Let the variance of the observed distribution be represented by s_o^2. The theoretical components would also have their respective variances, if the distributions were known. Since the true and error components are uncorrelated, the variance of the observed scores may be expressed as the summation of the variances of the component distributions. In keeping with our notation, the s_o^2 may be expressed as $s_o^2 = s_t^2 + s_e^2$. This expression is helpful in developing the concept of reliability which is discussed in the following section.

Reliability of Measurement

An important concept of measurement is *reliability*. In a word, reliability means consistency — consistency of the test in measuring whatever it does measure. Ross and Stanley [1] refer to reliability as the degree to which a test agrees with itself. Other common synonyms used for reliability are stability and dependability of the measurement.

In the previous section we discussed a theoretical partitioning of a test score into two parts. Correspondingly, the variance of the observed distribution was also partitioned into two variances: one, that of the true components and the other, that of the error components. A theoretical definition of reliability is the ratio of the true variance to the variance of the observed scores, that is, reliability is the proportion of the variance in the ob-

[1] Ross, C. C., and Stanley, J., *Measurement in Today's Schools*, 3rd ed. (Englewood Cliffs: Prentice-Hall, Inc., 1954), p. 121.

served scores that is non-error. If we let r represent the reliability, the expression $r = \dfrac{s_t^2}{s_o^2}$ defines the reliability. We know that $s_o^2 = s_t^2 + s_e^2$. Therefore, an equivalent expression for reliability is $r = 1 - \dfrac{s_e^2}{s_o^2}$. The symbol r is called the *coefficient of reliability* or the *reliability coefficient*. From the theoretical expression of reliability it can be seen that r can range from plus one when there is no error in the measurement, to zero when the measurement is all error. (If there is no error, s_e^2 is zero, and if measurement is all error, $s_e^2 = s_o^2$.) Empirically, negative reliability coefficients are possible.

Reliability is strictly a statistical concept. Coefficients of reliability cannot be determined by a subjective investigation of the test items. The test must actually be administered to a group of Ss and the reliability coefficient computed from the scores. The greater the value of the coefficient, the higher the reliability of the test. There are several different methods for empirically estimating the reliability of a test. For a specific test only one method is used, depending upon conditions of the test administration. Three methods commonly used are discussed in the following section.

Empirical Procedures for Determining Reliability

The publishers of standardized tests commonly use two or more equivalent forms of a test referred to as *parallel forms.* Parallel forms have equal means and variances when administered to a defined group of Ss. If more than two parallel forms exist, we would expect the intercorrelations between forms to be approximately equal. The parallel forms are usually administered to a group of Ss with a short time interval between the administrations. (As the time interval increases, the possibility of extraneous fluctuation of the scores also increases.) The scores of the two administrations are then correlated. If the test is reliable, we would expect a high positive correlation coefficient. Ss who score high on one form should be the high scorers on the other form. The correlation between the two forms is called the *coeffi-*

cient of *equivalence.* This coefficient is an indication of the extent to which the two forms are equivalent.

Parallel forms of a test are not always available. Sometimes, even if two forms are available, it is not feasible to administer two separate tests. When only one form of a test exists or only one test administration is feasible, it may still be possible to establish reliability. One technique is to use a test-retest procedure. This involves administering the same test to a group of Ss with an intervening time period. The correlation between the scores of the two administrations of the same test is a measure of reliability. Such a correlation is called the *coefficient of stability.*

The test-retest method may be unavailable for several reasons. It may be impossible to administer the test a second time. The second administration may be delayed for a considerable time. Such a delay is likely to introduce new and possibly relevant factors. In the educational setting, performance on achievement tests is especially susceptible to such factors. A one-form method which requires only one administration is the *split-half method.* The test is split into two halves, each half scored independently of the other. The items of the two halves should be matched on content and difficulty. The scores of the two halves are then correlated and this correlation coefficient is the reliability coefficient of the half-test. A special formula known as the *Spearman-Brown step-up* is used to estimate the reliability of the whole test. This formula is given by:

$$r_w = \frac{2r}{1 + r}$$

where r_w is the reliability of the whole test and r is the correlation between the two halves.

The split-half technique has the advantage of requiring only one administration of the test. A difficulty with the split-half method is that it requires matched halves of the test. If the test items are arranged in order of increasing difficulty, the odd-even method of splitting the test is commonly used. Nonetheless, the requirement of matched halves may be difficult to satisfy. Also, the application of the Spearman-Brown formula assumes equal variability in the two half-test distributions.

An inspection of the formula for the split-half method reveals that empirically the reliability coefficient could take on negative values if the correlation between the two halves is negative. If negative correlations appeared with parallel forms or test-retest methods, we would again have a negative reliability coefficient. However, negative correlations under these conditions would be very unusual and indicate a complete lack of reliability. In the theoretical formula this would mean that the error variance would exceed the total variance, a theoretical impossibility. However, due to lack of reliability and unique fluctuations of the scores, it is empirically possible to have a negative reliability coefficient.

Formulas exist for the estimation of reliability without splitting the test. These were devised by Kuder and Richardson and go by various KR numbers. Unfortunately the computational procedures are rather laborious. Books devoted to measurement usually contain detailed discussions of the Kuder-Richardson techniques.[1]

A word of caution relative to speeded tests at this point. A speeded test is one on which the Ss would perform better if given additional time. The Kuder-Richardson formulas and the split-half technique do not apply to speeded tests. They tend to over-estimate the reliability of a speeded test.

The empirical procedures for estimating reliability are susceptible to factors that can cause the scores to fluctuate. Thorndike and Hagan have identified four such sources as:

(1) Variations arising within the measurement procedure itself.
(2) Changes in the individual from day to day.
(3) Changes in the specific sample of tasks.
(4) Changes in the individual's speed of work.[2]

The test-retest method, if administered the second time after an intervening time interval, is susceptible to all sources except the changes in the specific sample of tasks. If the retest is immediate, it is susceptible to variations within the measurement procedure and changes in the individual's speed of work. If

[1] As an example the reader is referred to Ross, C. C., and Stanley, J., *Measurement in Today's Schools*, 3rd ed. (Englewood Cliffs: Prentice-Hall, Inc., 1954).
[2] Thorndike, R. L., and Hagen, E., *Measurement and Evaluation in Psychology and Education*, 2nd ed. (New York: John Wiley and Sons, Inc., 1961), p. 182.

parallel forms with an intervening time interval are used, all four sources of variation can be present. Parallel forms administered with a very short time interval between administrations eliminate changes in the individual from day-to-day. The split-half method and the Kuder-Richardson single test procedures are susceptible to variations arising within the measurement procedure and changes in the specific sample of tasks. These factors should be kept in mind when considering reliability coefficients based on the various procedures.

The educational researcher must pay close attention to the measuring devices used in his study. If standardized tests are used, the manuals usually contain discussions of reliability. A battery of standardized tests commonly has a table of reliability coefficients in the manual. The manual will also contain *norms* consisting of descriptive statistics about a reference group of Ss on whom the test was standardized. The researcher should check to be certain that his population corresponds adequately to the normative group. Reliability coefficients for one group will not necessarily hold for another group. When using information from a test manual, the researcher should keep in mind that norms must be relevant.

Objectivity in test scoring is defined as the extent to which equally competent scorers get the same results. Objectivity should not be confused with accuracy of scoring since inadequately trained scorers can exhibit a great deal of inaccuracy. Objectivity is closely associated with reliability, and generally an objective test has higher reliability than a subjective test. Note that the definition of objectivity does not specify a type of item. Objective tests do not necessarily consist of short answer or factual type items, although we often associate multiple-choice, short answer items with objective tests. The objectivity is in the scoring, not in the type of item.

Objective tests are occasionally criticized on the basis that they do not do the job, that is, they do not adequately measure. The criticism arises due to the fact that insuring objectivity may put undesirable characteristics on the items such as too much structure or providing the examinee with the alternatives. An overemphasis on objectivity may reduce the range and depth of measurement. However, since increased objectivity tends to increase reliability, it is advisable to retain as much objectivity as possible without sacrificing adequate measurement.

As was discussed in the previous chapter, the range of the group being tested also influences the size of the correlation coefficient. Since reliability is tied up with correlation, as the range increases, the reliability tends to be higher. The reliability coefficient is an indication of how consistently the test places each S relative to the others in the group. As the scores become more spread out it becomes easier to place the Ss. For example, it would not require very accurate testing to differentiate the mathematics achievement of engineering students and ninth graders. To place ninth graders accurately within an elementary algebra class would require a more accurate test.

The reliability of a test tends to increase with increased length. This assumes that any new items added are homogeneous with the original items. Homogeneous in this context means of equal difficulty and of similar content. In terms of the variances, the component of error variance is associated with individuals and will tend to remain stable as the length increases. The true variance component is associated with the content of the test, and as the length is increased, this component tends to increase. Thus, when we increase length, the true variance component tends to encompass a greater portion of the observed variance.

What is high and low reliability and, more appropriately, what is the minimum reliability that is acceptable? This question does not have a specific answer to cover all tests and situations. The business of high and low is, of course, a relative thing. The question must be answered in the light of existing information and previous results. An achievement test with a reliability of .65 might be undesirable if existing tests in the academic discipline have reliabilities in the .90's. On the other hand, a reliability of .65 on a theme-writing test may seem very good if previous results indicate reliability coefficients of .50 and less.

Validity of Measurement

A second important concept of measurement is validity. The *validity* of a test is defined as the extent to which a test measures what it is supposed to measure. The objective determination of validity is not a simple matter. There are two basic approaches to this problem. One through a logical analysis which is essentially concerned with the measurement of a trait. This is essentially a judgmental analysis. The other approach, through an empirical analysis, is concerned with criterion measurement. The criterion measure might be the performance on a task or test, or it may be a measure such as job performance. In the empirical approach we are basically interested in correlation between the test and the selected criteria.

Content Validity

An approach to validity through a logical analysis is the consideration of content validity. *Content validity* refers to the extent to which the test items reflect the academic discipline or behavior under study. It involves a systematic investigation of the test items to determine whether or not they make up a representative sample of the behavioral dimensions or traits to be measured. This approach to validity is commonly used in achievement tests.

The basic idea may appear to be simple but the actual procedure might be quite tedious and involved. Several precautions must be taken. For example, when using an achievement test the researcher must be certain that all the major topics are adequately covered and in the corresponding proportions. A difficulty which may arise is that a specific topic is over-represented because its content lends itself especially well to the construction of certain kinds of items.

The specific objectives of the instruction should be well defined so that they may be adequately reflected in the measurement device. An objective of instruction may be the acquisition of factual knowledge. However, this may be only one of several objectives. Yet the test may be so constructed that it reflects only a knowledge of factual information. It cannot be argued that all objectives are adequately measured by items requiring only factual knowledge. For this reason, content must be broad enough to include the application of procedures which reflect all objectives. The test items should reflect the desired behavior and not only an apparent behavior. An inspection of the test may fail to reveal the S's process in responding to the item.

The fallacy of over-generalization is one to be avoided. The previous example concerning objectives may be considered an over-generalization of content or objectives. Another case might be concerning the selection of reasons for statements in a geometry proof. The correct association of reasons with given statements should not be interpreted as meaning that the S could construct the entire proof, that is, actually select the statements. Also, identifying errors in a given proof does not measure the ability to construct a correct proof from memory.

Irrelevant factors may influence the performance. These factors are irrelevant to the achievement area but not to the item responses. Examples include the mechanics of marking a special answer sheet and confusion between item numbers and their response numbers on the answer sheet.

Content validity may be checked by some empirical analysis. If two parallel forms of a test are available, before and after instruction scores may be compared. From the standpoint of test construction, this procedure is entirely acceptable; however, for experimental purposes the validity may be confounded with the experimental effect. An analysis might reveal the types of errors or types of items in which errors are most frequent. A check of the frequency of unfinished tests gives an indication of the effect of speed upon test performance.

The determination of content validity usually involves detailed analyses of content, objectives, representativeness of a universe of items as well as the test items and opinions of experts in the area. These procedures are usually adequate for evaluating achievement tests. However, for measurement in the areas of aptitude and personality, content validity is not sufficient. Here some empirical analysis is necessary, usually involving concurrent validity or predictive validity.

Concurrent Validity and Predictive Validity

Concurrent and predictive validity involve the relationship between the test scores and measures of performance on an external criterion. Correlation coefficients are usually computed between the test score and the performance score on the criterion measure. *Concurrent validation* is used if the data on the two measures, test and criterion, are collected at or about the same time. *Predictive validation* involves the collection of the data on the criterion measure after an intervening period, say six months from the time of data collection for the test being validated. This is the basic operational distinction between the two. There is also a distinction in the objectives of validation. Concurrent validity is based on establishing an existing situation, in other words, what *is*, whereas predictive validity deals with what is *likely* to happen. Specifically, the question of concurrent validity is whether or not the test scores estimate a specified present performance; that of predictive validity, whether or not the test scores predict a specified future performance.

The criterion measure of concurrent validity is not necessarily another test score given at the same time as the test being validated. It may consist of concurrent measures such as job success or grade point average. The criteria measures used with predictive validity are often some types of job performance, certainly subsequent performance. Predictive validity is especially relevant when test results are used for the selection of personnel to fill positions.

Various techniques may be used for concurrent validation. Correlations may be computed between test scores on the new test and scores on a previously constructed test. This technique is often used when attempting to validate a more efficient test from the standpoint of time or administration. For example, a shorter test may be an adequate replacement for a longer test. This might be especially desirable in a research setting if a large sample were to be included in the study and long testing periods for data collection would not be feasible. It would then be well to test a small sample on both the short and long tests and determine the correlation between the measures. This correlation, along with the content of the shorter test, should indicate whether or not it is an adequate replacement for the longer test. The sample tested on both measures should be a random sample from the same population as the samples to be included in the research study.

A word might be said at this point concerning the selection of a suitable criterion measure. There are several possible sources of difficulty that may be associated with this selection.

For example, performance in many areas may be difficult to quantify. Various facets of performance on a task or job may not yield any objective information. Then too, extraneous factors over which there is essentially no control may affect performance especially during the measurement period. A S may be required to perform under less than desirable conditions, for example, with faulty equipment. Another difficulty is that criterion measures are only partial in that they do not measure the performance under study. Practical limitations impose this restriction. For example, it is impossible to measure everything that makes for success as a college student.

What, then, makes for a good criterion measure? Thorndike and Hagen identify four desirable qualities in a criterion measure. These are: (1) relevance, (2) freedom from bias, (3) reliability, and (4) availability.[1] The four qualities are defined below.

Relevance is the extent to which the performance on the criterion measure is determined by the same factors that determine performance on the original or predicted measure. The degree of relevance may be based on a professional judgment of the test content in terms of it adequately representing the measurement objectives. *Freedom from bias* means that all Ss have equal opportunity of performing on the test or task. Examples of a bias would be a portion of the Ss performing with faulty equipment or poorly printed tests. *Reliability* was discussed earlier and in this context it means that the criterion measure remain stable. Finally, *availability* simply means that the criterion measure be available and applicable for the specific situation.

Construct Validity

Construct validity is a type of validity which includes both logical and empirical analyses. This type of validity is also referred to as congruent validity. The construct refers to the theoretical construct or trait being measured, not the mechanical construction of the test items. A *construct* is a postulated attribute that certain individuals possess. Quite often we relate the attribute to behavior in that we expect individuals to behave (or not behave) in a specified manner. The theory of frustration em-

[1] Thorndike, R. L., and Hagen, E., *Measurement and Evaluation in Psychology and Education*, 2nd ed. (New York: John Wiley and Sons, Inc., 1961), p. 166.

braced by the researcher might include specific behavior patterns. For example, frustration increases as the individual unsuccessfully persists in a problem-solving task. The construct may be informally conceptualized with only a limited number of propositions or it may be part or all of a fully developed theory. When using construct validation, we are assuming that the individual's performance on the test reflects the attribute under study.

Construct validity involves a broader concept than the other types of validity. Also, establishing construct validity is more complex than establishing the other types of validity. Concurrent validity, for example, can be examined by a single statistic, the correlation coefficient between the test scores and the criterion scores. Not so with construct validity. It involves a more long-term procedure including imagination, reasoning, observations, and their interactions. There is an initial formulation of the construct, various deductions are made and tested through observation, and there is reformulation of the construct. The process is much like that of theory developing and testing. Cronbach has suggested three parts to construct validation:

(1) Suggesting what constructs might account for test performance. This is an act of imagination based on observation or logical study of the test. (2) deriving testable hypotheses from the theory surrounding the construct. This is a purely logical operation. (3) carrying out an empirical study to test this hypothesis.[1]

The three parts do not necessarily represent as neatly an ordered sequence of procedures in actual practice.

Establishing construct validity does not involve a single clear-cut procedure. However, we can suggest some general procedures that have proved effective for test validation. Certain informal procedures such as a close examination of the items and a pilot administration of the test with verbal description by the examiners can be used. The latter may reveal that the meaning of scores is not consistent across individuals. Two individuals attaining similar scores may have quite different verbal descriptions.

[1] Cronbach, L. J., *Essentials of Psychological Testing*, 2nd ed. (New York: Harper and Brothers, Publishers, 1960), p. 121.

Correlation coefficients between scores on the test and other tests related to the same general theory or construct are often cited as empirical evidence of construct validity.[1] When using such tests, moderately high correlations are usually involved; however, correlations that are too high may be undesirable since such correlations are indications that the test being validated measures nothing new. It may be desirable to show that the test is relatively free from the influence of other factors. For example, a spacial relations test should have a low correlation with performance on a reading achievement test. That is, we do not want the spacial relations test to be unduly influenced by reading achievement. A high correlation would tend to make the test invalid in that it is heavily influenced by reading achievement, a supposedly irrelevant factor. In a sense this is a negative approach since the low correlation does not guarantee that the test measures spacial relations. The fact that the test does not measure reading achievement does not mean that it measures spacial relations. It should be noted that test scores can also be correlated with performance on some practical criteria. It is not required that the measure be another test score.

We may also get some evidence of construct validity by studying the effect of an experimental treatment or some intervening variable on test performance. This involves a retest situation. Actually, the retest could be administered with only the normal events of the intervening time period coming between testings. This approach to validation is sometimes referred to as *test score stability*. Whether or not a high degree of stability is desirable depends on the theory underlying the construct. The intervention of certain factors might require a lack of stability in order to be consistent with the theory. The results of the test-retest must be interpreted accordingly.

The formulation of the construct may lead us to expect two groups, for example, men and women, to differ on the test. If the two groups are available for testing, this assumption may be tested. This is a relatively crude procedure for establishing validity since most constructs in educational research are of

[1] Correlation matrices and factor analysis can be used in construct validation. Although factor analysis for construct validity is beyond the scope of this book, the reader is referred to Cronbach, L. J., and Meehl, P. E., "Construct Validity in Psychological Tests," *Psychological Bulletin*, 1955, 52, pp. 281–302.

such a nature that we would expect considerable overlap. Therefore, too great a differentiation between groups may indicate a lack of validity. For example, physical ability test items may correspond somewhat to age, but if performance on a task correlated around .90 with age, the validity of the task would certainly be questioned.

Construct validity plays an important role in many research efforts. This is due in part to the fact that many research activities involve the formation of constructs that cannot be operationally defined, at least not immediately. Whenever this is the case, construct validity is involved in establishing the measurement of the attribute.

Validity and Variance

In the previous discussion on reliability we saw that, theoretically, reliability may be expressed as the proportion of the variance in the observed scores, that is, true variance. For validity, we consider the variances of two distributions, the scores on the test and those on the criterion measure. Then to relate the two we consider the variance that the two measures have in common. Suppose we theoretically quantify the variances in terms of Venn diagrams as in Figure 6.1. Let S_o^2 be the variance of the observed

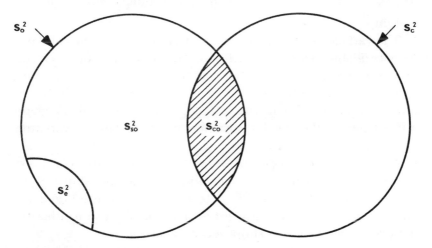

Figure 6.1 Theoretical partitioning of the variances of test and criterion measure distributions.

test scores, s_c^2 the variance of the criterion measure, and s_{co}^2 the *co-variation* or variance that the two have in common. This is also referred to as the *common factor* variance. In the diagram, s_o^2 would still contain error variance (s_e^2) and any variance not error or common with the criterion measure is variance specific to the observed distribution, represented in the diagram by s_{so}^2. The validity of a test is then defined as the proportion of the total observed variance that is common variance with the criterion measure. In symbol form validity $= \dfrac{s_{co}^2}{s_o^2}$, or validity $= 1 - \left(\dfrac{s_{so}^2 + s_e^2}{s_o^2}\right)$.

The variance relation between reliability and validity might also be explored at this point. The true variance or s_t^2 introduced with reliability would be made up of s_{so}^2 and s_{co}^2 of Figure 6.1. The total variance of the observed scores is composed of three parts, that is, $s_o^2 = s_{so}^2 + s_{co}^2 + s_e^2$. If we divide this equation by s_o^2 we get $\dfrac{s_o^2}{s_o^2} = \dfrac{s_{so}^2}{s_o^2} + \dfrac{s_{co}^2}{s_o^2} + \dfrac{s_e^2}{s_o^2}$. From this equation we can see that the proportion:

$$\frac{s_{so}^2}{s_o^2} + \frac{s_{co}^2}{s_o^2} = \frac{s_{so}^2 + s_{co}^2}{s_o^2} = \frac{s_t^2}{s_o^2}$$

represents the reliability and the proportion $\dfrac{s_{co}^2}{s_o^2}$ represents the validity.

The variance equations show us that a test can not be valid if it is not reliable. The s_{co}^2 is part of s_t^2 and hence if there were no true variance component there could be no co-variation component. However, the reverse is not true. The test could be reliable but not valid. The true variance component could be made up entirely of the specific variance and hence the co-variation component would be zero.

A test must be reliable in order to be valid, however a test can be reliable without being valid. This relationship can be logically pointed out. That is, a test may be consistently measuring the wrong thing. If a test is not consistent, it can hardly be measuring what it is supposed to measure.

The Validity Coefficient

The determination of validity by empirical techniques involves correlation between variables. The validity coefficients associated with tests are based on the correlations between tests and criterion measures. In some cases, especially when tests are used for prediction, parts of the criterion measure may be weighted differently. Validity is always specific to the particular measurement task. When a test manual or other literature reports that a test is valid (often supported by validity coefficients) the researcher must ask in what instance it is valid. The measuring device must be evaluated in the light of the specific objectives of the research study. A test that is valid for measuring the mathematics achievement of heterogeneous classes may not be valid for measuring the achievement of high-ability students in an experiment involving a modern mathematics curriculum. Validity coefficients must be interpreted in the context of the area of measurement and the specific research endeavor.

Necessity of Reliability and Validity

An ultimate objective of the educational researcher is to make a meaningful interpretation of his results. In order to do this, the measuring device or test must be reliable. Reliability is not a sufficient condition for good measurement but it is certainly a necessary condition. The lack of reliability causes difficult and essentially insurmountable problems. Suppose a researcher is interested in the effect of an experimental treatment upon spelling achievement. Two samples are drawn and one sample of Ss receives the experimental treatment while the other receives traditional instruction. A spelling test is used to measure spelling achievement, the dependent variable. The means for the two samples are determined and a Student's t-test is computed for the difference between two means. The statistical test shows no significant difference, but it is revealed that the spelling test used to measure achievement is unreliable. Is the statistical test not significant because there is no experimental effect or because of the low reliability of measurement? This question cannot be answered and no decision can be made on the results. The researcher's investigation has broken down for one apparent reason—the measurement was unreliable.

Validity is, of course, an essential requirement in a measuring device. In the above example, the researcher could hardly check on experimental effect upon spelling achievement if he did not have a test which measures spelling achievement. Inadequate measurement cannot be tolerated in educational research. The measuring devices must be examined logically and empirically for their validity and reliability.

Types of Measurement Devices

There are several different types of measurement devices in educational research. The term "types of measurement devices" is not used here in the sense of different measurement scales which were defined in an earlier chapter. Rather, we think of types of measuring devices as types of tests. We use the word test in a general sense. Earlier in this chapter we defined a test as a data gathering device for research purposes. At this point we will broaden that definition slightly so that we consider a test as generally consisting of a stimulus to which a S responds and gives a sampling of some pre-defined behavior.

Objectively Scored Items

A common measurement instrument is an objectively-scored set of items. Objectivity has been previously defined in connection with reliability. The S responds to each item, the items are then scored on the basis of right or wrong, and the S is assigned a numerical value which is his score. Inferences are then made from the score to the S's behavior and to the behavior of his group. Multiple-choice and simple response tests are examples of such measuring devices. However it should not be inferred that simplicity is a necessary condition for objectivity. An essay test might be objectively scored. The objectivity is in the scoring.

It should be noted that objectivity is a matter of degree. All tests contain some element of objectivity and there is not a sharp dichotomy between objective and non-objective techniques.

Direct Observation

A second measurement technique is the direct observation of behavior by a trained observer. This entails watching and noting what actually occurs. The basic problem with this technique is the interpretation of what is seen. Different observers see different things in the same situation. The problem of ambiguous definition of terminology is difficult to overcome. For example, in classroom observation, what is a dull class or a flexible class? What is a serious discipline problem? To be sure, much can be done to define the terms, but observed behavior often falls into a "gray" area of definition.

The data collected from direct observation are usually categorized as part of the analysis and may even be directly categorized during the observation. The establishment of categories is usually a subjective procedure on the part of the researcher. The researcher should be well informed in the area of study in order to establish a meaningful and valuable set of categories. Although the establishment of the categories may be quite subjective, the classification of observed behavior (or whatever is being observed) into the categories should be made as objective as possible. It should be noted that for various studies direct observation might be highly objective; for example, if we were simply counting the number of times a student leaves the classroom. However, for most research situations more complex variables are under study.

Although direct observation may have its limitations, many observational systems are presently available for the study of educational phenomena. An example of a direct observation scheme for classifying the interaction in a classroom is the Flanders Interaction Model.[1] This model for classifying class-

[1] Flanders, N. A., *Interaction Analysis in the Classroom* (Minneapolis, Minn.: University of Minnesota, 1960). Also for a more general discussion see Medley, D. M., and Mitzel, H. E., "Measuring Classroom Behavior by Systematic Observation," Gage, ed., in *Handbook of Research On Teaching* (Chicago: Rand McNally & Company, 1963).

room behavior has considerable use, especially in educational research. With adequate training, relatively high inter-observer reliability (coefficients in the neighborhood of .90) has been established with the use of such models. The Flanders Model involves a category system such that classroom interaction as interpreted by a trained observer is recorded (through a coding system) every three seconds. The coded information of the model presents a systematic account of the classroom proceedings. When direct observation is used in this manner, considerable effort and time must be reserved for the development of the system and mastery of its use. This is essential for usable data and interpretable results.

Direct observation does have some advantages. Assuming careful planning of the observational procedures and adequately trained observers, direct observation does provide a record of actual behavior which should be relatively free from observer bias. Direct observation can be effectively used in situations where other data gathering procedures are not applicable, for example, with young children for whom written communication is impossible and verbal communication difficult. Direct observation is usually used in a natural situation, eliminating some of the artificial factors that can arise in a testing situation.

Self-Report

Information may be acquired by having the S tell what happened or tell about an experience. This can become extremely tenuous, because now an interpretation by the S is included in addition to the interpretation of his remarks by the researcher. This procedure may also be quite laborious and time consuming, since in almost any group certain Ss become extremely verbal when asked to respond. This, as well as other factors associated with the Ss, may become extraneous variables which may have an effect on the data.

With all its limitations, self-report can provide useful information depending, of course, upon the conditions of the research situation. Suppose an educational psychologist is doing research on "learning to learn" and has his Ss perform on a unique learning task. The Ss are learning how to do the task. After successfully completing one or more trials, the S is asked how he learned to do the task. If the researcher expects a relatively unsophisticated description of mental procedures, this may be forthcoming; if, however, he expects a technical psychological description, he is likely to be disappointed. The adequacy of the self-report also depends upon the sophistication of the Ss. Under certain conditions the S may simply not know how to respond, and such situations should be avoided with self-report. When studying selected sociological and cultural variables in the natural situation, self-report may be effective and in essence be the only applicable procedure for securing the necessary information.

The Interview [1]

The interview is a type of self-report measuring device which may be used in educational research. This is a question and answer situation in which the interviewer asks questions supposedly pertinent to the research study. There is a great deal of variety in types of interviews, from a highly structured interview to one almost completely unstructured. The purposes of the interview and the type of situation will influence the amount of structure in the interview. The structure of an interview refers primarily to the types of questions and anticipated responses. (E.g., must the respondent select one and only one of three possible responses or can he say as much and what he wants as a response.) In any case, the procedures of the interview should be carefully planned and appropriate questions constructed.

The items or questions of an interview may take several forms, the two most common forms being the fixed-alternative response and the open-end response. The *fixed-alternative* items are exactly what the name implies: the respondent is asked to select one of two or more given alternatives. This type of item has the advantage of increasing the consistency of measurement and hence the reliability. The forced choice of one of the fixed alternatives is sometimes cited as a disadvantage since the S is *required* to select one of the given alternatives, his choice may only approximate his true feeling. Also this type of item in

[1] A more comprehensive discussion of the use of the interview and questionnaire appears in Chapter 8 in connection with survey research.

itself allows for no probing by the interviewer. Probing could be pursued 'with additional items leading out of the S's response.

The *open-end question* imposes no restrictions on the respondent except that he stay within the framework of the specific question. The open-end question has obvious advantages and disadvantages. Such questions are more flexible and allow for probing, if this is desirable. They enable the interviewer to detect things such as ambiguity, respondent's feelings, etc. The questions may elicit unanticipated answers which shed a new light on the research problem. Also, the respondent may be more cooperative when he is less restricted in his answer. If a misunderstanding exists, the interviewer may detect it and get it cleared up.

The open-end question may introduce additional variables associated with the Ss. The data may be quite diverse. This lack of uniformity may make the analysis difficult. The responses usually are categorized by the investigator to impose some degree of uniformity on the data. This procedure may itself be quite arbitrary and could introduce a possible bias.

The construction of questions for an interview is a task which should be approached carefully and critically. The questions should, of course, reflect the objectives of the research. The anticipated information should relate to the hypotheses. The statement of the question must be clear and unambiguous to the respondent. The fact that it is clear to the interviewer does not guarantee that it is clear to the respondent. The questions should not be personally offensive to the respondent. The question itself should not suggest that one response is more desirable than another. Responses which are socially or professionally preferable tend to invalidate the results. The respondent may choose these even though this is not the way he feels. The responsent should also be able to answer the questions. Lack of information on the part of the respondent will tend to produce invalid data.

The Measurement of Achievement

Academic achievement, or lack of it, is one of the principal outcomes of the educational experience. It stands to reason that considerable research is done on achievement. There are multitudes of achievement tests commercially available, commonly known as standardized achievement tests. The measurement aspect of a research study is not dispensed with by simply selecting a standardized test in the area of investigation and testing the Ss. To be sure, many standardized tests are excellent for research purposes, but the investigator must be careful in his selection. The test must be adequate for the objectives of the study and should not be inherently biased toward one or more of the groups. For example, it would hardly be adequate to use a standardized American social studies test to ascertain whether United States or British students have the greater knowledge in social studies.

Standardized tests are usually broad and based on general content of the achievement area. This may be an advantage or disadvantage, depending upon the objectives of the research. The same is true about the information in the manual concerning reliability, validity, and norms. If there are norms available for groups comparable to those being researched, this is a definite advantage. If the norms are not relevant, they may be interpreted to be relevant and thus give rise to a misconception. However, for many research studies it is not necessary to have norms.

The construction of a standardized test usually involves considerable effort on the part of experts. The researcher may not have comparable resources to devote to the construction of his measuring instrument. Standardized tests can often be quickly and efficiently scored by the publisher. This is a definite advantage, especially for research studies which involve large quantities of data.

The use of a standardized test greatly reduces the effort connected with the measurement of the data. However, it is not always possible to find a published test which will meet the objectives of the research. For example, in a study by Dessart,[1] various types of programmed learning materials and traditional teaching were used to ascertain the effects upon learning the concept of limit. The study was conducted with elementary algebra students at the junior high school level and involved an instructional period of ten days. The unit or topic to be learned

[1] Dessart, D. J., "A Study in Programmed Learning," *School Science and Mathematics* 62, Oct. 1962, pp. 513–20.

was very specific. It is unlikely that a standardized test could be found which deals specifically with that topic. There may be items in standardized mathematics tests which relate to the limit concept, but it would not be efficient to use the entire test just for a limited number of items. In such cases it is usually adequate to establish validity by a logical analysis. If at all possible, some reliability measures should be made on the test. Such tests should be subject to investigations of validity and reliability prior to their use in a research project.

When self-constructed tests are used for research in achievement, it is usually because they can meet the objectives of the measurement better than standardized tests. They may be preferred because of greater efficiency. A standardized test may be much longer than is actually needed. Whether or not a standardized or self-constructed test is more efficient depends on the research situation. Flexibility may be built into a self-constructed test which does not exist in a standardized test.

Achievement tests are usually made up of objectively scored items. The acquisition of factual knowledge can be adequately measured this way. Other outcomes of learning such as the application of concepts can also be measured using such items. Achievement tests need not be limited to short items. Free response items of varying types and lengths may also be used. For example, in geometry achievement the S might be required to produce an entire proof of a theorem. Such an item could be objectively scored although scoring time would be increased. Less objective items may also be used in achievement tests. The use of such items might raise some difficulties relative to validity and reliability.

The Measurement of Aptitude

Achievement and the potential ability for achievement are not the same thing. The potential for achievement is called *aptitude*. Intelligence tests are the most commonly known measures for aptitude in achievement. It should be recognized that the characteristics and definition of intelligence are far from being fully identified. However, there are several good group and individual intelligence tests available. *The Sixth Mental*

Measurements Yearbook[1] is an excellent source for information about such tests.

Aptitude tests may measure general aptitude or specific aptitude in a restricted area such as art or music. The group intelligence tests commonly used in the public schools are tests of general aptitude. A single test may include items related to different kinds of potential abilities such as verbal, numerical, or critical reasoning, to mention just three.

Aptitude measures find a great deal of use in educational research as control variables. For example, they may be built into an analysis as covariates. Intelligence scores are commonly used in this manner. There are relatively short tests available which measure different kinds of potential abilities. The construction of an aptitude test is a difficult matter and requires a great deal of effort and knowledge in the specific area.

The Measurement of Attitudes

Attitudes, in contrast to the ability or potential to achieve, deal with existing feelings of a S toward ideas, procedures, social institutions, etc. Note that the attitude is *toward* something. Usually we think of attitudes in terms such as acceptance-rejection or favorable-unfavorable. The intensity of feeling is not dichotomous but usually considered to be some kind of continuum between the extremes. It is placing the Ss on this continuum that is the job of the attitude inventory.

A scale is commonly used for the items of an attitude inventory. The scale consists of a number of points on the theoretical continuum to which the S can respond and thus indicate the intensity of his feeling. The minimum number of points would be two, although there are usually at least three, giving the S a neutral choice such as "undecided." A common type of attitude scale is the *Likert-type scale*. This scale consists of items which are assumed to have equal value. The various possible responses are assigned numerical values and these values are summed over all items to give the S an attitude score. The sum or average, computed by dividing the sum by the number of

[1] Buros, O. K., ed., *The Sixth Mental Measurements Yearbook* (Highland Park, N.J.: The Gryphon Press, 1965).

items, may be designated as the score. However, this average is not a mean in the sense of interval scale measurement. It is a score indicating position on an ordinal scale. This score places the S on the agree-disagree continuum of the attitude under investigation.

Consider an example in which a Likert-type scale could be used. A researcher is interested in the attitudes of high school seniors toward the school administration. A number of items are constructed consisting of statements to which the seniors respond. The possible choices for each item are: strongly disagree, disagree, undecided, agree, and strongly agree. The numerical values range from 1 to 5 respectively. (This assignment and the direction are arbitrary. For example, zero to 4 could have been used, or the agree end of the scale could have been assigned the low numbers.)

The responses of each senior are assigned the values and summed (or averaged) and this becomes his score. In this case a high score would indicate agreement with the items and presumably a favorable attitude toward the administration. It is important that the items are so constructed that they are consistent in direction and scoring. That is, an agree response should not reflect an unfavorable attitude and be scored 5. If there are items which reverse directions, they may be retained if a corresponding adjustment is made in the scoring procedure. Usually the items are constructed so that the scoring is not complicated by reversing directions.

The construction of a Likert-type attitude scale is not simply a matter of writing a set of statements. This is the initial step. The scale should be used in a trial run. The trial run may reveal items that are ambiguous or inconsistent with the rest of the items. A further step is to correlate the scores of each item with the scores of the total test. This may eliminate inconsistent items. The scale can be constructed with subscales and scores acquired for the various subscales. If it is difficult to place an item in a subscale, or if it seems to fit in more than one scale, the scores on this item can be correlated with the subscale scores. The item is then placed in the subscale with which it has the greatest correlation.

The number of possible responses in the scale is arbitrary. Five or seven responses are common. The advantage of additional responses is that it seems to be more sensitive to differences in attitudes due to the greater variance in scores. If the variance is truly due to the differences in attitudes this is fine. However, there may be confounded factors contributing to the variance. Ss have a tendency to develop a response-set. A *response-set* is a tendency to respond in a certain manner due to a reaction to the construction of the scale, independent of the attitude being measured. For example, we might have the middle-of-the-roader who will respond near the center of the scale no matter how strongly he feels. Sometimes reversing the direction of certain items is used as a deterrent against response set, but as was mentioned above, reversing directions complicates the scoring.

The Likert-type attitude inventory yields numerical scores which appear to be measured on an interval scale. Although the scores can certainly be ordered, it may be difficult to make a case for equal units. In the scoring, the difference between "undecided" and "agree" is one point, as is the difference between "agree" and "strongly agree." It would be difficult to say that the two one-point differences represent the same difference in feeling. This lack of an equal unit is, of course, reflected in the total score.

Thurstone grappled with this problem and developed what is called the *Thurstone Method* or equal-appearing interval scales. This was an attempt to place the Ss on a continuous scale having equal-appearing units. Thus, the difference in scores of 60 and 65 would be comparable to the difference in scores of 68 and 73. In the Thurstone method, each item is given a scale value ranging from zero to 11 from the unfavorable to favorable direction. Note that the items are scaled. The S then simply checks the items with which he agrees or a specified number with which he agrees most strongly. The score is an average of the numerical values of the items checked by the S.

A difficulty may arise in assigning the values to the items. The usual procedure is to have a panel of experts scale the items independently. If there is marked disagreement on the scaling of an item, the item is discarded. An item which is retained is given the median value assigned by the members of the panel. The initial choice of items to be used is the responsibility of the researcher. The choice is arbitrary, but the items should be carefully chosen in the light of existing knowledge and research about the attitudes.

The items retained by the panel should be tested in a trial run. Preferably the attitude inventory should be tested with Ss whose attitudes are known. This procedure may reveal items which are incorrectly scaled or measuring different factors than the remaining items. Items which are ambiguous or poorly constructed should be exposed by the trial run.

Both the Thurstone-type and the Likert-type scales assume unidimensionality. That is, they deal with a single trait or dimension of the trait. A difference between the two types of scales is the methods by which the unidimensionality is attained. The Likert-type empirically establishes the unidimensionality of the scale through correlation. This correlation was mentioned earlier and it consists of correlating the scores of each item with the total test score. Items correlating low with the total score are not measuring the same thing as the total score. Such items measure, if anything, a different trait. Items with low correlations are omitted and the remaining items measure one thing, thus arriving at the unidimensionality of the scale.

The unidimensionality of the Thurstone-type scale is arrived at through a judgmental process. The judges independently rate or scale the items, as was discussed before, and this results in each judge placing the items in position. If the items are unidimensional they will be rated in relatively the same positions by all judges. If judges fail to rank an item in about the same position then they are apparently ranking an item that is not unidimensional but multidimensional. Such an item is then discarded and by this process of elimination only the unidimensional items are retained.

A Thurstone-type scale is more laborious to construct than a Likert-type scale. Both scales are susceptible to invalid self-report by the S. However, the Thurstone-type is not affected by response-sets. The Likert-type may yield more information in that the S is required to respond to all items. In studies that used comparable scales of both types, the correlations between the scores were found to be quite high, some as high as the low .90's. On this basis, the scales may be considered interchangeable.

The Thurstone- and Likert-type scales are the most commonly used methods for measuring attitudes. Other techniques have been developed but will not be discussed in this text. This topic is discussed in greater detail in texts on psychological measurement.

Validity is a primary concern of attitude measurement. Any self-report device has the possibility of being faked, that is, in attitude measurement the S may report attitudes which are quite different from his true feelings. It is difficult to find an external criterion with which to compare the reported attitude. The actual behavior of Ss may provide such a criterion but be difficult to observe or measure.

Reliability coefficients on attitude inventories can be computed by usual techniques. The range on reliability coefficients is typically greater than for achievement tests in a specific area. Some coefficients go up into the .90's, but more modest coefficients are the usual result.

The construction of an attitude inventory requires a careful selection of items with a reworking of original statements. A trial run of some sort is essential and the elimination of ambiguity a requirement. This requirement is necessary but not sufficient. The items must measure and measure consistently the attitude under study.

Published attitude inventories are not as extensively available as achievement tests. However, there are some available in broad areas. The Minnesota Teacher Attitude Inventory[1] is one used in teacher education. In research projects, the purposes and topics of investigation are often so specific that the researcher has little alternative but to construct his own attitude inventory. The construction of the inventory may comprise a major part of the research effort.

The Measurement of Personality

Achievement, aptitudes, and attitudes are considered parts of personality. *Personality* refers to the sum total of a person's mental and emotional characteristics. The measurement of per-

[1] Published by The Psychological Corporation, New York, 1951.

sonality has certain inherent difficulties. One of these concerns what to measure. Although there is some ambiguity associated with the term, the consensus is that personality measurement deals with the measurement of traits. The term trait has been used previously and here it is more formally defined for use in the context of personality. A *trait* is a tendency for the individual to respond in a certain way to situations. For example, a pessimistic individual will tend to respond by emphasizing the unfavorable aspects of almost any situation. A person will tend to respond in a certain manner in any situation that tests his honesty. A trait, however, is not usually so "pure" that the response is consistent for all situations. An individual might be pessimistic about money matters but optimistic about other matters. Honesty may be reflected in business matters but be entirely lacking in a golf score. On the other hand, another sportsman would not consider adjusting his score. Thus, honesty may be different and yet two individuals might be viewed as possessing the same amount of this trait.

It would be inefficient to classify every habit or specific response as a trait. The attempt is made to identify general traits which encompass a large number of situations. The trait should adequately describe significant differences of behavior. Traits should be different in more than name only. Two supposedly different traits, upon careful analysis, may be comprised of the same factors, and essentially represent only one trait.

The methods of personality measurement may seem crude and inadequate when compared with analytical measurement in the chemistry laboratory. However, in a certain sense personality measurement is in its infancy and though techniques may not be precise, they may still be of value. The researcher should be aware of the measurement limitations and consider them in the interpretation of results.

The most straightforward approach to personality measurement would be by observing the S's responses, that is, his behavior. This procedure may prove satisfactory when a competent observer is working with a single S or a very limited number of Ss at one time. However, this technique is inefficient for large numbers of Ss. If the S is aware of the fact that he is being observed, his responses may be based on what he perceives to be acceptable rather than his usual response. This also applies to observing a group of Ss.

Personality measurement may take place through the opinions of associates of the individual. A formal rating scale of several items may be used in an attempt to instill some uniformity into the measurement. This method has a number of potential pitfalls, including the raters' own personalities and their ability to do the rating.

The obvious approach to personality measurement is to consult the individual himself. For large numbers of Ss a personal interview technique would hardly be efficient. So a paper and pencil personality inventory is commonly used. The S is asked to respond to an inventory which consists of one or more kinds of items. He may be asked about his preferences or asked to rate things or activities. A situation may be presented in the item and he is asked for his response to the situation. With a large number of items, the S is commonly given the possible response choices for each item, rather than permitting a free response.

An approach to constructing a personality inventory is the a priori approach. This is simply an attempt to construct items which reflect the trait under study. For example, to measure honestly, items are presented which involve situations in which a choice related to honesty is made. This approach to constructing a personality inventory may seem straightforward and inherently it is, but special care must be taken in constructing the items. Specific items may not measure what they are supposed to measure and the problem of ambiguity is usually present in the early stages. The validity of an inventory so constructed would likely involve both content and construct validity.

Empirical evidence may be used in constructing a personality inventory. The items may be tried out on a group whose personality characteristics are known. For example, with the honesty trait, the items would be given to a group whose honesty characteristics have been conclusively established. Suppose we would have a group considered to be 100 per cent honest. Their responses to the items would then reflect a 100 per cent honesty trait. The individual items would be separately analyzed. Items whose responses were not consistent would be deleted from the personality inventory. To strengthen this analysis, the items should also be tried out on a group of Ss known to be low in honesty. This is necessary to see how their responses differ from the honest group. Without the contrasting group, it would be necessary to assume that the responses of the two groups would be different. This assumption may not be tenable.

The items may be an indirect approach to the trait. Suppose we want to distinguish between authoritarian and democratic teachers. It might be undesirable because of certain terminology to use direct items. If the reading habits of these two types of teachers differ, this is a possible source for measuring the trait. Two groups of teachers who have been identified as democratic and authoritarian are administered the items on reading habits. The difference in responses of the two groups, if such a difference exists, is then attributed to a difference in the trait. There is no causative relationship implied here. Note that the point is to find something that differentiates the two groups, not to explain why the groups differ in reading habits. This procedure usually requires a great deal of searching for relevant items.

There are other measurement techniques for personality traits such as the projective technique which is essentially built around an unstructured task and allows for almost an unlimited number of possible responses. These techniques are not commonly used in educational research but find their use in clinical and diagnostic procedures. The discussion of this text only touches upon the business of personality measurement and then in the context of educational research. For comprehensive discussions of personality measurement it is suggested that the reader consult texts devoted to testing and measurement.[1]

The foremost problem of measuring personality is validity. The question of whether we are measuring what we claim to measure is often difficult to answer. The actual construction procedure using known groups does make an attempt at validation. The a priori approach is essentially a content-validity technique. The matter of estimating reliability is not as troublesome. It can be technically handled with the reliability procedures.

[1] As an example of such a text, Anastasi, A., *Psychological Testing*, 2nd ed. (New York: The Macmillan Company, 1961).

There are many personality inventories commercially available. The educational researcher will save a lot of time and effort if he can find a published test, adequate for his purposes. The construction of a satisfactory personality inventory requires someone well-trained in psychological testing. In the educational research setting, where we deal with relatively large numbers of "normal" Ss, traits are broadly defined, such as personal adjustment or social adjustment. Published inventories are available for such broad traits. For a very specific measurement, especially with an atypical group of Ss, the researcher may be required to construct his own measurement instrument. In such a case, a considerable amount of the research effort should be allotted for the construction of the instrument.

The educational researcher does not always find ready-made tests available for the purposes of his study. Suppose a study is conducted in which creativity is to be measured. It is difficult to define creativity, and even more difficult to measure what has been decided upon as a satisfactory definition. It may be possible to use modifications of existing tests. In a study by Klausmeier and Wiersma[1] in which divergent thinking tests were used, the measuring instruments included adaptations from tests by Guilford, Kettner, and Christensen.[2] The modifications were made in order to use the tests with fifth- and seventh-grade students.

Specific Task Measurement

The data for a research study need not consist of scores on some sort of paper and pencil inventory. For example, in a learning task the measure of learning may be time required to solve a problem, number of errors in a solution, or some measure of re-

[1] Klausmeier, H. J. and Wiersma, W., "Relationship of Sex, Grade Level, and Locale to Performance of High I.Q. Students on Divergent Thinking Tests," *Journal of Educational Psychology*, 55, 1964, pp. 114–119.

[2] Guilford, J. P., Kettner, N. W., and Christensen, P. R., "A Factor Analytic Study Across the Domains of Reasoning, Creativity and Evaluation: II. Administration of Tests and Analysis of Results. *University of Southern California Psychological Laboratory Reports*, 1956. No. 16. (Modifications in tests made by Frank B. May.)

dundancy, to mention just three. The definition of the task is often so specific that it exactly reflects the purposes of the research. In these situations, reliability and validity are often not treated in a technical manner.

All specific task measurement may not directly reflect the factors, characteristics, or behavior under study. For example, we might have a basketball skill test that involves putting coins in cups. The validity of such a task should be considered, namely, does it test basketball skill? Also, with certain specific task measurement dealing with skills such as selected motor skills or cognitive skills, the researcher may find it necessary to conduct one or more trials in order to secure the necessary reliability in the measurement. Certainly, if two or more examiners are used there should be some measure of inter-examiner consistency.

The type of research discussed in the preceding paragraph involves a very specific task. The rationale behind such research and its measurement must be carefully developed. It should reflect a definite and defined area of education or related matter such as a learning theory. The area may be general, such as learning, or very specific. In any event, the research procedures and the measurement should be carefully worked out and it should not appear as if the research is being conducted in an educational vacuum.

Special Considerations of Data Collection

A discussion of the use of the questionnaire appears in a latter chapter. However, the questionnaire as a data gathering device is introduced at this point to consider a problem of data collection associated with this device. When the questionnaire is mailed, invariably there will be Ss who fail to respond. The question of whether or not the respondents are responding truthfully is important. This is especially true of questions which have a socially or professionally desirable answer. It may be possible for the researcher to build into the questionnaire certain items which check the consistency of the respondent. For example, essentially the same item may appear later in the questionnaire, only in a different form or with a different wording.

Items may also be constructed so that a certain pattern of responses indicates inconsistency.

In this day of high-speed computers, measurement and data collection often comprise the greater amount of leg work of a research study. For example, a research study of the mathematics achievement in a large school system would require a great deal of data collection in order to have all grade levels and areas of mathematics included. The organization of the data collection plays an important role. A research study can easily go by the board, not because it is ill-conceived or the analysis facilities are unavailable, but because the data collection is so poorly organized that it becomes an overwhelming task.

The actual testing for the research endeavor should be allotted the necessary time. The scoring of the tests can be greatly facilitated by constructing an answer sheet which can be quickly hand-scored or better yet, scored by machine. The test publishers commonly have a scoring service. This scoring service is usually more economical and certainly more accurate than hand scoring.

Assembling Data for Analysis

The computer usually does not analyze the answer sheets or the scores as they appear on the answer sheets. The scores must be transmitted from the data sheets to data cards, commonly IBM cards which feed the information to the computer. The standard IBM card has 80 columns. A single number or letter may be punched into each column.

The format for the data card should be carefully defined. That is, the information that goes into each column should be spelled out. Information is commonly of two types — identification and test scores. If the number of bits of information on a S does not exceed the 80 columns, one card per S is sufficient. The identification information consists of such things as the S's classification on the independent variables and his unique number. It may include other information such as age or sex. Usually the identification comes in the early columns of the card, but this is not essential. The test scores, commonly the dependent variables, are punched into the card using as many columns as necessary. For example, a two digit test score requires two columns. If there are 10 different tests, each giving a two digit score, these data would require 20 columns. If tests with varying numbers of digits in the scores are used, the numbers of columns used for each score is sometimes held constant, namely the greatest number of digits for any score. This may facilitate setting up the analysis for the computer. It is not essential that the number of columns be the same for all test scores.

The data should be so organized that a minimum of effort is required to transmit the data from its original form to the IBM card. Also, any confusion should be eliminated to minimize the number of copy errors. The person punching the cards can work most efficiently if the data for each S are presented in a line or row on a sheet in the exact order as they are to appear on the card. It is very inefficient for a key punch operator to be fishing around trying to assemble the data. In any event, the punched cards should be verified, a process of checking for possible errors in the original card punching operation. The corresponding information for all Ss appears in corresponding columns on the IBM cards.

If the data are analyzed on a desk calculator, it is important to classify and organize all scores so that there is no confusion as to the identification of a score. Also, the scores should be presented so that errors are minimized in transmitting the scores from the data sheets to the calculator. The computations on the calculator should be performed in such a manner that several internal checks may be made during the calculations.

Measurement and data collection are very important aspects of the research study. The measurement should be carefully defined in terms of the objectives of the research. The measurement follows the conception of the research objectives. It is not acceptable research procedure to collect a mass of data and then begin searching for some research objectives to fit the data. Validity and reliability should be considered and coefficients reported if available. Good measurement does not insure a good research study, but poor measurement certainly dooms the study to failure. Recall that adequate measurement is a necessary but not sufficient condition for good educational research.

Suggested Study Exercises

6.1 Discuss the distinction between the concepts of validity and reliability. Why do we say that measurement can be reliable without being valid, but that the reverse cannot be true?

6.2 Examine a standardized achievement test and propose a research problem for which it might serve as the measurement device. Identify the Ss for which the test would be appropriate and the population under study. State one or more hypotheses for your proposed research study. Identify possible statistics that could come out of the test data and would be necessary in the light of your hypotheses.

6.3 A researcher wants to do a study about the extent of hostility in upper elementary classrooms taught by teachers classified as autocratic or democratic. Discuss some of the measurement difficulties that the researcher is likely to encounter. Is it possible to quantify hostility in any way? How would you define hostility? Assume that hostility can go both ways: from students to teacher and vice versa. Suggest a type of measurement device that might be used for data collection.

6.4 Construct a short "culture fair" intelligence test. By culture fair is meant a test that does not reflect a specific culture. That is, the performance of a S is not influenced by his culture. Thus, assuming communication, the test should be as valid for a South Pacific native as an American high school student. Consider such things as the types of possible items and the content of the items.

6.5 Suppose a teacher wants to do a study on the attitudes of junior high students toward a compulsory "orientation to the school" program. Assume that the Ss have completed the program. Construct five items that would fit into such an attitude inventory. Designate the scoring for your items.

6.6 Select an article from a research journal which involves the measurement of attitudes or personality characteristics. Read the article carefully and check to see if the author discusses such things as validity, reliability, and type of measuring device. Are the data quantified in some way? Were standardized tests used for the study?

6.7 Define objectivity of a measurement device. Why is it an error to conclude that objectivity is limited to short answer, factual type items? Construct one (or more) objective items from your field of study which requires more than a short answer response. Consider short answer as consisting of two sentences or less.

6.8 Discuss the advantages and disadvantages of the interview as a measurement device as compared to some kind of a paper and pencil response test or inventory.

6.9 A research director for a large city school system conducts an extensive study of achievement in grades three through eight. He measures achievement in several areas with subscores in the areas so that there are 18 different achievement scores for each participating student. Ten of the scores require two digits and the remainder three digits. The sample of students is drawn from 74 city schools. The total sample size is over 1,000 and each student in the sample is to be identified by a number. In addition to the specific school and grade level, the students are classified according to sex and ability level: high, average and low. The student's age is recorded. The city is divided into eight socio-economic districts and this information is also recorded in terms of the location of the school that the student attends. Produce a possible card layout for an IBM card that includes all of the above information. Consider the number of columns you would use for identification and achievement scores. The order is somewhat arbitrary, but construct a possible grouping of scores. Recall that 80 columns are available on an IBM card.

7 Experimental Design

The Meaning of Experiment

The word experiment has a generally familiar but broad meaning in our society. Many research and for that matter non-research procedures are referred to as experiments. When we refer to an experiment in educational research or experimentation in education, we are referring to a research situation which is quite specifically defined, even though the definition is broad enough to include a large number of types of investigations. An experiment in education is a research situation in which one or more factors are systematically varied according to some preconceived plan, in order to determine the effects of this variation. The preconceived plan, which is superimposed upon and essentially lends structure to the research, is the experimental design. Note that the design is preconceived, that is, preconceived to actually doing the research. The research is not carried out and then a design sought to give meaning to the results, although this is not unheard of in education. Experimental design in education is not limited to research in a laboratory setting, such as a learning laboratory. Design also applies to studies in the classroom or school setting.

Criteria for a Well-Designed Experiment

There are certain general comments which can be made relative to the characteristics of a well-designed experiment. A primary characteristic is that the experimental design provides sufficient control to meet the objectives of the research and adequately answer the questions or test the hypotheses. Control in this context is used as a noun and may be defined as restraints placed upon the experimental conditions. The word control may also be used as a verb; that is, we say the researcher controls certain experimental variables or factors. Maximum control is attained when only the experimental effects and random chance effects are operating in the experiment. It is not always possible or necessary to attain maximum control.

Control is also used as an adjective to describe a specific group involved in the experiment. This group is a control group. (All experiments do not involve a control group.) The control group is essentially a group of Ss who do not receive an experimental treatment. A group of students taught by traditional methods might serve as a control group in an educational experiment dealing with new teaching methods.

A well-designed experiment results in data that are free from bias. A lack of bias means that the scores do not vary in a systematic manner but only as expected on the basis of random chance variation. Thus any significant differences can be attributed to the effect of experimental treatments. Recall from the discussions on testing hypotheses that the probability statements had the general form of: What is the probability of the statistic appearing by chance? If this probability is less than the predetermined significance level, we reject the hypothesis that the statistic (for example, a difference in means) is due to chance, and attribute it to the experimental effect. Now, if there is both a bias and an experimental effect operating, then we cannot be certain what has brought about the statistic. So in order to make a conclusion about the experimental effect, it is necessary to have bias-free data. Bias may enter into the experiment by a haphazard or non-random assignment of Ss to the experimental units. It may also enter in when larger units such as classes are assigned as experimental units.

The data should not only be free from bias but also contain the necessary information that the researcher needs to test his hypotheses and make his inferences. The design must provide for the extraction of this information from the data. The purposes of the experiment, reflected specifically in the hypotheses or questions, will dictate the data to be collected in the context of the design. It is essential that the hypotheses can be tested individually and validly.

The testing of hypotheses by statistical procedures such as the parametric techniques requires an estimate of random error or fluctuation. Such an estimate should be available from the data. In order to adequately test the hypotheses and provide answers, this error term must not be unreasonably inflated. The experimental design should provide for the removal or control of factors inflating the error estimate. In some experiments it may be necessary to build in certain factors as independent variables so that their contribution to the variation is not included in the error estimate. Recall that in the F-test of the analysis of variance, for example, the denominator of the F-ratio is the error estimate of variance. As the F-ratio increases in size, its probability of appearing by chance decreases and hence the likelihood of a significant difference, that is, experimental effect, increases. If the error estimate is inflated, the F-test will be insensitive to an existing experimental effect. A design which does not provide a good error estimate cannot lead to conclusions. However, since conclusions are usually drawn, they may very well be in error when adequate error estimates are not available. Of course, the measuring instrument must be precise enough to detect the existence of real differences. A good experimental design, then, provides an accurate estimate of random error, when such an estimate is necessary for testing hypotheses.

A common experimental error is the omission of a control group when the objectives of the research require such a group. The hypotheses may imply that an experimental treatment has an effect. In order to test the hypotheses, a comparison group which has not had the experimental treatment may be necessary. The change in the experimental group between the initiation of the experiment and the time of data collection may have occurred because of the passing of time, regardless of the experimental treatment. In other words, the experimental group may have shown a similar change without the experimental treatment. Such a situation requires that the control group be built into the design so that a valid comparison can be made to determine whether or not there is an experimental effect. It is not satisfactory to begin searching for a comparison group after the experiment has been conducted.

The well-designed experiment guards against the contamination of the data. Contamination may enter into the data if the Ss of the experimental groups and control group are allowed considerable interaction, and this interaction has an effect upon the dependent variable. For example, in an achievement study involving different techniques with several groups of seventh graders, if the students of the various groups study together after school this would undoubtedly affect the achievement scores. This might also be considered as a lack of control over a relevant factor, but obviously a very difficult factor to control. In some experiments it is considered undesirable if the experimental group is aware of its experimental status. This awareness alone may affect the performance of the group.

A possible experimental error is having relevant factors confounded with the independent variables. In any research, when two variables are confounded, it is impossible to separate the effects of the two variables. In an experiment of relatively limited scope, only one teacher may be using a specific teaching technique. Thus, in the experiment there are as many teachers as experimental treatments, but each teacher is involved in only one. Teacher is therefore confounded with the experimental treatment which is teaching technique. To be sure, the teachers may be equated on several factors but it is difficult to equate teachers on teaching effectiveness. In many situations it is not feasible to have all teachers teach with all techniques. A better design would involve several teachers for each technique. If we compare two teachers they may be quite different, but if we compare two groups of teachers, the two groups may in fact be quite similar. The inclusion of several teachers for each technique would extend the scope of the experiment. Preferably, the teachers would be randomly assigned to the techniques. The reader should note that confounding variables is not the same as having variables inflate the error variance. In the case of confounding, the effect of an extraneous variable cannot be separated from the effect of an experimental treatment. When the error variance is inflated, an uncontrolled source of variation is included in the error variance, thus decreasing precision. A good experimental design guards against both of these errors.

There are several other errors which may enter into an experimental design. An incorrect sampling unit may be used relative to the analysis of data. The experiment may be weak because of insufficient numbers of Ss or unwarranted assumptions may be made about the nature of the measuring instrument. For example, it may be much more difficult or even impossible for high scoring Ss to show a comparable increment as low scorers. This is not because the gain does not exist among the high scorers, but because the test cannot measure it due to the test ceiling. This is an example of an inadequate measuring instrument. If any sizable number of Ss score either at the bottom or top of the test, there is no way to make an estimate of the performance mean or the error variance. The above are examples of possible experimental errors.

With all of the possible pitfalls, the reader might wonder that satisfactory experiments are designed at all. The development of an appropriate design and adequate execution of the experiment take considerable and careful planning. It is an exacting task in which several things must be considered simultaneously. Carrying out the experiment in a haphazard manner or using an inadequate experimental design will result in an experiment lacking in validity.

Experimental Validity

Experimental validity is used in this discussion as defined by Campbell and Stanley.[1] Validity is considered to be of two types: internal validity and external validity. *Internal validity* is the basic minimum necessary to make the results of the experiment interpretable. Internal validity questions whether the experimental treatment really makes a difference in the dependent variable. An adequate answer to this question requires adequate internal validity. Before it can be answered, the researcher must be confident that extraneous variables have not produced an effect that is being mistaken as an effect of the experimental treatment.

External validity of an experiment deals with the generalizability of the results of the experiment. To what populations, variables, situations, etc., do the results generalize? Securing answers to this question that are in keeping with the objectives of the experiment requires adequate external validity.

We desire to use experimental designs that are high in both types of validity. However, in some cases, securing one type of validity tends to jeopardize the other type. As more rigorous controls are applied in the experiment, less carry-over can be anticipated between what occurred in the experiment and what would occur in a field situation. For example, in research on instructional techniques, the control of the experiment may be so extensive that essentially an artificial situation is created and only the experimental variables are operating. This would greatly enhance internal validity but the generalization might be so limited that the results could not be applied to a real classroom situation. This is not to say that it is never desirable to achieve maximum control. The objectives of the experiment dictate the necessary validity requirements. Obviously an experiment whose results are uninterpretable is useless, even if wide generalizability would have been possible. On the other

[1] Campbell, D., and Stanley, J. "Experimental and Quasi-Experimental Designs for Research on Teaching," Gage, ed., in *Handbook of Research on Teaching* (Chicago: Rand McNally & Company, 1963), pp. 171–246.

hand, it is unsatisfactory to do an experiment and then discover that the results cannot be generalized as anticipated in the objectives of the experiment.

Internal validity involves securing adequate control over extraneous variables, selection procedures, measurement procedures, and the like. The experimental design should be so developed that the researcher can adequately check on the factors that might threaten the internal validity. To be sure, all possible factors are not operating in all experiments, but the researcher should have some knowledge about his variables and the possible difficulties that may arise in connection with internal validity. Then he can design his experiment accordingly so that his results can be interpreted adequately.

External validity certainly concerns the populations to which the researcher expects to generalize his results, but it is not limited to these. It also may include generalizing his findings to other related independent variables or modifications of the experimental variable. There may be factors such as size of class, type of school, etc., across which the researcher hopes to generalize. For example, suppose an experiment is being conducted in a suburban school with fourth-grade pupils. Would the results apply to an inner city school? To eighth graders? Most likely not, but again this depends on the variables and the details of the experiment. The researcher may also desire to generalize to different measurement variations. For example, would the results of an experiment including pretesting be applicable to a classroom situation with no pretesting? External validity is concerned with these types of questions.

Experimental designs in educational research are rarely, if ever, perfect. Both internal and external validity are important, and through experimental design we attempt to embrace adequate validity. Since enhancing one type of validity may tend to jeopardize the other, we often attempt to secure an adequate compromise. The compromise is essentially that of attaining sufficient control to make the results interpretable while maintaining enough realism so that the results will generalize adequately to the intended situations. As we consider the various experimental designs, comments will be made about the experimental validity of the designs.

Posttest-Only Control Group Design

The terms pretest and posttest are commonly used in connection with experimental design. *Pretest* refers to a measure or test given to the Ss prior to the experimental treatment; *posttest* is a measure taken after the experimental treatment. Certainly not all designs involve pretesting. The designs discussed in this chapter are those commonly found in the educational research literature.

Experimental designs commonly involve two or more groups: a group for each of the experimental treatments and a control group. The *Posttest-Only Control Group Design* is such a design. This design, in its simplest form, involves just two groups: the group which receives the experimental treatment and the control group. The Ss are randomly assigned to the two groups. Note that the random assignment of Ss takes place prior to the experiment. The experimental group receives the experimental treatment. Upon the conclusion of the experimental period, the two groups are measured on the dependent variable under study. Preferably, this measurement takes place immediately after the conclusion of the experiment, especially if the dependent variable is likely to change with the passing of time.

The posttest-only control group design is an efficient design to administer. It does not require pretesting, which for many situations is not desirable or applicable. Pretesting and posttesting require that each individual S be identified so that the pre- and posttest scores may be matched. The posttest-only design requires the Ss to be identified only in terms of their group and possibly other independent variables, if such variables are in the design.

The posttest-only control group design is high in internal validity. The random assignment of Ss rules out selection bias. Any effects of extraneous factors are, of course, functions of the experimental control; but with the random assignment such effects should be equally spread over the groups at the beginning of the experiment. Such effects may not be eliminated, but if they do not interact with the experimental treatment, they do not threaten the internal validity.

However, the posttest-only control group design does have some possible weaknesses that could threaten internal validity. If there is considerable subject mortality during the experiment, the design is weak for checking on differential mortality between the groups. *Differential mortality* means that the dropouts in one group have different characteristics than those of the other group and that these characteristics may be relevant to the experimental and dependent variables. Without additional information it is essentially impossible to rule out a possible effect of differential mortality, if there is a considerable dropout of Ss. If there is a suspicion that it will be difficult to keep the initial groups intact, it might be well to consider another design. Another possible threat to internal validity is if some relevant but non-experimental factors enter during the experiment and operate in one and not the other group. (The entrance of such factors would be due to a lack of control.) These factors may have a direct effect upon the dependent variable or they may interact with the experimental or control treatment to affect the dependent variable. Such factors are relevant only as they, in one way or another, affect the dependent variable.

The external validity of the posttest-only control group design is high, provided that the generalizations can be made from the experimental to the nonexperimental setting. The random assignment of Ss is assumed to have eliminated the possibility of selection biases interfering with generalization.

The posttest-only control group design may be extended to include more than two groups. Two or more experimental treatments may be used, increasing the number of groups to three or more. The Ss would be randomly assigned to the groups from the population. The effects of the various experimental treatments could be investigated by comparing means or some statistics of the treatment groups and the control group. This brings us to possible analyses of the data.

The analysis of data for the posttest-only control group design, as for any design, depends upon the type of data and the underlying assumptions. If the parametric assumptions can be met, the simplest analysis would be a Student's t-test for the difference between means. If more than two groups are included in the design, a one-way analysis of variance would be appropriate. An analysis of covariance may be used if suitable data on possible covariates are available, for example, prior test scores or grades. Any covariate would likely be some type of antecedent variable, otherwise it may have been affected by the experimental treatment. The inclusion of relevant covariates would increase the power of the statistical test. By removing a component of variance due to the covariate, the inclusion of a relevant covariate would provide a more precise estimate of error variance over, say, an analysis of variance.

Pretest-Posttest Control Group Design

The addition of a pretest given prior to the experimental period essentially extends the posttest-only control group design to the pretest-posttest control group design. The Ss are randomly assigned to the two groups. In this design, the Ss are tested just prior to the experiment on a supposedly relevant antecedent variable, possibly a second form of the test which measures the dependent variable.

What is gained by pretesting? It has already been pointed out that the inclusion of relevant covariates will result in a more powerful statistical test if an analysis of covariance is the statistical technique. The design is strong in internal validity. It has an advantage over the posttest-only design if subject mortality is a problem. The dropouts can be checked on the pretest and thus the researcher has an indication as to whether or not there is a differential mortality between the two groups.

The external validity of the pretest-posttest control group design has a possible threat from the existence of an interaction between the pretesting and the experimental treatment. The pretesting itself may have some sort of an effect upon the Ss so that the results do not generalize to the non-pretested population. The problem of pretesting effects must be considered in the context of the specific experiment. For some dependent variables, it may have a substantial effect and for others no effect at all. For example, an attitude inventory administered prior to the experimental period might arouse certain feelings and yield different end results than if there had been no pretest. In an achievement study with different teaching techniques as the experimental and control treatments, covering a substantial instructional period such as one or two semesters, pretesting is unlikely to be a threat to validity.

The random assignment of Ss is assumed to remove selection bias as a threat to external validity. The question of generalizing to the non-experimental setting may be raised. External validity cannot be pinned down through objective computations. It has a logical context about it, relative to the specific experiment. The researcher should have some knowledge about what is operating in his experiment relative to external validity.

The pretest-posttest control group design may be extended to additional groups. In all cases, the Ss of all groups are randomly assigned. The pretests for all groups are given at the same time. The same is true for the posttests.

An analysis of the data has already been suggested as an analysis of covariance. This is an appropriate technique if the parametric assumptions are tenable. The gain scores of the groups may be determined and a Student's t-test computed on the difference between the gain score means. If there are more than two groups, the gain scores would likely be analyzed by an analysis of variance. As the number of groups increases, the number of required t-tests also increases quite rapidly.

Solomon Four-Group Design[1]

The extension of the pretest-posttest control group design to the Solomon four-group design is sort of a "have your cake and eat it too" situation when it comes to pretesting and the possible effects of pretesting. This design in its four-group form includes two control and two experimental groups. One and only one of each of the two types of groups is pretested. The four groups are posttested at the conclusion of the experimental period. The assignment of Ss to all groups is random.

By including the groups that are not pretested, the researcher is able to determine both the main effects of pretesting and the interaction of pretesting with the experimental variable. Thus, of the three designs discussed so far, the Solomon four-group

[1] Solomon, R. L., "An Extension of Control Group Design," *Psychological Bulletin*, 1949, 46, pp. 137–150.

would seem to be the highest in validity. The comments made for the pretest-posttest control group design relative to generalizing to the non-experimental setting hold for this design. The design may be extended to include additional experimental treatments, but two groups—one pretested and one not—are required for each treatment.

The asymmetries of the design rule out an analysis of covariance including all groups, since only one-half the groups are pretested. An analysis of covariance could be done on the data of the pretested groups if the effects of testing are negligible. For the same reason, an analysis of variance on gain scores is not possible for all groups. Pretest may be considered an independent variable, and a two-way analysis of variance could be computed on the posttest data. The two independent variables would be experimental versus control treatment and pretest versus non-pretest. The dependent variable would be the posttest score. The parametric assumptions would, of course, be required for any of these analyses.

Various additional comparisons may be made on the data of a Solomon four-group design. The pretest data may be compared with the posttest scores of the non-pretested control group. If the assignment of Ss has been genuinely random, this comparison is a measure of the effect of the passing of time in the usual (control) situation. The comparison would be between statistics computed for the groups, not between scores of individual Ss. In this comparison, the Ss pretested are not the same as those supplying the posttest data. By various comparisons in combinations of two, the effect of the experimental treatment may be checked in four different ways. The comparison of the pre- and posttest scores within the experimental group gives an indication of the actual gain due to the experimental treatment. The comparison of the posttest scores of the two pretested groups (one experimental and one control group) is an indication of the effect (or lack of effect) of the experimental treatment when the Ss are pretested. A similar comparison in the remaining two groups checks the same thing for non-pretested Ss. A comparison of the pretest scores of the control group and the posttest scores of the non-pretested experimental group is the fourth comparison involving the effect of the experimental treatment. This comparison is again an indication of the gain due to the experimental treatment when Ss are not pretested. With the exception of the first, these comparisons cross over groups. The random assignment of Ss enables us to assume that the groups were initially the same, thus making these cross-groups comparisons possible. The individual comparisons could be made using an appropriate two-sample technique such as Student's *t*-test for the difference between two means.

Factorial Designs

The next design is one which is becoming increasingly more common in the educational research literature. It actually comprises a family of designs called the *factorial designs*. The basic construction of a factorial design is that all levels of each independent variable are taken in combination with the levels of the other independent variables. (Technically this is referred to as a complete factorial.) The design requires a minimum of two independent variables with at least two levels of each variable. This minimum design is called a 2 by 2 (2×2) factorial. Theoretically there could be any number of independent variables with any number of levels of each. The number of digits indicates the number of independent variables. The numerical values of the digits indicate the number of levels for the specific independent variables. These numbers need not be the same for the independent variables. Consider a $2 \times 3 \times 5$ factorial. This means there are three independent variables, with two, three, and five levels respectively. An example which fits this factorial is two teaching methods, three ability levels, and five grades.

The number of different groups involved in a factorial design increases very rapidly with the increase of the number of independent variables and number of levels. The 2×2 factorial has four groups. To add just one independent variable with two levels would increase this to a $2 \times 2 \times 2$ (commonly denoted by 2^3) factorial with eight cells. If one level is added to each of the independent variables of a 2×2 factorial, the number of groups is increased to nine. Since the levels must be taken in all combinations, the number of groups is the product of the digits which specify the factorial design.

TABLE 7.1

Diagram of a $2 \times 3 \times 5$ factorial design [1]

		Variable A					
		1			2		
		Variable B			Variable B		
		1	2	3	1	2	3
Variable C	1	$A_1B_1C_1$	$A_1B_2C_1$	$A_1B_3C_1$	$A_2B_1C_1$	$A_2B_2C_1$	$A_2B_3C_1$
	2	$A_1B_1C_2$	$A_1B_2C_2$	$A_1B_3C_2$	$A_2B_1C_2$	$A_2B_2C_2$	$A_2B_3C_2$
	3	$A_1B_1C_3$	$A_1B_2C_3$	$A_1B_3C_3$	$A_2B_1C_3$	$A_2B_2C_3$	$A_2B_3C_3$
	4	$A_1B_1C_4$	$A_1B_2C_4$	$A_1B_3C_4$	$A_2B_1C_4$	$A_2B_2C_4$	$A_2B_3C_4$
	5	$A_1B_1C_5$	$A_1B_2C_5$	$A_1B_3C_5$	$A_2B_1C_5$	$A_2B_2C_5$	$A_2B_3C_5$

[1] The 30 cells (groups) could all be designated by the letters with subscripts, as they are in the figure. Note that no cell designation is exactly like any other. Any two cell designations differ in at least one subscript.

The $2 \times 3 \times 5$ factorial mentioned above would contain 30 groups. Suppose we designate the independent variables by A, B, and C respectively. The different levels of the independent variables may be designated by the subscripts 1, 2, etc., to the required number. The groups of the $2 \times 3 \times 5$ factorial design are diagrammed in Table 7.1.

The control group may be built into the factorial design by considering "no experimental treatment" as one of the levels of the independent variable—experimental treatment. In an experiment involving only an experimental treatment and no experimental treatment in combination with other independent variables, one half of the Ss would be in control groups. It should be noted that a control group is not a requirement of the factorial design. Its inclusion depends upon the objectives of the experiment.

The factorial design enables the researcher to check the effects of several independent variables simultaneously. Also, the interaction effects may be determined. These points were discussed in connection with analysis of variance in Chapter 3. The assignment of Ss to the various groups is a random assignment from a single population.

The factorial design is considered high in internal validity. The design may be used whether or not the Ss have been pretested. However, it is more often used for experiments in which no pretests are administered. Under these conditions, the validity comments are essentially the same for the factorial design as for the posttest-only control group design. The design is not commonly used unless the parametric assumptions are met. The analysis of variance is an appropriate analysis technique. In fact, the factorial designs are commonly referred to as factorial analyses of variance.

If an analysis of covariance is anticipated, the design must, of course, include pretesting of the Ss. The assembling of the data is a bit more tedious, not only because now there is more of it, but because the pre- and posttest scores of each S must be matched. The actual statistical analysis is usually done on a high-speed computer. When analyzing the data, the researcher should be careful that the computer program will test the hypotheses of his study. The calculations of a factorial design are greatly simplified if there are equal numbers of Ss in the various groups.

The real advantages of a factorial design over alternative designs are not necessarily great gains in validity. The principal advantages are twofold. One is the economy of a single design rather than separate designs for each of the factors or variables. Secondly, the factorial design provides the possibility of investigating the interactions between the variables. Theoretically, the factorial design may be extended to include any finite number of variables and levels. However, complex designs should be considered with caution, one reason being that such a design may not be economically feasible in terms of the available Ss. Also, the interpretation of higher-order interactions may, for all practical purposes, be impossible.

The use of a complete factorial may, for some reason, be impossible or undesirable. In such a situation a fractional factorial may be an appropriate design. A fractional factorial design is one in which only selected combinations of variable levels are used. The valid use of a fractional factorial requires the assumption that certain higher-order interactions are of little interest and do not contribute a significant effect. This assumption is necessary for the technique of confounding. The reader is reminded that confounding involves an effect being attributable to more than one variable (or interaction) and the single effects of the variables confounded cannot be separated. The fractional factorial confounds higher-order interactions with main effects on the assumption that the higher-order interac-actions do not contribute to an effect. The procedure for setting up such a design is beyond the scope of this text. Extensive discussion of both complete and fractional factorial designs appear in the more advanced experimental design texts.[1]

Counterbalanced Designs

The counterbalanced designs make up a family of designs in which experimental control is enhanced by entering all Ss into all levels of the experimental treatment variable. They also go by other names such as cross-over, switch-over, or rotation designs. (It should be noted that this is not a unique usage of the term rotation in experimental design.) Sometimes these designs are referred to as multiple-observation or re-peated measures designs if any one S is observed more than once. Campbell and Stanley[2] discuss these designs under the heading of quasi-experimental designs. They direct their ap-plication to naturally assembled groups rather than groups to which the Ss have been randomly assigned. In this discussion we will assume the random assignment of Ss.

The device by which the design is structured is a *Latin square*. A Latin square is an $n \times n$ array in which the n letters or num-bers appear once and once only in each row and column. The size of the square may vary from a 2×2 as minimum to, at least theoretically, any finite number. The number of different pos-sible squares increases greatly with an increase in n. For ex-ample, there are twelve different ways of arranging the letters of a 3×3 square and 161,280 ways for a 5×5 square. The size of the Latin square used in a specific experiment depends upon the number of experimental treatments to be assigned by the square.

An illustration of a counterbalanced design follows. Suppose

[1] See for example, Cox, D. R., *Planning of Experiments* (New York: John Wiley and Sons, Inc., 1958).

[2] Campbell, D. T., and Stanley, J. C., "Experimental and Quasi-Experimental Designs for Research on Teaching," Gage, ed., in *Handbook for Research on Teaching* (Chicago: Rand McNally & Company, 1963), pp. 220–222.

a researcher has randomly selected three groups of Ss: a group each of eighth graders, tenth graders, and twelfth graders. Each S is to solve singly three different problems, say P_1, P_2, and P_3, in some sequence. These might be unique problems administered under standardized conditions in a learning laboratory. The dependent variable could be one of several measures such as time required for solution or number of errors. (More than one dependent variable might be measured, but the design would apply in the same manner for each dependent variable.) The different positions in the sequence of problems make up different ordinal positions which are actually the first, second, and third times in the solution sequence.

The above experiment would require a 3×3 Latin square. Suppose the researcher has six Ss in each of the three grade levels. The diagram of the experimental design appears in Table 7.2. In the diagram, the eighteen Ss are numbered consecutively with the first six subscripts assigned to the eighth grade, etc., T_1, T_2, and T_3 represent the three times. The specific Latin square used in this design is:

$$
\begin{array}{ccc}
1 & 2 & 3 \\
3 & 1 & 2 \\
2 & 3 & 1
\end{array}
$$

Note that the numbers of the Latin square make up the subscripts on the problems as assigned to the first three Ss. After this, the Latin square repeats for each group of three Ss. The Latin square has only complete replications and is repeated the same number of times for each grade level. Thus, all sequences of problems, as designated by the rows of the Latin square, appear an equal number of times in each grade level. The problems appear the same number of times in the ordinal positions, designated by T_1, T_2, and T_3 in the diagram. In this respect the design is balanced.

The Latin square defines three unique sequences of problems, but this does not exhaust the possible sequences. For example, the sequence $P_3 P_2 P_1$ does not appear. The specific Latin square used in a design is randomly determined.

The counterbalanced design is appropriate only if it can be assumed that there are no interactions of the variables involved.

TABLE 7.2

Diagram for counterbalanced design using a 3×3 Latin square and a total of eighteen Ss

		T_1	T_2	T_3
	S_1	P_1	P_2	P_3
	S_2	P_3	P_1	P_2
8th grade	S_3	P_2	P_3	P_1
	S_4	P_1	P_2	P_3
	S_5	P_3	P_1	P_2
	S_6	P_2	P_3	P_1
	S_7	P_1	P_2	P_3
10th grade	⋮	⋮	⋮	⋮
	S_{12}	P_2	P_3	P_1
	S_{13}	P_1	P_2	P_3
12th grade	⋮	⋮	⋮	⋮
	S_{18}	P_2	P_3	P_1

For example, the effect of problems in the diagram could instead be an interaction effect between the grade levels and the ordinal positions. The design is strengthened if replications of Ss are assigned to different Latin squares. In the diagrammed design, a replication of the same square is indicated. This replication would enable the researchers to compute a within grade level and sequence error term. This may or may not be necessary, depending upon the hypotheses and the variables of the experiment.

A modification of this design may be made by having an entire group follow the same sequence, but no two groups following the same sequence, instead of having each S follow a sequence and all sequences represented at least once in a group. This would apply to an experiment in which the group participated as a unit. In such a design, the assumption of no interactions is likely to be less tenable than for the other design. A threat to validity under this condition is that selection factors may be operating in groups already established by some criterion other than random selection.

A measurement is made on the dependent variable following each experimental treatment. To illustrate, in the example of Table 7.2, each S would be measured three times, once after each problem. Thus, that particular design would yield 54 scores on a dependent variable. The counterbalanced designs are preferred if no pretesting is necessary. The designs are not considered control group designs, although it may be possible to build in a control group.

The counterbalanced designs have a potential threat to external validity not encountered in designs discussed earlier. That threat is multiple-treatment interference. This interference is the effect of prior treatments upon subsequent treatments. For example, in the illustration of Table 7.2, the solution of the first problem may affect performance on the remaining two problems. The S's performance may be different than what it would have been had there been no previous problem. In educational research it is difficult to erase the effects of prior treatments. The other factors, such as not being able to generalize to the non-experimental setting, may be operating in counterbalanced designs as in the posttest-only designs.

The counterbalanced designs have the potential for high internal validity, especially if random assignment is employed along with sufficient replications with different Latin squares. The problem of an interaction effect being interpreted as a main effect may be intuitively checked by inspection. If an experimental treatment is consistently high, say in the treatment means, it is unlikely that this is caused by an interaction, since the interaction is unlikely to imitate the main effect throughout the design. On the other hand, if one experimental treatment mean is significantly different from the others, and the big difference lies in only one group, then the alternative conclusion of an interaction is highly tenable. It should be noted that this intuitive inspection is not a statistical test of a hypothesis.

The usual analysis procedure associated with a counterbalanced design is an analysis of variance. The parametric assumption of independent observations may give some difficulty since multiple observations are taken on the Ss. It may be necessary to introduce computational adjustments due to the multiple observations. The analyses of these designs often become quite complex. The discussion of this text is a general overview of the designs. Theoretical and computational details are commonly discussed in advance design texts.[1]

Quasi-Experimental Designs

The educational researcher, especially one who carries on his experiments in the classroom setting, often finds that he has little control over the assignment of Ss to groups. Random assignment requires that all members of a population have an equal probability of being included in the sample. In looking at classes or other natural social assemblages, it soon becomes apparent that various selection factors are operating and that the group is hardly a random selection of a larger population. However, though full experimental control cannot be attained when such groups are involved, it is possible to design studies which have some of the aspects of experimental design. The risk of misinterpretation exists, but the use of such groups may prove valuable. These are called *quasi-experimental* designs by Campbell and Stanley.[2] The use of such designs is recommended only when better designs are not applicable or are impossible to administer.

Time Designs

The researcher who employs a less than true experimental design should be aware of the variables that are not controlled by the design. Many of the quasi-experimental designs involve only a single group. *Longitudinal* or *time designs* as applied to a single group belong to the quasi-experimental type of design. The time designs essentially involve periodic measurement on some dependent variable, with the experimental treatment injected between two of the measurements. The real question in

[1] The reader is referred to Lindquist, E. F., *Design and Analysis of Experiments in Psychology and Education* (Boston: Houghton Mifflin Co., 1953).

[2] Campbell, D. T., and Stanley, J. C., "Experimental and Quasi-Experimental Designs for Research on Teaching," Gage, ed., in *Handbook for Research on Teaching* (Chicago: Rand McNally and Company, 1963), p. 204.

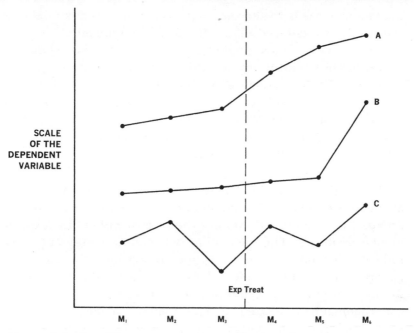

Figure 7.1 Possible outcome patterns of a time design.

this design is whether the experimental treatment has an effect on the performance (as measured by the dependent variable) of this group.

The patterns of the means or whatever the statistic of the dependent variable is, have almost an unlimited number of possible forms. The major problem of internal validity is that of alternative explanations for the pattern, other than the effect of the experimental treatment. Figure 7.1 contains three possible patterns. The M_i's on the horizontal axis represent the measurement occasions and the vertical axis represents the scale of the dependent variable. Data are collected at each of the M_i points. For any one particular experiment and dependent variable, there would be only one pattern. The interpretation of Pattern A would be that the experimental treatment is likely to have had an effect. The slope of the line returns to approximately the pre-experimental treatment level, especially between the fifth and sixth measurements. Pattern B appears, on the surface, to include no experimental treatment effect. However, the marked increase between the final two measurements might be the result of a delayed effect. If there is no apparent external event which could have produced this effect, the researcher is in somewhat of a bind to explain this increase. The experimenter should anticipate in advance the time interval between the introduction of the experimental treatment and the appearance of its effect. For certain variables, the effect in B is about as definite as that of Pattern A. It should be noted that as the time interval increases, the likelihood of an intervening extraneous event also increases.

The erratic pattern of C almost excludes drawing a conclusion about an experimental treatment effect. Since there is no control group, it is most difficult to infer the pattern without the experimental treatment. The fluctuation between measurements may indicate that other factors are operating which override any experimental treatment effect. It is possible that the experiment requires an increase in control before there is sensitivity to an experimental treatment effect. The definite conclusion of no experimental treatment effect cannot be drawn from Pattern C.

The most serious threat to the internal validity of the time designs is the possibility of external events which are uncontrolled, giving rise to alternative explanations. The interpretation of the results hangs on the plausibility of ruling out the effects of such external events. The possibility of such events increases as the experimental period is extended in time. The validity of a time design may also be affected by a change in the use of the measuring instruments. Since several measurements occur, a lack of consistency in measurement might produce an effect which in turn would be interpreted as an experimental treatment effect. This could occur, of course, between any two measurements or it could be a gradual deterioration which would make the final measurement considerably changed from earlier measurements.

The external validity of a time design may or may not be good. With the multiple measurements, the design takes on a sort of sequential pretesting characteristic. Thus, the possibility exists of some kind of interaction effect of pretesting which would not be manifest in the unpretested population. However, in conducting research in an actual classroom situation, this is hardly considered a limitation. The measurements can be timed to coincide with the usual testing routine. The possible threats to external validity are not considered serious if the experiment and its measurement are not artificial.

The analysis of the data of quasi-experimental designs is not as straightforward as for the true designs. In the time designs, usually some kind of comparison between pre- and posttest data is made. A pooled pretest and posttest comparison is inadequate because it will not distinguish between certain patterns. Also, such a comparison may not be sensitive to an experimental treatment effect. For example, suppose the group drops back down on subsequent measurements following the measurement immediately after the experimental treatment. The pooling of all these measurements will tend to wash out any experimental treatment effect.

The comparison of the measurements immediately preceding and following the introduction of the experimental treatment is certainly unsatisfactory for a pattern such as B in Figure 7.1. In essentially all cases, a single test of significance between the two measurements is insufficient.

The test of significance used will be determined in part by the hypothesized pattern. In a pattern such as A, some type of pooled (or other extrapolated) data from the pre-experimental treatment measures might be compared with M_4. Some kind of investigation of the slope and intercept of the straight line fit to the pattern may be involved. Changes in either slope or intercept may be evidence of an experimental effect. The assumption of linearity, that is, a straight line fit, is not always tenable. The researcher should possess sufficient knowledge about the variables to make a judgment about the linearity assumption.

A modification of the time designs discussed above is a design in which there is repeated introduction of the experimental treatment into the sequence. The experimental treatment is inserted randomly into the sequence. Time is controlled by having equal intervals between measurements. The internal validity of a design with repeated introduction of the experimental treatment is strengthened over the other time design in that the repeated application of the experimental treatment gives a check on the influence of extraneous events. It is unlikely that an extraneous event would consistently coincide with the experimental treatment.

The repeated measurement of this design is a possible threat to external validity, as it was in the designs discussed earlier. The Ss may be quite sensitive to the experimental arrangements of the change in conditions from experimental treatment to no experimental treatment. For example, suppose that the use of programmed learning materials was the experimental treatment. The Ss would undoubtedly become aware of the experimental nature of the situation. This could be a possible limitation on the generalizability of the results.

A second possible threat to external validity is the multiple treatment interference discussed in connection with the counterbalanced designs. The experimental treatment-no experimental treatment, alternating characteristic of this design, makes generalizations to situations in which the experimental treatment is continually present very hazardous. Any one experimental condition (or lack of it) cannot be isolated from the sequence and interpreted as being representative of extended periods under this condition and this condition alone.

In analyzing the data of a time design with repeated applications of the experimental treatment, it is advisable not to make a comparison between single measurements of the experimental treatment and the lack thereof. The effect of an extraneous event could be easily misinterpreted as a significant experimental effect. If the parametric assumptions are tenable, some type of a significance test for the difference between treatment means is possible. There should be at least two measurements contained within each treatment. The patterns of the individual Ss might be inspected for consistency with the experimental effect.

The time design can also be constructed to include multiple groups. In this sense, it takes on the characteristics of a control group design. The second group, again taken intact as found in some educational setting, would be measured at the same times as the other group, but would not have the experimental treatment inserted anywhere in the sequence.

The inclusion of the additional group in the design facilitates interpretation of the experimental treatment effect. The postexperimental treatment data can now be checked against the pre-experimental treatment data of its own group and the data of the control group. Internal validity is strengthened in that it is possible to check if any selection factors are operating in the groups prior to the introduction of the experimental treatment. It is still possible that some type of selection-experimental treatment or testing and experimental treatment interaction is operating and this may be a threat to external validity.

The data analysis of the time design with a control group can be extended to comparisons between the two groups. Such comparisons are in addition to the between measurement, within the groups, comparisons. The difference between the statistics of the two groups can be plotted over the several measurements. These differences are likely to be linearly related to time. The time design with the control group is especially well adapted for research in the actual school situation. The multiple measurements can be built into the routine testing schedule. The researcher can often locate another class or even another school to serve as the control group.

Any experiment requires some finite amount of time from initiation to completion. The amount of time required varies greatly from experiment to experiment. The time for a specific laboratory task may be relatively short. The time designs may appear to be extended because of the multiple measurements. The blocks of time between measurements are specific to the experiment. However, the longitudinal studies in which Ss are measured at various intervals for several years are generally not considered to be this type of design. In a loose sense, such studies could be considered to be based on time designs, but usually no controlled experimental treatment is introduced. Such studies are often strictly of a non-experimental nature, in which a multitude of factors are operating simultaneously, and experimentation in the formal sense is absent. That is, the researcher is not deliberately manipulating and controlling variables. The time designs in this discussion refer to designs used in an actual pre-meditated experiment.

Nonequivalent Control Group Design

One of the most commonly used experimental designs in educational research is the nonequivalent control group design.[1] In this design, both the group which receives the experimental

[1] Campbell, D. T., and Stanley, J. C., "Experimental and Quasi-Experimental Designs for Research on Teaching," Gage, ed., in *Handbook of Research on Teaching* (Chicago: Rand McNally & Company, 1963), pp. 217–220.

treatment and the control group are pretested and posttested. This design resembles very closely the pretest-posttest control group design but should not be confused with it. The primary difference (and an extremely important experimental difference) is that there is no random assignment of Ss to the groups of the nonequivalent control group design. The groups are taken intact as they exist in some educational setting. Thus, the aspect of sampling equivalence prior to the experiment is missing.

The major threats to the internal validity of a nonequivalent control group design are possibilities of interactions between selection factors and other factors. These interactions might be mistaken for an experimental treatment effect. The external validity of this design may be somewhat questionable. The pretesting gives the possibility of some kind of interaction which would not be present in the nonpretested population. The experiment being carried out in a natural setting lessens the experimental awareness. A selection bias might also be interacting with the experimental treatment. Again, the external validity must be considered in the light of the specific variables and conditions of the experiment.

The real crux of control in the nonequivalent control group design is the similarity between the two groups. The measure of similarity is commonly considered to be the pretest, assuming the pretest has some marked relationship to the dependent variable. It should be noted, however, that the control will not reach the level attained in the pretest-posttest control group design. The occurrence of similar pretest results for the two groups does not rule out the possibility of selection factors interacting with other factors.

Another possible threat to the internal validity of the nonequivalent control group design is regression. Regression has heretofore not been introduced in this context, but the regression effect is a possible threat to validity whenever extreme groups, relative to the dependent variable, are used in the experiment. The regression effect is an inherent tendency for the extreme scores to regress toward the common mean on subsequent measurements. For example, the highest scorer on an I.Q. test would unlikely be the highest scorer on a subsequent I.Q. test. A shift between pretest and posttest scores due to regression could be interpreted as some kind of experimental effect. In designs discussed earlier, the random assignment of Ss is assumed (and rightly so) to control for possible regression effects.

The nonequivalent control group design with its pretests suggests an analysis of covariance as an appropriate analysis technique. If the parametric assumptions can be met, this is certainly a possibility. Caution should be exercised, however. An unreliable covariate or lack of homogeneity of regression can make such an analysis quite dubious. Gain scores between the two test scores can be computed for each S, and some kind of comparison made on the gain scores of the groups. This is usually a less desirable procedure than the analysis of covariance.

The nonequivalent control group design might be strengthened by extending the design to two or more replications of the experimental and control conditions. A disadvantage of this extension is that it quickly runs into large numbers of Ss. Also, because of lack of control, the additional groups may introduce additional uncontrolled factors. For example, suppose several classes were involved in an achievement study. In order to complete the testing, the classroom teachers administer the tests. If any ambiguity or extensive flexibility existed in test administration directions, the experiment would be very susceptible to inconsistent measurement procedures, a most undesirable factor.

The replication of the groups might still be worthwhile, for example, in a study involving achievement of average students. The replicated experimental treatment groups now give an added dimension of comparison. Comparisons between the experimental treatment groups can be made to check the consistency or inconsistency of any experimental effect. It is also unlikely that some extraneous event would affect all experimental groups and be misinterpreted as an experimental effect.

The assignment of the experimental treatment to the groups should, if at all possible, be a random assignment. If several groups of both types are included in a relatively homogeneous situation, factors such as the difference in teachers will tend to be equalized over the experimental and control conditions. If a systematic assignment, such as all the "adventurous teachers" are given experimental groups, is followed, a bias is definitely introduced. For some experiments in which a new teaching technique is the experimental variable, volunteers are recruited from the teacher ranks. This procedure is somewhat dubious, although sometimes a case is presented for teachers being most effective with techniques toward which they are favorably disposed. By this reasoning, the teachers of the control groups are not less effective, since they are using their preferred method. However, they may be more or less effective for other reasons.

A modification of the nonequivalent control group design may be used if an interaction between pretesting and the experimental treatment is likely. This modification requires a minimum of four comparable groups. The groups which are pretested are not posttested and vice versa. Thus, two experimental and two control groups are required. The decision of which group receives the pretest is based on a random selection. No S is tested twice.

As with the usual nonequivalent control group design, this design can be strengthened by extending the number of groups. As the number of groups is increased, the likelihood of a selection interaction with some other factor decreases. The extension of this design involves a marked increase in the number of groups.

The external validity of the nonequivalent control group design with separate groups being pre- and posttested is very good. Since no S is tested twice, there is no possibility of an interaction between the pretesting and the experimental treatment. With the multiple groups, the likelihood of a selection and an experimental treatment interaction is small.

Selection of Subjects

An important aspect of experimental design is the selection of the Ss or the groups to be involved in the experiment. It has certainly been implied in the discussion that it is desirable to have some type of randomization in the assignment. We noted that pre-experimental equivalence of groups is attained by a random assignment of Ss to the groups. Sampling for an experiment is a matter that should be taken seriously. A haphazard or take-them-as-they-come procedure is completely unsatisfactory and essentially invalidates the experiment.

Entire texts have been written on the matter of sampling. Sampling can become very complex, both theoretically and in practice. A few comments are presented here and in a later chapter concerning some of the more common sampling procedures.

The definition of a random sample as given earlier is that all members of the population have an equal chance of inclusion in the sample. Suppose a group of Ss are to participate in an experiment and every S is to be assigned to one of the experimental treatment or control groups. Random assignment means that all Ss, before assignment, have the same probability of being assigned to any one of the groups. A random number table is commonly used to make the assignment. If the experimental design does not exhaust the pool of Ss, those not participating may simply be considered another group.

The procedure of matching Ss, in setting up the groups, has found some use in educational research. Two Ss are matched on some factor, supposedly related to the dependent variable and then one is randomly assigned to the experimental treatment group and the other to the control group. Matching is an attempt to make the groups equivalent prior to the experiment. It should be noted that matching is not a substitute for randomization in establishing equivalence of groups. In some designs it can serve as a useful technique with randomization. As the number of groups increases, matching becomes more difficult. Effective matching requires that the researcher can select relevant matching variables. Trying to match Ss on several variables simultaneously generally meets with very limited success. If the variables are highly correlated it may not prove too difficult, but in that case it would be about as effective to match on only one of the variables.

Threats to Experimental Validity

There are several factors which are possible threats to the validity of any experiment. The specific conditions of the experiment determine the extent to which such factors are an influence on the validity. One of these factors is subject mortality. In a laboratory experiment the conditions may be so structured that all selected Ss participate. It is not serious if a S must be omitted for a reason external to the experiment, especially if the S can be replaced by a comparable substitute. However, if a selective factor is operating among the non-showers, this can be serious.

Experiments carried on with classes should involve no more

absences and dropouts than normal. Suppose the Ss correctly anticipate the posttest date and a group of low achievers are absent at that time. This would certainly bias the results. Mortality may be encouraged if the experimental treatment group is required to attend special sessions. The elimination of non-showers is almost certain to selectively shrink the group. Even if dropout rates in the two or more groups are the same, there may be some type of interaction operating causing differences in the characteristics of the dropouts of the two groups. Any of these difficulties with subject mortality are threats to experimental validity.

Lack of consistency in the administration of the measuring instruments, by threatening the reliability of measurement, is a threat to the validity of the experiment. The lack of consistency could exist between the groups or between administrations of tests to the same group. This problem is minimized when a fixed measurement device such as a standardized achievement test is used with standardized administration procedures. The grading of essay exams is difficult to standardize. The standards may shift between separate administrations or a single scorer may shift in his own scoring. Interviews and direct observations are very susceptible to change between administrations. Interviewers differ both between and within themselves. Maximum standardization without destroying the objectives of the interviews or observations is a necessity. Interviewers or observers should be randomly assigned to Ss or groups.

External events, regression effects, and possible effects of pretesting have been discussed in connection with various designs. Undesirable practice effects may appear as a result of pretesting. With groups lacking in pre-experimental equivalence, differential maturation may take place. *Maturation* consists of processes operating within the Ss that are functions of time. We usually think of maturation as growing older, but it also includes factors such as fatigue. Differential maturation is a likely threat to validity when different aged classes make up the experimental treatment and control groups. The random assignment of Ss is assumed to eliminate differential maturation as a threat to validity.

Inadequate Experimental Designs

There are research procedures in education which seemingly take on characteristics of experiments but in fact are inadequate as experimental designs. These are the procedures termed Pre-experimental designs by Campbell and Stanley[1] and Faulty designs by Kerlinger.[2] Unfortunately these designs are still used in educational research, although with the development of adequate experimental designs, the poor designs are on the decrease. The basic weakness of these procedures is that they are completely or almost completely lacking in control and hence for all practical purposes are entirely void of experimental validity.

A single group, taken intact, pretested and posttested, is an inadequate design. The group receives the experimental treatment between the two testings. No control group is included in the investigation. Thus, there is no comparison group and any number of extraneous factors could have produced the difference between the pre- and posttest scores. These extraneous factors are confounded with the experimental treatment effect.

An attempt may be made to compare the results of the single pre- and posttested experimental treatment group with some group which has previously had the measures but did not receive the experimental treatment. This extension is entirely inadequate. There is still a lack of control. There is no way of certifying that the groups were equivalent at the respective pretest occasions. Attempts at after-the-fact matching is ineffectual. Thus, there is a complete lack of selection control.

A procedure in which there is a comparison made between two groups posttested at the same time is the Static-group comparison.[3] The groups are not pretested and there is essentially no

[1] Campbell, D. T., and Stanley, J. C., "Experimental and Quasi-Experimental Designs for Research on Teaching," Gage, ed., in *Handbook for Research on Teaching* (Chicago: Rand McNally and Company, 1963), pp. 176–183.

[2] Kerlinger, F. N., *Foundations of Behavioral Research* (New York: Holt, Rinehart and Winston, Inc., 1964), pp. 292–297.

[3] Campbell, D. T., and Stanley, J. C., "Experimental and Quasi-Experimental Designs for Research on Teaching," Gage, ed., in *Handbook of Research on Teaching* (Chicago: Rand McNally & Company, 1963), pp. 182–183.

control, except possibly over the measurement, since both groups are measured at the same time. An example involving the use of a static-group comparison would be ascertaining the effects of a college education by comparing measures on incoming freshmen with those of graduating seniors. The experimental treatment is a college education. A selective dropout has undoubtedly occurred in one of the groups, namely the graduating seniors. There is no certification that the groups were equivalent at their respective points in time of college entrance. The experimental treatment spans an interval of such magnitude that a multitude of extraneous factors are likely to be confounded with the experimental effect. At this age level, maturation is likely to have an effect on variables such as social finesse and attitudes.

The posttesting of a single group or single S which has had the experimental treatment is an inadequate procedure for experimentation. There is no pretesting and no control group. Inferences made from the data are based on guesses of what the results would have been if the experimental treatment had been omitted. This is a most unsatisfactory procedure for drawing valid conclusions.

Statistical analyses of the data collected in the inadequate procedures serve essentially no experimental purpose. A serious error is to apply statistical techniques and then interpret them as appropriate procedures. A descriptive analysis of the data may be made and possibly some descriptive statistics of a distribution of scores reported. However, this in itself does not comprise an experiment in education. A perceptive educator might be able to make some subjective inferences from the data, but as an experiment, the inadequate procedures discussed above do not make the grade.

Concluding Remarks

The discussion of this chapter has attempted to give the reader a general overview of experimental design in educational research. The designs presented are general patterns for the pursuit of an experiment. The comments relative to analyses were general, and for a design as it applies to a specific experiment, the details of the analysis would need to be worked out. For example, a very important detail of designs for which an analysis of variance is appropriate is the decision about how many independent variables can be meaningfully and practically included in the same design. In the effort for gaining control and efficiency, designs may become very complex. Entire texts are devoted to the intricacies of such designs.

The distinguishing characteristic of experimental research is the manipulation of variables. The variables are deliberately manipulated and controlled by the researcher. The experimental design provides the structure for the experiment. It might be mistakenly inferred that complexity is a desirable characteristic of an experimental design and that increased complexity is a mark of a sophisticated experimenter. The mark of a sophisticated experimenter is to come up with an experimental design that will do the job. To do the job is to meet the objectives of the research and be adequate for testing the hypotheses. An experiment should have definitely stated hypotheses and the design should test the hypotheses. A meaningful interpretation of the results is a necessary requirement of an adequate design. The statistical analysis of the data is a very intricate part of the design. However, a statistical analysis does not necessarily imply that an experiment has been done. This fact is elaborated on in a subsequent chapter.

At this point, the reader should possess a feeling of the underlying reasoning of experimental design and the logic of the various design structures. Characteristics of a good design were discussed early in the chapter. A well-conceived design will not guarantee valid results. However, an inappropriate and inadequate design is certain to lead to uninterpretable results and faulty conclusions, if any are drawn. No amount of post-experiment statistical manipulation can be brought to the fore that will straighten out an inadequate design. The design is conceived prior to the experimentation and should be carefully planned and applied. There are no post-experiment manipulations, statistical or otherwise, that can take the place of a well-conceived experimental design.

Suggested Study Exercises

7.1 Define the concepts of internal and external validity of an experiment. Why do we say that for some experiments an attempt at increasing one type tends to jeopardize the other type?

7.2 A researcher plans to do an experiment in the school setting concerning the effects of class size upon achievement in chemistry. He defines class size as an independent variable and has four levels of size, namely, 12, 20, 30, and 38 students. Four high schools are involved in the study, each having eight chemistry classes, two of each class size. The researcher can assign students at random to a class within a school but he cannot assign students randomly to a school. Two chemistry teachers are used in each school; all teachers teaching four classes. The dependent variable is chemistry achievement measured after an instructional period of one semester. Discuss the aspect of control in this situation. Consider possible uncontrolled variables and variables which are or might be controlled. Is there a possibility of confounding of variables in this research situation? Suppose that chemistry achievement is measured on an interval scale. State one or more hypotheses for this experiment and suggest an appropriate analysis technique. Discuss one or more experimental designs which would apply to this situation.

7.3 Discuss two methods by which experimental control over extraneous variables may be increased.

7.4 Discuss in detail an example of an experiment for which the posttest only control group design is appropriate. Consider such points as why you would not need pretests and the number of groups you would include (you may want to extend the design to more than two groups). Identify how you are enhancing control in your proposed experiment. Also identify the independent variable(s), dependent variable(s), and constants.

7.5 A researcher is doing an experiment on problem solutions. The experiment is done in a learning laboratory. The Ss for the experiment are college students enrolled in a sophomore level education course. The problems, although similar, are of two types: geometrical and algebraic. Type of problem is an independent variable. Other independent variables are sex of the student and group size. There are two group sizes: individual and pair. The dependent variable is number of errors to solution and this is considered to be measured on an interval scale measurement. There are 160 Ss (96 girls and 64 boys) available for the experiment. Each S is to solve only one problem. Present a factorial design that would be appropriate for this experiment. Discuss how you would assign the Ss and how many would be assigned to the various cells. How would you build randomization into the assignment? Identify the null hypotheses for the main effects, that is, the three independent variables.

7.6 Suppose in the factorial analysis of Exercise 7.5 a significant interaction is found between the independent variables of group size and sex of student. What does this mean that such an interaction exists? Present a possible plot of the means of the four groups involved and interpret your plot.

7.7 Discuss the gains of internal validity when going from the pretest-posttest control group design to the Solomon four-group design.

7.8 To ascertain the effect of Boy Scout training it is proposed to measure a group of fourteen-year-old Boy Scouts and a group of eight-year-old boys who have not yet had Boy Scout training. The boys are measured at the same time on proficiency in various skills. This is not a true experimental situation, but what design is being applied? Discuss the weaknesses related to experimental validity.

7.9 A teacher is interested in the effects of the use of programmed learning materials as supplementary aids in an advanced algebra course. He is interested in the amount of algebra learned during one semester of instruction. There are 83 students enrolled in four advanced algebra classes that are taught by this teacher. These students make up the Ss for the experiment. One group of students has access to the programmed materials and the other has not. Suggest an experimental design that would apply to this situation. Is it necessary that the teacher use a pretest? Consider the matter of control. What procedures would be necessary for adequate internal validity? Comment on the external validity of this experiment.

7.10 Discuss an experimental situation for which a counterbalanced design would be applicable. We say that multiple-treatment interference is a threat to validity when using a counterbalanced design. What does this mean?

7.11 Discuss the differences between "true" experimental designs and quasi-experimental designs. Discuss some of the difficulties introduced when less than a true design is introduced.

7.12 A researcher desired to do a study of the effects of individual versus massed practice on fifth-grade spelling achievement. He found three elementary school principals willing to cooperate and then allowed the fifth grade teachers to use the method they preferred. (A single teacher used only one method.) After an eight week period, which began about November 1st, the students were given a common spelling test. Discuss the experimental errors in the above procedure. Comment on both internal and external validity for this situation.

7.13 A teacher does a research study on third grade reading achievement with a class. Two methods of instruction are used, but not simultaneously. The students are tested every four weeks and a particular method is used for a four week session. The methods are randomly assigned to the four week instructional periods and the procedure continues for the school year. What type of design is being applied in this situation? Discuss its weaknesses and advantages. What might be a special measurement problem that might arise? Assuming the parametric assumptions discuss possible analysis techniques.

7.14 Summarize the general characteristics of a well-designed experiment.

7.15 Select one or more research articles which involve experimentation from such publications as the *Journal of Experimental Education* or the *Journal of Educational Psychology*. Read the article carefully to determine the design used, the methods and adequacy of control, and the analysis procedures. Comment on the experimental validity of the study.

8 *Non-Experimental Research*

The experiment is not always an appropriate technique in educational research. There are many variables in the educational setting which, because of their nature, cannot be manipulated by the researcher. For example, intelligence, aptitude, socioeconomic background and the like cannot be randomly assigned to Ss and manipulated in an experiment. This chapter deals with procedures which are not experimental in nature but can be used as research tools. To be sure, experimental research, with its high degree of control and subsequent unambiguous (relatively) interpretation, can be very valuable. However, it is not a matter of choosing sides and getting two camps — one experimental and the other non-experimental. Non-experimental research can be well done and also make very valuable contributions to the field of education. Each type of research has its place in the educational context.

Ex Post Facto Research

The first type of non-experimental research discussed in this chapter is *ex post facto* research. There is some ambiguity as to the definition of this type of research. However, for the purposes of this discussion we will use the definition put forth by Kerlinger. That definition as given is:

> . . . research in which the independent variable or variables have already occurred and in which the researcher starts with the observation of a dependent variable or variables. He then studies the independent variables in retrospect for their possible relations to, and effects on, the dependent variable or variables.[1]

This is actually a broad definition of *ex post facto* research. The reader is reminded that other definitions may appear in educational literature.

The definition forcefully implies a lack of control over the independent variables. The independent variables exist in the situation and are not placed there or manipulated by the researcher. If the researcher draws a sample from a larger population, the sample should be drawn at random. However, there is a difference between drawing Ss at random and assigning Ss at random for experimental treatments. Suppose a study was being done on the divergent thinking abilities of high school students in New York and Los Angeles. "City" here takes on the characteristics of the independent variable. It would not be possible to randomly assign high school students to the cities. The students have, in essence, self-selected themselves by living in their respective cities. However, since it is unlikely that it would be feasible to measure all the high school students of both cities, random samples would be drawn. Thus, in *ex post facto* research

[1] Kerlinger, F. N., *Foundations of Behavioral Research* (New York: Holt, Rinehart and Winston, 1964), p. 360.

the researcher does not possess the option to randomize in the experimental sense. Randomization comes in through the sampling process.

The matter of self-selection introduced above requires close attention. Often the groups under study are designated because they differentially possess certain characteristics. Such characteristics may be extraneous to the research problem but may in fact have an effect upon the variables under study. Suppose a study was being conducted dealing with mental retardation and the Ss under study were divided into two groups — those mentally retarded and those not. Now the presence or absence of mental retardation becomes the dependent variable and the Ss have self-selected themselves into the two levels. Suppose that the researcher discovered that the incidence of extremely high fever in connection with childhood diseases was considerably greater for the mentally retarded group. He might conclude that high fevers caused mental retardation. Maybe a statistical test for the difference between the proportions of high fever for the two groups was significant. The researcher can conclude that there is a relationship between the two variables, but not the causal connection that high fevers cause mental retardation. The reason for this is that there are any number of other variables which singly or in combination could have caused the mental retardation.

A structure which resembles an experimental design may be superimposed upon the data, primarily for analysis purposes. Obviously the analysis technique and the computer do not know the source of the data. The superimposed structure should not be misinterpreted to be an experimental design. Note that in the definition a retrospective search for the independent variables is implied. The independent variables may be identified, usually before the data are collected, but because of the lack of control, it is very tenuous to conclude that a causal connection exists between the independent and dependent variables. In most situations there are several uncontrolled extraneous variables. While due to the control in the experimental studies, a direct effect may be concluded, in the *ex post facto* investigations this is much more of a gray area. Thus, the researcher runs a relatively high risk of misinterpreting his results if he begins concluding cause and effect relationships. The naive researcher, completely oblivious to the variables operating in the situation, is very likely to reach tenuous and unfounded conclusions. The researcher should be sensitive to alternative explanations of the results.

Ex post facto research should be carried on in the framework of some defined hypotheses and related theory. Unfortunately, this is not always the case. Sometimes data are collected with apparently no other direction than to see what it looks like and to see what comes out of it. Such studies, undirected by hypotheses, are *ex post facto* in nature. However, this is usually a less efficient and less desirable approach than using defined hypotheses in conducting the research.

An example of *ex post facto* research was a study of characteristics of college students in the United States and British Isles.[1] This was a cross-national study in which the two cultures or countries comprised the two levels of at least one independent variable. Additional independent variables were identified, such as type of college, either public or private, size of student enrollment, and regional location of the college. (Many more independent variables could have been identified.) In most large-scale *ex post facto* studies, several dependent variables are also included in the same study. The dependent variables of this study included performance on achievement measures and scores on attitude inventories. These were called the "characteristics" of the students.

It is quite apparent that college students cannot be randomly assigned to the country in which they attend college or to the type of college they attend. In this sense they have self-selected themselves. Within a country it would be very likely that some kind of selection factors would be operating in terms of type of college. In looking at the student samples of private and public institutions of higher learning, it would be impossible to make a convincing case for the fact that these two populations are random selections from a common population prior to their entry into college. The Ss of the study could be classified in terms of

[1] Dickson, G. E., *et al.*, *The Characteristics of Teacher Education Students in the British Isles and the United States*, USOE, CRP 2518, The University of Toledo, 1965.

the independent variables (assuming unambiguous definitions) but not randomly assigned to the levels of these variables.

The data of a study such as the one discussed above, assuming adequate sampling, measurement, and data collection, could reveal whether or not the college students of the two countries differ significantly on the dependent variable or variables. If the parametric assumptions are tenable, a Student's t-test could be used to test the null hypothesis of no difference between the countries. If additional independent variables were included, an analysis of variance would be a more likely technique. However, it should be carefully noted that to say that the college students of the two countries differ does not reveal why they differ. Now the search begins for cause and effect relationships between the independent and dependent variables. The differences between countries, which might bring about a difference in college student characteristics, are many. The point of embarkation upon the retrospective search would undoubtedly begin with an analysis of basic differences in the college programs of the two countries. But there are any number of other variables, any one of which singly or in combination with others could have brought about, or at least contributed to, the difference. For example, the domestic financial situations may be such that the majority of the students in the two countries come from basically different backgrounds. Also, motivational factors may differ widely between the two countries. Alternate explanations would be plausible and should be entertained as possible explanations of the results.

Two or more independent variables might be identified and the data analyzed by a factorial analysis of variance, for example. It would be easy enough to classify the students on such variables as country and population of metropolitan location of the college. Classification on variables such as type of college or type of program may not be as straightforward, due to lack of consistency in the meaning. However, operational definitions could be developed for the purpose of classifying the students. In any event, an analysis of variance could be computed and main and interaction effects determined. Again, the definite cause and effect relationship is not clear. Main effects might be the cause of extraneous, confounded variables. Any interaction effect might be the result of one or more unidentified variables. The more complex analysis would undoubtedly give a more precise estimate of within variation and thus result in a more powerful statistical test than a Student's t-test.

Although there is considerable risk of misinterpretation, *ex post facto* investigations can make valuable contributions to educational knowledge and improvement. A large portion of educational research is *ex post facto* in nature. Many non-experimental, empirical studies provide a considerable amount of information, even if cause and effect relationships are not definitely established. In the cross-cultural example discussed above, it might be important to know if and how the student characteristics differ even if we do not know precisely why they differ. Sometimes educational investigations begin on the assumption that a difference exists without any empirical evidence that this assumption is tenable. It behooves researchers to have evidence about the facts of a situation before an attempt is made to explain the situation. Otherwise the researcher runs an additional risk of trying to explain a situation which does not even exist. Such a procedure really goes out of the realm of research and into pure conjecturing or guessing. Conjecturing about the interpretations is tenuous enough without conjecturing about the results.

Ex post facto investigations can be improved by adhering to some relatively simple guidelines. Hypotheses should be stated and tested whenever possible. The study should state alternate hypotheses and whenever possible these hypotheses should be tested as well. The researchers should be extremely cautious in interpreting the results. A thorough knowledge of the independent variables in the context of the dependent variables is essential and will tend to guard against profuse and improper interpretations. Any conjectures should be recognized as just that. The researcher should recognize the empirical results of the study and, if necessary, should limit the discussion to these results in preference to pursuing conjectures for which there is little or no basis.

Correlational studies often take on characteristics of *ex post facto* research. A group of Ss are observed on two variables, the variables to be correlated. There is no prior manipulation of variables and no random assignment of Ss to experimental treatments. If the researcher plans to generalize to a larger population, the Ss observed would comprise a random sample from the population. Suppose a substantial correlation is found between the two variables. This does not necessarily imply causation. In the non-experimental setting, alternate explanations involving uncontrolled variables cannot be experimentally discounted. Thus, the relationship which exists between two variables may be caused by one or more other variables. The lack of correlation between two variables certainly lessens the credibility of a causal hypothesis. A high correlation, on the other hand, has allowed the causal hypothesis to survive this first possibility of disconformation.

It should be noted that correlational studies are not necessarily *ex post facto* in nature. The correlation coefficient might be another measure taken on the experimental and control groups of designs such as those discussed in Chapter 7. If two dependent variables were observed, it would be possible to consider the difference between the correlation coefficient of the two groups. We could compute a statistical test for such a significant difference in a manner similar to, say, testing for a significant difference between means.

Sampling from Large Populations

The next non-experimental type of research to be discussed is survey research. However, between the discussions of *ex post facto* and survey research, it is appropriate to make some additional comments on sampling. In many cases, for both *ex post facto* and survey research, relatively large populations are studied. The measurement of the entire population is often a practical impossibility, hence the selection of a sample. The usual criteria for selection is that the sample be a random sample. The selection of a random sample from a large population may be an extensive task involving quite sophisticated techniques. For example, in selecting a random sample of United States college students, how are we to insure an equal probability of selection for all students? There are often practical restrictions on the sample, such as the number of colleges that can be included. Thus, the matter of sampling, always extremely important when used, may take on an especially important role because of its complexity. In fact, one of the major contributions of survey research has been its contributions to both the theory and application of sampling.

If a finite population is relatively small, readily accessible, and homogeneous, a simple random sample would be feasible. To meet the criteria of a random sample, each member of the population would have the same probability of inclusion. (If sampling from a finite population without replacement, every possible sample of a given size would have an equal probability of inclusion.) The probability would equal the sampling fraction. The sampling fraction is the ratio of sample size to population size.

Stratified Random Sampling

The population may not be homogeneous but in essence consist of several subpopulations. Rather than select randomly from the entire population, the researcher might use stratified random sampling. This in essence involves separating the population into its subpopulations or strata. Once the strata allotments have been determined, the selection within the strata is random.

The decision must be made as to the numbers, that is, allotments, that will be selected from each stratum for the sample. One method is to use *proportional allocation*. With this procedure, each stratum contributes to the sample a number proportional to its size in the population. For example, if stratum A contains one-fourth of the population, then one-fourth of the sample members will be drawn from stratum A.

Stratified sampling guards against wild samples. It insures that no subpopulation will be omitted from the sample. It guards against overloading in certain subpopulations. Simple random samples have a tendency to distribute themselves according to the population proportions. Stratified random sampling with proportional allocation will build this proportionality into the sample.

Another advantage of proportional allocation may be realized if there is considerable variability between strata means relative to the variable under study. Proportional allocation will make the estimate of the variance of the estimate of the population mean [1] more precise. What this means is that it will make this estimate of the variance smaller. The estimate of the variance of the estimate of the population mean under simple random sampling contains a component due to the variance between strata means. Proportional allocation removes this component. Thus, in constructing confidence intervals for the population mean, the estimate of the variance from proportional allocation would produce an interval with a smaller span. The result is a more precise interval-estimate of the population mean. This is an example of an outcome of using a more precise estimate of the variance. If there is no difference between strata means, there is no gain in precision in going from simple random sampling to proportional allocation.

A second method of allocation is *optimum allocation*. In optimum allocation, the strata contributions to the sample are proportional not only to the strata populations but also to the strata variances. (In determining strata sample sizes, they are proportional to the products of strata population sizes and strata standard deviations.) With all other factors held constant, the strata with the larger variances will contribute the greater numbers to the sample. Optimum allocation requires a prior knowledge or at least a good estimate of the variances of the individual strata.

The gain in going from proportional to optimum allocation is again a gain in precision. If the strata variances differ, the estimate of the variance of the estimate of the population mean under proportional allocation contains a component due to the variance in the strata variances. Optimum allocation removes this component, thus giving a more precise estimate of the variance of the estimate of the population mean.

The use of proportional allocation requires information about the relative sizes of the strata in the population. Preferably, the

---

[1] The population mean is a parameter and therefore has no variance. However, since we are sampling and presumably using inferential statistics, we would be estimating the population mean from the sample data. This estimate of the population mean has variance and we would also be estimating this variance from the sample data. Hence the somewhat cumbersome wording.

exact population numbers or good estimates of these numbers should be available. In addition to the size information, optimum allocation requires good estimates or exact values of the variances of the strata in the population. The use of poor or inaccurate estimates may result in a sample such that the estimate of the variance of the estimate of the population mean becomes inflated rather than more precise.

The choice of sample size is, more often than not, an arbitrary choice dictated by available resources. However, the idea of precision as reflected in the proportional and optimum allocations may provide a rationale for the sample size. If the researcher has some basis for designating a desired precision and the variance information is available, a necessary sample size could be computed. This sample size is the size necessary to attain the desired precision. If the variance information is not available, a sample may be drawn and the sample variance used as an estimate. Additional members are then selected for the sample if necessary.

Systematic Sampling

The use of *systematic sampling* is quite common in educational research where large populations are studied, and alphabetical or possibly other lists of the population members are available. Directors of institutional research often use this technique in selecting a sample. The primary advantage of systematic sampling in educational research is one of convenience.

The method of systematic sampling is a procedure by which the selection of the first sample member determines the entire sample. The members (that is, their names or type of identification) are in some type of order. For example, the names of the population members may be placed in random order on a list. The sample size is chosen and the sampling fraction determined. Let us say the sampling fraction is $1/k$. Then the first member of the sample is randomly selected from the first k members of the population as they appear in the order. Following this first selection, every k^{th} member of the population is selected for the sample.

In terms of simple random sampling, systematic sampling

greatly reduces the number of different possible samples. In fact, with systematic sampling only k different samples are possible. The case for systematic sampling in educational research rests upon the justification for considering the sample to be a random sample. This consists of making a case for the assumption that the population as ordered for the selection is in random order.

The most serious and really the only threat to systematic sampling is the existence of periodicity in the population order that is reflected in the dependent variable. *Periodicity* means that every k^{th} member of the population has some characteristics, unique to only those members, which are related to, or have an effect upon, the dependent variable. In that case, the sample estimates are entirely in error. If the researcher suspects the existence of periodicity, he should take additional samples or use another sampling method. If no periodicity exists and the population is assumed to be in random order, the sample may be considered a random sample.

Periodicity may inadvertently enter into the order of the list. Suppose a sample of fifth graders is being selected from a large school system population. The sample is to be measured on an ability test in order to estimate the ability level of the fifth-grade population of the school system. The researcher in charge of the study decides to take a one-in-thirty sample and notes that he can conveniently use class lists. The fifth-grade classes all contain 30 or very close to 30 students. The researcher calls for class lists but the fifth-grade teachers, instead of sending alphabetical lists, send lists on which the student names in each class are arranged from high to low, according to performance on a recent achievement test. The researcher puts the lists together, one class following another, and selects his systematic sample. Since achievement and performance on an ability test are quite conclusively related, marked periodicity has entered into the sampling list. Suppose the first random selection would give the third name on the list, meaning the 3rd, 33rd, 63rd, etc., students on list would comprise the sample. This sample would differ from other samples, especially those beginning with names such as the 26th on the list. Any list used for systematic sampling should be checked carefully to determine how the list is ordered.

Cluster Sampling

Cluster sampling is a method which has found some use in education. It is commonly used when entire schools or classrooms are to be included in the sample. An entire group or *cluster* is taken as a unit. The clusters are randomly selected from the larger population of clusters. Once a cluster has been selected, all the members of the cluster are included in the sample. A cluster is not to be confused with a stratum. Usually all strata are represented in a sample, if stratified sampling is used, and selections are then randomly made within strata. In cluster sampling, the randomization appears in selecting the clusters. There is no random selection within clusters. All individual members of the selected clusters are measured on the dependent variable.

Sampling Through an Intermediate Unit

The technique of sampling through an intermediate unit is practically a necessity in some educational research studies. In the cross-national example discussed under *ex post facto* research, the individual college students were the primary units of the study. However, the students attended colleges and the practical considerations of the study limited the number of colleges that could be included. The colleges became the intermediate units in the sampling procedure. The probability of a student being included now involved two probabilities: the probability of his college being selected and his probability of inclusion if his college was selected. In a probability sense, we can consider these two selections as independent events. Thus, the student's probability of selection was the product of these two probabilities.[1]

---

[1] This is somewhat analogous to the situation in which we determine the probability of getting two consecutive 6's on two rolls of a single unbiased die. This probability is 1/6 times 1/6 or 1/36. If we do not get a 6 on the first roll we have no chance of getting the two 6's. By the same token, if a student's college was not selected he no longer could get into the sample. If we have a 6 on the first roll we still need a 6 on the second to meet the criterion of two 6's. If a student's college was selected he must still be selected from his college population in order to get into the sample.

The selection of the sample requires information about the number of primary units in each of the intermediate units of the population. One selection procedure is to list all the intermediate units and select the sample of intermediate units, with probability proportional to size. By algebraic manipulation it can be shown that this selection procedure requires the selection of an equal number of primary units from each of the intermediate units.

The order of listing the intermediate units, prior to their selection, requires some aspect of randomization. If there are stratifying variables which subdivide the intermediate unit population, it may be well to order the intermediate units by strata. The order within strata should be random. The stratifying technique will insure that no strata are inadvertently missed and also that the strata will have proportional representation.

Special problems may arise such as what to do if a small intermediate unit is selected and it does not have sufficient primary units. Another problem might be a very large intermediate unit that is selected twice. The resolution of these problems should be considered prior to selecting the sample. There are alternative procedures which can be used. For example, if a large intermediate unit is selected twice, a double sample of primary units could be selected within the intermediate unit; or a single sample; or a sample proportional to its size. Unique characteristics of the research study may influence the type of procedure most appropriate.

The intermediate units in a large-scale study are often of such a nature that all those selected will not choose to participate. This is especially true for educational research when the intermediate units are individual colleges, school districts, or schools. Thus, a selection procedure for alternates is necessary. Again, this procedure should be developed prior to selecting the initial sample. Suppose that the intermediate units have been ordered by strata and then randomly listed within strata. If an intermediate unit chooses not to participate, it can be replaced by the unit immediately following it on the list. This retains the unit within the original stratum. If the intermediate unit being replaced happens to be the final unit of the stratum, the immediately preceding unit may be used as a replacement if the researcher wants to make the selection within the same stratum.

The matter of sampling is an important aspect of any research study in which we hope to generalize from a sample to a population. The idea of random sampling is relatively simple. The procedures necessary to achieve random sampling may not be at all simple. The foregoing discussion is essentially a brief definition of some of the more common techniques. For detailed procedures when applying a specific technique, the researcher should consult texts devoted to sampling theory and procedures.[1]

Survey Research

A large number of studies in education are conducted to determine the status quo. Such studies go by names such as school surveys, status surveys, or just surveys. They are studies which are not concerned with the manipulation of variables. A school survey often includes the gathering of facts, such as number of students that eat in the school cafeteria, number of students who ride the buses, average student load per teacher, etc. Under a broad definition of research such surveys might qualify, but in many instances they take on more of the characteristics of skilled clerical work with sorting and tabulating. In large status studies for which sampling is used, the most sophisticated part is often the selection of the sample. School surveys provide many facts which are not only important but necessary to the educational enterprise.

Status studies are certainly not the only educational research endeavors that come under the survey umbrella. Survey has a broader meaning and occasionally some confusion is associated with the meaning of this type of educational research. It remains to define more precisely what is meant by survey and to distinguish between different types of survey studies. Regardless of the type of survey, surveys specifically deal with questions about *what is* rather than *why it is so*.

The status surveys already discussed deal primarily with

[1] Examples of such texts are Cochran, W., *Sampling Techniques*, 2nd ed. (New York: John Wiley and Sons, Inc., 1963), and Kish, L., *Survey Sampling* (New York: John Wiley and Sons, Inc., 1965).

tabulations of tangible variables. Survey research as defined by Kerlinger[1] deals with the incidence, distribution, and inter-relations of sociological and psychological variables. These studies deal with how people feel or perceive and how they be-have, in addition to things such as role and group status. (Both role and group status could be actual or perceived.) The objec-tives of a survey research study might be to determine how the psychological and sociological variables are related. Often the relationships between the psychological (or sociological) vari-ables are studied as well. In any event, there is more involved in what we will call survey research than a tabulation of tangible objects.

Classification of Survey Studies

In educational research we often classify studies according to some criteria in order to enhance definition and understanding. Experimental designs, as discussed in Chapter 7, were classi-fied into various types. One criteria used for classifying experi-mental research was basically the extent of experimental valid-ity of the design. There exist different criteria for classifying types of educational research and survey studies. The classifi-cation schemes are quite arbitrary. For the purposes of this dis-cussion we will use three different criteria. Each criterion will be a dichotomy.

One criterion has already been presented in the definition of status surveys and survey research. This might be called the nature of the variables that are under investigation. If a survey study involves the tabulation of tangible variables it is classi-fied as a status survey. A survey dealing with people's percep-tions and feelings in connection with sociological and psycho-logical variables would be classified as survey research.

A second dichotomous criterion for the classification of sur-veys is the group measured, a sample or a population. We shall refer to these as a sample survey and a population survey. Popu-lation surveys (sometimes called census) can be used effectively

[1] Kerlinger, F. N., *Foundations of Behavioral Research* (New York: Holt, Rinehart and Winston, Inc., 1964), Chapter 22. The definition given by Dr. Kerlinger includes sampling from a population.

with small populations; however, they are rarely used with large populations. It may be physically or financially impossible to include the entire population. In the case of large populations, the time involved in measuring the entire population might actually reduce the accuracy of measurement. That is, during the extended time required for measurement, the population might change with respect to the dependent variable, and the passing of time would reflect a change in the measurement between Ss measured earlier and those measured later in the survey. Thus, a random sample could actually provide greater accuracy than measuring the entire population because it would not contain this effect of the larger time span.

A sample survey involves selecting a random sample and attempting to make inferences about the population from the sample observations. If the entire population is measured, there is no inferential aspect concerning the statistics of the study. It would not be proper to use inferential statistics to generalize to the population when the entire population is included. Descriptive statistics would undoubtedly be used. However, for a sample survey, inferential statistics would be expected to play a major and important role. Surveys often are concerned with large populations and generally a sample survey is more efficient than a population survey.

A third classification of surveys is by the criterion method of data collection. There are several procedures for data collection but for the purposes of this discussion on surveys consider two methods — the personal interview and the mail questionnaire. These types of data collection were introduced in an earlier chapter but they are discussed in greater detail here since their primary use is in connection with surveys. Other data collection procedures, such as a telephone survey, for example, are rarely used in education.

Up to this point we have three dichotomous criteria for the classification of surveys. Any one survey fits into one of the two classifications of each criterion. Thus, when we superimpose the three criteria upon each other, we arrive at a single classification schema with eight mutually exclusive classes or cells. This schema can be represented by a cube partitioned into two parts on each of its three dimensions. Each dimension represents one

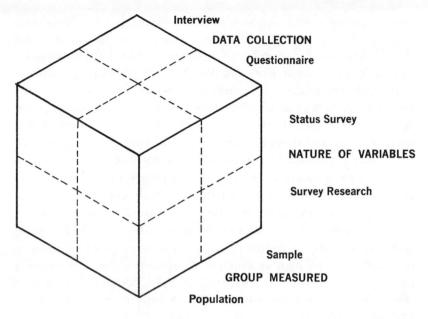

Figure 8.1 Diagram for a two by two by two classification of surveys.

of the three criteria. The classification schema is presented in Figure 8.1. Note that classifying a survey in any one of the eight cells identifies it in terms of all three criteria. Other classification schemes are certainly possible, and this particular system may not cover all possible types of surveys. However, from a practical standpoint, it is adequate for surveys in education.

The three criteria used in the above classification scheme comprise the factors determining the survey. Decisions on these three criteria provide direction for the entire survey. The nature of the variables is essentially the basis for doing the survey. The definition and identification of the variables should be precise enough so that there exists no ambiguity about what is being studied.

The group measured will influence the quantity of data collected as well as subsequent analysis procedures. The analysis for a sample survey will be directed toward inferential statistics while that of a population survey toward descriptive techniques. If a sample survey is done, it may be necessary to apply rather complex and sophisticated sampling procedures. It is not sufficient to open a text and follow some sampling procedure as a recipe. The researcher will have to weigh the advantages and disadvantages of several different procedures and consider available information. For example, if stratified random sampling with optimum allocation is anticipated, are adequate estimates for strata variances available? If any type of stratified sampling is to be used, the stratifying variables must be considered and identified. If a systematic sample is anticipated, the necessary lists must be available and arranged according to the requirements of the procedure. It may be necessary to use some type of "captive" clusters in order to successfully complete the data collection. For example, it might be feasible to administer a questionnaire to entire college classes, whereas mailing it to individual students would result in few returns. The question of whether or not captive clusters would introduce a bias would need to be considered. Attention to many details is required when developing and conducting the sampling procedures for a sample survey.

Interview and Questionnaire — Definitions

Both the interview and questionnaire as data collection procedures were mentioned in Chapter 6. However, the two types of data collection will now be discussed more fully in the context of surveys. These data collection procedures are closely associated with surveys, although they are not necessarily limited to this type of research. The *interview* is a face-to-face confrontation between an interviewer and a S or a group of Ss. It is an oral exchange between individuals. The *questionnaire* is a list of questions or statements to which the S is asked to respond by a written response. A response may range from a check mark to an extensive written statement. In the case of the interview, a response may be limited to a single word, for example, yes or no, or it may require a rather lengthy oral discussion.

A questionnaire is sometimes referred to as a written, self-administered interview, and by the same token we could consider an interview as an oral questionnaire. The two types of data collection have a great deal in common relative to item construction and use. Interview and questionnaire have rather broad meaning in educational research. The author recognizes that there are other definitions for these terms. Since there is some ambiguity associated with the terminology, the reader should check the definitions in any discussion.

Use of Interviews

The interview has the advantage of being a flexible measurement device. The items of the interview usually contain open-ended questions to which the S can offer pretty much of a free response. An open-ended question is one for which the S constructs his own response rather than selecting from a group of alternative responses. The interview provides a unique flexibility in that the interviewer may pursue the response with the S. The interviewer may ask for an elaboration or a redefinition of the response if it appears incomplete or ambiguous. Also, the S's response may reveal other factors or feelings which the interviewer can choose to pursue and probe.

Interview items may allow varying degrees of flexibility. Flexibility is basically a matter of item structure. We can put items on a continuum from unstructured to completely structured. An example of an unstructured item would be: What do you think of the honors program in mathematics? A partially structured question would be: What do you think about the effectiveness of the mathematics honors program relative to advanced placement in college? A structured question would be: Do you feel that the present honors program in mathematics should be (a) continued without modification, (b) continued but modified, or (c) discontinued? For the above example questions, the term "honors program in mathematics" is assumed to refer to a specific program with which the respondent is familiar. The items of a single interview would undoubtedly vary in degree of flexibility. Items may follow some type of sequence, in which they become more structured as the interviewer focuses on specific feelings or points. Flexibility and the opportunity to probe are two desirable characteristics of the interview and should not be eliminated by overstructuring the items.

The interview may be applicable as a data collection procedure when other procedures are not possible. An illiterate or near-illiterate could not respond to a written inventory. A study involving the responses of educationally disadvantaged adults might require an interview, since motivation for responding to a written inventory might be entirely lacking, even if the items were written in a manner that the respondent could understand.

The interview is well suited for probing the feelings and perceptions of the Ss. However, the items of the interview itself will not insure accurate measurement of these feelings. Obviously, the S must be able to respond accurately with adequate oral expression. Not only must the S be able to respond, but he must also be willing to do so. Difficulties arise if the S does not have the information necessary to answer the question, or if he feels uneasy about divulging the information. A S may misunderstand the question or misinterpret the type of response needed. The interviewer must be able to recognize misunderstanding and uneasiness. He must be able to make on-the-spot decisions as to what the S is saying and what additional probing is necessary.

The interview is a face-to-face confrontation between individuals. As such, a good rapport is essential between S and interviewer. Perceptive probing is of little value if some hostility has developed and the S will not respond accurately. Usually the interview begins with gathering factual information about the S and it is during this period that the rapport of the interview is established. Personal and controversial questions generally appear later in the interview, if they appear at all. The timing and inclusion of such questions must be left to the judgment of the interviewer. The interview should proceed in a businesslike manner with a friendly atmosphere, but excessive informality should be avoided.

The data of the interview are the responses of the S. The question arises as to whether or not the S is telling the truth. Does he really feel the way he says he feels? Reliability of the data is always a potential problem when conducting an interview because an interview can be faked. Any of several factors may threaten the reliability of the data: the S may be inclined to give a response that he thinks is socially or professionally preferable, regardless of the way he really feels. The S may have suspicions about the interviewer or the reason for being interviewed that influence the reliability of his responses. Personal or controversial information may not be readily forthcoming. If the S is forced (or feels that he is forced) into responding when he does not have adequate background or does not want to reveal the information, he is likely to prefabricate responses.

There is no methodological technique that can insure the reliability of the data. However, it may be possible to enhance truthful responses and to construct somewhat crude reliability checks. The interviewer must be careful not to imply preferable responses. Controversial questions should be avoided until the proper background and rapport have been established. In the context of the interview, the interviewer may form an opinion of whether or not the S is telling the truth. It may be possible to construct questions which check on the consistency of responses. The observation of past, present, or future behavior may provide a possible reliability check. For example, if a S responds very favorably toward building new schools and then vigorously campaigns against a school bond issue, his responses might be questioned. The direct observation of behavior in this context is not always possible, and even if possible, may be prohibitive in terms of time and effort.

The data-recording of the interview should be efficiently structured so that it does not interfere with conducting the interview. If tape recorders are used, the entire oral communication is retained. However, taping an interview requires special equipment that is not always available. Therefore, in many studies involving an interview, shorthand records of the interview must be developed. Structured questions may require only a check mark indicating one of several alternative responses. The responses to unstructured questions should be recorded briefly but completely, covering all main points. The recording of data should be as unpretentious as possible and should not arouse suspicions in the S. For example, if the S gives a short response, the interviewer should not engage in extensive writing. The materials for data-recording should be arranged prior to the interview so that there is no confusion on this matter.

All of the activity of conducting an interview requires that the interviewer be well trained in the procedures. The interviewer should be well informed about the variables under investigation

so that he can make perceptive probes. There should be a training period for the interviewers. If there is no training period,
the early interviews essentially become the training sessions
and may differ in style and competency from the later interviews
by the same interviewer. When two or more interviewers are
used for a survey, attention must be given to training for inter-
interviewer consistency. Each interviewer should conduct a
number (depending on the complexity of the interview schedule) of practice interviews so that he has mastery of the technique to be used. During the training period there should also
be some provision for multiple interviewers to interview the
same S independently, in order to check on inter-interviewer consistency. Possibly a single S's responses could be taped and the
responses recorded independently by the two or more interviewers. The records of different interviewers could then be
compared and differences discussed, with the process repeated
until the consistency is judged adequate. The S's responses
should not be a function of the specific interviewer. The requirement of considerable manpower, training, and time is often
viewed as a disadvantage of the interview.

There has been very little said up to this point about the construction of questions for an interview. By no means should the
questions be a haphazard or off-the-cuff collection. The principles that apply to item construction for questionnaires also
apply to interviews. This matter is discussed in greater detail
in the following section.

Use of Questionnaires

The initial task of a survey involving a questionnaire, as in any
research study, is to spell out the objectives of the study. Assuming this task to be adequately done, the researcher is confronted with the task of constructing the questionnaire. The
questionnaire as a whole must cover the objectives by providing
adequate data for the survey. Constructing the individual items
is a task that requires careful attention to detail. As in the case
of the interview, items may range from unstructured to structured. There are several criteria that can be used in constructing items for questionnaires. A discussion of the criteria is presented below.

The burden of communication is upon the questionnaire constructor and once the questionnaire has been sent or administered, there is no longer an opportunity to straighten out any ambiguities. Obviously, ambiguities should be eliminated as much as possible. An item should not include several questions to be answered by one response. For example, "Are you in favor of team-teaching and the use of teaching machines?" If the S responds "no" it is not clear whether he does not favor either one or both, team-teaching or the use of teaching machines. The S may also misinterpret the question to mean that if he favors either or both he should respond yes. Items should be phrased and partitioned so that the response can be definite and there is no confusion as to meaning of a response.

When constructing an item, the question of whether or not the item can convey to the S a meaning different from the intended meaning should be raised. For example, suppose the question of where you teach is posed. The S may conclude that the type of school—elementary, high school, inner city, suburban—is required. Another S may conclude that a geographical region is wanted, and still a third S may give the name and address of a specific school. A S hurriedly responding may simply state that he teaches in a classroom. Such an item would be improved by rephrasing the question as: List the name and address of the school in which you teach. Or, if the type of school is desired, and to avoid confusion as to what criterion is being used to define type, it would be well to provide a set of alternative responses such as: (a) elementary (b) junior high (c) senior high.

The items should not be personally offensive or embarrassing to the S and he should not be asked questions which he cannot possibly answer. The items should fit the informational background of the Ss. Suspicions should not be raised by the items and there should not be an indication of hidden motives for securing the information. Items should not be pedestrian and monotonous nor should they be suggestive as to preference of response. The items should be so constructed that responses will not be superficial but contain adequate depth for the purposes of the study.

When check lists or categories for responses are used, they should be exhaustive and the different possible responses mutually exclusive. For many kinds of items it is necessary to provide a middle of the road or neutral response such as "no definite feeling" or "undecided." This avoids forcing the S to an undesirable choice. Form of response should be straight-forward and uniform.

The items of a questionnaire should be constructed in a manner that facilitates data tabulation. Many times this is simply a mechanical matter of arranging the space for responses appropriately on the questionnaire. Anticipated coding schemes should be developed in advance. For example, responses on a five-point ordinal scale may be assigned numerical codes. If a computer is to be used in the analyses, coding schemes must conform to IBM card formats. The space allotted for open-ended items should conform to the extent of anticipated response. The S may take a cue from the space as to what is expected of his response. Specified space also lessens the likelihood of a rambling response. However, space should be adequate so that the S does not feel restricted in his response.

Before preparing the final form of the questionnaire, the items should be tried out with a small group. This is sort of a pilot run. The group need not be a random sample of prospective Ss, but the members of the group should be familiar with the variables under study and be in a position to make valid judgments about the items. The results of the pilot run should identify misunderstandings, ambiguities, useless items, and inadequate items. Additional items may be implied. Mechanical difficulties in matters such as data tabulation may be identified. Difficulties with the directions for completing the questionnaire may be uncovered. On the basis of the pilot-run results, necessary revisions should be made for the preparation of the final form.

The questionnaire as a whole should be attractive to the S. Certain physical characteristics can be utilized such a multicolor printing that aid in drawing attention and making the questionnaire more appealing. The length should be such that responding does not become a tedious or burdensome task. Unreasonable demands should not be made upon the S's time. The items should be of interest to the S. For many questionnaires, the items follow a logical sequence which, if developed properly, can enhance the interest of the S.

Before the S responds to a questionnaire, he must be introduced to it. The "cover" letter is the vehicle of introduction and it is the device that gets the S to respond to the questionnaire. In a sense, the cover letter is the rapport-establishing device. It is a very important item and should be carefully constructed.

The cover letter should be straightforward and explain the purposes and value of the survey. The S should be made to feel that his response is important. There should be nothing in the cover letter that raises suspicions. The S should be assured that the researcher is interested in the overall responses of the group and that individual responses will not be singled out and associated with the S. There may be a procedure set up by which replies remain anonymous. In any event, the S should be assured that all responses are confidential.

The matter of who signs the cover letter can be of some importance. Response may be improved if the cover letter carries the signature of someone in some way associated (or appears to be) with the Ss. For example, the cover letter of a questionnaire about guidance institutes being sent to guidance counselors might well carry the signature of the institute director on staff at a university that conducts such institutes. A graduate student who sends out a questionnaire, giving as a reason the data collection for a thesis, can expect a limited and disappointing response.

The problem of non-response is often viewed as the primary disadvantage of questionnaire surveys. The problem is what to do in such a situation. Unfortunately, a rather common practice is to ignore the problem which, without preplanning, may be the only alternative. There exist procedures for increasing the number of returns. Often these procedures meet with limited success, but this depends upon the unique conditions of the survey.

The cover letter signature has already been mentioned as having some influence upon the rate of response. The length of the questionnaire also should be considered. Lengthy questionnaires discourage response. If a S can respond in a matter of five minutes, he is more likely to do so than if he must spend an hour or two in order to adequately respond to the items. It may be well to search for items that can be eliminated if a questionnaire seems overly long. Items may be reconstructed to lessen the time of response.

The S should be encouraged to respond immediately to the questionnaire. A deadline of two weeks or a month should not be implied; this will tend to encourage the S to put off responding and, although his intentions are good, he is likely to forget the entire matter. Of course, a self-addressed, stamped, return envelope should be provided. Mechanically, it should be as easy as possible for the S to return the questionnaire.

Follow-up questionnaires are a must for practically any questionnaire survey. The follow-ups should come shortly after the initial mailing and, as in the original cover letter, the S should be encouraged to respond immediately. Follow-ups should be planned in advance and in some cases two or more follow-ups may be desirable. Sometimes an appeal to professional interest is made or inducements such as money or a report of research findings are offered to encourage returns. The use of telegrams, telephone calls, or special delivery letters may prove effective, but expensive. Promised anonymity may increase returns, depending on the type of survey.

Unless the researcher administers the questionnaire to a captive audience and collects them on the spot, some non-response is inevitable and should be anticipated. The researcher should decide in advance what percentage of non-response can be tolerated. This will be determined somewhat by the variables and population under study. Generally 75 per cent is considered a minimum rate of return. The difficulty with a low return rate is that the data may be biased. If this is true, the data do not represent the group under study. For example, suppose a survey on need for mathematics teachers was being conducted on a statewide basis. Most of the small schools for some reason did not return the questionnaire, while large systems did. This could result in an average need (based on the data of the returned questionnaires) of mathematics teachers in excess of the total number of mathematics teachers found in most schools throughout the state. Non-response results in a data gap that may markedly distort the real situation. It is very tenuous to assume that non-response is randomly distributed throughout the group.

The researcher should plan in advance some procedure for dealing with non-response. It may be possible to interview a sample of non-respondents and acquire some information about their characteristics and reasons for not returning the questionnaire. Another alternative is to identify subgroups in the sample (or population) and check if certain subgroups are high in non-response. This procedure does not reveal the feelings of the non-respondents but it does identify the non-responding groups. Non-response may be associated with a certain type of feeling toward the questionnaire items. That is, non-respondents may have what they interpret as unfavorable attitudes toward the items. If this is operating the sample of responses will be definitely biased, since response and non-response is associated with the variables under study. A check of subgroups may indicate this type of phenomenon. However, it does not eliminate or correct it. The researcher will be required to take this into consideration when he reports the results.

One possibility of dealing with non-response when discussing results is for the researcher to calculate the effect on the statistics if all non-respondents had responded in a manner to cause the greatest change in the results. This would be relatively easy to do for items that have only two alternative choices. For example, suppose an item has yes-no alternatives, and 800 out of 1,000 questionnaires sent had been returned. Of the 800, 500 or 62.5 per cent responded "yes." The extremes would be that the 200 non-responders would have all responded either "yes" or "no." If all had responded "yes," the "yes" responses would have totaled 700 out of 1,000 or 70 per cent. If all had responded "no," we still would have 500 out of 1,000, or 50 per cent "yes" response. Therefore, although the actual observed percentage of "yes" response was 62.5 per cent, the range of 50 per cent to 70 per cent represents the possible extremes. The researcher would then take this into consideration when reporting the pattern of results.

The researcher should keep an accurate and complete record of outgoing and incoming questionnaires. Mailing dates, destinations, dates of return, and by whom, should be recorded. Incoming questionnaires should be inspected for ambiguous and incomplete responses. Questionnaires returned late after repeated follow-ups may be inadequate or worthless. The date of return may be a basis for checking bias in the responses. The responses to the various follow-ups should be kept separate and checked against the initial responses for any bias due to persistence. Reluctant respondents, returning their questionnaires late, may be quite different in response than earlier respondents. Factors such as the above may aid in the interpretation of the data.

Methodology of Survey Research

The methodology of conducting a survey involves a series of detailed steps, each of which should be carefully planned. The lack of planning is certain to result in confusion of data collection, unorganized data, and uninterpretable results. The initial step is to define the objectives of the study and to outline the sequential steps of conducting the survey. The definition of objectives should include a good background of the variables to be studied. Variables involved in the survey must be operationally defined. The investigator should have information about the relationships of the sociological and psychological variables from past studies. This information is valuable in constructing the items for the measuring device.

The next step is the development of the sampling plan. (Actually, the initial decision is whether to sample or measure the entire population.) Various factors related to sampling must be considered. The population to be sampled must be defined. If stratification is used, stratifying variables must be identified. Factual information about the population is necessary for the selection of a stratified sample. For example, suppose a sample of teachers is to be selected and a stratifying variable is level taught: primary, intermediate, junior high, and senior high. It would then be necessary to know the proportions of teachers in each of the strata. The individual teachers of the population would need to be identified in terms of the different strata. The overall sampling plan must be operational. The sample selection must be conducted in such a manner that valid inferences can be made to the population and any subpopulations.

Although some activities can be conducted simultaneously,

the construction of the interview or questionnaire items is the next major step. This is often the most difficult and taxing part of the survey. Since it is so crucial to the success of the survey, considerable time and effort should be reserved for this task. Considerable revision of items is commonly involved. The items should be tried out on small groups. If interviews are used, the interviewers will need to be trained. This in itself is no small task.

The analysis procedures should be considered during construction of the items. It is necessary that the items produce data that can be analyzed and analyzed in an analytic manner. The initial questions of both interview and questionnaire often pertain to factual information about the S, such as sex, marital status, etc. This information is important in that it identifies the S in terms of classifying variables for the analysis. For example, if the responses of men and women are to be analyzed separately or comparatively, it is important to know the sex of the S. The final measuring device should reflect the anticipated analysis procedures.

When the measurement instrument is judged to be satisfactory, the data collection begins. It is important to adhere to the sampling plan in collecting the data. If interviews are used, there should be some provision for systematically checking the interviewers. This may be accomplished by having multiple interviews (usually no more than two) of the same S by different interviewers. For example, every fifteenth interview may be checked by having two interviewers interview the same S. It is important that some measure of consistency be taken between interviewers. For certain types of interviews it is well to get a measure of the consistency of a specific interviewer. This may by accomplished by taping subject responses and having the interviewer record the responses on two independent occasions.

The data analysis must of necessity depend upon several factors, but before anything is analyzed the responses must be translated into a form which can be analyzed. This involves some kind of quantification such as assigning numbers to responses. Responses will need categorization. Category systems for open-ended questions will need to be constructed. Such systems may be based on a content analysis of responses or on an a priori basis. The translation of data is known as *coding*. There is usually considerable counting and categorization involved in assembling and coding the data.

The data and corresponding analyses must ultimately take a form that allows the researcher to meet the objectives of the survey. If inferences are to be made to populations, the analyses should provide for making such inferences. A number of separate analyses are commonly conducted on the data of a single survey. Not only separate analyses but different types of analyses may be in order. For example, data comprised of frequencies on factual information items would be analyzed differently than the data of an attitude scale. The former might involve proportions while the latter would most likely involve ordinal scale measurement. If some items involved interval scale measurement and the parametric assumptions were tenable, a parametric technique could be applied. Correlation coefficients are often computed between responses from various items. (These are not necessarily Pearson-product moment correlation coefficients.) Such coefficients indicate the relationship between responses but they do not explain the relationship as a cause and effect situation. Note that determining the relationship deals with the question of what is, not necessarily why it is so. The results of the various analyses are usually synthesized by the researcher. Sometimes multivariate techniques are used for analyzing several variables simultaneously.

The methodology of conducting a survey can be summarized in a flow chart which illustrates the major steps and the sequence of these steps. Although some procedures can be done simultaneously, the various steps do follow a definable sequence. Such a flow chart for the steps of conducting a survey is presented in Figure 8.2. (The details for any specific survey would, of course, be provided at each step such as do we have simple random sampling, systematic sampling, stratified random sampling, etc.) The left part of the figure includes the major steps of the survey. The activities on the right suggest the major procedures that come under each step. In some cases procedures overlap into two steps. Not all of the procedures would necessarily be applicable for a specific survey, for example, training of interviewers is not necessary for a mail questionnaire study.

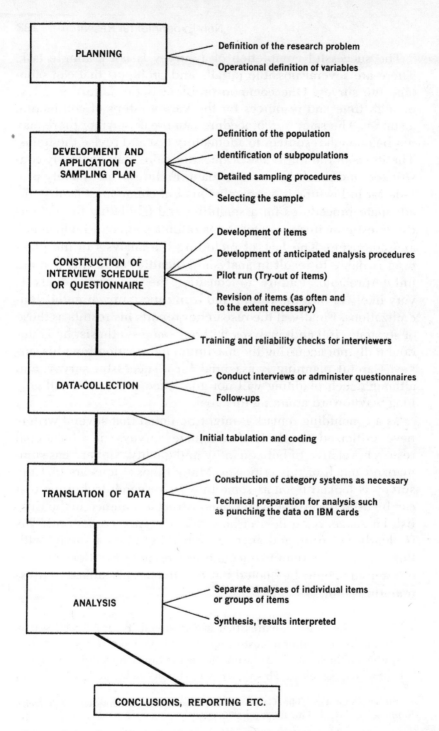

Figure 8.2 Flow chart for the steps of conducting a survey.

The successful completion of a survey is not a simple task. There are several possible pitfalls and problems that can sabotage the survey. One common problem is the failure to allow enough time and resources for the various steps of conducting a survey. The sampling procedure can break down or there may not be enough resources to adequately test and revise the items. The items of the interview or questionnaire may be poorly constructed and result in unusable data. Failure to adequately provide for follow-ups is a very obvious but common difficulty. Inadequate procedures for assembling and tabulating the data as the questionnaires are returned is often a source of inefficiency and confusion. The lack of including the analysis in the planning is liable to result in analysis difficulties or results that are uninterpretable. Failure to consider the non-respondents is very likely to bias the results and bring about unwarranted generalizations. Finally, if the researcher reports his results as those of separate, isolated analyses without some synthesis, he is undoubtedly not acquiring the maximum information from his survey. Careful planning is essential for a successful survey, and although such planning will not guarantee success, it will go a long way toward attaining this goal.

As a concluding remark it might be noted that several writers have criticized the lack of adequate surveys in educational research, relative to both quantity and quality. Sieber[1] has summarized much of this criticism. Many times it appears that the survey is looked upon as some inferior research technique that can be used by anyone who can construct a sentence in the English language, regardless of how that sentence comes out. This is clearly not true, and anyone embarking upon a survey with this concept is certain to encounter extreme difficulties. Numerous authors could be quoted but two quotations suffice to illustrate this point.

Many of the questionnaires that are received by principals, superintendents, and other educators appear to have been thrown together by the graduate student during the short break between lunch and his two o'clock class. This type of questionnaire has led many school

[1] Sieber, Sam D., "The Case of the Misconstrued Technique," *Phi Delta Kappan*, Vol. XLIX, Jan. 1968, pp. 273–276.

administrators to develop negative attitudes about the questionnaire as a research approach.[1]

Too often surveys are made of problems that lead nowhere, that have
no significant purpose or that are oriented toward meaningless topics.
On the other hand, it does not follow that the survey is an inferior
type of research; the concept of inferiority does not belong here since
the answer that is needed depends on the type of question that is
raised . . .[2]

The individual who anticipates doing a survey, as with any research endeavor, should give careful attention to the appropriate
methods and master these methods for the application in his
specific study.

Historical Research

When used in the context of educational research, history may be
defined as "an integrated narrative or description of past events
or facts, written in the spirit of critical inquiry, to find the whole
truth and report it." [3] Since historical research involves a description of past events, there is no possibility of control or manipulation of variables in the experimental sense. The aspect of critical inquiry is an important part of historical research. As control
and manipulation of variables are essential to the experimental
approach, so critical inquiry is essential to historical research.

A review of related literature is necessary for any research
endeavor and in a sense this is historical research. To be sure,
it may be a relatively modest portion of the overall research
project, but nonetheless, a review of related literature serves an
important function. Essentially, it provides a context for conducting the research and interpreting the results. On a larger scale, a
research study consisting entirely of historical research provides

[1] Borg, Walter R., *Educational Research: An Introduction* (New York: David
McKay, Inc., 1963), p. 206.

[2] Mouly, George J., *The Science of Educational Research* (New York: American Book Co., 1963), p. 234.

[3] Good, C. V., *Essentials of Educational Research* (New York: Appleton-Century-Crofts, 1966), p. 145.

perspective for interpreting a part of the contemporary educational context. Historical research provides information that aids in making educational decisions. In order to adequately meet this function, the information must be accurate and viewed in the context of when the events occurred. Historical research requires as demanding standards of objectivity as other methods of educational research. Due to the nature of historical data, that is, events that cannot be observed firsthand, it is often more difficult to meet these standards.

Sources of Information in Historical Research

Historical research concerns the critical evaluation and interpretation of a defined segment of the past. Therefore it is necessary to acquire some records of the period under study. The most common source is some type of written record of the past: books, newspapers, periodicals, diaries, letters, minutes of organizational meetings, etc. However, written documents are not the only sources. Physical remains and objects (relics) of the past are other possible sources. Information may be orally transmitted through media such as folksongs and legends. Pictures, records and various other audio-visual media may serve as sources of information about the past.

The sources of historical information are commonly classified as primary and secondary. A *primary source* is an original or first-hand account of the event or experience. A *secondary source* is an account which is at least once removed from the event. The written record of a war correspondent as he viewed a battle would be an example of a primary source of information about the battle. The memoirs of a general who was not present at the battle would be a secondary source, assuming he reconstructed the battle from the description given him by officers and enlisted men of his command. The writings of John Dewey himself are primary sources of his views, whereas an interpretation of John Dewey by one of his students would be considered a secondary source.

Hypotheses in Historical Research

The methodology of historical research does not consist of the undirected collection of information. A collection of unrelated or loosely related bits of information would not be viewed as a valuable research contribution. The historical researcher will want to use his information to explain and interpret conditions, events, and phenomena that existed during the period under study. As the experimenter works in the context of hypotheses, so the historical researcher also formulates hypotheses to direct his research activities. The hypotheses are attempts at explaining and interpreting the phenomena of the period under study. After the hypotheses have been formulated, the search begins for information that will confirm or reject the hypotheses.

Hypotheses in historical research are usually not stated in a statistical sense. The null hypothesis form is not used in the context of testing hypotheses by statistical techniques as discussed earlier. Rather, in the context of historical research, hypothesis takes on a broader meaning as a tentative statement or conjecture of the situation. In historical research, as in any research endeavor, more than one hypothesis may be used. Some examples of hypotheses in historical research now follow.

Suppose a researcher were conducting historical research concerning the decline of the humanistic curriculum during the seventeenth and eighteenth centuries. Undoubtedly this decline was due to a combination of several factors. One hypothesis might be that the elevation of the common man and his vernacular through the industrial revolution reduced the importance of the humanities as an avenue to culture. A second hypothesis might be that the advances of science made unwelcome inroads into the curriculum and this reluctant acceptance actually was detrimental to the humanities.

It should be noted that the above hypotheses rest on an assumption or fact, that is, that the humanistic curriculum did decline during this period. If this assumption were not correct, the hypotheses would have no basis. Having established any necessary assumptions (or facts) and stated the hypotheses, the researcher would then set out to assemble the necessary information to confirm or refute his hypotheses. In the above case, when dealing with the initial hypothesis, he would look for increased use of the common vernacular in the curriculum materials of the period. The researcher would investigate the different avenues to culture that developed during the period and the relationships between these and the humanities. On the basis of the evidence he would then retain or discard his hypothesis.

Consider a second example. Suppose a researcher is doing historical research on the development of professional education in the United States specifically as it relates to secondary teachers. Undoubtedly there would be several hypotheses but one might be that the teachers college developed as an outgrowth of the normal school, due primarily to the inadequate supply of teachers produced by the colleges and universities. The researcher would then collect evidence about the various possible factors that influenced the development of the teachers college. He would need information about the supply and demand of secondary teachers and how this was related to the numbers of teachers produced by colleges and universities. This hypothesis is based on the assumption that the teachers college was an outgrowth of the normal school. Also, the hypothesis not only considers the inadequate supply as a factor but as the primary factor.

The matter of basing hypotheses on accurate assumptions may seem obvious, but failure to do so is not unknown. A false assumption or misconception is likely to persist in leading to a false conclusion. For example, in the late nineteenth century many liberal arts colleges took the position that it was unwarranted to grant a baccalaureate to graduates of professional schools. This position was based on the assumption that it was not in the tradition of higher education to award bachelors degrees for the profession of education. Careful historical research would have revealed that the arts degree of the medieval university originated almost exclusively for teaching purposes.

Methodology of Historical Research

The methodology of historical research may be summarized into four essentially overlapping steps. Assuming that a research problem has been adequately identified and initial hypotheses formulated, the first step is the collection of source materials. (If the researcher has no information upon which to base initial hypotheses, it may be necessary to collect some source materials prior to formulating hypotheses.)

The second step consists of subjecting the materials to a critical evaluation as to their trustworthiness and value in the light of the research problem. The third step is a synthesis of the information from the source materials. It is at the third step that the hypotheses may be revised or new ones formulated. Additional inferences may be made relative to the problem. Initial and tentative interpretations are made at the third step. The fourth step is a continuation of the third and involves an analysis and synthesis procedure by which the historical researcher rejects or accepts hypotheses, makes final interpretations, and draws conclusions.

Collection and Evaluation of Source Materials

The collection of source material does not consist of simply assembling all available documents, etc., which appear to have some relevance to the research problem. A basic rule of historical research is to use primary sources whenever possible. The researcher must decide which are primary and which are secondary sources. It is not always possible to find primary sources. The source materials must be subjected to external criticism.[1] External criticism is the tool for establishing the validity of the document. The question to be answered: Is the document genuine, authentic, and what it seems to be?

The problem of establishing the validity of materials must concern several possible factors, any of which could make the document invalid. The status of the author (if it is written material) in the context of the event is important. Was the author in a position to make a valid record of the event? Was he an on-the-spot observer, if the document appears to be a primary source? Are factors such as time and place consistent with what is known about the event?

The practice of using ghost writers has been (and still is) quite

[1] Good, C. V., *Introduction to Educational Research* (New York: Appleton-Century-Crofts, 1963), pp. 200–211.

common. Thus, a document which appears to be the product of a direct observer may in fact be a secondary source. The ghost writer's unique contributions may inadvertently or deliberately threaten the validity of the document. There are also possibilities of inadvertent, mechanical errors. A word may be mistranslated or an error made in typing or transcribing documents. For source materials produced before the advent of printing, copy errors in reproduced documents are very likely. (Printing has not eliminated the possibility of such errors but has reduced their likelihood.)

The possibility of deliberate frauds, distortions, and forgeries may be very real. Modern technology has developed methods of checking the authenticity of objects and documents. X-ray and radioactivity procedures may be used in establishing age of the materials. Alterations in the original document may be detected by technological methods. In subjecting material to external criticism, the historical researcher must make a decision as to whether or not he finds the material genuine. Obviously, the researcher cannot relive the experience of when the material first came into being. Thus, the decision is somewhat arbitrary. If the researcher finds damaging evidence, the acceptance of the material is highly questionable. Lack of such evidence does not guarantee authenticity but does have a positive aspect in that the material has survived the initial round of scrutiny.

The second step of critical evaluation is the step of internal criticism.[1] This is the step of establishing the meaning of the material along with its trustworthiness. There may be some overlap between the external and internal criticism, but the shift in emphasis is from the actual material to the content of the material. The external criticism in a broad sense precedes internal criticism in the sequence since there is little point in dealing with the content of the material if its authenticity is doubtful. However, consider the external criticism directed toward the author of what appears to be a historical document. In establishing his status it may very well be necessary to evaluate some of the content that he has written. This essentially becomes internal criticism. The distinction between external and internal criticism is not one of method but one of purpose.

[1] Good, C. V., *Introduction to Educational Research* (New York: Appleton-Century-Crofts, 1963), pp. 211–220.

The author is an important factor in evaluating the content of a document as well as establishing the authenticity of the document. A pertinent question of internal criticism is whether the author was predisposed, because of his position or otherwise, to present a biased rather than an objective account. Biographies and autobiographies may tend to shift the emphasis from the event to the person. Fictitious details may be included by the author because of some personal factor. An author who was opposed to an existing educational policy will tend to emphasize different factors than one who was favorable toward the same policy at the same time. For situations such as this, the position or status of the author is very important in ascribing meaning to his statements.

An analysis of the author's style and use of rhetoric is important in evaluating his statements. Does the author have a tendency to color his writings by eloquent but misleading phrases? Is part of the writing figurative rather than a record of the real event? If the question of figurative and real meaning arises, the researcher must be able to distinguish between the two. Does the author borrow heavily from documents already in existence at the time of his writing? If he does, is his document an objective restatement of the facts or do his own interpretations come into his writings? The latter is more likely the case. The researcher should check the reporting of the author for consistency with the earlier sources. This process should also give indications of the separation of fact and interpretation.

The question of accuracy runs through all of internal criticism (as well as external criticism). There are two parts to the question of the accuracy of a specific author. Was he competent to give an accurate report and secondly, if competent, was he predisposed to do so? A competent reporter may, for some reason, give a distorted account of the event. In checking several authors there may be inconsistencies even about facts such as the date of a specific event. In such a case, the researcher must weigh the evidence and decide upon what appears to be the most accurate account.

A single document, even a primary source, can seldom stand on its own. Internal criticism involves considerable cross-referencing of several documents. If certain facts are omitted from an account, this should not be interpreted to mean that the author was unaware of them or that they did not occur. Each document should be evaluated in its chronological position. That is, it should be evaluated in the light of the documents that preceded it, not in the light of documents that appeared later. If several sources contain the same errors, they are likely to have originated from a common erroneous source. If two sources are contradictory it is certain that at least one is in error, but it is also possible that both are in error. The discounting of one account does not establish the trustworthiness of another. A specific document may prove valuable for certain parts of the overall research problem and essentially useless for other parts.

Synthesis, Analysis, and Conclusions

The business of internal criticism actually carries over into the third step of the methodology, that of synthesis of the information. The researcher now has his materials and, at least to his own satisfaction, has established the authenticity and value of the materials. However, the relative value of the various materials must be considered. As the researcher systematically checks through the evidence on which he will retain or reject his hypotheses, he must weigh the evidence of the various sources. It is a serious error either to overestimate or underestimate a source. The researcher guards against such errors by taking into account the factors used to establish the validity and value of the sources. For example, a primary source may be given more weight than a secondary one.

The researcher is now about to move into the fourth and final step of the methodology of historical research. It should be pointed out that there is no clear-cut separation between the third and fourth steps. Nonetheless, this final step is characterized by final decision making on the research problem. The entire evidence must be weighed, central ideas or points pulled together, and inconsistencies resolved at least to the satisfaction of the researcher.

The researcher must be careful at this fourth step not to introduce a source of inaccuracy that he attempted to detect in other documents by his internal criticism. That is the error of bias. For example, bias could enter if the researcher is partial to a hypothesis and tends to retain the hypothesis even if the evidence points against it.

The problem of avoiding the error of bias is that of remaining objective in analyzing the data. Judgments will need to be made but they should be as objective as possible.

The educational research problems investigated by historical research generally deal with either policy or processes. The nature of history and historical inquiry places this limitation on historical research. In a certain sense the problems investigated by historical research have an ongoing characteristic. Many of the important educational issues are temporarily dealt with by relying on the perspective supplied by the history of the issue. This perspective is acquired through historical research. Curriculum change is often viewed in the light of past philosophy, ideas, developments, and curriculums. Historical research is necessary to define the situation of the past and its meaning in the light of the present problem. Interpretations based on historical research may aid in defining a course of action dealing with a present educational problem.

The historical researcher may be looking for any one or a combination of things in his research endeavor. He may be searching only for accuracy of the facts. More likely, he will be looking for cause and effect situations of the past. He may carefully scrutinize the interactions of two or more relevant factors that were present during the period under study. A valid and adequate interpretation, whether new or old, of some event or idea may be the basic purpose of the research. The specific goals will depend upon the specific research problem. Sometimes problems need redefinition. This could go in both directions — narrowing and broadening the problem. It may be that the initial statement of the research problem is too broad to provide a direction of attack. On the other hand, the available source material may be too limited to provide a satisfactory resolution of the problem. Additional related ideas, points, or topics may be required in order to research the problem adequately. The isolation of the problem may be impossible and a broadening may be necessary for this reason. That is, the materials cannot be adequately evaluated and interpreted without the addition of factors which broaden the original problem.

This has been a brief discussion of the methodology of historical research in education. A good summary of the methodology of historical research is presented in the definition of historical research given by Borg: "The systematic and objective location, evaluation, and synthesis of evidence in order to establish facts and draw conclusions concerning past events."[1] A historical research study involves a great deal of attention to detail. In addition to a knowledge of the methodology, as with any research study, the researcher must possess a background knowledge of the problem. Critical appraisal and adequate evaluation are necessary for historical research. The researcher who is planning to do historical research should prepare himself in the methodology just as an experimenter learns about experimental design.

Concluding Remarks

This chapter has discussed research methodology of a non-experimental nature. Specifically, three broad types of research were discussed: *ex post facto*, survey, and historical research. Other non-experimental methods of inquiry might have been included. Examples of such are case studies and philosophic research. The fact that they are not discussed in this text should not be interpreted to mean that these methods are not recognized as legitimate research methods. Rather, they have limited application in education as research techniques. Case studies, for example, find greater use for guidance and diagnostic purposes than for research purposes.

The research situation in education, as in any behavioral discipline, is one in which both experimental and non-experimental research is conducted. Both types of research have their functions and unique situations of application. Since this is the case, the general question of which type is better is not applicable.

Research methodology should be continually scrutinized for the purpose of improvement and development, whether it be experimental or non-experimental. It would hardly be adequate, in this age of rapid developments, if educational research

[1] Borg, W. R., *Educational Research: An Introduction* (New York: David McKay, Inc., 1963), p. 188.

methodology became static. New techniques are being developed and older ones revised in all types of educational research. New procedures and extensions of existing procedures are continually appearing in the literature. Certainly no one method of educational research has a monopoly on future development and improvement.

Suggested Study Exercises

8.1   A researcher is interested in what effects location of the school, grade level, and sex of the student have upon performance on a critical thinking test. He locates his population, draws a random sample, and measures the sample. Discuss why this is an example of *ex post facto* research rather than an experiment. Assume that the parametric assumptions can be met and suggest possible analysis techniques. If critical thinking cannot be measured on an interval scale, what would be possible analysis techniques? Three grade levels, seven through nine, are used in the study and location of school is defined as a dichotomy: rural and urban.

8.2   Discuss stratified random sampling. Consider the techniques of proportional and optimum allocation. Give an example of a situation for which you would use each technique.

8.3   A study is proposed to determine the mathematics achievement of high school seniors of a statewide area. A sample of seniors is to be measured. Discuss some of the sampling difficulties that would be likely with such a large population. Discuss the possibilities of using stratified or cluster sampling. What would be possible stratifying variables if a stratified random sample were selected?

8.4   The dean of a College of Education is interested in why staff members resign to take other positions. He instructs a research committee to interview *all* resigning staff members with the purpose of determining why they are leaving and hopefully acquiring information which will help retain staff members in the future. With this in mind, plan a structured interview which will secure the necessary information. Discuss the underlying reasoning that would go into the questions of your interview. Suggest possible checks on the validity of the responses. Classify this type of survey in the classification schema presented in this chapter.

8.5 A survey is made of the attitudes of teachers toward the new mathematics. A brief one-page questionnaire of items is sent to a random sample of teachers in a tri-state area. Elementary, junior high and senior high teachers are included in the sample. Discuss a possible sampling technique for this study. Construct three or four items for the questionnaire that might reflect the relationship between the attitudes and one or more other educational variables. Discuss how you would deal with non-response which is likely to occur. What provisions would you make ahead of time for checking the non-respondents?

8.6 Suppose the study of Exercise 8.5 were changed to a status survey, involving the same sample and a questionnaire, with the purpose of determining the number of teachers and the extent to which teachers use the new mathematics in instruction. Construct a short questionnaire (one page or less) of items whose responses are fixed and easily tabulated. With this change in the purpose of the study, do you think your non-responding group would change? If so, how?

8.7 Discuss the advantages and disadvantages of the use of an interview for survey research. Do the same for the questionnaire and then compare the circumstances under which each would be the preferable technique.

8.8 Select an article from a research (or other) publication which deals with an example of historical research. Read the article carefully to detect the methodology used by the author in collecting information and arriving at conclusions. Consider such things as whether or not primary sources were used and the synthesis of the available information. Identify the author's hypotheses and the evidence used in making decisions about the hypotheses.

8.9 The individual who engages in historical research is limited in the matter of validity in terms of the documents from which he acquires information. Discuss possible procedures that might be used in establishing validity of information. Contrast this with the validity of information when conducting an experiment.

8.10 We talk about experimental and non-experimental research. Consider individually and possibly discuss in small groups a criterion for deciding when to use an experimental or a non-experimental approach. Develop some specific points in your criterion.

9 Organizing and Doing a Research Project

The primary emphasis of this chapter is on the steps of carrying out a research project and the order of these steps in doing the research. Many of the comments of this chapter have been made in earlier chapters but are worth repeating here in a consideration of the entire project. The word project has a very broad meaning for this discussion. It can mean any research endeavor from the simplest of short duration, to the most complex and extensive. It should be noted that a short project is not necessarily simple nor is an extended project necessarily complex.

The Need for Organization

The case for organization can hardly be overstated when a research project is to be undertaken. The basic reason for planning and organizing is to facilitate the research. Organization is the map by which the researcher proceeds. Research endeavors have been completed, and with apparent success, which initially seemed lacking in organization. However, the odds are extremely high against the successful and efficient completion of such a project.

Any one research project is made up of specifics. For example, we can talk about the formulation of hypotheses in general, but for a certain project the specific hypotheses are required. These hypotheses specifically refer to the variables, conditions, factors, or Ss of the project. When we speak in terms of generalities, the reader should keep in mind that to complete a research project the generalities must be applied or translated into the specifics. The specifics vary with the nature and complexity of the research study. However, it is the attention to the details of the specifics which brings a research project to a successful conclusion. The specifics must be put together to produce the final product. Organization will avoid haphazard activities when dealing with the specifics.

The novice, or any researcher for that matter, may feel overwhelmed as he begins a research project. The first impulse may be to acquire something tangible, possibly collect some data. To follow such an impulse will very likely lead to an unfortunate beginning. In the interest of efficiency and acceptability (or possibly excellence), one of the purposes of organization is to avoid making mistakes, if not altogether, at least keeping them at a minimum. It is implied that graduate students are very susceptible to making mistakes as they pursue the research for their degrees. It should be hastily added that graduate students have no monopoly on errors. Any researcher is susceptible to errors and the sophisticated researcher will take precautions against making mistakes. Adequate organization is such a precaution, although it will not necessarily eliminate all errors. Possible errors are mentioned at various points in the discussion of this chapter.

(They are mentioned for the purpose of illustration and should not be viewed as an exhaustive list of possible errors.) The mistiming of data collection, mentioned above, is such an error.

An Organization Format

The format presented in this chapter is a general format for organizing and conducting a research project. The author recognizes that there is considerable flexibility in procedure from project to project. In fact, there may be considerable flexibility within a single project. In discussing a general format, the aspect of flexibility should be kept in mind.

The organization of a research project is divided into four general parts, with several subtopics under each part. The subtopics are flexible so that for certain projects their order may be concurrent or even possibly reversed. For example, the delimiting of the problem might involve simultaneous review of the literature. The four major parts would generally follow the order indicated, although there might be some overlap. For example, in a study quite exploratory in nature, some data collection might actually precede the final identification of the necessary data. It should also be mentioned that for certain studies one or more of the subtopics may not apply. Test revision is unnecessary if a standardized test is used for a population or sample for which the test was intended. An outline of the organization of procedures with subtopics is as follows:

I. Identification of the problem
    Review of the literature
    Delimiting and stating the problem
    Identification of independent and dependent variables
    Formulation of hypotheses
    Identification of necessary data
II. Data collection
    Development or selection of the measuring instrument(s)
    Training for data collection procedures
    Pilot study or trial run with the measuring instruments
    Reliability checks and any necessary revision
    Sample selection for the actual project

      Application of experimental treatments
      Data collection for the actual project
      Assembling the data

III. Analysis
      Superimposing the analysis design on the data
      Completion of the actual analysis procedures
      Assembling the results

IV. Conclusion
      Interpretation of the results
      Synthesis
      Preparation for writing

The climax of a research endeavor is usually the writing of a report, thesis, or some other similar means of written communication. This is an extremely important part of research since research findings are of limited value unless communicated to other people. The following chapter is concerned with writing about research.

Identification of the Problem

The clear and concise identification of the problem is not an easy matter. Some research studies are pursued in such a way that it is difficult to determine what the investigator is trying to find out. In fact, the literature contains reports in which the problem is never clearly identified. This may take the form of a study which seems to have no problem but proceeds with little except technical direction. Other studies tend to leave the problem too general, making it difficult to identify the specifics by which to proceed. Either situation is unsatisfactory.

An early task, then, is to satisfactorily identify the research problem. (Several comments were made in Chapter 1 about the statement of the problem.) Initial ideas will require a pulling together and initial statements will need to be revised. The identification of the problem should develop through a background of information. Once the topic of interest has been selected (supposedly the researcher knows what general topic he wants to research), the review of related literature will aid in the satisfactory identification of the problem.

Review of Related Literature

The review of related literature serves multiple purposes when conducting a research project. One use has already been mentioned, that of helping to identify the problem. The review of literature should supply information that will more minutely and accurately describe the problem. Upon the selection of a topic for research, the researcher must determine what has already been done concerning this topic. Additional information may aid in bringing the problem into better focus.

Research is not done in a vacuum. The review of literature provides a setting for the research. The research should fit in the educational context of its specific area and more indirectly in the overall educational setting. If a direct case is not made for the value of the research, such importance should certainly be implied by relating the research to what has been done.

The review of literature should be an enlightening experience for the prospective researcher; although it may not make him a scholar in the area, he can pick up considerable information and ideas. Design and experimental procedures may be implied. Such procedures described in the literature may be the initial step toward worthwhile modifications in the proposed research. The existing literature may give indications as to what are considered orthodox methods. Unanticipated difficulties may appear which can be circumvented if they are revealed by the review of literature. Specific information about the distributions of the variables under study may be valuable in deciding on sample size. Although we usually associate the review of literature with the identification of the problem and the research setting, it can contribute valuable information to any part of the research project. In the time sequence, however, the review comes early and is initially associated with the identification of the problem.

The establishment of the limits of the problem is facilitated by the review of the literature. (The resources for the research project, of course, bear upon the extensiveness of the study.) This is the step of delimiting the problem (stating it in as precise terms as possible). The researcher should be careful that his definitions and terminology are consistent with the literature. If terms are used which have multiple or ambiguous meanings, they should be precisely defined within the context of the research project.

Statement of the Problem

The problem may be identified in the form of a statement, a question, or a series of either. A statement such as "the secondary curriculum" is far too broad to be considered an adequate identification of a problem. To be sure, the investigator may want to pursue a problem in secondary curriculum. A better choice of a topic might be: The effects of two types of curriculum materials upon achievement in geometry at the tenth-grade level. Even this statement might need additional delimiting; for example, if the researcher is proposing to consider only students enrolled in a college preparatory course. The statement of a problem that is too broad will lead to confusion and lack of direction in pursuing the research project.

The choice of form for stating the problem (question or direct statement) is arbitrary. The question may have an advantage in that it is more direct and brings the problem into clearer focus. When stated in question form, the goal of the research is to provide an adequate answer to the question.

The statement of the problem requires additional information for an adequate identification of the problem. For example, the problem mentioned above concerning geometry achievement has no stated hypotheses, although they may be implied. Before an attempt is made at stating hypotheses we need something by which we can express the hypotheses, namely the independent and dependent variables. Other parallel terms might be used for independent and dependent variables in the context of non-experimental research.

The dependent variable implied in the statement of the problem for the geometry example is geometry achievement. However, geometry achievement needs more precise definition. Are the students to be tested only on factual knowledge? Are the students to be tested on some combination or all of the elements that make the discipline—logical reasoning, constructions, proof development, factual knowledge? If all of these areas comprise achievement, are they to be combined or measured separately?

These are examples of questions that must be considered in identifying the dependent variables.

The independent variable implied in our hypothetical geometry example is type of material. Two levels of this variable were mentioned and these would require complete definition. However, there might be other independent variables identified which could be included for control purposes. For example, the students might be classified according to high and average ability. Students within an ability group would tend to be more homogeneous in geometry achievement than those not so grouped. Additional independent variables would have to be clearly defined. It would be an error to ignore relevant factors that could be controlled as independent variables. This is the point in the research activity—to clearly identify the independent variables. It is not good research procedure to leave the identification ambiguous and then attempt to control relevant factors after the data has been collected.

The matter of research design, or experimental design if an experiment is being conducted, begins coming to the fore at this point. The reader might wonder why design is not separately identified in the overall organization since an entire chapter was devoted to experimental design alone. The design is closely associated with the final three parts of the identification of the problem and after that influences and permeates the remaining activities of the research project. The identification of the independent variables raises design questions. For example, what number of independent variables can be simultaneously handled in a meaningful manner? Will the inclusion of certain independent variables alter the appropriate error term if analysis of variance is anticipated? These are questions, the answers to which have direct bearing upon the design. The dependent variable and its measurement have design implications. The practicality of conducting the research influences the design. A design requiring 200 Ss would have little value if only 50 Ss are available.

Formulation of Hypotheses

The intuitive formulation of hypotheses may be mixed in with the identification of the variables. Certainly there would be some idea about what to hypothesize before the variables are specifically spelled out. However, the precise formulation of the hypotheses requires the use of the independent variables or factors under study. The hypotheses as stated also imply the statistics (if sampling is used) and the statistical procedures to be used for testing the hypotheses. The matter of design, which insures that anticipated procedures will adequately test the hypotheses, is important at this point. An error not uncommon in educational research is to state quite complex hypotheses, implying a test for interaction between independent variables, and then realizing that there is no provision for a test of the interaction hypothesis, either because the variables are confounded in the design or separated so that they could not possibly interact. The precise statement of hypotheses should sharpen the focus on the specifics of the research design.

The hypotheses may be stated in different forms. One form is to indicate the direction of expected results, based on previous experience or on some a priori reasoning. Another form is the null hypothesis form. The null hypothesis was discussed in detail in the earlier chapters on hypothesis testing. The statistical procedures commonly test the null hypothesis directly in terms of the statistical theory. The researcher should check his hypotheses so that there is no confusion between the results of the statistical test and the acceptance or rejection of the hypotheses. Research such as historical research would possibly not include a statistical test of a hypothesis. If hypotheses are not tested in this manner, the term null hypothesis is usually not associated with the research.

Identification of Necessary Data

The identification of the variables and the formulation of hypotheses leads to an identification of the necessary data. The independent variables may require personal data on the S. This would be true in *ex post facto* research where the levels of independent variables are not assigned to Ss. The existing classifications essentially become the levels of the independent variables. There may be additional data required such as socio-economic information.

A good deal of the necessary data is identified by the dependent variables. The identification may need some refinement at this point. Also, the researcher should be certain that the type of measurement scale is adequate. For example, suppose the researcher plans to use a parametric test for the difference between means. The necessary measurement scale would then be at least an interval scale. Whatever statistics the researcher is planning to compute must be available from the data. This may seem trivial but it is important to remember when preparing for adequate data collection.

Data Collection

The second major part of the research project, that of data collection, follows directly from the identification of the necessary data. The researcher knows what data he needs, now he must work out the procedures for collecting that data. The first matter is what to measure the dependent variables with and thus secure the necessary data.

The researcher may have available to him existing measuring instruments, whether published or otherwise, that will secure the necessary data for him. If this is the case, the initial step in data collection is considerably simplified. If this is not the case, then considerable effort must be put into the development of the instruments. The items must be carefully constructed according to the technical procedures for item construction, and the content of the items must reflect the objectives of the research. This is true whether it is a test battery, an interview, or a questionnaire that is being developed. The items may differ considerably between measuring instruments but the construction of items is a major task in the development of any measuring instrument.

The selection of measuring instruments is not always a case of what is or is not available. The researcher may have existing instruments but they may serve only as a starting point or base and may need considerable revision for the purpose of the particular research project. Consider the cross-cultural example discussed in the *ex post facto* section of the preceding chapter. There are quite a number of achievement tests available (in the United States at least). An achievement test in an area such as mathematics could be used in both countries without revision.

However, a test on professional education knowledge would be unsatisfactory for use in both countries in its original form, as published in the United States. The items themselves are used as the basis for the measurement but they would need considerable revision. The revision would need be of such a nature that the meaning of the item is consistent across the countries. If the meaning of an item cannot remain consistent, the item would have to be eliminated or replaced. Of course, the final instruments for both countries should be constructed so that they measure the same thing and the scoring is consistent. Inconsistent scoring procedures would introduce a bias and hence be a methods error.

The measuring instruments need not be tests, attitude inventories, questionnaires, interviews, or the like. It may be necessary to develop some sort of equipment for the measurement. A researcher in physical education may require quantitative measurements of hand grip or muscle strength. An experiment in the learning laboratory may require arrangement of blocks or selections on pictorial boards. Learning psychologists working with animals often use a maze or some kind of lever device to induce the animal to learn a procedure by offering a reward. Thus, the step of developing or selecting the measurement instruments can be viewed very broadly in the general context of educational research. In any one research project, however, the development and selection is very specific, dictated by the data necessary for the project.

The training for data collection procedures covers a wide variety of possibilities, depending again upon the specific research project. There may be very little training necessary if the administration of a test is straightforward and simple. A brief review of the administration procedures with the testers may be all that is required. On the other hand, complex experiments or extensive interviews may require a great deal of effort to master and standardize the procedures.

The data collection procedures should be carefully developed before a pilot study is attempted, if the pilot study is specifically concerned with the effectiveness of the measuring instrument itself. Otherwise, inconsistencies or other defects may be due to the data collection procedures rather than the instrument. Not all research projects require a trial run of the measuring instruments; however, if such a run is required, it is for the purpose of revising items, eliminating ambiguities, and the like. It may not be possible to eliminate all adjustments in the data collection procedures during the trial run. For some studies, it is essentially impossible to refine the procedures without a trial run.

The results of the pilot study lead directly into revisions and reliability checks, if these are considered necessary. If extensive revisions are made, it would be necessary to have a second trial run with the revised instrument. When self-developed tests are used, reliability checks are a necessity. If standardized tests are used for any populations except those designated in the test manual, reliability checks are necessary. The lack of a pilot study does not eliminate the possibility of a reliability check. Reliability coefficients can and should be computed on the data collected for the analysis. Such coefficients should be computed whenever applicable and necessary. Of course, this computation would follow the actual data-collection of the project.

The choice of Ss for the trial run should correspond with the population from which the anticipated sample (assuming a sampling study) will be selected. In some cases, instruments are pre-tested on any Ss that are readily available. The value of such a procedure is questionable. The desirable situation is to have a representative sample of the population. Sometimes a special subpopulation is sampled or entirely included for the trial run. The effectiveness of this procedure depends upon whether or not the use of such subpopulations adequately reflect the use of the instrument with the proposed population or sample. This is really a trial run in a very limited sense. It is essentially part of instrument development and would likely have little or no value in establishing reliability.

The researcher should not attempt to generalize the use of an instrument across diverse populations. For example, a mathematics test constructed for junior high arithmetic should not be given to fifth graders and expect the procedures, reliability coefficients, etc., to apply. By the same token, an instrument constructed for fifth graders should not be administered to eighth graders for the trial run. The error of using inappropriate Ss for a trial run is usually not as glaring as this example. Such an error can lead to difficulties in securing valid data for the research study.

Before data can be collected, there must be someone (or something) from which to collect the data. If an entire population is to be measured, the researcher must be certain that all members are included. An experiment may require all the members of a subpopulation, such as all the third graders enrolled in a certain school. However, the members will need to be randomly assigned to the experimental groups. The same situation would apply to an experiment in a learning laboratory, for example. The Ss would be randomly selected from the population and assigned to the experimental treatments.

The selection of a random sample has been discussed in previous chapters. As was pointed out, this is often a task of considerable magnitude, especially for research projects like large surveys. The researcher should have his sampling procedures carefully developed so that this step can proceed efficiently and with a minimum of difficulty.

The time between sample selection and the data collection for the project varies with the type of study. In the case of an experiment, the application of the experimental treatments takes place during this interval. The time interval may vary considerably for different experiments. Consider a learning laboratory experiment. The Ss may participate shortly after being assigned, and the data consist of measures of their performance during the experimental session. On the other hand, a considerable period may elapse while the Ss are exposed to the experimental treatments, with the data consisting of measures taken at the close of the experimental treatment. An experiment involving the use of different types of materials over an instructional period of several weeks would be an example. In the case of a survey when no experimental treatments are applied, the interval between sample selection and data collection is usually quite short.

The data collection may take place at different times either for the same or different Ss. Longitudinal studies requiring several measures on the same Ss would be an example. Any studies involving pre- and posttesting would require some time interval between testing the same Ss. Different Ss would be measured at different times in the case of cross-cultural studies, if, for example, they were measured at the end of the school year. School years conclude at different times in different countries. The important thing in this example would be to measure the Ss at the same point in their training.

The total time required for the data collection also varies considerably. All Ss may be measured simultaneously within a very short interval or the time span may be considerable as Ss are measured individually or in small groups. Examples of the latter are interviews or individual learning tasks. The researcher should be careful to allow sufficient time for the data collection. Insufficient time may introduce error and possibly invalidate the data.

The data collection should proceed according to the specified plan as developed by the researcher or indicated in the test manual that accompanies the test. This activity, as with all activities throughout the entire research project, requires concentrated attention to detail — not only the detail of administering the instrument but the associated details as well. The data collector must be certain that he has the appropriate tests for the Ss he is planning to test. Special pencils, answer sheets, stop watches, etc., are often necessary. The matter of being at the right place at the appointed time is important. Careless data collection will undoubtedly lead to difficulties immediately following this step in the research endeavor.

Once the data are acquired, the researcher prepares for the analysis. However, the data in their original form are usually not ready for the process of analysis. If tests, questionnaires, interviews, and the like have been used, the responses of Ss will have to be transmitted from the answer sheet to a data card or data sheet. If data are put on IBM cards, the data must be assembled in such a manner that the keypunch operator can transmit the information to the cards efficiently and with a minimum of error.

The data may require some coding when transferred to an IBM card. The levels of the independent variables are usually coded into the identification columns of the card. This requires at least one column (but seldom more) for each independent variable, where the levels are identified by some numerical code. If pre- and posttesting have been done, the pre- and posttest scores of each S must be put into proper order, or *collated*. Often the Ss are assigned numbers for identification. All of this type of information must be assembled before cards can be punched.

The researcher may not anticipate using a computer for the

analysis. A desk calculator may be sufficient if the necessary computations are not extensive. Qualitative data may not require any computations. However, if the researcher has quantitative data such as test scores, some grouping and assembling is necessary prior to analysis. The scores of each dependent variable must at least be grouped together. Responses on questionnaires, especially responses to open-end questions, require categorization. The quantitative responses require tabulation. Data of the type collected in an historical study require sorting, categorization, and evaluation. Thus, any type of research project that involves quantitative data requires some assembling of the data after having been collected.

The researcher may encounter the problem of missing data. This difficulty is often associated with studies involving large samples; however, it can occur in situations with few Ss and small amounts of data. The seriousness of missing data depends upon the research study. If a correlation study involves a large number of Ss, the absence of a single S's observations is of little concern. On the other hand, one or more missing observations in an experimental design requiring equal numbers of observations for all groups will introduce serious analysis and interpretation difficulties.

There is no completely satisfactory procedure for dealing with the problem of missing data, although operational procedures exist which enable the researcher to continue assembling the data in preparation for the analysis. One procedure has already been indicated, that is, to delete a S who has missing data. Before many Ss are deleted, however, some checking must be done on the possible introduction of bias. For example, in a study involving achievement it would not be satisfactory to delete the low ability students because they had managed to be absent the day of the achievement testing. In such a situation it is best not to announce the testing beforehand, and to provide for immediate make-up testing.

A second procedure for dealing with missing data is to substitute values for the missing observation. The question, of course, is what values to substitute. One procedure is to substitute the mean value of the group, on the assumption that for a single value the mean is the most likely to appear. If some other information is available for the S, it may be possible to substitute some predicted value. For example, if we knew a S's I.Q. score, it might be possible to predict an achievement score. This would require information about the relationship between I.Q. and the achievement score and the assumption that the relationship holds for the group under study. The use of substitute scores may be quite tenuous and if this procedure is followed, a rationale for the substitution must be developed.

A research project may involve some unusable data. A response may be completely out of context so that it is obvious that the S misunderstood the question. Scores may be unreasonably high or low due to a technical error in the data collection. If an observation falls outside of the range of possible values it is clearly unusable. The rules for discarding unusable data should be developed and then applied during the data-assembling process. It is not proper to analyze the data and then discard data so that the results will more closely resemble expectations. If considerable data are unusable, a check on the Ss should be made to determine whether a certain group of Ss consistently produced unusable data. If this is true, it is likely that a bias has been introduced.

Accuracy checks should be made on the data recording and coding. A possible source of error is the copy error when making entries onto a data sheet. The recorder may copy the entry incorrectly or place the entry in the wrong box on the data sheet. If IBM cards are punched, they should be verified. This is a process by which errors in putting the data on the cards can be identified.

Analysis

The third major step in organizing and conducting a research project is the analysis of the data. If careful preparation has been made in the identification of the problem and the data collection has been adequate, the analysis should proceed with little difficulty. The formulation of the hypotheses and the type of data collected dictate to a large extent the specific analysis procedures. The analysis design is implied by the statement of the hypotheses. For example, suppose the hypotheses deal with the interactions of independent variables. The identification of necessary data should then make provision for the parametric assumptions. The implied analysis is then a parametric technique which will consider independent variables simultaneously and account for an interaction effect, if such an effect exists. An analysis of variance, possibly a factorial, is an example of such an analysis. The analysis is superimposed upon the data and the data must "fit" the analysis.

The final steps of identification of the problem included setting up the anticipated analysis procedures. The analysis is not an end in itself but a means to an end; it is the tool by which the results are generated from the data. The analysis can only be altered within the bounds of the hypotheses. Usually adjustments consist of only minor alterations in things such as the number of Ss in a cell. Unexpected mortality may necessitate such an adjustment. However, the basic analysis would not be changed. Side analyses that were not initially anticipated may be carried out due to some interesting results in the data. These are peripheral to the major problem and should not be viewed as a replacement for the major or primary analysis.

A serious error can be made by departing markedly from the analysis as set up by the identification of the problem. The researcher may unwittingly and in varying degrees depart from his problem and hypotheses; sometimes, because of unfortunate data collection, major adjustments in the analysis seem unavoidable. This is a very tenuous procedure when it comes to research methods. Actually the research procedures have begun to break down prior to this step in the matter of data collection. The researcher will have to decide whether or not he can salvage enough of the data to proceed with the original problem; if not, it may be necessary to redo the data collection.

When the analysis design is satisfactorily superimposed upon the data, the researcher is ready to proceed with the actual analysis. If the data are in good shape and the analysis procedures well defined and applicable, this step should proceed efficiently. Yet on many research projects this is the step where difficulties and frustrations are encountered. Inadequate data and inappropriate analysis procedures are common sources of difficulty. Lack of sufficient resources occasionally poses a problem. An example of such a difficulty is the absence of a computer when one is required. Although it manifests itself at this point, it is a result of poor planning earlier in the research project. If difficulties of this type occur, a careful reassessment of the research project must be made to determine what can be retained in the light of available data and resources. Sometimes it is possible to use an alternate but more feasible analysis technique.

Technical difficulties can usually be overcome. A more serious resource deficiency would be one in which the results of the data collected are not appropriate or meaningful in terms of the proposed study. Again, by careful planning, this situation could be avoided. This is more likely to appear in a project where several people are working on a single problem and there is lack of communication and coordination between members. The outcome of this difficulty becomes more apparent when interpreting the results.

Upon the completion of the analysis, some assembling of the results is necessary, regardless of the type of research project. If the analysis is done by a computer, some translation and reorganization of the computer output is necessary. An analysis done on a desk calculator requires reorganization and computations are usually deleted. An historical researcher will need to pull together various facets of his results. The assembling of results may be more of an ongoing process with the historical researcher, and not quite as defintive a step as in a project requiring statistical analysis.

The assembly of results should not be confused with the assembly of data. The distinction is illustrated by an example. Suppose a researcher does a survey study and assembles the responses in categories or in some other manner pulls them together. This is assembling data. Then he analyzes these categories. The tabulations represent results and this is assembling the results.

Descriptive statistics and results of statistical tests are commonly reported in tables. The researcher will have to decide upon the organization for the tables. Suppose that he has means, standard deviations, etc., for several dependent variables. Then he must consider whether it is more meaningful to group by statistics such as putting means only or means and standard deviations only in a table, or by variables, that is, place all the statistics relative to a variable or group of variables in the same table. The organization of a table is a flexible matter and several forms are acceptable. (This point is discussed further in the following chapter on writing the research report.) The organization of the tables should facilitate the interpretation of results. The tables should have all items clearly defined. Confusion may result not only because of poorly defined headings but also by putting an excessive amount of information in a single table. Tables that have many different types of entries and are spread over more than one page are often difficult to read. The use of tables is often a necessary technique but it should facilitate the reporting of results and not be a source of confusion.

Conclusion

The reader is reminded that the emphasis of this chapter is upon doing the research and not upon writing the research report. To be sure, these two activities cannot be completely separated since in doing the research many things are written which may appear (likely with revision) in the research report. The following chapter deals with the formal approach to producing a finished written product. In the final part of this discussion we are dealing with the activities prior to writing the report; these should not be confused with the "conclusions" section of the final written research report.

The interpretation of the results should not be confused with the results themselves. This confusion is a common error. The results in a certain sense are the facts and the interpretations are what the researcher makes of the facts. Alternative interpretations should be presented and entertained if there is no basis for discrediting them. If hypotheses have been tested, the researcher should interpret the meaning of the results (reject or fail to reject) in the context of the specific project. The interpretations should be based on the results which, of course, are based on the data. The use of appropriate research methods up to this point is necessary but not the only condition for valid interpretations. Where much of the methods may have been of a technical nature, the interpretations involve more than technical procedures. The researcher should be well informed about the problem under study so that he can make valid interpretations. Being informed is necessary but not the only qualification.

A synthesis or pulling together of the various parts of a research project is a necessity. Actually, this process should be going on during the entire project so that no one part (or researcher) gets too far afield and also to avoid duplication and "excess baggage." Examples of excess baggage would be retaining unnecessary procedures or collecting data which initially seemed necessary but were replaced or deleted.

The synthesis also guards against inadvertently overlooking important segments of the research. The researcher should have an overall grasp of the entire project as it approaches completion. This is not to say that this overall grasp should be lacking at earlier stages; rather, this grasp should now be in terms of what has been done. The synthesis will help to tie things together and reveal the connections between the various parts of the research.

The three subtitles of the conclusion part as presented in the outline early in this chapter cannot really be separated. The synthesis may be done prior to or simultaneous with the interpretation of the results. For example, certain conditions or irregularities of data collection may have a direct bearing on the interpretation of the results. The synthesis may have revealed these conditions to the researcher. The interpretation of results, almost without exception, does require some synthesis, so that these two steps should be considered as taking place simultaneously.

The finished, tangible product of a research project is usually the written report. In a general sense, all of the research activities are done as a preparation for writing. As the research is completed, the activities and results more directly reflect this preparation. The researcher is beginning to consider such questions as: How will I present these results and how will I discuss these interpretations? The preparation for writing, again, is not an isolated activity but is occurring simultaneously with other activities of the project. The researcher should conduct the study in such a manner that he can account adequately and accurately for all he does. Haphazard and isolated procedures make the writing very difficult and inefficient.

The writing of the research report is not something to be taken lightly. Preparation for such writing can be a great help in reducing the confusion and inefficiency which often accompanies this activity. A common error is not having all of the necessary information and references readily available. Another difficulty is a lack of time. Reasonably sized blocks of time should be available. This increases efficiency since whenever the writer stops and starts with considerable intervening time and events, some repetition is necessary in order to get acclimated again to the task. Also, continuity is enhanced by persisting with the writing task.

A serious error in the overall research endeavor is to delay the writing after the completion of the analysis and interpretation of results. Actually, the research project is not completed until the report is finished. Often a good deal of persistence is required to bring the research to the writing stage. Then the writing task remains as the concluding activity and climax. At this point persistence should be increased rather than diminished. If there is a marked delay with the writing task, the research has a tendency to become cold and unfamiliar and the report may never be written. Sometimes the research report is completed at a later date, but reactivating the research project involves a great deal of additional effort and relearning. Many research problems lose their pertinence with the passing of time. Certainly delay results in a reduction of enthusiasm on the part of the researcher.

Doing a research project is a matter of separate but interrelated activities or parts. Some activities can be more easily separated than others and many follow a logical sequence. The overall scope of the research project is important and should be well identified. But getting the research completed is a matter of doing it piece by piece. Various generalizations are considered and applied, but for a single research project it is the specifics and the attention to detail that gets the job done. Detailed planning is an important aspect of doing a research project. Resources and effort will be required. Attending to all of these matters will not guarantee an adequate research study, but it will help to enhance efficiency, avoid errors, and improve the research effort.

Suggested Study Exercises

9.1 Discuss possible reasons for the review of the literature early in a research project. What are some items of specific information that may be supplied by the review? Produce a list of specifics. Would there be any reason for doing additional literature review toward the close of a research project? If so, why?

9.2 A researcher plans to do a study for which the dependent variable is "history achievement" at the secondary level. Discuss how you would arrive at a more precise definition of history achievement. Consider the various facets of history achievement and develop what you consider a satisfactory definition. Compare the definitions of the various class members.

9.3 Discuss an educational research study which is an example of a project that would require a pilot study. Consider such points as why the pilot study is necessary and how it could be efficiently and successfully conducted.

9.4 Discuss some of the more common errors or difficulties that arise in the mechanics of data collection. By mechanics is meant actually securing the necessary data and not constructing the measuring instruments.

9.5 Select an article from a research journal which is the report of a research project. Read the article carefully and attempt to detect the specific parts of the organization discussed in this chapter. (Some of the subtitles may not apply to the specific study you are reading.) This will require some reading between the lines on your part since you will be essentially reconstructing the doing of the research from the written report. That is, you are not an eyewitness to the research study.

9.6 Select a research problem which would require a research project of modest duration. Present an overview of the specifics of your project which would follow the organization presented in this chapter. Again, it may not be necessary for you to include all suggested subtitles. Make your remarks brief and try to limit the entire overview to, say, the equivalent of eight to ten double spaced, typewritten pages.

10 *Reading and Writing About Research*

The individual who engages in a research endeavor eventually arrives at the point when he wishes to communicate his findings. Some communication may take place through informal or formal discussions, but usually a larger audience is sought. The mode of communication is commonly through writing. The written document may take the form of a thesis, journal article, monograph, or a technical report to a funding agency, to mention just a few. The significance of a research study, both academically and practically, is usually judged on the content of its written report. The importance of precise and clear reporting can hardly be overestimated.

The communication of the information in a written document takes more than a writer; it also requires a reader. The burden of communication does not rest entirely on the writer. Not all individuals connected with the educational enterprise are writers but all should be readers of research. Therefore, in this chapter some attention is directed toward reading as well as writing about research. Also, some reading is a necessary prerequisite to research activity, if only for the review of literature.

Meaningful reading of research is not something which is automatically assured by the passing of time. Research periodicals are often avoided by educational practitioners simply because when they are read the articles are not understood. Meaningful and efficient reading is a learned skill. The skill may seem somewhat elusive and it may seem trite to say "read critically" without any additional direction. However, there are some guidelines that can be used in doing a critical reading of a research report. These guidelines are often stated in question form as points to look for. For the purpose of this discussion, research report is very broadly defined to mean a written account of a research study. This could be a thesis, article, or a similar report and is not limited to mean only a technical report.

Meaningful Reading and Critical Analysis

The critical analysis of one or more research articles is often a requirement of an introductory course in educational research. It is well to have the analysis preceded by an abstract or outline of the article. This helps to acquire a necessary understanding of the content, prior to the critical analysis. The abstract should hit the main points of the article and should reveal a general overview of the content. Some specifics should be included such as a statement of the problem or the hypotheses. A brief outline for an abstract might be as follows:

A. Statement of the problem
B. General methods and procedures
C. Results
D. Conclusion

The amount of information under each of these subheadings should be brief and to the point. For an article of average (six to ten pages) length, three to five sentences under each subheading should suffice.

The evaluation of the content of a research report may be considered from two points of view. First, there is the consideration of the value of the research in the educational context, and second, the methodology of the research per se, that is, whether the research was carefully planned and executed. Both points are important. The most perfectly planned piece of research has little value if it has no place in the educational context. On the other hand, a brilliant research idea pursued haphazardly is essentially worthless.

The worth of a problem and the complexity of the methodology are independent factors. Trivial problems may be camouflaged in complex designs. Problems with far-reaching implications may be pursued with relatively simple procedures. The research reader should not infer that because a report involves complex procedures the problem is necessarily of comparable importance. This is one reason why it is important that the researchers know the area under study.

The criticism of a research report may be approached through the posing of specific questions, which, when answered satisfactorily, provide a clear analysis. Most of the questions in the following discussion are directed to methodology, while some are related to the value of the research. The questions are organized according to the usual parts of a research report. This is the same as suggested for the abstract.

The statement of the problem is the first item the reader looks for in a research report. A clear, concise statement is very important, for without it the reader may wonder whether or not the researcher had a clear concept of the problem in mind. The questions commonly associated with the statement of the problem are as follows:

1. Is the problem clearly and concisely stated?
2. Is the problem delimited so that it can be researched? The problems of educational research must be spelled out and delimited. For example, "the teaching of arithmetic" is not

a satisfactory way to propose a problem because it is far too broad.

3. Are the hypotheses and objectives stated in the context of the research problem?
4. Does the research have a setting in the overall educational context or at least in its own research area? Is there evidence that the researcher is aware of the research in the area? Is there a conceptual framework for pursuing the research?
5. Are the terms well defined? Is there confusion in the definition of terms? Do they have multiple or arbitrary meanings? An example would be the use of terms such as "nonconforming student." Are the independent and dependent variables clearly identified?
6. Is there a basic rationale on which the study rests? The rationale may be implied through assumptions. If this is done, are the assumptions tenable and in keeping with existing knowledge?

A discussion of procedures usually follows the statement of the problem. The amount of procedural detail given depends upon the type of research report. A journal article often does not spell out a great deal of detail. A graduate thesis or technical report, on the other hand, commonly has one or more chapters devoted to procedures. Whatever the case, the writer must convey to his readers that he understands the details of his procedures.

The list of questions dealing with procedures concerns such matters as sampling and testing. Obviously, if no sample was drawn or no tests given, these questions need not be considered. Some questions are, of course, unique to the type of study. The questions concerning general procedures and methodology are as follows:

1. Are the procedures appropriate for meeting the objectives and testing the hypotheses? Were the assumptions met for the statistical tests used? If an experiment was involved, was adequate time allowed for the appearance of an experimental effect? In the case of an historical study, were primary or secondary sources used?

2. What variables were controlled in the design and were there any uncontrolled variables? If there were uncontrolled variables, were they relevant to the study and how were they likely to have affected the results? A researcher may be under the impression that it is sufficient to acknowledge the existence of the uncontrolled variables. A recognition that they exist does not account for the effects they may have on the study. The researcher should systematically account for their possible influence. Since there is no way to empirically measure the effects of uncontrolled variables, a knowledge and background of the variables is invaluable.

3. Are the variables of the study categorized and quantified adequately? Were tests assumed to be valid and reliable without being checked? Are reliability coefficients reported? If standardized tests were used, is there reference to normative data? If measuring instruments were constructed, were they tried out on a pilot group? Are there adequate descriptions of the measuring instruments? Is there a description of the critical evaluation of historical materials and if so, were the evaluation procedures adequate?

4. Were the data accurately and objectively collected and recorded? Did the data collection proceed according to plan? Were checks made to guard against possible errors in collecting and tabulating the data? Was a reasonable time schedule followed for the data collection?

5. Is there an adequate description of the population? (This may be included with the statement of the problem.) Was the sample a random sample? Was there any possibility of the introduction of a sampling bias? Was there any mortality in the sample and if so, is there a discussion of the possible relevancy of the mortality? If replacement procedures were used, were such procedures adequate?

6. If the study deals with an experiment, is the design discussed? Does the design seem applicable and carefully administered? Is the design oversimplified or unnecessarily complicated in the context of the problem? Is it clear how the independent variables were manipulated?

7. Are the analysis procedures clearly and completely identified? If several different analyses were done, is it clear how they are related and what contribution is made by each? Were

the analysis procedures appropriate for the research problem and the data? Were there violations of necessary assumptions or tenuous assumptions included without being checked?

The results of a research study should be clearly identified in the research report. The results are the products of the data and the analysis. At this point, the results should not be mixed with the results of other studies discussed in the background of the problem. The questions dealing with results follow:

1. Are the results a logical product of the analyses? This may seem like a trivial question but occasionally results appear which seem to have no basis in the procedures and analysis. If this occurs, the research writer either did not adequately discuss the procedures or he has a misconception of what the procedures were to accomplish.
2. Are the results presented in clear and orderly fashion? If tables were used in reporting results, are the tables well organized and understandable? Are the results complete? Is important information implied which was actually not reported? Was there considerable information in the data which has no corresponding results?
3. If several related variables were investigated, are the results consistent? Do the results seem reasonable in the light of what is known about the data? Also, are the results consistent within themselves? For example, suppose the range or distribution of scores was reported and then the mean of the distribution is reported and its value exceeds the greatest score used in computing the range.
4. Are the results, which are facts, mixed with conjecture? Results and conjecture should be clearly separated. Conjecture should not appear in this part. If it does, confusion is introduced and the impression develops that the researcher is attempting to pass off conjecture as fact.

The conclusions section of a research report is usually the climax. The perceptual ability, knowledge, and insight of the researcher come to the fore at this point. Preceding sections of the report are more technical in nature. This is not to say that insight, knowledge, etc., are lacking in the prior sections. Questions associated with the conclusions of a research report follow:

1. Are the conclusions based upon the results? Are there inconsistencies between the results and conclusions? Are the conjectures based upon the results and the existing knowledge of the problem being researched?
2. Is the discussion of the results related to findings from previous research? Are the conclusions consistent with previous knowledge about the problem? Does the discussion follow the outcomes of the research or is there considerable wandering from the main point? Are the conclusions incorporated into the larger educational frame of reference?
3. Are alternate hypotheses discussed?
4. Is there a discussion of limitations and weaknesses of the study? Additional questions are implied by almost all research studies. Is the researcher aware of additional questions?
5. Is there confusion with the meaning of non-significant statistical tests? Are these interpreted to be meaningless or unimportant findings? Non-significant statistical tests have meaning and the fact that a statistical test is significant does not necessarily mean great substantive importance.
6. Does the research generalize to other populations? If so, is there a rationale for making a valid generalization?

The conclusions section should indicate the significance of the research in the educational context. Many of the questions asked above relate to this matter as well as to the matter of the methodology. The basic question on the significance of the research in the educational context considers how the results might be used. (An answer to this question may have been implied in the statement of the problem.) Note that the results need not necessarily be ends in themselves. Results could be used for theory building, for example. Part of the significance of the research is the uses the reader can make of it. The reader of research should ask himself questions such as: Do I find these results useful? What are other possible approaches to the problem? What would be likely to produce more useful results?

In order to understand a research report, one must be able to read critically. The discussion of this section poses many questions which could be raised when considering a research report. These questions could be considered a checklist for criticizing a report. The questions should not, however, be viewed as an exhaustive list; other questions could be raised in reference to specific research reports and inappropriate questions disregarded.

The questions deal with specific items as the reader progresses through the usual organization of a research report. In any research report, it is necessary to deal with specifics, but the reader should not lose the general overview and meaning of the research. It is a good idea to read a research report over for the general overview without being too concerned with the specifics. Then, with the general problem in mind, the reader can reread the report, concentrating on the specifics.

The suggestions put forth by the questions provide a yardstick by which the reader can evaluate the research report. However, the reader should have some familiarity with research procedures in order to adequately understand and evaluate the methods of the reported research. Research methods are learned. The previous chapters of this text have research methods as the major emphasis. Even with a minimal background, the reader will improve with experience in understanding and evaluating research reports.

Preparing a Research Proposal

At this point in the discussion we will consider the matter of writing a research proposal. This activity involves writing about research; it concerns, however, a proposed rather than a completed research project. In proposal writing we discuss *what* research is contemplated, *why* it is being contemplated, and *how* we intend doing it. Proposal writing has developed into somewhat of a necessary art within recent years. Many educators who a short time ago did no proposal writing now find themselves engaging in this activity. One motivating factor (among others) was the Elementary and Secondary Education Act of 1965. Although many projects funded under this act are not strictly research, many of the comments about proposal writing do apply. The comments of this section are general suggestions for preparing a research proposal. They are directed toward proposals required by the Bureau of Research, United States Office of Education, and the research branches of various foundations or agencies. However, many of the comments would also apply to the dissertation proposal required of students in many graduate schools. There may be certain comments such as those dealing with budget procedures that are not directly applicable to the dissertation proposal. However, such comments are easily recognized.

The first consideration when writing a research proposal is where to apply. Once a decision has been made concerning the foundation or agency, the researcher should secure the specific guidelines from the agency for preparing the proposal. The guidelines provide specific details as to format, number of copies, deadlines, sections required, necessary subheadings, and the like. The researcher should follow the guidelines accurately and any deviation should be avoided, and, if unavoidable, thoroughly explained. Funding of proposals is generally competitive and there is usually an excess of proposals that meet the standards of format. Therefore, any proposals not meeting the standards will be rejected immediately.

The procedure for decision-making on proposals invariably involves a review by anonymous and impartial readers. The reader will decide whether or not to recommend funding. If funding is recommended, there may be other factors such as budgetary considerations that delay or prevent approval. If the reader does not recommend funding, the proposal will be rejected. Therefore, it is extremely important that the writer present an adequate case for the reader. Generally, the proposal will stand or fall on what is contained in the main body of the proposal. The writer should not assume that the reader will read between the lines. Readers are generally sophisticated individuals, but research projects are specific and the writer should not assume that the reader will possess specific information about the research topic. The proposal should be written so that the uninformed reader can understand the ideas and procedures.

The names of headings and subheadings within the proposal may differ somewhat for different agencies. For example, some may require a section entitled "Procedures," others a "Description of Activities," and still others a "Narrative" section in which the writer can supply his own subheadings. However, the general format for the development of a research proposal is common to essentially all agencies. It develops in a logical manner from the statement of the problem within an adequate context through the methodology and procedures, concluding with a budget. Normally, one section requires a discussion of the significance of the proposed research project. It is in this section that the writer makes his case for the value of the project. In other sections, primary emphasis is directed toward the case that the writer can adequately do the project. It is in these other sections that research methods play an important role.

Research Problem and Background

The research problem should be specific and clearly identified. The problem must be delimited and defined within the educational context and the particular area under study. Somewhere early in the proposal there should be a statement clearly indicating what the researcher specifically intends to cover. No single project can cover the entire educational concern and no researcher should attempt to accomplish everything. Sometimes writers are oversensitive to the idea that they will be criticized for not making the problem all-inclusive. They are more likely to be criticized for having a problem that is too broad.

Consider an example. Suppose a writer indicated his problem as the improvement of teacher education. This is far too broad a statement. Although readers may be sympathetic to the idea that teacher education can be improved, this type of statement will be viewed unfavorably. There is also an implied conclusion that whatever it is the researcher is intending to do will result in the improvement of teacher education. If this is already conclusive the researcher is no longer at the research stage but ready for implementation.

Since the above example is so broad, almost any aspect of teacher education could be included. However, an example of a delimited research problem in teacher education might be to assess and compare the academic achievement and personality characteristics of secondary education students being trained with three different programs. This statement would be followed by operational definitions of terms such as compare, academic achievement, personality characteristics, and the different programs. The type of study implied is not an experiment, but *ex post facto* in nature. There are no foredrawn conclusions implied in the statement of the problem. The statement of the problem would undoubtedly be followed by specific objectives. The significance of the study would be implied, although it would be discussed in greater detail later in the proposal. The problem implies a search for facts and it could certainly be indicated that such facts are necessary and helpful in making decisions about program procedures that might improve secondary teacher education.

After the statement of the problem, it is important that the writer provide a background, usually through a review of the literature relating to his area of study. This section should demonstrate to the reader that the writer has a comprehensive knowledge of the research area. Not only should the writer exhibit adequate historical knowledge but also his familiarity with present activity and developments concerning the problem. The information in the literature concerning the specific problem may be quite extensive, while the review of literature in the proposal will be somewhat limited. (A suggested length for the proposal is usually provided in the guidelines and the writer must decide as to space allotments for the various sections.) Therefore, one of the marks of a knowledgable writer is the ability to select the pertinent facts and tie them together for an understandable and accurate background. It is important to provide continuity between the ideas from the literature and the research problem. The position of the research problem should be clearly indicated in the content of the educational area. There should be an indication as to how the proposed research will contribute to the knowledge of the area. The writer should avoid statements inferring that information of this problem is very limited or a review of the literature has revealed no information about the problem. The reader will be very suspicious (and rightly so) of such statements, and will likely interpret them as a lack of knowledge on the part of the writer rather than as a gap in the literature.

Many research proposals, especially those involving experiments or *ex post facto* studies, include statements of hypotheses. Other types of studies such as status surveys may include questions that will presumably be answered through the proposed research. Hypotheses and questions should be specific and to the point. In terms of hypotheses, any acceptable form which enhances the understanding may be used. For example, if statistical tests for differences are anticipated, the null hypothesis may seem most appropriate. If a theoretical construct has been developed, alternate hypotheses may be appropriate. Of course, hypotheses that cannot be tested by the results of the research should be omitted. Also, the writer should not base his hypotheses on only one possible outcome of the results. The researcher should be able to make decisions about his hypotheses or questions with any possible outcome of the results.

What, then, are some of the possible errors that can be made in the research proposal section dealing with the problem and its background? Some errors have already been identified above. These are errors such as not delimiting the problem or presenting an inadequate review of related literature. The failure to clearly identifying the research problem is quite common. The writer must remember that although he may have the problem clearly in mind, the reader must conceptualize it from the written account. Smith[1] identifies the errors of a trivial problem and a problem peripheral to education. The former is exactly what the name implies, that is, a research problem of little significance to education. The latter, a peripheral problem, is a problem that is not central to education. An example might be a problem dealing with physical activity and its relationship to heart disease. This would undoubtedly be viewed as a significant problem and would touch upon physical education problems. However, the central focus of the problem would be more applicable for a heart or medical association than an educational agency. Another example might be certain problems concerning adult education which would be more appropriate for an agency doing research in gerontology than an education agency. The statement of the problem, coming as it does early in the proposal, should make a favorable impression upon the reader. If

[1] Smith, G. R., "A Critique of Proposals Submitted to The Cooperative Research Program," Culbertson and Hencley, eds., In *Educational Research: New Perspectives* (Danville, Ill.: The Interstate Printers and Publishers, 1963).

this is not the case, the remainder of the proposal will carry the burden of changing this initial impression.

Research Methodology and Procedures

This section of the research proposal describes in detail what is to be done and how. Although some proposal guidelines may not require subheadings, the writer should include subheadings such as Design, Sample, Data Analysis, and any others that might apply to his specific research problem. Subheadings not only aid the writer in identifying and describing the various activities, but they should aid the reader in understanding the continuity of the activities. One of the most common errors of this section is that the methods and procedures are lacking in detail. The explanation should be complete enough so that the reader has no question about what is anticipated and how it will be accomplished.

The early part of the methodology and procedures section usually contains a discussion of the research design. This discussion sets the stage for the specific procedures. The design should reflect the objectives and specifically the hypotheses or questions. The design should be appropriate for the complexity of the research problem. A common error is to present a simple design for a complex problem. (The reverse could also occur.) Another common error is to provide a design that does not test all of the hypotheses. Hypotheses dealing with interactions between independent variables are susceptible to being ignored in the design. All hypotheses or questions must be covered by the design.

The design should be identified as specifically as possible in acceptable design terminology. In the case of an experiment, it should be apparent how the independent variables will fit into the design; for example, 2×3 factorial design with the type of materials and ability level as independent variables is a specific way of indicating a design. The term factorial conveys a great deal of meaning in this context. Additional information should be specified such as the levels of the independent variables and number of replications in the cells.

The writer should also consider possible weaknesses in the design and describe what will be done to compensate for or eliminate the weaknesses. A common difficulty is the influence of extraneous variables. The writer should discuss their possible effects and indicate how they will be controlled or eliminated. A second similar type of difficulty is that of confounded variables. A serious error is to ignore or dismiss lightly extraneous and confounded variables. Occasionally writers are under the misconception that identifying the difficulty but not providing for the solution is sufficient; for example, the effects of variable X are confounded with the experimental treatments, but in the context of the situation the variables cannot be separated and hence we are doing the best we can. The reader is not judging whether or not the researcher is doing the best he can; rather, he is trying to decide whether or not the design is adequate for the proposed research. The fact that the researcher is putting forth his best is not justification for approval.

The discussion of the procedures usually follows somewhat of a chronological order in terms of conducting the research project. If sampling is to be used, the technique is usually presented early in the procedures section. The instruments used for measuring the variables should be specified early. If instrument development is involved, this will require a detailed discussion.

Consider the matter of sampling. The sampling plan must be viewed in terms of the external and internal validity of the research project. These concepts were discussed in an earlier chapter but for purposes of review, external validity deals with generalizing the results and internal validity with interpreting the results. When sampling is used, the researcher is invariably attempting to make inferences to a larger population. The sample must be selected so that it represents the population. If inferential statistics are used, the sample must provide appropriate estimates of random variability which involves some type of random sample.

Suppose a study is anticipated which would involve a sample of high school seniors from a single state. It is not adequate to say that a random sample of seniors will be selected from the high schools of the state. The sampling plan should be described in detail. Assuming an adequate operational definition of a high school senior, the writer should indicate how he will identify all members of the population. What types of information will be available that will include all seniors fitting the definition? Are there safeguards against omitting segments of the population? Are stratifying variables to be used? If so, what are they and why are they important? Will it be necessary to sample through an intermediate unit? What will be the replacement procedure if selected units decline to participate? These types of questions should be carefully answered. For example, stratified random sampling with proportional allocation would be a possible sampling plan. The stratifying variables should be operationally defined and it should be clear to the reader that students can be identified in terms of stratifying variables from the population information. For example, it is not adequate to simply indicate that size of district will be a stratifying variable. The number and definition of categories for this stratifying variable should be indicated: less than 2,000 students, 2,000 to 5,000 students, etc., with size of the district based on the 1967–68 average daily attendance as reported in State Document X. A complete description of this type will provide the reader with the evidence as to how and why the researcher will select the sample.

A lack of detail about the sampling plan will leave the reader with the impression that a sample of convenience will be used, another very serious methodology defect. Samples of volunteers should also be avoided. Another possible error is that the sampling procedure will not secure a sample adequate for inferring to the intended population. For example, a sample of seniors from a few large city systems willing to cooperate is not adequate for inferring to the state population of high school seniors.

The anticipated measurement instruments should be identified carefully since they usually provide the operational definitions of the dependent variables and possibly some independent variables. When applicable, the procedures for dealing with matters such as reliability should be discussed.

The data collection procedures should be presented with some type of flow chart or time schedule. The reader must be assured that the data collection is in accord with the general design for the research project. The writer should guard against the introduction of undesirable factors. For example, if several groups are involved, how is consistent measurement maintained? In Chapter 7, designs involving Latin squares were discussed. A Latin square design might be used to balance sequence effects during the data collection. Points such as these should be made to convince the reader that the data collection will be adequate.

The specific procedures of the data analysis should be identified and, of course, such procedures must be in accordance with the design. If statistical techniques are anticipated, it is not adequate to say that statistical procedures will be used. Be specific in identifying the technique; for example, a one-way analysis of variance will be used to test for significant differences between the achievement means of the three experimental groups. The analysis procedures must not only reflect the hypotheses, but the reader must be assured that necessary conditions for the analysis are met. In a case involving the use of a parametric technique, interval scale measurement (among other assumptions) is necessary. Other assumptions about distribution shape and variability may be necessary. A common error is to ignore assumptions which may be tenuous.

The writer should also indicate the availability of necessary equipment or special resources for the analysis. Research projects involving large quantities of data and/or complex analyses invariably require access to a computer or automatic test scoring machines. The writer should specifically indicate what equipment he expects to use and whether or not it is available at his institution.

The methodology and procedures section of a proposal should explain clearly and in detail how the research activity will lead to the results. The amount of detail will depend somewhat on the type of project. If a project involves considerable instrument development, this may limit the amount of detail that can be specified in the analysis. Some projects are complete within themselves, others set the stage for continuing research. Whatever the case, the narrative for this section should specify the what and how of the research activity.

Significance of the Proposed Research

Whether or not a special heading is allocated to the significance of the research in the proposal guidelines, the writer should include a discussion of this topic. The significance may be implied in the review of literature and statement of the problem. If a section entitled Use To Be Made of the Findings is required, the significance of the research can certainly be emphasized in this section. (The Bureau of Research, USOE, requires such a section.)

Research is seldom conducted for the sole purpose of accumulating empirical results. Certainly these results may be important and the writer can indicate the contribution to the existing knowledge in the area. A scholarly contribution to the field is significant. However, the writer must project his goals beyond the information purpose to the practical significance of his research. What will the research mean to the practicing educator? Will the results, regardless of outcome, influence programs or methods? If the research will set the stage for deciding on alternate courses of action for improving education, this can be a significant contribution. What will be improved or changed as the result of the proposed research? How will the results of the study be implemented and what innovations will come about?

In considering the significance, the writer should not assume that he already knows the outcome. Also, an unreasonable course of action should not be suggested. For example, a writer should not imply that the results of his study will require immediate and extensive curriculum reorganization of all senior high schools. Any suggested course of action should be reasonable in the usual context of educational innovation and change.

The significance of the proposed research need not be limited to a broad application or improvement. Its significance in a specific district or institution may also be stressed. For example, a research project in teacher education may have important implications for the program in the researcher's institution. The research project itself, regardless of the results, may generate new interest, ideas, and morale for the institution. All of the above provide possibilities through which the research project can make a noteworthy contribution.

Other Items of the Research Proposal

There are several other items that are usually required in the proposal document. The fact that these items are grouped together for this discussion does not mean that they are relatively unimportant. However, most of these items are quite straightforward and the proposal guidelines very specific as to the necessary information.

The cover page of a research proposal contains information such as the names of the proposed research project, principal investigator, and institution with which he is associated. This page is often followed by an abstract limited either to a number of pages or words. Although the abstract precedes the proposal document, it is usually one of the last steps in the preparation of the proposal. The abstract should be a concise, straightforward summary of the proposed research. The abstract usually makes the initial impression upon the reader and it is very important that the content of the abstract be understandable and include the major points about the research project. The abstract is really the defining statement of the proposed research in terms of its objectives, procedures, and type of research study.

The budget section is required for any research proposal seeking funds. Although budget guidelines are usually very specific, it is well for the writer to discuss the budget with someone familiar with financial procedures in his institution or school district. Detailed budgets are required. There are matters such as partial salaries, fringe benefits, retirement contributions, and overhead that require a knowledge of institutional policy. Sometimes overhead rates (such as 15 per cent of total budget) are specified by the funding agency. Overhead rates can also vary according to types of research projects. It is not the writer's task to establish financial policy, but it is his responsibility to be aware of policy that apply to his proposal.

There are basically two types of errors (excluding arithmetic errors) that can occur when constructing a budget. The first is to be misinformed on financial policy and apply incorrect formulas in computing budget items. The second error is that of omitting items. Research projects may require travel allowances and special equipment. The researcher will be required to submit several copies (possibly several hundred) of a final report to the funding agency. This will involve publication costs. The proposal writer should consider all financial requirements from the time that the project is approved until the final report is submitted to the funding agency.

The writer should consider each budget item carefully in the light of its contribution to the research project. The proposal will be evaluated on the basis of economic efficiency and the needs of the proposed research. That is, the funding agency will consider what it is getting for its money. The budget should reflect the extensiveness of the proposed research. If expensive items or procedures are included that will contribute little to the overall research project, it would be well for the writer to consider ways to eliminate or replace such procedures. Sometimes minor cutbacks in the amount of information to be secured can result in major budgetary reductions. Unusual procedures for developing a budget such as excessive overhead rates should be avoided. The overall budget should appear reasonable in the light of the anticipated contribution of the proposed research.

Another required section of the proposal document is a section discussing the personnel to be associated with the research project. Information about each individual having major responsibility in the research project should be provided. This information consists of name, present position, degrees, publications, background related to the project, and percentage of time committed to the project. For many projects, research assistants are written in, although they need not be specifically identified. This section of the proposal may also include a description of special facilities or resources that will be necessary for the project. The writer should assure the reader that such facilities have already been committed to the project if it is funded.

The researcher may want to include some appended items in his proposal document. Such items, of course, appear at the end of the proposal. Appended items consist of any other relevant information that is not contained in another section of the proposal. Examples of information for this section might be letters of support from leading educators who are familiar with the proposed research, names of consultants who were involved in developing the research ideas, and possible support for parts of the research project from another funding agency.

Preparing a research proposal for a funding agency is a major writing task. It requires a great deal of attention to detail and considerable rewriting is often involved before the proposal is considered satisfactory for submittal. In this discussion, several sources of errors have been identified. Generally, the proposal must meet the requirements of technical excellence in order to be recommended for funding. Various agencies establish their own criteria for evaluating proposals. However, the Bureau of

Research, USOE,[1] indicates four general criteria that can be viewed as general evaluation criteria. These four are:

1. educational significance
2. soundness of design or operational plan
3. adequacy of personnel and facilities
4. economic efficiency

Suggestions have been made throughout this discussion that should aid the writer in meeting these four general criteria.

Writing the Research Report

The writing of the research report is usually the concluding task of the research endeavor. In contrast to a research proposal which concerns a proposed research project, the research report deals with a completed research project. The task of pulling everything together is finalized during the writing of the report. This is the point at which the research must be essentially reproduced in written form. It is a matter of telling what was done, what occurred, and what it means in a concise, understandable, accurate, and logical manner.

Since much of what is written is a reproduction of what has gone before, it would intuitively seem that writing would not be a difficult task. Yet many research reports are detained in the writing stage for an exorbitantly long period. Some reports become permanently bogged down at this stage. The anticipated but nonexistent article, the unfinished thesis, and the time-extended technical report are not uncommon. Good research reports are not easily written. Writing, like any skill that must be acquired, demands specific and concentrated attention.

Since the written report is an account of the research project, the organization of the report follows quite closely the organization of the research project as discussed in the preceding chapter. Also, since a reader reads what someone else has written, suggestions about what to look for when reading a report also apply

[1] "Support for Research and Related Activities," Bureau of Research, USOE, October 1965, p. 5.

to writing a report. The questions discussed in an earlier section about reading a research report could be viewed by a writer as requiring satisfactory answers in the written report.

The extensiveness of content depends to some extent upon the type of research report. A journal article commonly has a brief lead into the statement of the problem. A brief review of literature is provided with relatively few references, say between three and ten. On the other hand, a technical report to a funding agency or a thesis usually requires a considerable amount of background information. Research procedures and analysis techniques are usually discussed in greater detail for a thesis than for an article.

Although the writing of the report is usually associated with the close of the research project, portions of the writing may be done while the research study is in progress. Certainly, preliminary drafts of review of the literature can be written; such drafts may be revised and brought up to date later. Research procedures can be recorded as the project is conducted and while they are fresh in the researcher's mind. In any event, precise records should be carefully kept during the progress of the research project. It is extremely difficult to write from memory and avoid serious omissions.

The writer should assemble the available information before beginning the writing task. Mechanical procedures for including footnotes, figures, tables, and the like should be well in mind. The writer should familiarize himself with style and procedures. These are the technical aspects in the production of a written report. Several references concerning writing procedures are listed at the end of this chapter and should prove helpful when dealing with these matters. In the interest of efficiency and continuity, relatively large blocks of time should be reserved for the writing task. Each time the writer leaves the task, some repetition is necessary to become reoriented when the task is resumed. The writer should have the necessary physical resources for efficient pursuit of the writing task. Preferably the writer should work with a minimum of interruption.

The research report should contain all the necessary data and at the same time be brief and to the point. First drafts are rarely adequate and there is usually considerable changing and rewriting before the final draft is prepared. Nonetheless, the writer should write as carefully as he can and should not put just anything down, with the view that it will be changed later anyway. A general outline of what is to be included in the report is a necessity. For a more extensive report it might be well to outline each chapter.

Statement of the Problem and Review of the Literature

The comments on writing a research report follow the same organization as that used in the preceding section on reading research reports. The first part, that of the Statement of the Problem, includes the review of related literature which was not emphasized in the section on reading. For the writer, the review of literature may involve considerable effort. Most theses have an entire chapter devoted to this review.

The statement of the problem should be concise and to the point. It should come early in the report. Long, drawn-out introductions are usually unnecessary. The reader is interested in the research problem and he should be led directly to it, not through a forest of unnecessary effusion. The introduction has the purpose of setting the stage for the statement of the problem. When this has been adequately done, the problem should be stated.

The task of reviewing the literature usually comes quite early in the research project. The review serves multiple purposes, one of which may be aiding in producing a more definitive statement of the problem. When reviewing the literature, complete bibliographical entries should be made and some kind of abstracting form set up. Three by five or four by six cards can serve quite effectively. A separate card (or cards) should be used for each source. The relevant points of the specific source should be noted in enough detail so that the researcher has the necessary information when he writes the report. This will avoid repeated returns to the original sources to determine what was really said. Also, since the final research report will require a bibliography, the initial entries should be accurately and carefully recorded. The card entry procedure facilitates arranging the bibliography in alphabetical order.

The length of the review of literature section or chapter of a research report varies with the type of report. An article commonly has a relatively brief review. The review should aid in putting the problem into perspective. There is usually some rationale for the importance of the research problem which leads to the purpose for doing the research and how this purpose ties in with what has already been done in the area.

The researcher should decide upon some type of organization for presenting the information from the review of literature. In an extensive research study the various sources are usually grouped according to the parts of the study to which they pertain. The information may also be discussed in order of relevance to the problem, the more relevant sources being discussed first. Sometimes the items of the review are discussed in a chronological order, usually beginning with the one most distant in time. This can be especially effective if the research on a topic has been closely related to the passing of time. The progress of the problem can be followed up to its present stage, an especially effective means for putting it in perspective.

The ideas from the various studies referred to in the review of literature should relate to each other and the research problem. A common error is to present ideas from individual studies as little packages within themselves. This makes for a disjointed presentation. A related error is to treat each study in a mechanical way, regardless of relative importance. The writer should avoid the excessive use of quotations. In the context of the research problem, the ideas from several sources can usually be tied together better by the writer's own words than by a series of quotations. The ideas from the review of literature should be integrated into a logical discussion with the focus upon the research problem.

The researcher is not obligated to discuss information from every source listed in the bibliography. Often in an article three or four main points are brought in from an equal number of sources. Additional references may be listed in the bibliography, complementing the information from the sources discussed. The researcher should indicate by the review of literature that he is well acquainted with the problem and the research related to the problem. This must be brought out in the discussion. An extensive bibliography with almost no discussion is not evidence of an adequate review of literature. It is only evidence of an extensive bibliography.

Methods and Procedures

The methods and procedures sections of a report may include several topics. For an extensive report, these topics may be discussed in separate chapters. Such things as measurement, experimental procedures, sampling procedures, design, analysis, and significance levels (if hypotheses are tested) are included under procedures. A good rule to follow concerning the detail of this section is that the description should be detailed enough so that a reader could replicate the study. There should be no areas in which it is uncertain as to what was done. For example, it is not sufficient to say that the creativity of a sample of third graders was measured. The procedures and tests used for measuring creativity should be carefully described. The measurement of creativity should, of course, reflect the definition of creativity as given in the statement of the problem.

The procedures section should contain a rationale for the research methodology. This is especially important in a research report such as a thesis. Shorter reports often do not have a stated rationale for applying, for example, a specific statistical test. The rationale for the procedure is implied and a statement given as to what was done. In writing his thesis, a graduate student may be required to present quite a detailed rationale for using a statistical test since mastery of the research methods may be the primary reason for doing the research. This rationale may include a description of the general purpose of the statistical test. For example, in an article, the statement that a Student's t-test for the significant difference between two means was computed may appear and be sufficient. In a thesis there would probably be a discussion of the Student's t-test and how it can be applied to the difference between two means. This detailed rationale may not always be required of a thesis. However, it facilitates the understanding of the research, not only for the writer but also for a reader who is not familiar with the specific techniques. Research reports such as those submitted to the Bureau of Research, USOE, should contain such a rationale if uncommon or complex statistical procedures have been used. A reader may assume that what was done is accurate, but if he can get no meaning out of the procedures, it is unlikely that he will continue reading the report.

The order of discussing the various items under a procedures section is somewhat arbitrary. One logical order is the sequence in time according to which the items were carried out in the research project. It is possible that two or more items were worked on simultaneously. Usually the research project progresses through the stages of preparation for data collection, data collection, and data analysis, in that order. The results are the products of the data analysis. Therefore, it is often desirable to discuss the analysis near the close of the procedures section. In that way, the analysis is relatively fresh in the mind of the reader when he comes to the results section.

Results

The results follow directly from the analysis and it should be apparent that the results are based upon the analysis. The writer should not mix results of his study with those of studies reported in the review of literature. Probably the most important concern in writing the results section is to present them in a clear, concise, and well-organized manner. A common error when reporting results is to mix results with conjectures and conclusions. The reader should be able to concentrate on the results themselves without spending considerable effort trying to sort and organize the results.

The organization of results depends upon the specific research project. If several dependent variables are involved, the results may be grouped according to dependent variables. For example, achievement measures might be grouped together, separate from attitude measures. Independent variables may also be used as a basis for organization. An extensive experimental research project may involve several experiments. Assuming the experiments to be somehow sequentially related, the discussion of results could be organized according to experiment. The important thing about the organization of the results is that it can be easily followed, thus facilitating the reporting of the research.

The use of tables can be a very helpful device for organizing results. In fact, for research reports which involve large amounts of statistical results, tables are a necessity. The forms of tables are somewhat flexible. Publication manuals such as that of the American Psychological Association are quite specific as to the table requirements for the Association's journals. Some general comments may be made concerning the construction of tables.

The title of a table should state specifically what the table contains. If a table contains means and standard deviations, this should be stated. The means and standard deviations should not be referred to simply as results. The title should also include information as to what means and standard deviations. It is not sufficient to title a table simply as Means and Standard Deviations. An example of a table title would be: Means and Standard Deviations of Fifth-Grade Students on Academic Measures. The part of the table immediately below the title should contain subheadings indicating the content of the columns. For the table entitled as the example above, the far left column would contain the academic measures. The sources of the means and standard deviations should be identified, such as experimental groups and control group. Finally, means and standard deviations should be differentiated. The upper title and subheadings of the table for the example would be as follows:

TABLE 10.1

Means and Standard Deviations of Fifth-Grade Students on Academic Measures

	Exp. Group 1		Exp. Group 2		Control Group	
Measure	Mean	S.D.	Mean	S.D.	Mean	S.D.

More than one type of statistic can be reported in a single table, but the writer should avoid running in a large number of different types. Means and standard deviations often go together. A correlation matrix may comprise a single table. Sometimes means and standard deviations appear with correlation coefficients. This can become cumbersome because correlation coefficients involve two variables and it may be confusing as to which mean goes with what variable.

The writer should put things together which facilitates communicating the results. The contents of a table should be directed toward a single idea or facet of the research. Tables should not be crowded and confusing. Spacing is relative and depends upon the type of printing, size of characters, and number of digits in the entries. For the table in the example presented earlier, the spacing is adequate for four- or five-digit entries. If means or standard deviations contained exceeded five digits, it would be wise to provide additional space. With rare exception it is good policy to limit tables to one page in length. A table should follow as closely as possible the first reference to it in the research report. A table that will not fit into the remaining space on the page should be placed on the page immediately following, at the end of the first paragraph. A table of one page or less in length should not be split between two pages. Certain periodicals require that all tables appear at the end of the article. When used, this procedure facilitates printing, but it should not be viewed as a general procedure for including tables.

Tables are used for grouping results. However, not all results, including statistical results, appear in tables. If the number of entries is small, say three or four, it is not necessary to construct a table. Such results can be reported directly in the prose. For example, if the researcher had three means to report, he might insert a sentence such as: The means of the three experimental groups were 87, 84, and 95, respectively. In the context of the paragraph it should be clear as to what respectively means.

The results section should contain all of the necessary information for meeting the objectives of the research project. Things like hypotheses should be checked to see if they have been adequately tested and the results of these tests reported. Existing patterns should be pointed out. If supplementary analyses are done, these results should appear. (Extensive tables of supplementary results may be placed in an appendix if their inclusion makes this part of the report cumbersome.) Only results should be reported. If a pattern appears, the pattern should be carefully described but a discussion of why the pattern emerged should be deferred for the conclusions section.

Conclusions, Recommendations, and Implications

The final section of the research report consists of conclusions, recommendations, and implications. Commonly called the conclusions section, it may also go by names such as Conclusion and Discussion, Conclusions and Recommendations, etc. In any event, Conclusions almost invariably appears in the title of the section.

This final section is the key of the research report and should contain the highlights of the study. In many ways this is the most difficult section to write. The writer's perceptive ability in the area being researched is probably taxed more in writing this section than any other. The results must be interpreted and the entire study synthesized.

The final section may open with a brief review of the problem and procedures of the research project. This focuses the reader's attention on the problem and objectives of the study. The focus may have become somewhat blurred because of the attention to details in the analyses. This review should be brief and the writer should move quickly to the conclusions and the corresponding discussion. The review should not break the continuity with the results section.

The conclusions must follow logically from the results of the investigation. Here the writer must be careful not to pass off results as conclusions, an error which is less likely to occur than passing off conclusions in the results section of the report. The number of conclusions drawn would depend in part upon the complexity of the results. Supposedly at least one substantive conclusion could be drawn, otherwise it would hardly be worthwhile pursuing, much less reporting, the research. A study could, of course, contain a series of conclusions. The organization would be similar to the reporting of results.

The common error of writing the final section is to draw conclusions that are too broad. Educational research, especially research conducted in the classroom and other natural educational settings, involves situations for which there is less than maximum control. Also, there may be inexactness in the data. Caution should be exercised when drawing the conclusions.

Qualifying statements such as under specific conditions or subject to such and such conditions are often appropriate, especially when arriving at generalizations. The writer must keep in mind that the conclusions must be backed up by factual information.

The other extreme is for the writer to be too narrow and restrictive in drawing conclusions. This situation reflects a lack of information about the research problem. Usually this difficulty is not as likely to appear in drawing specific conclusions, since they follow from the results. Conclusions that are overly restrictive are more likely to appear in the generalizations.

The final section should contain, in addition to the conclusions, a summary and a discussion. The discussion should be enlightening and creative, characteristics which depend largely on a scholarly understanding of the area under study, past research in the area, and the specific research project under concern. Such knowledge will not necessarily guarantee such a discussion but without it such a discussion is most unlikely.

The discussion should include implications for educational practice and possibly educational theory. At this point (as at other points) in the research endeavor, the writer should be aware of any weaknesses in his design or procedures. Assumptions should be reviewed. This usually leads to suggestions for additional research in the area. Research in most areas is of a continuing nature; answers or partial answers to research questions invariably raise or imply additional questions. A question may be raised about a variable that was either uncontrolled or not considered in the research at hand. The writer should be aware of the limitations of his research and have accounted for such; he should not need to apologize for any shortcomings.

The conclusions and summary should be to the point. Conjecture and speculation should be clearly distinguished from direct conclusions. Implications should stay within the mainstream of the research study. Tangential points should be brought in only when they are relevant to the point under discussion.

The writing of the research report is not a task which can be taken lightly or approached haphazardly. Careful preparation is a prerequisite for this task. The writer should not expect to produce a satisfactory final product without some revision. Gen-

erally the report is improved with subsequent revisions, addi-
tions, and deletions. Research writing is a complex and exacting activity and revision should be considered a normal part of
this task.

Revision may be initiated either by the author himself or
someone else's criticism of the report. Self-criticism may be most
valuable after the writer has let the report sit for a short time,
say ten days to two weeks. This is not to be viewed as a lack of
persistence. Rather it is easier to get a critical perspective of
the report if a short time has passed. Explanations may not be as
obvious as they seemed to be during the initial writing. Omissions and confusing statements become more apparent. Contra-
dictions may come to the fore which were undetected the first
time through. Before releasing the final draft of the manuscript
for typing, the writer should make a critical and comprehensive
search for omissions, inconsistencies, ambiguous statements,
and inaccurate information.

As a matter of course, the writer should subject his report to
the criticism of his peers. A graduate student is forced into this
due to the channels already set up for submitting a thesis and
getting it approved. Criticism is offered in a positive and constructive attitude and should be accepted in the same manner.
The writer should not interpret criticism as a personal assault.
No one is obligated to accept the criticism, but assuming that
the critics are competent, their suggestions are likely to improve
the report and the manner of presentation.

As a concluding statement, the reader is reminded of two important points. The first is not to underestimate the task. Prepare for it carefully and attack the problem systematically,
with attention to detail. Secondly, be persistent. Do not put off
the writing when the facts are fresh.

Bibliography and Appendix

A bibliography is a necessary part of the research report. Even
if no footnote references are made in the body of the report, a
bibliography should still be included. The writer should adopt
a standard procedure for the bibliographical entries. A good
policy, one which has been mentioned previously, is to make an
accurate and technically correct entry when the source is ini-

tially reviewed. This will save considerable time and effort when the final bibliography is being prepared. Entries made on three by five cards can greatly facilitate putting them in alphabetical order.

A bibliography should always be included but an appendix only if it is necessary. An appendix is necessary when there are materials which do not fit well in the main body of the report. Several types of materials can be placed in an appendix: self-constructed measuring instruments such as tests or questionnaires, tables of raw scores, or related data. Great bulks of related results tend to make the main report cumbersome and difficult reading. Such results can be placed in the appendix. For example, in discussing hypotheses about testing means, the means are necessary in the results section. However, the standard deviations and other measures of the distributions may be of interest and could be placed in an appendix. Separate appendices should be used for different types of materials. The appendices appear at the end of the report, following the bibliography.

Concluding Remarks

The satisfactory completion of the written research report concludes the specific research project. In a sense this is true, but this should not be the conclusion of an individual's research efforts. A well-done piece of research should be a source of satisfaction and pride. It will undoubtedly be a valuable learning experience, whether done by a novice or the most sophisticated researcher. To abandon the area of research is an injustice to the educator himself and very likely to the field of education. The association with his and others' research should stimulate the educator to pursue new and related ideas. Research should be a continuing phenomena with each specific project adding to the store of knowledge. The research methods provide the necessary tools by which the specific projects are completed.

Suggested Study Exercises

10.1 Select one or more research articles about an educational topic and write an abstract for each article. Follow the four parts of the outline as suggested in this chapter. Limit yourself to not more than five sentences under each of the four parts of the outline.

10.2 Present a critical review of one or more research articles. You may use the articles suggested in Exercise 10.1. The questions presented in this chapter may serve as a guide for your review. However, for your specific articles, all of the questions may not be applicable. If the members of a class or group review a common article, compare and discuss the individual reviews. The sharing of views and ideas on matters such as critical reviews can be a worthwhile learning experience.

10.3 Select a research topic of limited magnitude and write a hypothetical research report including the statement of the problem and the anticipated procedures and analysis. Since this is a hypothetical study, it is not expected that you collect data or produce any results and conclusions. Therefore, the sections dealing with these matters would be missing from your report. Do a brief review of the literature and limit your review and statement of the problem to two or three typewritten pages. Be brief and concise and pay special attention to the continuity of ideas. Use your mastery of the content of previous chapters to present an adequate and correct methodology for doing the research study. Include a bibliography. This suggests a writing task of the magnitude of a short term paper.

10.4 Select a research report, probably an article, which deals with an educational topic in your area or one about which you have some knowledge. Read the report through the results section but do not read the conclusions. Write a conclusions section of your own. After you have completed your conclusions, subject them to your own critical review and compare them to the conclusions of the report.

Selected References on Writing Procedures

The following bibliography presents a cross-section of helpful references for the mechanics and procedures of writing a research report. The references provide suggestions concerning style, presentation of headings and subheadings, typing requirements, and the like. This is in no sense an exhaustive bibliography. Many associations have their own publication manuals. There are many similarities between such manuals and the content is primarily oriented toward publication in the professional journals. The publication manual of the American Psychological Association is included in this bibliography. If a writer is preparing an article for a professional journal that has special publication requirements, he should secure the publication manual prior to writing the report.

American Psychological Association, Council of Editors. *Publication Manual of the American Psychological Association,* rev. ed. Washington, D.C.: American Psychological Association, 1967.

Ball, John, and Williams, C. B. *Report Writing.* New York: Ronald Press, 1955.

Cambell, W. G. *Form and Style in Thesis Writing.* Boston: Houghton Mifflin Co., 1954.

Dugdale, K. *A Manual on Writing Research.* Bloomington, Ind.: Indiana University Bookstore, 1962.

Emberger, M. R., and Hall, M. R. *Scientific Writing.* New York: Harcourt, Brace & Co., 1955.

Faculty of Teachers College, University of Cincinnati. *A Guide for the Preparation of Dissertations, Theses, and Field Reports.* Cincinnati: University of Cincinnati, 1952.

Flesch, R. F., and Lass, A. H. *The Way to Write,* 2nd ed. New York: McGraw-Hill Book Co., 1955.

Good, C. V., ed. *Dictionary of Education,* 2nd ed. New York: McGraw-Hill Book Co., 1959.

Leggett, G., Mead, C. D., and Charvat, W. *Prentice-Hall Handbook for Writers,* 3rd ed. Englewood Cliffs, N.J.: Prentice-Hall, 1960.

Shannon, J. R. "Tips to Writers from Seventy-Five Editors of Educational Periodicals," *Journal of Educational Research*. 1950, 44, 241–68.

Turabian, K. L. *A Manual for Writers of Term Papers, Theses, and Dissertations*. Chicago: The University of Chicago Press, 1960.

U.S. Government Style Manual, rev. ed. Washington, D.C.: Government Printing Office, 1959.

Van Hagan, C. E. *Report Writers' Handbook*. Englewood Cliffs, N.J.: Prentice-Hall, 1961.

Williams, C. B., and Stevenson, A. H. *A Research Manual for College Studies and Papers*. New York: Harper and Brothers, 1951.

Bibliography

American Association for Health, Physical Education, and Recreation. *Research Methods Applied to Health, Physical Education, and Recreation,* rev. ed. Washington, D.C.: NEA, 1952.

American Psychological Association. *Standards for Educational and Psychological Tests and Manuals.* Washington, D.C.: American Psychological Association, Inc., 1966.

Anastasi, A. *Psychological Testing,* 2nd ed. New York: The Macmillan Co., 1961.

Barnes, F. P. *Research for the Practitioner in Education.* Washington, D.C.: Department of Elementary School Principals, NEA, 1964.

Barnes, J. B. *Educational Research for Classroom Teachers.* New York: G. P. Putnam's Sons, 1960.

Best, J. W. *Research in Education.* Englewood Cliffs, N.J.: Prentice-Hall, Inc., 1959.

Biometrics. The Biometric Society, Tucson, Arizona.

Borg, W. R. *Educational Research: An Introduction.* New York: David McKay, Inc., 1963.

Borko, H., ed. *Computer Applications in the Behavioral Sciences.* Englewood Cliffs, N.J.: Prentice-Hall, Inc., 1962.

Brickman, W. W. *Guide to Research in Educational History.* New York: New York University Bookstore, 1949.

Campbell, D. T., and Stanley, J. C. *Experimental and Quasi-Experimental Designs for Research.* Chicago: Rand McNally & Company, 1963. (Reprint from *Handbook of Research on Teaching,* Gage, ed.)

Clarke, R. B., Coladarci, A. P., and Caffrey, J. *Statistical Reasoning and Procedures.* Columbus, Ohio: Charles E. Merrill Books, Inc., 1965.

Cochran, W. G. *Sampling Techniques,* 2nd ed. New York: John Wiley and Sons, Inc., 1963.

Collier, R. O., Jr., and Elam, S. M., eds. *Research Design and Analysis:* Second Annual Phi Delta Kappa Symposium on Educational Research. Bloomington, Ind.: Phi Delta Kappa, 1961.

Cook, D. R. *A Guide to Educational Research.* Boston: Allyn and Bacon, Inc., 1965.

Cornell, F. G. *The Essentials of Educational Statistics.* New York: John Wiley and Sons, Inc., 1956.

Cox, D. R. *Planning of Experiments.* New York: John Wiley and Sons, Inc., 1958.

Cronbach, L. J. *Essentials of Psychological Testing,* 2nd ed. New York: Harper & Row, Publishers, 1960.

Culbertson, J. A. and Hencley, S. P., eds. *Educational Research: New Perspectives.* Danville, Ill.: The Interstate Printers and Publishers, Inc., 1963.

Ebel, Robert L. *Measuring Educational Achievement.* Englewood Cliffs, N.J.: Prentice-Hall, Inc., 1965.

Edwards, A. L. *Experimental Design in Psychological Research,* rev. ed. New York: Holt, Rinehart and Winston, Inc., 1960.

────── *Statistical Methods in the Behavioral Sciences.* New York: Holt, Rinehart and Winston, Inc., 1954.

────── *Techniques of Attitude Scale Construction.* New York: Appleton-Century-Crofts, Inc., 1957.

Ferguson, G. A. *Statistical Analysis in Psychology and Education,* 2nd ed. New York: McGraw-Hill Book Co., Inc., 1966.

Festinger, L., and Katz, D., eds. *Research Methods in the Behavioral Sciences.* New York: Dryden Press, 1953.

Finney, D. J. *An Introduction to the Theory of Experimental Design.* Chicago: The University of Chicago Press, 1955.

Fisher, R. A. *The Design of Experiments,* 6th ed. New York: Hafner Publishing Corp., 1951.

Furst, E. J. *Constructing Evaluation Instruments.* New York: David McKay, Inc., 1958.

Galfo, A. J., and Miller, E. *Interpreting Educational Research.* Dubuque, Iowa: Wm. C. Brown Company, Publishers, 1965.

Good, C. V. *Introduction to Educational Research,* 2nd ed. New York: Appleton-Century-Crofts, 1963.

Good, C. V. and Scates, D. E. *Methods of Research: Educational, Psychological, Sociological.* New York: Appleton-Century-Crofts, 1954.

Goodwin, William L. "The Effects on Achievement Test Results of Varying Conditions of Experimental Atmosphere, Notice of Test, Test Administration and Test Scoring," Technical Report No. 2, Research and Development Center for Learning and Re-Education, Madison, Wis.: University of Wisconsin, 1965.

Gregory, R. H., and VanHorn, R. L. *Automatic Data Processing Systems: Principles and Procedures.* Belmont, Calif.: Wadsworth Publishing Co., Inc., 1960.

Guba, E., and Elam, S., eds. *The Training and Nurture of Educational Researchers.* Bloomington, Ind.: Phi Delta Kappa, Inc., 1965.

Guenther, W. C. *Concepts of Statistical Inference.* New York: McGraw-Hill Book Co., Inc., 1965.

Guilford, J. P. *Fundamental Statistics in Psychology and Education,* 4th ed. New York: McGraw-Hill Book Co., Inc., 1965.

———— *Psychometric Methods,* 2nd ed. New York: McGraw-Hill Book Co., Inc., 1954.

Guilford, J. P., Kettner, N. W., and Christensen, P. R., "A Factor Analytic Study Across the Domains of Reasoning, Creativity, and Evaluation: II. Administration of Tests and Analysis of Results," *University of Southern California Psychological Laboratory Report,* No. 16, 1956.

Harris, C. W., ed. *Problems in Measuring Change.* Madison, Wis.: University of Wisconsin Press, 1963.

Hays, W. L. *Quantification in Psychology.* Belmont, Calif.: Brooks/Cole Publishing Co., 1967.

Hockett, H. C. *The Critical Method in Historical Research and Writing.* New York: The Macmillan Co., 1955.

Huntsberger, D. V. *Elements of Statistical Inference,* 2nd ed. Boston: Allyn and Bacon, Inc., 1967.

Hyman, Herbert H. *Survey Design and Analysis.* New York: Free Press, 1955.

Journal of Applied Physiology, American Physiological Society, Washington, D.C.

Kahn, R. L., and Cannell, C. F. *The Dynamics of Inteviewing.* New York: John Wiley and Sons, Inc., 1957.

Kaimann, R. A., and Marker, R. W. *Educational Data Processing, New Dimensions and Prospects.* New York: Houghton Mifflin Co., 1967.

Kerlinger, F. N. *Foundations of Behavioral Research; Educational and Psychological Inquiry.* New York: Holt, Rinehart and Winston, Inc., 1964.

Kish, L. *Survey Sampling.* New York: John Wiley and Sons, Inc., 1965.

Lindquist, E. F. *Design and Analysis of Experiments in Psychology and Education.* Boston: Houghton Mifflin Co., 1953.

McGrath, G. D., Jelinek, J. J., and Wochner, R. E. *Educational Research Methods.* New York: The Ronald Press Co., 1963.

McNemar, Q. *Psychological Statistics,* 3rd ed. New York: John Wiley and Sons, Inc., 1962.

Mehrens, W. A. and Ebel, R. L., eds. *Principles of Educational and Psychological Measurement: A Book of Selected Readings.* Chicago: Rand McNally & Company, 1967.

Mouly, G. J. *The Science of Educational Research.* New York: American Book Co., 1963.

Mussen, P., ed. *Handbook of Research Methods in Child Development.* New York: John Wiley and Sons, Inc., 1960.

Payne, S. L. *The Art of Asking Questions.* Princeton, N.J.: Princeton University Press, 1951.

Popham, W. J. *Educational Statistics; Use and Interpretation.* New York: Harper & Row, Publishers, 1967.

Psychological Monographs, The American Psychological Association, Washington, D.C.

Psychometrika, The Psychometric Society, Richmond, Virginia.

Ray, W. S., *An Introduction to Experimental Design.* New York: The Macmillan Co., 1960.

Remmers, H. H., Gage, N. L., and Rummel, J. F. *A Practical Introduction to Measurement and Evaluation.* New York: Harper & Brothers, Publishers, 1960.

Ross, C. C., Stanley, J. C. *Measurement in Today's Schools.* 3rd ed. Englewood Cliffs, N.J.: Prentice-Hall, Inc., 1954.

Rummel, J. F. *An Introduction to Research Procedures in Education,* 2nd ed. New York: Harper & Brothers, Publishers, 1964.

Scott, W. A., and Wertheimer, M. *Introduction to Psychological Research.* New York: John Wiley and Sons, Inc., 1962.

Sieber, S. D., and Lazarsfeld, P. F. *The Organization of Educational Research*, CRP 1974, Bureau of Applied Social Research, Columbia University, 1966.

Siegel, S. *Nonparametric Statistics for the Behavioral Sciences*. New York: McGraw-Hill Book Co., Inc., 1956.

Stanley, J. C., ed. *Improving Experimental Design and Statistical Analysis: Proceedings of the Seventh Annual Phi Delta Kappa Symposium of Educational Research*. Chicago: Rand McNally & Company, 1967.

Stanley, J. C., "Controlled Experimentation in the Classroom," *Journal of Experimental Education*, 1957, 15, 195–201.

Thorndike, R. L. and Hagen, E. *Measurement and Evaluation in Psychology and Education*, 2nd ed. New York: John Wiley and Sons, Inc., 1961.

Travers, R. M. W. *An Introduction to Educational Research*, 2nd ed. New York: The Macmillan Co., 1964.

Van Dalen, D. D. *Understanding Educational Research—An Introduction*, enlarged and revised. New York: McGraw-Hill Book Co., Inc., 1966.

Walker, H. M., and Lev, J. *Elementary Statistical Methods*, rev. ed. New York: Holt, Rinehart and Winston, Inc., 1958.

Wandt, E. *A Cross-Section of Educational Research*. New York: David McKay, Inc., 1965.

Wise, J. E., Nordberg, R. B. and Reitz, D. J. *Methods of Research in Education*. Boston: D. C. Heath & Company, 1967.

Appendix A: Solutions to Suggested Study Exercises

Note

Exercises which have flexible answers or direct the reader to a journal article are not included in this solutions section. Brief responses are provided for exercises in which class discussion may be helpful. For some exercises which require a rather lengthy discussion or response, the solution given here is an overview. The purpose of this solutions section is to help the student evaluate his own mastery of concepts and to make the consideration of the exercises a more profitable learning experience. The purpose is not to exhaust the discussion of every detail associated with the exercises.

Chapter 1

1.3 The null hypothesis has stated or implied in its form the characteristic of nondirection. For example, this may take the form of no difference between two parameters. The non-directional form indicates that we do not hypothesize one parameter to be less than or greater than the other.

Chapter 2

2.1 (a) The *type* of residential dwelling would be nominal scale. If we were interested in number of family units we could go to ratio scale. However, such a quantitative characteristic is not defined when we simply classify according to type.

   (b) Calcium deposits could be measured on a ratio scale.

   (c) Performance on an essay part of a history test would be measured on an ordinal scale. Considerable objectivity and quantification would have to be defined before such a performance could be measured on an equal unit or ratio scale.

(d) Ratings of student teacher performance would be measured on an ordinal scale.

*(e) Ratio scale measurement would be involved.

2.2 The constants are grade level, sex, and school. The independent variables are instructional materials and teacher, although these two cannot be separated since it is implied that each teacher uses only one type of instructional material. The dependent variable is reading achievement.

2.3

Frequency Distribution for the 80 Scores

Score	f	Score	f	Score	f
20	1	31	2	42	3
21	0	32	4	43	2
22	0	33	5	44	3
23	1	34	3	45	3
24	2	35	6	46	2
25	1	36	4	47	2
26	0	37	5	48	1
27	3	38	4	49	1
28	2	39	3	50	0
29	3	40	3	51	1
30	5	41	4	52	1

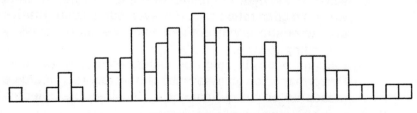

Histogram for the 80 Scores above

2.4

Interval	f
19.5–22.5	1
22.5–25.5	4
25.5–28.5	5
28.5–31.5	10
31.5–34.5	12
34.5–37.5	15
37.5–40.5	10
40.5–43.5	9
43.5–46.5	8
46.5–49.5	4
49.5–52.5	2

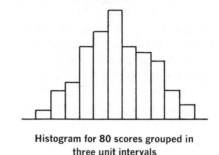

Histogram for 80 scores grouped in three unit intervals

In comparing the two histograms we appear to get more of a pulling together when the data are grouped. Frequencies within the intervals are generally increased over the frequencies of the individual scores which is, of course, due to the combination of single score frequencies. Note that the range of the histograms has not changed in this case.

2.5 Measures of central tendency are points in a distribution that locate the distribution on a scale. Measures of variability are intervals that indicate the dispersion or spread in the distribution. These two types of measures provide different information, essential in defining a specific distribution.

2.6 Figure 2.7 indicates that 16 blocks occupy the area for less than 5 or greater than 8. Thus, the probability of getting such a sum is $^{16}/_{36}$ or .444. The probability of getting either a 6 or an 8 is $^{10}/_{36}$ or .278.

2.7 The 57 is 1.4 standard deviation units above the mean. Table A indicates that .0808 of the area lies to the right of a standard score of 1.4. Hence, the probability of getting a score of 57 or greater is .0808. In like manner, between 55 and 65, the probability is .6826; between 40 and 55, the probability is .8185. (It should be noted that for these solutions the actual values were used. The accuracy of measurement was not discussed, but for more precise results this would be necessary. If, for example, measurement was to the nearest integer, then the true boundary for the 57 or greater would be 56.5, since any score exceeding 56.5 would be considered 57 or greater. This would slightly change the standard scores and hence the probabilities.)

2.8 The researcher would select a random sample from which he could compute statistics. The sample would reflect the population within the boundary of sampling fluctuation. Hence, the statistics are used to infer to the parameters, again within the bounds of sampling fluctuations. The statistic involved would be the mean reading level of the sample of first graders measured; the corresponding parameter is the mean reading level of the entire first-grade population. The chain of reasoning follows the inference implied above. The population has certain characteristics called parameters (which will not be known for certain). The random sample which reflects the population has certain characteristics called statistics. The statistics are determined and known and from these we reason back to the corresponding parameters and draw conclusions about the parameters. In this particular situation the researcher draws conclusions about the population mean from the observed sample mean.

2.9 A statistic is a measure of a sample and a parameter a measure of a population. The underlying distribution is the distribution which provides the theoretical base for how the statistic under study behaves; that is, what is the shape, location, and dispersion of the distribution of which we have one observation—namely, the statistic. It is the underlying distribution of the statistic.

Chapter 3

3.1 The dependent variable is the score on the history achievement test. Since each student will produce one score or observation, the assumption of independence requires that no student influence the score of any other student during the testing. To meet this assumption it would be necessary to exclude any group efforts and guard against cheating while the test is being taken. Note that it is not necessary to exclude group study prior to the testing. The thing being measured is knowledge of history at the time of testing, regardless of how the student prepared himself prior to the test.

3.2 The null hypothesis tested is that the population means are equal; that is, no difference between the population means. In symbols this is given by $H_0: \mu_1 - \mu_2 = 0$. Since

the statistical test was significant the probability statement is: the probability that the observed difference in
sample means would occur by chance, if, in fact, there is
no difference in population means, is less than .05. Note
that the difference in sample means is a statistic and the
difference in population means a parameter.

3.3 The independent variables are materials, age, and class
size. The dependent variable is reading achievement. The
constants are teacher and sex.

3.4 Assuming the parametric assumptions, a Student's t-
test or an analysis of variance would be appropriate techniques. The null hypothesis is that the two treatment
means of the population are equal; that is, $H_0: \mu_{T_1} = \mu_{T_2}$.
The null hypothesis is rejected. The possible error being
made here is rejecting a true hypothesis (type I or alpha
error). The probability of making such an error is less than
.01. The test is significant at the .05 level, since if the
probability is less than .01 it is certainly less than .05.

3.5 The population means of sixth-grade arithmetic achievement for boys and girls are equal; that is, $H_0: \mu_B = \mu_G$ or
$H_0: \mu_B - \mu_G = 0$. Since the statistical test was significant
at the .05 level, the probability statement is as follows:
the probability that the observed difference between the
sample means would occur by chance, if, in fact, the population means are equal, is less than .05. The conclusion
is that the population means are different; population
means referring to those of boys and girls on sixth-grade
arithmetic achievement. There is not enough information
to decide whether or not the test is significant at the .01
level. The probability may be less than .05 but greater
than .01, that is, it could fall between the .05 and .01
levels.

3.6 We would reject the hypothesis since with 19 degrees of
freedom and a two-tailed test (no direction is hypothesized) a t-value of 2.09 is required for significance at the
.05 level. Since the t-value was positive, the sample mean
was larger than the hypothesized mean.

3.7 Since there are 6 levels and 8 Ss in each level, there is a
total of 48 Ss. Five degrees of freedom are associated with
the independent variable and 42 with the within or error
term. Thus, the appropriate F-distribution has 5 and 42
degrees of freedom. With these degrees of freedom, values of 2.44 and 3.49 are required for significance at the

.05 and .01 levels respectively. Thus, the observed F-value is significant at the .05 level but not at the .01 level. In educational research the .05 level is generally considered conservative enough, hence we would probably reject the null hypothesis. The probability statement is: the probability that the observed sample means would appear if the population means are equal is less than .05. (However, this probability is greater than .01.)

3.8 The analysis of variance would be an appropriate technique. The three null hypotheses deal with (1) the effect of stimulus; (2) the effect of display; and (3) the interaction of display and stimulus. The null hypotheses could be stated as follows: (1) There is no difference in the population means of those students using nonsense symbols and those using learning materials. (2) There is no difference in the population means of those students using random and those using ordered displays. (3) This hypothesis involves four population means which we will denote by μ_{NR}, μ_{NO}, μ_{MR}, μ_{MO}, where the subscripts N and M stand for nonsense symbols or meaningful materials, and R and O denote random or ordered displays. The null hypothesis is that these four population means are equal after the main effects of stimulus and display have been removed. The main effects and the interaction each have one degree of freedom associated with them. If there is a total of 80 Ss, the within or error term has 76 degrees of freedom. Therefore, the appropriate underlying distribution in all three cases is the F-distribution with one and 76 degrees of freedom. This distribution requires a value of 3.97 for significance at the .05 level.

3.9 The concept of interaction between two independent variables is sometimes referred to as the effect that one independent variable has upon another. The effect of one of the variables does not remain constant over the levels of the other.

3.10 An analysis of covariance would be used when it is necessary to include a statistical control over a relevant factor. The analysis of covariance may be necessary if it is suspected that the groups differ markedly on a factor relevant to the dependent variable. The hypothesis may be so stated that it becomes necessary for the researcher to adjust for initial differences; for example, if we are interested in the amount learned during a period rather than the absolute amount known at a point in time. The analysis of variance is preferred if no adjustment on dependent variable scores is necessary. Initial differences of S's may be randomly distributed among the groups.

3.11 The null hypothesis is that the *adjusted* population reading achievement means of students taught using the three sets of instructional materials are equal. Adjusted means of the dependent variable are actually tested. If the statistical test is significant, the conclusion is that the instructional materials have different effects upon fourth-grade reading achievement.

3.12 The two possible types of errors in hypothesis testing are (1) rejecting a true hypothesis, and (2) accepting a false hypothesis. Hypotheses are neither proved nor disproved because there is always the probability, however small, that an error is being made in the decision on the hypothesis.

Chapter 4

4.1 The parametric techniques assume that the data are measured on at least an interval scale. This is not a necessary assumption for the non-parametric techniques. The non-parametric techniques do not require assumptions about the shape of the population distribution which are crucial with the parametric techniques when sample size is small. Since non-parametric techniques deal with nominal or ordinal data, the parametric assumption of homogeneity of variance does not apply. Both techniques require the assumption of random sampling since this is a necessary part of any inferential technique. Also, under certain conditions the assumption of a continuous underlying distribution of the dependent variable (variable measured) is common to both types of techniques.

4.3 The null hypothesis can be stated as such: there is no difference between the population distribution (from which the sample was drawn) and the expected distribution. An equivalent statement is that the population distribution is the expected distribution. The probability statement: the probability that the observed sample distribution would appear by chance, if the population distribution is the expected distribution, is less than .01. We conclude that the population distribution is not the expected distribution. This statistical test is significant at the .05 level since probability less than .01 is certainly less than .05.

4.4 The null hypothesis: the frequency of blue eyes equals the frequency of brown eyes in the university population. An equivalent statement would be: the proportion of blue eyes equals the proportion of brown eyes in the university population. A chi-square test can be used to test this hypothesis.

4.5 An inspection of Table E reveals that a χ^2-value of 3.84 with one degree of freedom is required for significance at the .05 level. Therefore, the value of 4.81 is significant. The null hypothesis tested: the populations from which the sample were drawn have a common median. The null hypothesis is rejected.

4.6 The appropriate chi-square distribution has 12 degrees of freedom, therefore a value of 21.03 is necessary for significance at the .05 level. A χ^2-value of 23.81 is significant and we would reject the hypothesis that the four samples were drawn from a common population and conclude that the sample distributions came from different population distributions. Probability statement: the probability that the four observed sample distributions would appear by chance, if drawn from the same population, is less than .05.

4.7 The parametric analysis of variance analyzes actual observed scores measured on an interval or ratio scale. The Kruskal-Wallis analysis, in contrast, analyzes ranks which are based on ordinal measurement. The parametric technique deals with the ratio of two variances while the Kruskal-Wallis technique involves a statistic defined as "H." The Kruskal-Wallis technique is a one-way analysis whereas the parametric technique may include two or more independent variables and their interactions. Null hypothesis: the population distributions from which the five samples were drawn have the same average (or have identical averages). An equivalent statement is to hypothesize that the samples were drawn from a common population with respect to averages.

4.8 Since the sample size exceeds 25, the normal distribution may be used as an adequate approximation to the binomial distribution. Since the significance level is .01, a value of 2.58 is necessary for a significant test. The value

3.21 is significant and we would reject the null hypothesis. Therefore we conclude that the median difference of the before and after scores in the population is *not* zero.

4.9 It would be undesirable to use the same type of analysis for both dependent variables because the mathematics achievement has interval scale measurement and the handedness data are only nominal scale measurement. Frequencies or proportions would be tested statistically in the handedness data and means in the mathematics achievement data. A chi-square test could be used for the handedness data, an analysis of variance or Student's *t*-test for the mathematics achievement data. We would conclude that in the population, athletes and non-athletes differ in frequency or proportion of handedness. Assume that we have been dealing with the null hypothesis, that is, there is no difference in the population proportions of athletes and non-athletes; we could be making the error of rejecting a true hypothesis.

4.10 Errors of reasoning or procedure:
   (1) A Student's *t*-test does not apply to data measured on an ordinal scale.
   (2) there is confusion on significance; a test significant at the .01 level is significant at the .05.
   (3) rejecting the null hypothesis would result in concluding that the *population,* not sample, measures are different.
   (4) since the null hypothesis is rejected, there is no probability of having made a Type II or beta error. The possibility does exist of having made a Type I or alpha error.

Chapter 5

5.1 A correlation coefficient is an index of the relationship between two variables. The coefficient can take on values between plus and minus one inclusive. The end points of plus and minus one indicate perfect relationships. The algebraic sign indicates the direction of the relationship. For a negative correlation, high scores on one variable are associated with low scores on the other variable.

5.2 This coefficient is significantly different from zero since Table F indicates that a value of approximately .31 or greater is necessary for a significant test, with 38 degrees of freedom and the .05 level (two-tailed test). The null hypothesis: the population correlation coefficient between the two variables is zero. Probability statement: the probability that a sample correlation of .413 would occur by chance, if, in fact, the population correlation is zero, is less than .05. We conclude that the population correlation is not zero.

5.4 Null hypothesis: the correlation coefficients of the populations from which the samples were drawn are equal. Probability statement: the probability that the observed difference in sample correlation coefficients would occur by chance, if there is no difference between the population correlation coefficients, is less than .05. We reject the null hypothesis and conclude that there is a difference between the population correlation coefficients. Possible error: reject a true hypothesis (Type I or alpha error). With this amount of information we cannot conclude anything about the .01 level. Probability less than .05 does not indicate whether it is greater or less than .01.

5.5 The Pearson-product moment correlation coefficient requires that both variables possess at least interval scale measurement and that their underlying distributions are continuous, somewhat symmetrical, and homoscedastic. The Spearman rank coefficient does not require interval measurement but only that the scores can be ordered. If the Spearman rank coefficient is used as a substitute for the Pearson-product moment coefficient, the underlying distributions should be continuous and homoscedastic. Both coefficients assume a linear relationship between the two variables being correlated. The scores that actually go into the computation of a Spearman rho are the ranks and not the observed scores.

5.7 The biserial coefficient would likely apply in this situation. Oration performance could be reduced to a dichotomy, and although measured on an ordinal scale, has a continuous underlying distribution. Null hypothesis: the correlation between oration performance and English mastery in the population is zero. An equivalent statement: there is no relationship between oration performance and English mastery in the student population. With a significant statistical test we would reject the null hypothesis and conclude that there exists a relationship between these two variables in the population.

5.8 (a) Point biserial, assuming color of eyes to be dichotomy of either blue or brown.
(b) Pearson-product moment
(c) Spearman rho
(d) Biserial

5.9 With sample size of 120 we would interpret the coefficient of .62 as reflecting a relationship (in the population) between reading for comprehension and punctuation
skill. Whether this is a low, modest, or high correlation
is a relative matter and must be interpreted in the light of
other information about the two variables. Possible hypotheses: (1) the population correlation is zero; (2) considering the classes as representing different populations,
there exists no difference between pairs of population correlations (3) since most high school classes contain both
boys and girls, there is no difference between the population correlations of boys and girls. The population under
study appears to be sophomore English students enrolled
in this specific type of high school. A difficulty in sampling arises in that the students of the four classes may
not be a random sample of the entire sophomore population of the specific high school. Scheduling of classes or
other factors may have introduced a bias.

5.11 We want to make some decisions about the population
characteristics which are parameters. We draw a sample
and compute characteristics of the sample which are statistics. The statistics reflect the corresponding parameters within the bounds of random sampling fluctuations.
We hypothesize about parameters and infer from the statistics to the parameters and thus make decisions about
the population.

Chapter 6

6.1 Validity has to do with whether or not a test measures
what it is supposed to measure, while reliability concerns
whether or not it is consistent in measuring whatever it
does measure. A test can be reliable but not valid by consistently measuring something it was not designed to
measure and failing to measure what it was designed to
measure. An unreliable test cannot be valid since lack of

consistency eliminates the possibility of measuring what it is supposed to measure.

6.3 The primary measurement difficulties deal with classifying teachers as autocratic and democratic and quantifying the variable hostility. A possible method for quantifying hostility would be the proportion of hostile words used either by the teacher or the students. This would require some kind of definition and list of hostile words, most likely constructed by experts in this area. Hostility would then be defined in terms of the proportion of "hostile" words. Some kind of direct observation by trained observers might be used for data collection. The above procedure would not take into account the context and voice inflection associated with the word. This may be necessary since certain words may be hostile in one context and neutral in another.

6.7 Objectivity of a measuring device is defined as the extent to which equally competent scorers get the same results. The objectivity is in the scoring and not in the length of response.

6.8 The interview has the advantage of a face-to-face situation and thus allows for probing and clearing up of any ambiguities or misunderstandings. Information may be secured in an interview because of the personal contact which would not be forthcoming with a paper and pencil device. The disadvantage of the interview is the amount of necessary resources in terms of time, money, and personnel. Other advantages and disadvantages may be unique to a specific situation. For example, if there is little response to a mailed questionnaire, an interview may produce a considerably higher rate of response.

6.9 The following is one possible card layout. Consider first the identification information. There are seven items of information in identification. These items are listed below with the corresponding number of necessary columns.

1. City school number: two columns; there are 74 schools and each would be assigned a two-digit number.
2. Student identification number: four columns; since there are over 1,000 students and we assume there are less than 10,000 in the sample.
3. Grade level: one column; numbers 3 through 8.
4. Sex: one column; boys assigned zero and girls one.
5. Ability level: one column; since there are only three

classifications — one number assigned to each classification.
6. Age: two columns; record the actual age of the student;
   if age is measured to the nearest tenth of a year, three
   columns would be necessary.
7. Socio-economic classification of the school: one
   column; assign different one-digit numbers to each of
   the eight districts.

The achievement variables would require a minimum total
of 44 columns since the ten two-digit variables would require 20 columns and the remaining eight variables, 24
columns. Since there is sufficient room on the card, it
might be desirable to allow three columns for each variable, requiring a total of 54 columns. In that case the two-
digit variables would all have their scores preceded by a
zero (or blank). That is, a score of, say, 86 would be recorded as 086 on the card. Either 12 or 13 columns would
be required for identification but it might be well to reserve
the first 15 or 20 columns for identification, in case it
would become desirable to add information later. It is not
necessary that the identification information appear first,
or that it be grouped together. Such grouping may facilitate the programming.

Chapter 7

7.1   Internal validity concerns the basic minimum control, etc.,
      which are necessary in order for the results to be inter-
      pretable. External validity is the extent to which the results
      of the experiment are generalizable to existing conditions,
      populations, and the like. Internal validity is often en-
      hanced by increasing control and thus reducing factors
      which may be operating in the real situation. This tends to
      jeopardize external validity. The reverse may also occur:
      when the experiment is essentially a replication of the real
      situation (high external validity) but so many factors are
      operating that it is impossible to interpret cause and effect.
7.2   The fact that the researcher can assign students at ran-
      dom within the school gives a measure of control which
      would be missing if he had to take existing classes. Exist-
      ing classes may contain ability biases and any number of
      relevant factors. The researcher can enhance control by

building "school" into the design as an independent variable. Since each teacher teaches four classes, the researcher could assign one class size per teacher. However, teacher would be confounded with the independent variable school since any one teacher would teach in only one school. The variable school might have several uncontrolled but relevant variables associated with it such as student ability and lab facilities. These variables are essentially confounded with the variable school. Possible hypotheses: (1) class size has no effect upon the mean chemistry achievement of the population from which these classes were drawn; (2) there is no difference between the chemistry achievement means of the four school populations. The posttest-only control group extended to four groups is a possible design if one class size, say 30, is considered the control group. If it is necessary to gain statistical control over student ability, the pretest-posttest control group design with the appropriate extension could be used. A factorial design may seem desirable if it is possible to experimentally control additional variables, but the unequality of class size would almost require unequal cell frequencies.

7.3 Possible methods for increasing control over extraneous variables: (1) build them into the design as independent variables, (2) balance their effect over the levels of the other independent variables, (3) the obvious procedure of eliminating the extraneous variable. The various procedures discussed in this chapter for increasing internal validity are essentially procedures for increasing control.

7.5 There are three independent variables with two levels of each, therefore a $2 \times 2 \times 2$ or 2^3 factorial would be an appropriate factorial design. This factorial design has eight cells. However, one-half of the eight cells involve pairs and require two Ss. Therefore, one complete replication requires 12 Ss, six boys and six girls. Since there are only 64 boys and it requires six boys for a replication, the greatest multiple of six we can use is 60. So we would randomly eliminate 36 girls and four boys and proceed with 120 Ss. Sex is a fixed variable but we would *randomly* assign the 60 boys (and girls) to the levels of the independent variables type of problem and class size, assigning 40 to pairs and 20 to individuals, and 30 to each type of problem. Actually we would have the eight cells and the frequencies would be 10 and 20, depending on whether the cell includes an individual or a pair. Thus, randomization is built in by assigning Ss to cells. The null hypotheses for the main effects may be identified in symbol form by: $H_0: \mu_g = \mu_a; H_0: \mu_I = \mu_p; H_0: \mu_b = \mu_g$ where the μ_i's are population means and the subscripts represent the various levels of the independent variables, type of problem, group size, and sex, in that order.

7.6 An interaction between the variables sex and class size indicates that effect of class size does *not* remain constant over the two levels of sex. In presenting a plot of means, a change in slope of the two lines would appear. This change may or may not involve a crossover of the two lines.

7.7 The primary gain in validity is that the Solomon four-group design makes it possible to check any effects of pretesting or the interaction of pretesting with the experimental treatment.

7.8 The procedure applied here is a static-group comparison. This procedure is almost entirely lacking in control and hence lacking in experimental validity. There are a multitude of factors in addition to Boy Scout training that could affect performance in the skills. The greater maturity due to age differential, selective dropout, and additional external (to Boy Scout training) experience are examples of factors that would undoubtedly affect the performance and favor the fourteen-year-old boys. It is impossible to partition out an effect due singly to Boy Scout training.

7.9 Since it is implied that the teacher does not have the option of randomly assigning students, the nonequivalent control group design applies. He could randomly assign two of the classes to the use of programmed materials (experimental treatment) but this does not meet the requirement of a true experimental design. The teacher is interested in the amount of algebra learned during the semester, therefore pretesting is necessary but it would also be necessary as a statistical control. The statistical control of covariance would be essential for adequate internal validity. This experiment would most likely be quite high in external validity since testing could occur at natural times and the experiment would be carried on in a natural field setting. The population to which the results are generalized would have to be carefully defined in terms of the students that are enrolled in advanced algebra classes in this specific type of high school.

7.10 Multiple treatment interference means that observations taken on the same S immediately following a specific treatment are affected by prior treatments. Thus, a S receives more than one treatment and prior treatments interfere with the effects of subsequent treatments. This is a threat to validity since it becomes impossible to separate the effects due to specific treatments.

7.11 True experimental designs possess the feature of random assignment of Ss or experimental treatments which is lacking in the quasi-experimental designs. Thus, complete experimental control is lacking in the latter designs. The quasi-experimental designs commonly are used when pre-assembled groups of Ss must be taken intact. The primary difficulty comes with the lack of control, thus making the interpretation of the results tenuous. Also, the matter of inference and applying analysis techniques becomes "muddied" and more difficult.

7.12 There exists no random assignment of Ss to the practice treatments. The use of volunteering schools through the principal may have introduced bias and would certainly limit the generalizability of the results. The teacher variable is very apparent and essentially uncontrolled. The assumption is that teachers are most effective with techniques that they prefer. Even if this is true there is no evidence that different teachers, independent of practice method, are equally effective. With only three schools it would be difficult to make a case for the assumption that the teachers of each method are a random sample of fifth-grade teachers, either in general or a more specific group. There may exist other relevant uncontrolled factors within the schools, and since the method is optional to the teacher, there is no reason to assume a balance between schools on such factors. Thus, internal validity is low because of lack of control. The external validity is also low because of the limits on generalization mentioned above.

7.13 This is an example of a time design. A design such as this is susceptible to multiple treatment interference. In this case, delayed effects may begin appearing on subsequent observations. The pattern of results may be difficult to interpret. The advantage of using such a design is that it can be applied in the natural setting and provide information on the reading profile of a specific class. A special measurement problem would be attaining equivalent difficulty levels for the various tests given at four week intervals. Suppose there was a marked drop in performance after one period. This would be interpreted as an effect of the method of instruction when in fact the drop may be due to a more difficult test. Possible parametric analyses: (1) comparisons between means of adjacent periods when method of instruction changed; (2) a comparison between some kind of pooled means for each method. The pattern of means would have to be considered prior to an analysis.

7.14 Basically, a well-designed experiment meets the requirements for internal and external validity. This requires the general characteristics of (1) sufficient control to meet the objectives of the research project; (2) bias free data; (3) possess necessary information to test the hypotheses and, if a statistical test is used, an appropriate and accurate estimate of random error is available when necessary; and (4) the design fits the basic objectives and purposes of the research project.

Chapter 8

8.1 This is not an experiment because there is no manipulation of independent variables. This study is *ex post facto* in nature, since the independent variables have already occurred and a retrospective search for cause and effect relationships is implied. An analysis of variance, possibly a factorial, could be used if the parametric assumptions are tenable. If the parametric assumptions cannot be met, a technique such as the median test might be used. The Kruskal-Wallis analysis of variance by ranks could be used if we consider the six-grade level by location of school classifications as independent samples.

8.2 Stratified random sampling is the technique of dividing the population into nonoverlapping subpopulations and then making random selections from these subpopulations on the basis of some predetermined allocation. Proportional allocation involves sample sizes proportional to the corresponding strata populations. Optimum allocation involves sample sizes proportional to strata variances as well as strata populations. Both types of allocation may produce gains in precision over simple random sampling.

Proportional allocation removes a component from the error variance due to variance between strata means. Optimum allocation will remove this component, as well as a component due to variance between strata variances.

8.4 This study clearly involves a population and an interview. Since the interview would deal with the feelings, perceptions, etc., of the resigning staff members, we would classify the nature of the variables as survey research. Thus, we have a survey research study of a population using an interview.

8.7 The interview has the advantages of (1) allowing for deeper probing of the S and possibly pursuing a response, (2) clearing ambiguities, (3) securing information that would not be forthcoming with a written questionnaire, and (4) the problem of non-response is many times eliminated and usually not as great as with a questionnaire. The primary disadvantage of the interview is that it requires considerable resources in terms of time, effort, and personnel. The questionnaire has the advantage of not requiring the personnel resources of the interview. The questionnaires can all be sent at the same time so there is not a large lapse of time that may occur between interviews. This could be a disadvantage of the interview if external events occur which affect the responses. The primary disadvantage of the questionnaire is the usual high percentage of non-response. If a great deal of written material is necessary to communicate to the S and elicit his response, the length of the questionnaire may be a disadvantage. Also, if communication breaks down there is no opportunity, at the time, to eliminate ambiguities.

8.9 Possible procedures for securing information concerning the validity of documents used for historical research are as follows:

(1) check consistency of the document with related primary and secondary sources; this may involve considerable cross-referencing.

(2) evaluate the writer in terms of his position, possible bias, possibility of deliberate frauds, etc.

(3) use of X-ray and radioactivity procedures for establishing age of documents.

It should be noted that the above procedures will not conclusively insure validity. The advantage that the experimenter has is that of being an eyewitness to the event. The information of the experiment is received firsthand, and assuming that the experimenter knows what he sees, presumably the information is accurate and valid. (Note that having valid information does not necessarily make its interpretation valid.)

Chapter 9

9.1 The review of the literature can serve multiple purposes, especially early in (or prior to) the research project. Possible reasons (which reflect the specific information supplied) include (1) provide a background for the research study, (2) inform the researcher what has been done in the area, (3) provide information about possible procedures or designs, and (4) reveal possible gaps or omissions in the area. Additional review of the literature toward the close of the research project is desirable if enough time has passed since previous review that an updating is required. Also, such a review is an aid to writing conclusions and tying the specific research project with other research in the area.

9.4 There are any number of specific errors which can occur in the mechanics of data collection such as failure of the tester to appear at the proper place or time, lack of necessary equipment such as electrographic pencils, and failure to give proper instructions. A more subtle but common error is the lack of efficient assembly of the data during the collection stage. This can result in considerable inefficiency and possibly missing data. Using a measuring device whose administration procedures are improper (usually too complex) for the Ss is a possible error. A related error is having inadequately trained personnel administering the measuring device. Also, an inadequate manual can be a source of difficulty in data collection.

Chapter 10

The exercises of Chapter 10 suggest that the reader select either research articles to read or research topics to report. Although there are only four exercises for this chapter, any one exercise may require considerable effort. The exercises could be combined and directed toward the writing of a thesis or graduate paper. That is, the critical reviews, review of literature, identification of data, and the like, could be used as part of the preparation for a thesis. The exercises should not be viewed as necessarily meeting the requirements for a graduate paper, since such requirements are determined by the major professor, type of research topic, and the institution.

Appendix B: Selected References for Locating Research Information on Educational Topics

The educational researcher must know where to locate the research studies of his specialized area or areas. It is essential that the researcher keep up with current developments and ideas. Considerable reading of related research is often necessary for adequately identifying and formulating a research problem. An adequate background of the current research literature is necessary for the researcher to put his problem in its proper context and perspective. The research literature can also be an excellent source of ideas about how to effectively initiate a research study in a specific area.

This bibliography is divided into two parts: (1) a list of books, including selected review periodicals, and (2) a list of journals which are either directly research-oriented or often contain articles dealing with research ideas and specific research studies. Comments are made about several of the entries on the first list.

This bibliography should not be viewed as an exhaustive list. Also, this is not a bibliography of research methodology references. However, research methodology may appear in the context of the specific areas. The prospective educational researcher should find the sources helpful in locating ideas and information about his research topic.

Books and Review Periodicals

Alexander, C., and Burke, A. J. *How to Locate Educational Information and Data*, 4th ed. New York: Bureau of Publications, Teachers College, Columbia University, 1958.

This volume lists sources for locating educational data and information. A substantial part of the book is devoted to the technique of using the library, including the location of books and periodicals.

Buros, O. K., ed. *The Sixth Mental Measurements Yearbook.* Highland Park, N.J.: Gryphon Press, 1965.

> This volume contains references on the construction and use of specific tests. There is a list of almost 2,000 commercially available tests in the areas of achievement, attitudes, and aptitude.

Cooperative Research Program Project Reports. Washington, D.C.: U.S. Office of Education, Department of Health, Education and Welfare.

> A research project supported by U.S. Office of Education funds requires that a formal report be submitted to USOE at the conclusion of the project. These reports are usually detailed descriptions of the specific projects. The project names and abstracts appear in publications such as *Research in Education* (noted later in this bibliography). The entire report of a project can be made available by requesting it from the USOE.

Dissertation Abstracts. Ann Arbor, Michigan: University Microfilms, Inc.

> This is a monthly compilation of doctoral dissertation abstracts submitted by over 115 cooperating institutions. The abstracts are arranged under subject categories as assigned by the author. A subject index and an author index are also included.

Education Index. New York: The H. W. Wilson Co.

> An author and subject index of educational books, periodicals, and other materials. The periodicals from which information is indexed are listed near the beginning of each volume. Paper-bound copies of current months are available to keep the index up-to-date. Volumes are accumulated every three years, the first being published in 1932 and containing materials from the period 1929–1932.

Gage, N. L., ed. *Handbook of Research on Teaching.* Chicago: Rand McNally & Company, 1963. Sponsored by the American Educational Research Association.

> This is a comprehensive presentation of research on teaching, including theoretical bases, methodology, major variables, and the teaching of grade levels and subject matter. The volume contains 23 chapters and includes contributions of 31 authors recognized as specialists in their various areas.

Harris, C. W. *Encyclopedia of Educational Research,* 3rd ed.

New York: The Macmillan Company, 1960. Sponsored by the American Educational Research Association.

The encyclopedia presents a synthesis, interpretation, and evaluation of the research on topics which cover the entire range of education. There is an extensive bibliography at the conclusion of each topic which covers related books and periodicals. Two earlier editions of the encyclopedia have been published: 1941 and 1950.

Harris, T. L. "Summary of Investigations Relating to Reading, July 1, 1960 to June 30, 1961," *Journal of Educational Research*, 55:197–220; February 1962.

Lyda, M. L. et al. *Research Studies in Education; 1953–63*, Bloomington, Indiana: Phi Delta Kappa, Inc., 1965.

This volume is a cumulated edition of the titles and authors of doctoral dissertations completed during an eleven-year period. The titles are categorized according to 28 dissertation categories. Over 100 colleges and universities reported the work of their doctoral candidates to the compilers of this volume. An earlier volume of the *Research Studies* was published in 1952. Additional monographs with the same title are added annually to keep the publication up-to-date.

Psychological Abstracts. Washington, D.C.: American Psychological Association.

This publication contains abstracts of studies dealing with all major areas and problems of psychology, including those related to education. Editions are published monthly to keep the abstract current. Volumes are accumulated each calendar year and are indexed by author and subject.

Psychological Review. Washington, D.C.: American Psychological Association, Inc.

This review is published bimonthly. A substantial part of this publication is concerned with reports of theoretical significance. Reports of original research are included only when they are parts of theoretical discussions.

Research in Education. Washington, D.C.: U.S. Government Printing Office, A publication of the U.S. Department of Health, Education and Welfare.

This is a publication issued monthly in connection with the Educational Resources Information Center (ERIC). It contains four sections: (1) report résumés, (2) report indexes, (3) project résumés, and (4) project indexes. The report résumés provide brief descriptions of the research reports that are available. Project résumés provide similar descriptions of research projects. The indexes provide listings of reports and projects indexed not only by subject, but also by author (investigator) and institution. The publication is brought up-to-date each month so it does provide an excellent source of information for current and recent research activities.

Review of Educational Research. Washington, D.C.: American Educational Research Association.

The *Review* is published five times per year. Each issue is devoted to the research on a single educational topic. Topics are reviewed in three-year cycles, with the more active topics reviewed every cycle and less active topics on alternate cycles. An extensive bibliography of significant studies is included in the *Review.*

Shores, L. *Basic Reference Sources.* Chicago: American Library Association, 1954.

Suggested Research Journals

American Educational Research Journal. Washington, D.C.: American Educational Research Association, NEA.

British Journal of Educational Psychology. London, England: British Psychological Society.

British Journal of Educational Studies. London, England: Faber & Faber, Ltd.

California Journal of Educational Research. Burlingame, California: California Teachers Association.

Canadian Education and Research Digest. Toronto, Ontario: Canadian Education Association.

Child Development. Purdue University, Lafayette, Indiana: The Society for Research in Child Development, Inc.

Educational and Psychological Measurement. Durham, North Carolina: G. Frederic Kuder.

Elementary School Journal. Chicago, Illinois: Department of Education of The University of Chicago.

Exceptional Children. Washington, D.C.: Council for Exceptional Children, NEA.

Florida Journal of Educational Research. Tallahassee, Florida: Florida Education Association.

Journal of Educational Psychology. Washington, D.C.: American Psychological Association.

Journal of Educational Research. Madison, Wisconsin: Dembar Publications, Inc.

Journal of Educational Sociology. New York University, New York: The Payne Educational Sociology Foundation.

Journal of Experimental Education. Madison, Wisconsin: Dembar Publications, Inc.

Journal of Experimental Psychology. Washington, D.C.: American Psychological Association, Inc.

Journal of Research in Science Teaching. National Association for Research in Science Teaching and Association for the Education of Teachers in Science. New York: John Wiley & Sons, Inc.

NEA Research Bulletin. Washington, D.C.: National Education Association.

National Elementary Principal. Washington, D.C.: Department of Elementary School Principals, NEA.

Phi Delta Kappan. Bloomington, Indiana: Phi Delta Kappa.

Psychological Bulletin. Washington, D.C.: American Psychological Association.

Psychological Reports. Missoula, Montana: Southern Universities Press.

Psychometrika. Richmond, Virginia: The Psychometrika Society.

School Science and Mathematics. Kalamazoo, Michigan: Central Association of Science and Mathematics Teachers, Inc.

The Research Quarterly. Washington, D.C.: American Association for Health, Physical Education, and Recreation, NEA.

What Research Says To The Teacher. (A Series of Monographs.) Washington, D.C.: Department of Classroom Teachers and American Educational Research Association, NEA.

Appendix C: Tables

TABLE A

Ordinates and areas of the normal curve °

(In terms of σ units)

$\frac{x}{\sigma}$	Area	Ordinate	$\frac{x}{\sigma}$	Area	Ordinate	$\frac{x}{\sigma}$	Area	Ordinate
.00	.0000	.3989	.50	.1915	.3521	1.00	.3413	.2420
.01	.0040	.3989	.51	.1950	.3503	1.01	.3438	.2396
.02	.0080	.3989	.52	.1985	.3485	1.02	.3461	.2371
.03	.0120	.3988	.53	.2019	.3467	1.03	.3485	.2347
.04	.0160	.3986	.54	.2054	.3448	1.04	.3508	.2323
.05	.0199	.3984	.55	.2088	.3429	1.05	.3531	.2299
.06	.0239	.3982	.56	.2123	.3410	1.06	.3554	.2275
.07	.0279	.3980	.57	.2157	.3391	1.07	.3577	.2251
.08	.0319	.3977	.58	.2190	.3372	1.08	.3599	.2227
.09	.0359	.3973	.59	.2224	.3352	1.09	.3621	.2203
.10	.0398	.3970	.60	.2257	.3332	1.10	.3643	.2179
.11	.0438	.3965	.61	.2291	.3312	1.11	.3665	.2155
.12	.0478	.3961	.62	.2324	.3292	1.12	.3686	.2131
.13	.0517	.3956	.63	.2357	.3271	1.13	.3708	.2107
.14	.0557	.3951	.64	.2389	.3251	1.14	.3729	.2083
.15	.0596	.3945	.65	.2422	.3230	1.15	.3749	.2059
.16	.0636	.3939	.66	.2454	.3209	1.16	.3770	.2036
.17	.0675	.3932	.67	.2486	.3187	1.17	.3790	.2012
.18	.0714	.3925	.68	.2517	.3166	1.18	.3810	.1989
.19	.0753	.3918	.69	.2549	.3144	1.19	.3830	.1965
.20	.0793	.3910	.70	.2580	.3123	1.20	.3849	.1942
.21	.0832	.3902	.71	.2611	.3101	1.21	.3869	.1919
.22	.0871	.3894	.72	.2642	.3079	1.22	.3888	.1895
.23	.0910	.3885	.73	.2673	.3056	1.23	.3907	.1872
.24	.0948	.3876	.74	.2703	.3034	1.24	.3925	.1849
.25	.0987	.3867	.75	.2734	.3011	1.25	.3944	.1826
.26	.1026	.3857	.76	.2764	.2989	1.26	.3962	.1804
.27	.1064	.3847	.77	.2794	.2966	1.27	.3980	.1781
.28	.1103	.3836	.78	.2823	.2943	1.28	.3997	.1758
.29	.1141	.3825	.79	.2852	.2920	1.29	.4015	.1736
.30	.1179	.3814	.80	.2881	.2897	1.30	.4032	.1714
.31	.1217	.3802	.81	.2910	.2874	1.31	.4049	.1691
.32	.1255	.3790	.82	.2939	.2850	1.32	.4066	.1669
.33	.1293	.3778	.83	.2967	.2827	1.33	.4082	.1647
.34	.1331	.3765	.84	.2995	.2803	1.34	.4099	.1626
.35	.1368	.3752	.85	.3023	.2780	1.35	.4115	.1604
.36	.1406	.3739	.86	.3051	.2756	1.36	.4131	.1582
.37	.1443	.3725	.87	.3078	.2732	1.37	.4147	.1561
.38	.1480	.3712	.88	.3106	.2709	1.38	.4162	.1539
.39	.1517	.3697	.89	.3133	.2685	1.39	.4177	.1518
.40	.1554	.3683	.90	.3159	.2661	1.40	.4192	.1497
.41	.1591	.3668	.91	.3186	.2637	1.41	.4207	.1476
.42	.1628	.3653	.92	.3212	.2613	1.42	.4222	.1456
.43	.1664	.3637	.93	.3238	.2589	1.43	.4236	.1435
.44	.1700	.3621	.94	.3264	.2565	1.44	.4251	.1415
.45	.1736	.3605	.95	.3289	.2541	1.45	.4265	.1394
.46	.1772	.3589	.96	.3315	.2516	1.46	.4279	.1374
.47	.1808	.3572	.97	.3340	.2492	1.47	.4292	.1354
.48	.1844	.3555	.98	.3365	.2468	1.48	.4306	.1334
.49	.1879	.3538	.99	.3389	.2444	1.49	.4319	.1315
.50	.1915	.3521	1.00	.3413	.2420	1.50	.4332	.1295

° From *Educational Statistics* by J. E. Wert. Copyright 1938 by McGraw-Hill Book Company. Used by permission of McGraw-Hill Book Company.

$\frac{x}{\sigma}$	Area	Ordinate	$\frac{x}{\sigma}$	Area	Ordinate	$\frac{x}{\sigma}$	Area	Ordinate
1.50	.4332	.1295	2.00	.4772	.0540	2.50	.4938	.0175
1.51	.4345	.1276	2.01	.4778	.0529	2.51	.4940	.0171
1.52	.4357	.1257	2.02	.4783	.0519	2.52	.4941	.0167
1.53	.4370	.1238	2.03	.4788	.0508	2.53	.4943	.0163
1.54	.4382	.1219	2.04	.4793	.0498	2.54	.4945	.0158
1.55	.4394	.1200	2.05	.4798	.0488	2.55	.4946	.0154
1.56	.4406	.1182	2.06	.4803	.0478	2.56	.4948	.0151
1.57	.4418	.1163	2.07	.4808	.0468	2.57	.4949	.0147
1.58	.4429	.1145	2.08	.4812	.0459	2.58	.4951	.0143
1.59	.4441	.1127	2.09	.4817	.0449	2.59	.4952	.0139
1.60	.4452	.1109	2.10	.4821	.0440	2.60	.4953	.0136
1.61	.4463	.1092	2.11	.4826	.0431	2.61	.4955	.0132
1.62	.4474	.1074	2.12	.4830	.0422	2.62	.4956	.0129
1.63	.4484	.1057	2.13	.4834	.0413	2.63	.4957	.0126
1.64	.4495	.1040	2.14	.4838	.0404	2.64	.4959	.0122
1.65	.4505	.1023	2.15	.4842	.0395	2.65	.4960	.0119
1.66	.4515	.1006	2.16	.4846	.0387	2.66	.4961	.0116
1.67	.4525	.0989	2.17	.4850	.0379	2.67	.4962	.0113
1.68	.4535	.0973	2.18	.4854	.0371	2.68	.4963	.0110
1.69	.4545	.0957	2.19	.4857	.0363	2.69	.4964	.0107
1.70	.4554	.0940	2.20	.4861	.0355	2.70	.4965	.0104
1.71	.4564	.0925	2.21	.4864	.0347	2.71	.4966	.0101
1.72	.4573	.0909	2.22	.4868	.0339	2.72	.4967	.0099
1.73	.4582	.0893	2.23	.4871	.0332	2.73	.4968	.0096
1.74	.4591	.0878	2.24	.4875	.0325	2.74	.4969	.0093
1.75	.4599	.0863	2.25	.4878	.0317	2.75	.4970	.0091
1.76	.4608	.0848	2.26	.4881	.0310	2.76	.4971	.0088
1.77	.4616	.0833	2.27	.4884	.0303	2.77	.4972	.0086
1.78	.4625	.0818	2.28	.4887	.0297	2.78	.4973	.0084
1.79	.4633	.0804	2.29	.4890	.0290	2.79	.4974	.0081
1.80	.4641	.0790	2.30	.4893	.0283	2.80	.4974	.0079
1.81	.4649	.0775	2.31	.4896	.0277	2.81	.4975	.0077
1.82	.4656	.0761	2.32	.4898	.0270	2.82	.4976	.0075
1.83	.4664	.0748	2.33	.4901	.0264	2.83	.4977	.0073
1.84	.4671	.0734	2.34	.4904	.0258	2.84	.4977	.0071
1.85	.4678	.0721	2.35	.4906	.0252	2.85	.4978	.0069
1.86	.4686	.0707	2.36	.4909	.0246	2.86	.4979	.0067
1.87	.4693	.0694	2.37	.4911	.0241	2.87	.4979	.0065
1.88	.4699	.0681	2.38	.4913	.0235	2.88	.4980	.0063
1.89	.4706	.0669	2.39	.4916	.0229	2.89	.4981	.0061
1.90	.4713	.0656	2.40	.4918	.0224	2.90	.4981	.0060
1.91	.4719	.0644	2.41	.4920	.0219	2.91	.4982	.0058
1.92	.4726	.0632	2.42	.4922	.0213	2.92	.4982	.0056
1.93	.4732	.0620	2.43	.4925	.0208	2.93	.4983	.0055
1.94	.4738	.0608	2.44	.4927	.0203	2.94	.4984	.0053
1.95	.4744	.0596	2.45	.4929	.0198	2.95	.4984	.0051
1.96	.4750	.0584	2.46	.4931	.0194	2.96	.4985	.0050
1.97	.4756	.0573	2.47	.4932	.0189	2.97	.4985	.0048
1.98	.4761	.0562	2.48	.4934	.0184	2.98	.4986	.0047
1.99	.4767	.0551	2.49	.4936	.0180	2.99	.4986	.0046
2.00	.4772	.0540	2.50	.4938	.0175	3.00	.4987	.0044

TABLE B
Critical values of t °

df	Level of significance for one-tailed test					
	.10	.05	.025	.01	.005	.0005
	Level of significance for two-tailed test					
	.20	.10	.05	.02	.01	.001
1	3.078	6.314	12.706	31.821	63.657	636.619
2	1.886	2.920	4.303	6.965	9.925	31.598
3	1.638	2.353	3.182	4.541	5.841	12.941
4	1.533	2.132	2.776	3.747	4.604	8.610
5	1.476	2.015	2.571	3.365	4.032	6.859
6	1.440	1.943	2.447	3.143	3.707	5.959
7	1.415	1.895	2.365	2.998	3.499	5.405
8	1.397	1.860	2.306	2.896	3.355	5.041
9	1.383	1.833	2.262	2.821	3.250	4.781
10	1.372	1.812	2.228	2.764	3.169	4.587
11	1.363	1.796	2.201	2.718	3.106	4.437
12	1.356	1.782	2.179	2.681	3.055	4.318
13	1.350	1.771	2.160	2.650	3.012	4.221
14	1.345	1.761	2.145	2.624	2.977	4.140
15	1.341	1.753	2.131	2.602	2.947	4.073
16	1.337	1.746	2.120	2.583	2.921	4.015
17	1.333	1.740	2.110	2.567	2.898	3.965
18	1.330	1.734	2.101	2.552	2.878	3.922
19	1.328	1.729	2.093	2.539	2.861	3.883
20	1.325	1.725	2.086	2.528	2.845	3.850
21	1.323	1.721	2.080	2.518	2.831	3.819
22	1.321	1.717	2.074	2.508	2.819	3.792
23	1.319	1.714	2.069	2.500	2.807	3.767
24	1.318	1.711	2.064	2.492	2.797	3.745
25	1.316	1.708	2.060	2.485	2.787	3.725
26	1.315	1.706	2.056	2.479	2.779	3.707
27	1.314	1.703	2.052	2.473	2.771	3.690
28	1.313	1.701	2.048	2.467	2.763	3.674
29	1.311	1.699	2.045	2.462	2.756	3.659
30	1.310	1.697	2.042	2.457	2.750	3.646
40	1.303	1.684	2.021	2.423	2.704	3.551
60	1.296	1.671	2.000	2.390	2.660	3.460
120	1.289	1.658	1.980	2.358	2.617	3.373
∞	1.282	1.645	1.960	2.326	2.576	3.291

° Abridged from Table III of R. A. Fisher and F. Yates, *Statistical Tables for Biological, Agricultural, and Medical Research,* published by Oliver & Boyd, Ltd., Edinburgh, by permission of the authors and publishers.

TABLE C
Table of probabilities associated with values as small as observed values of x in the binomial test °

Given in the body of this table are one-tailed probabilities under H_0 for the binomial test when $P = Q = \frac{1}{2}$. To save space, decimal points are omitted in the p's.

N \ x	0	1	2	3	4	5	6	7	8	9	10	11	12	13	14	15
5	031	188	500	812	969	†										
6	016	109	344	656	891	984	†									
7	008	062	227	500	773	938	992	†								
8	004	035	145	363	637	855	965	996	†							
9	002	020	090	254	500	746	910	980	998	†						
10	001	011	055	172	377	623	828	945	989	999	†					
11		006	033	113	274	500	726	887	967	994	†	†				
12		003	019	073	194	387	613	806	927	981	997	†	†			
13		002	011	046	133	291	500	709	867	954	989	998	†	†		
14		001	006	029	090	212	395	605	788	910	971	994	999	†	†	
15			004	018	059	151	304	500	696	849	941	982	996	†	†	†
16			002	011	038	105	227	402	598	773	895	962	989	998	†	†
17			001	006	025	072	166	315	500	685	834	928	975	994	999	†
18			001	004	015	048	119	240	407	593	760	881	952	985	996	999
19				002	010	032	084	180	324	500	676	820	916	968	990	998
20				001	006	021	058	132	252	412	588	748	868	942	979	994
21				001	004	013	039	095	192	332	500	668	808	905	961	987
22					002	008	026	067	143	262	416	584	738	857	933	974
23					001	005	017	047	105	202	339	500	661	798	895	953
24					001	003	011	032	076	154	271	419	581	729	846	924
25						002	007	022	054	115	212	345	500	655	788	885

° Adapted from Table IV B of *Statistical Inference* by Helen M. Walker and Joseph Lev. Copyright 1953 by Holt, Rinehart and Winston, Inc. Adapted and reprinted by permission of Holt, Rinehart and Winston, Inc.

† 1.0 or approximately 1.0.

TABLE D
Critical values of $F°$
5 per cent (roman type) and 1 per cent (bold-face type) points for the distribution of $F°$

Degrees of freedom for greater mean square

Each cell shows the 5 per cent point (roman) / 1 per cent point (bold-face). Rows give degrees of freedom for lesser mean square.

df lesser	1	2	3	4	5	6	7	8	9	10	11	12	14	16	20	24	30	40	50	75	100	200	500	∞
1	161 / 4052	200 / 4999	216 / 5403	225 / 5625	230 / 5764	234 / 5859	237 / 5928	239 / 5981	241 / 6022	242 / 6056	243 / 6082	244 / 6106	245 / 6142	246 / 6169	248 / 6208	249 / 6234	250 / 6258	251 / 6286	252 / 6302	253 / 6323	253 / 6334	254 / 6352	254 / 6361	254 / 6366
2	18.51 / 98.49	19.00 / 99.01	19.16 / 99.17	19.25 / 99.25	19.30 / 99.30	19.33 / 99.33	19.36 / 99.34	19.37 / 99.36	19.38 / 99.38	19.39 / 99.40	19.40 / 99.41	19.41 / 99.42	19.42 / 99.43	19.43 / 99.44	19.44 / 99.45	19.45 / 99.46	19.46 / 99.47	19.47 / 99.48	19.47 / 99.48	19.48 / 99.49	19.49 / 99.49	19.49 / 99.49	19.50 / 99.50	19.50 / 99.50
3	10.13 / 34.12	9.55 / 30.81	9.28 / 29.46	9.12 / 28.71	9.01 / 28.24	8.94 / 27.91	8.88 / 27.67	8.84 / 27.49	8.81 / 27.34	8.78 / 27.23	8.76 / 27.13	8.74 / 27.05	8.71 / 26.92	8.69 / 26.83	8.66 / 26.69	8.64 / 26.60	8.62 / 26.50	8.60 / 26.41	8.58 / 26.35	8.57 / 26.27	8.56 / 26.23	8.54 / 26.18	8.54 / 26.14	8.53 / 26.12
4	7.71 / 21.20	6.94 / 18.00	6.59 / 16.69	6.39 / 15.98	6.26 / 15.52	6.16 / 15.21	6.09 / 14.98	6.04 / 14.80	6.00 / 14.66	5.96 / 14.54	5.93 / 14.45	5.91 / 14.37	5.87 / 14.24	5.84 / 14.15	5.80 / 14.02	5.77 / 13.93	5.74 / 13.83	5.71 / 13.74	5.70 / 13.69	5.68 / 13.61	5.66 / 13.57	5.65 / 13.52	5.64 / 13.48	5.63 / 13.46
5	6.61 / 16.26	5.79 / 13.27	5.41 / 12.06	5.19 / 11.39	5.05 / 10.97	4.95 / 10.67	4.88 / 10.45	4.82 / 10.27	4.78 / 10.15	4.74 / 10.05	4.70 / 9.96	4.68 / 9.89	4.64 / 9.77	4.60 / 9.68	4.56 / 9.55	4.53 / 9.47	4.50 / 9.38	4.46 / 9.29	4.44 / 9.24	4.42 / 9.17	4.40 / 9.13	4.38 / 9.07	4.37 / 9.04	4.36 / 9.02
6	5.99 / 13.74	5.14 / 10.92	4.76 / 9.78	4.53 / 9.15	4.39 / 8.75	4.28 / 8.47	4.21 / 8.26	4.15 / 8.10	4.10 / 7.98	4.06 / 7.87	4.03 / 7.79	4.00 / 7.72	3.96 / 7.60	3.92 / 7.52	3.87 / 7.39	3.84 / 7.31	3.81 / 7.23	3.77 / 7.14	3.75 / 7.09	3.72 / 7.02	3.71 / 6.99	3.69 / 6.94	3.68 / 6.90	3.67 / 6.88
7	5.59 / 12.25	4.74 / 9.55	4.35 / 8.45	4.12 / 7.85	3.97 / 7.46	3.87 / 7.19	3.79 / 7.00	3.73 / 6.84	3.68 / 6.71	3.63 / 6.62	3.60 / 6.54	3.57 / 6.47	3.52 / 6.35	3.49 / 6.27	3.44 / 6.15	3.41 / 6.07	3.38 / 5.98	3.34 / 5.90	3.32 / 5.85	3.29 / 5.78	3.28 / 5.75	3.25 / 5.70	3.24 / 5.67	3.23 / 5.65
8	5.32 / 11.26	4.46 / 8.65	4.07 / 7.59	3.84 / 7.01	3.69 / 6.63	3.58 / 6.37	3.50 / 6.19	3.44 / 6.03	3.39 / 5.91	3.34 / 5.82	3.31 / 5.74	3.28 / 5.67	3.23 / 5.56	3.20 / 5.48	3.15 / 5.36	3.12 / 5.28	3.08 / 5.20	3.05 / 5.11	3.03 / 5.06	3.00 / 5.00	2.98 / 4.96	2.96 / 4.91	2.94 / 4.88	2.93 / 4.86
9	5.12 / 10.56	4.26 / 8.02	3.86 / 6.99	3.63 / 6.42	3.48 / 6.06	3.37 / 5.80	3.29 / 5.62	3.23 / 5.47	3.18 / 5.35	3.13 / 5.26	3.10 / 5.18	3.07 / 5.11	3.02 / 5.00	2.98 / 4.92	2.93 / 4.80	2.90 / 4.73	2.86 / 4.64	2.82 / 4.56	2.80 / 4.51	2.77 / 4.45	2.76 / 4.41	2.73 / 4.36	2.72 / 4.33	2.71 / 4.31
10	4.96 / 10.04	4.10 / 7.56	3.71 / 6.55	3.48 / 5.99	3.33 / 5.64	3.22 / 5.39	3.14 / 5.21	3.07 / 5.06	3.02 / 4.95	2.97 / 4.85	2.94 / 4.78	2.91 / 4.71	2.86 / 4.60	2.82 / 4.52	2.77 / 4.41	2.74 / 4.33	2.70 / 4.25	2.67 / 4.17	2.64 / 4.12	2.61 / 4.05	2.59 / 4.01	2.56 / 3.96	2.55 / 3.93	2.54 / 3.91
11	4.84 / 9.65	3.98 / 7.20	3.59 / 6.22	3.36 / 5.67	3.20 / 5.32	3.09 / 5.07	3.01 / 4.88	2.95 / 4.74	2.90 / 4.63	2.86 / 4.54	2.82 / 4.46	2.79 / 4.40	2.74 / 4.29	2.70 / 4.21	2.65 / 4.10	2.61 / 4.02	2.57 / 3.94	2.53 / 3.86	2.50 / 3.80	2.47 / 3.74	2.45 / 3.70	2.42 / 3.66	2.41 / 3.62	2.40 / 3.60
12	4.75 / 9.33	3.88 / 6.93	3.49 / 5.95	3.26 / 5.41	3.11 / 5.06	3.00 / 4.82	2.92 / 4.65	2.85 / 4.50	2.80 / 4.39	2.76 / 4.30	2.72 / 4.22	2.69 / 4.16	2.64 / 4.05	2.60 / 3.98	2.54 / 3.86	2.50 / 3.78	2.46 / 3.70	2.42 / 3.61	2.40 / 3.56	2.36 / 3.49	2.35 / 3.46	2.32 / 3.41	2.31 / 3.38	2.30 / 3.36
13	4.67 / 9.07	3.80 / 6.70	3.41 / 5.74	3.18 / 5.20	3.02 / 4.86	2.92 / 4.62	2.84 / 4.44	2.77 / 4.30	2.72 / 4.19	2.67 / 4.10	2.64 / 4.02	2.60 / 3.96	2.55 / 3.85	2.51 / 3.78	2.46 / 3.67	2.42 / 3.59	2.38 / 3.51	2.34 / 3.42	2.32 / 3.37	2.28 / 3.30	2.26 / 3.27	2.24 / 3.21	2.22 / 3.18	2.21 / 3.16

df																								
14	4.60 / 8.86	3.74 / 6.51	3.34 / 5.56	3.11 / 5.03	2.96 / 4.69	2.85 / 4.46	2.77 / 4.28	2.70 / 4.14	2.65 / 4.03	2.60 / 3.94	2.56 / 3.86	2.53 / 3.80	2.48 / 3.70	2.44 / 3.62	2.39 / 3.51	2.35 / 3.43	2.31 / 3.34	2.27 / 3.26	2.24 / 3.21	2.21 / 3.14	2.19 / 3.11	2.16 / 3.06	2.14 / 3.02	2.13 / 3.00
15	4.54 / 8.68	3.68 / 6.36	3.29 / 5.42	3.06 / 4.89	2.90 / 4.56	2.79 / 4.32	2.70 / 4.14	2.64 / 4.00	2.59 / 3.89	2.55 / 3.80	2.51 / 3.73	2.48 / 3.67	2.43 / 3.56	2.39 / 3.48	2.33 / 3.36	2.29 / 3.29	2.25 / 3.20	2.21 / 3.12	2.18 / 3.07	2.15 / 3.00	2.12 / 2.97	2.10 / 2.92	2.08 / 2.89	2.07 / 2.87
16	4.49 / 8.53	3.63 / 6.23	3.24 / 5.29	3.01 / 4.77	2.85 / 4.44	2.74 / 4.20	2.66 / 4.03	2.59 / 3.89	2.54 / 3.78	2.49 / 3.69	2.45 / 3.61	2.42 / 3.55	2.37 / 3.45	2.33 / 3.37	2.28 / 3.25	2.24 / 3.18	2.20 / 3.10	2.16 / 3.01	2.13 / 2.96	2.09 / 2.89	2.07 / 2.86	2.04 / 2.80	2.02 / 2.77	2.01 / 2.75
17	4.45 / 8.40	3.59 / 6.11	3.20 / 5.18	2.96 / 4.67	2.81 / 4.34	2.70 / 4.10	2.62 / 3.93	2.55 / 3.79	2.50 / 3.68	2.45 / 3.59	2.41 / 3.52	2.38 / 3.45	2.33 / 3.35	2.29 / 3.27	2.23 / 3.16	2.19 / 3.08	2.15 / 3.00	2.11 / 2.92	2.08 / 2.86	2.04 / 2.79	2.02 / 2.76	1.99 / 2.70	1.97 / 2.67	1.96 / 2.65
18	4.41 / 8.28	3.55 / 6.01	3.16 / 5.09	2.93 / 4.58	2.77 / 4.25	2.66 / 4.01	2.58 / 3.85	2.51 / 3.71	2.46 / 3.60	2.41 / 3.51	2.37 / 3.44	2.34 / 3.37	2.29 / 3.27	2.25 / 3.19	2.19 / 3.07	2.15 / 3.00	2.11 / 2.91	2.07 / 2.83	2.04 / 2.78	2.00 / 2.71	1.98 / 2.68	1.95 / 2.62	1.93 / 2.59	1.92 / 2.57
19	4.38 / 8.18	3.52 / 5.93	3.13 / 5.01	2.90 / 4.50	2.74 / 4.17	2.63 / 3.94	2.55 / 3.77	2.48 / 3.63	2.43 / 3.52	2.38 / 3.43	2.34 / 3.36	2.31 / 3.30	2.26 / 3.19	2.21 / 3.12	2.15 / 3.00	2.11 / 2.92	2.07 / 2.84	2.02 / 2.76	2.00 / 2.70	1.96 / 2.63	1.94 / 2.60	1.91 / 2.54	1.90 / 2.51	1.88 / 2.49
20	4.35 / 8.10	3.49 / 5.85	3.10 / 4.94	2.87 / 4.43	2.71 / 4.10	2.60 / 3.87	2.52 / 3.71	2.45 / 3.56	2.40 / 3.45	2.35 / 3.37	2.31 / 3.30	2.28 / 3.23	2.23 / 3.13	2.18 / 3.05	2.12 / 2.94	2.08 / 2.86	2.04 / 2.77	1.99 / 2.69	1.96 / 2.63	1.92 / 2.56	1.90 / 2.53	1.87 / 2.47	1.85 / 2.44	1.84 / 2.42
21	4.32 / 8.02	3.47 / 5.78	3.07 / 4.87	2.84 / 4.37	2.68 / 4.04	2.57 / 3.81	2.49 / 3.65	2.42 / 3.51	2.37 / 3.40	2.32 / 3.31	2.28 / 3.24	2.25 / 3.17	2.20 / 3.07	2.15 / 2.99	2.09 / 2.88	2.05 / 2.80	2.00 / 2.72	1.96 / 2.63	1.93 / 2.58	1.89 / 2.51	1.87 / 2.47	1.84 / 2.42	1.82 / 2.38	1.81 / 2.36
22	4.30 / 7.94	3.44 / 5.72	3.05 / 4.82	2.82 / 4.31	2.66 / 3.99	2.55 / 3.76	2.47 / 3.59	2.40 / 3.45	2.35 / 3.35	2.30 / 3.26	2.26 / 3.18	2.23 / 3.12	2.18 / 3.02	2.13 / 2.94	2.07 / 2.83	2.03 / 2.75	1.98 / 2.67	1.93 / 2.58	1.91 / 2.53	1.87 / 2.46	1.84 / 2.42	1.81 / 2.37	1.80 / 2.33	1.78 / 2.31
23	4.28 / 7.88	3.42 / 5.66	3.03 / 4.76	2.80 / 4.26	2.64 / 3.94	2.53 / 3.71	2.45 / 3.54	2.38 / 3.41	2.32 / 3.30	2.28 / 3.21	2.24 / 3.14	2.20 / 3.07	2.14 / 2.97	2.10 / 2.89	2.04 / 2.78	2.00 / 2.70	1.96 / 2.62	1.91 / 2.53	1.88 / 2.48	1.84 / 2.41	1.82 / 2.37	1.79 / 2.32	1.77 / 2.28	1.76 / 2.26
24	4.26 / 7.82	3.40 / 5.61	3.01 / 4.72	2.78 / 4.22	2.62 / 3.90	2.51 / 3.67	2.43 / 3.50	2.36 / 3.36	2.30 / 3.25	2.26 / 3.17	2.22 / 3.09	2.18 / 3.03	2.13 / 2.93	2.09 / 2.85	2.02 / 2.74	1.98 / 2.66	1.94 / 2.58	1.89 / 2.49	1.86 / 2.44	1.82 / 2.36	1.80 / 2.33	1.76 / 2.27	1.74 / 2.23	1.73 / 2.21
25	4.24 / 7.77	3.38 / 5.57	2.99 / 4.68	2.76 / 4.18	2.60 / 3.86	2.49 / 3.63	2.41 / 3.46	2.34 / 3.32	2.28 / 3.21	2.24 / 3.13	2.20 / 3.05	2.16 / 2.99	2.11 / 2.89	2.06 / 2.81	2.00 / 2.70	1.96 / 2.62	1.92 / 2.54	1.87 / 2.45	1.84 / 2.40	1.80 / 2.32	1.77 / 2.29	1.74 / 2.23	1.72 / 2.19	1.71 / 2.17
26	4.22 / 7.72	3.37 / 5.53	2.98 / 4.64	2.74 / 4.14	2.59 / 3.82	2.47 / 3.59	2.39 / 3.42	2.32 / 3.29	2.27 / 3.17	2.22 / 3.09	2.18 / 3.02	2.15 / 2.96	2.10 / 2.86	2.05 / 2.77	1.99 / 2.66	1.95 / 2.58	1.90 / 2.50	1.85 / 2.41	1.82 / 2.36	1.78 / 2.28	1.76 / 2.25	1.72 / 2.19	1.70 / 2.15	1.69 / 2.13
27	4.21 / 7.68	3.35 / 5.49	2.96 / 4.60	2.73 / 4.11	2.57 / 3.79	2.46 / 3.56	2.37 / 3.39	2.30 / 3.26	2.25 / 3.14	2.20 / 3.06	2.16 / 2.98	2.13 / 2.93	2.08 / 2.83	2.03 / 2.74	1.97 / 2.63	1.93 / 2.55	1.88 / 2.47	1.84 / 2.38	1.80 / 2.33	1.76 / 2.25	1.74 / 2.21	1.71 / 2.16	1.68 / 2.12	1.67 / 2.10
28	4.20 / 7.64	3.34 / 5.45	2.95 / 4.57	2.71 / 4.07	2.56 / 3.76	2.44 / 3.53	2.36 / 3.36	2.29 / 3.23	2.24 / 3.11	2.19 / 3.03	2.15 / 2.95	2.12 / 2.90	2.06 / 2.80	2.02 / 2.71	1.96 / 2.60	1.91 / 2.52	1.87 / 2.44	1.81 / 2.35	1.78 / 2.30	1.75 / 2.22	1.72 / 2.18	1.69 / 2.13	1.67 / 2.09	1.65 / 2.06
29	4.18 / 7.60	3.33 / 5.42	2.93 / 4.54	2.70 / 4.04	2.54 / 3.73	2.43 / 3.50	2.35 / 3.33	2.28 / 3.20	2.22 / 3.08	2.18 / 3.00	2.14 / 2.92	2.10 / 2.87	2.05 / 2.77	2.00 / 2.68	1.94 / 2.57	1.90 / 2.49	1.85 / 2.41	1.80 / 2.32	1.77 / 2.27	1.73 / 2.19	1.71 / 2.15	1.68 / 2.10	1.65 / 2.06	1.64 / 2.03

* Reproduced by permission from *Statistical Methods*, 5th Edition, by George W. Snedecor, © 1956 by the Iowa State University Press.

TABLE D (continued)

Degrees of freedom for lesser mean square	Degrees of freedom for greater mean square																							
	1	2	3	4	5	6	7	8	9	10	11	12	14	16	20	24	30	40	50	75	100	200	500	∞
30	4.17 / 7.56	3.32 / 5.39	2.92 / 4.51	2.69 / 4.02	2.53 / 3.70	2.42 / 3.47	2.34 / 3.30	2.27 / 3.17	2.21 / 3.06	2.16 / 2.98	2.12 / 2.90	2.09 / 2.84	2.04 / 2.74	1.99 / 2.66	1.93 / 2.55	1.89 / 2.47	1.84 / 2.38	1.79 / 2.29	1.76 / 2.24	1.72 / 2.16	1.69 / 2.13	1.66 / 2.07	1.64 / 2.03	1.62 / 2.01
32	4.15 / 7.50	3.30 / 5.34	2.90 / 4.46	2.67 / 3.97	2.51 / 3.66	2.40 / 3.42	2.32 / 3.25	2.25 / 3.12	2.19 / 3.01	2.14 / 2.94	2.10 / 2.86	2.07 / 2.80	2.02 / 2.70	1.97 / 2.62	1.91 / 2.51	1.86 / 2.42	1.82 / 2.34	1.76 / 2.25	1.74 / 2.20	1.69 / 2.12	1.67 / 2.08	1.64 / 2.02	1.61 / 1.98	1.59 / 1.96
34	4.13 / 7.44	3.28 / 5.29	2.88 / 4.42	2.65 / 3.93	2.49 / 3.61	2.38 / 3.38	2.30 / 3.21	2.23 / 3.08	2.17 / 2.97	2.12 / 2.89	2.08 / 2.82	2.05 / 2.76	2.00 / 2.66	1.95 / 2.58	1.89 / 2.47	1.84 / 2.38	1.80 / 2.30	1.74 / 2.21	1.71 / 2.15	1.67 / 2.08	1.64 / 2.04	1.61 / 1.98	1.59 / 1.94	1.57 / 1.91
36	4.11 / 7.39	3.26 / 5.25	2.86 / 4.38	2.63 / 3.89	2.48 / 3.58	2.36 / 3.35	2.28 / 3.18	2.21 / 3.04	2.15 / 2.94	2.10 / 2.86	2.06 / 2.78	2.03 / 2.72	1.98 / 2.62	1.93 / 2.54	1.87 / 2.43	1.82 / 2.35	1.78 / 2.26	1.72 / 2.17	1.69 / 2.12	1.65 / 2.04	1.62 / 2.00	1.59 / 1.94	1.56 / 1.90	1.55 / 1.87
38	4.10 / 7.35	3.25 / 5.21	2.85 / 4.34	2.62 / 3.86	2.46 / 3.54	2.35 / 3.32	2.26 / 3.15	2.19 / 3.02	2.14 / 2.91	2.09 / 2.82	2.05 / 2.75	2.02 / 2.69	1.96 / 2.59	1.92 / 2.51	1.85 / 2.40	1.80 / 2.32	1.76 / 2.22	1.71 / 2.14	1.67 / 2.08	1.63 / 2.00	1.60 / 1.97	1.57 / 1.90	1.54 / 1.86	1.53 / 1.84
40	4.08 / 7.31	3.23 / 5.18	2.84 / 4.31	2.61 / 3.83	2.45 / 3.51	2.34 / 3.29	2.25 / 3.12	2.18 / 2.99	2.12 / 2.88	2.07 / 2.80	2.04 / 2.73	2.00 / 2.66	1.95 / 2.56	1.90 / 2.49	1.84 / 2.37	1.79 / 2.29	1.74 / 2.20	1.69 / 2.11	1.66 / 2.05	1.61 / 1.97	1.59 / 1.94	1.55 / 1.88	1.53 / 1.84	1.51 / 1.81
42	4.07 / 7.27	3.22 / 5.15	2.83 / 4.29	2.59 / 3.80	2.44 / 3.49	2.32 / 3.26	2.24 / 3.10	2.17 / 2.96	2.11 / 2.86	2.06 / 2.77	2.02 / 2.70	1.99 / 2.64	1.94 / 2.54	1.89 / 2.46	1.82 / 2.35	1.78 / 2.26	1.73 / 2.17	1.68 / 2.08	1.64 / 2.02	1.60 / 1.94	1.57 / 1.91	1.54 / 1.85	1.51 / 1.80	1.49 / 1.78
44	4.06 / 7.24	3.21 / 5.12	2.82 / 4.26	2.58 / 3.78	2.43 / 3.46	2.31 / 3.24	2.23 / 3.07	2.16 / 2.94	2.10 / 2.84	2.05 / 2.75	2.01 / 2.68	1.98 / 2.62	1.92 / 2.52	1.88 / 2.44	1.81 / 2.32	1.76 / 2.24	1.72 / 2.15	1.66 / 2.06	1.63 / 2.00	1.58 / 1.92	1.56 / 1.88	1.52 / 1.82	1.50 / 1.78	1.48 / 1.75
46	4.05 / 7.21	3.20 / 5.10	2.81 / 4.24	2.57 / 3.76	2.42 / 3.44	2.30 / 3.22	2.22 / 3.05	2.14 / 2.92	2.09 / 2.82	2.04 / 2.73	2.00 / 2.66	1.97 / 2.60	1.91 / 2.50	1.87 / 2.42	1.80 / 2.30	1.75 / 2.22	1.71 / 2.13	1.65 / 2.04	1.62 / 1.98	1.57 / 1.90	1.54 / 1.86	1.51 / 1.80	1.48 / 1.76	1.46 / 1.72
48	4.04 / 7.19	3.19 / 5.08	2.80 / 4.22	2.56 / 3.74	2.41 / 3.42	2.30 / 3.20	2.21 / 3.04	2.14 / 2.90	2.08 / 2.80	2.03 / 2.71	1.99 / 2.64	1.96 / 2.58	1.90 / 2.48	1.86 / 2.40	1.79 / 2.28	1.74 / 2.20	1.70 / 2.11	1.64 / 2.02	1.61 / 1.96	1.56 / 1.88	1.53 / 1.84	1.50 / 1.78	1.47 / 1.73	1.45 / 1.70
50	4.03 / 7.17	3.18 / 5.06	2.79 / 4.20	2.56 / 3.72	2.40 / 3.41	2.29 / 3.18	2.20 / 3.02	2.13 / 2.88	2.07 / 2.78	2.02 / 2.70	1.98 / 2.62	1.95 / 2.56	1.90 / 2.46	1.85 / 2.39	1.78 / 2.26	1.74 / 2.18	1.69 / 2.10	1.63 / 2.00	1.60 / 1.94	1.55 / 1.86	1.52 / 1.82	1.48 / 1.76	1.46 / 1.71	1.44 / 1.68
55	4.02 / 7.12	3.17 / 5.01	2.78 / 4.16	2.54 / 3.68	2.38 / 3.37	2.27 / 3.15	2.18 / 2.98	2.11 / 2.85	2.05 / 2.75	2.00 / 2.66	1.97 / 2.59	1.93 / 2.53	1.88 / 2.43	1.83 / 2.35	1.76 / 2.23	1.72 / 2.15	1.67 / 2.06	1.61 / 1.96	1.58 / 1.90	1.52 / 1.82	1.50 / 1.78	1.46 / 1.71	1.43 / 1.66	1.41 / 1.64
60	4.00 / 7.08	3.15 / 4.98	2.76 / 4.13	2.52 / 3.65	2.37 / 3.34	2.25 / 3.12	2.17 / 2.95	2.10 / 2.82	2.04 / 2.72	1.99 / 2.63	1.95 / 2.56	1.92 / 2.50	1.86 / 2.40	1.81 / 2.32	1.75 / 2.20	1.70 / 2.12	1.65 / 2.03	1.59 / 1.93	1.56 / 1.87	1.50 / 1.79	1.48 / 1.74	1.44 / 1.68	1.41 / 1.63	1.39 / 1.60
65	3.99 / 7.04	3.14 / 4.95	2.75 / 4.10	2.51 / 3.62	2.36 / 3.31	2.24 / 3.09	2.15 / 2.93	2.08 / 2.79	2.02 / 2.70	1.98 / 2.61	1.94 / 2.54	1.90 / 2.47	1.85 / 2.37	1.80 / 2.30	1.73 / 2.18	1.68 / 2.09	1.63 / 2.00	1.57 / 1.90	1.54 / 1.84	1.49 / 1.76	1.46 / 1.71	1.42 / 1.64	1.39 / 1.60	1.37 / 1.56

70	1.35 / 1.53	1.37 / 1.56	1.40 / 1.62	1.45 / 1.69	1.47 / 1.74	1.53 / 1.82	1.56 / 1.88	1.62 / 1.98	1.67 / 2.07	1.72 / 2.15	1.79 / 2.28	1.84 / 2.35	1.89 / 2.45	1.93 / 2.51	1.97 / 2.59	2.01 / 2.67	2.07 / 2.77	2.14 / 2.91	2.23 / 3.07	2.35 / 3.29	2.50 / 3.60	2.74 / 4.08	3.13 / 4.92	3.98 / 7.01
80	1.32 / 1.49	1.35 / 1.52	1.38 / 1.57	1.42 / 1.65	1.45 / 1.70	1.51 / 1.78	1.54 / 1.84	1.60 / 1.94	1.65 / 2.03	1.70 / 2.11	1.77 / 2.24	1.82 / 2.32	1.88 / 2.41	1.91 / 2.48	1.95 / 2.55	1.99 / 2.64	2.05 / 2.74	2.12 / 2.87	2.21 / 3.04	2.33 / 3.25	2.48 / 3.56	2.72 / 4.04	3.11 / 4.88	3.96 / 6.96
100	1.28 / 1.43	1.30 / 1.46	1.34 / 1.51	1.39 / 1.59	1.42 / 1.64	1.48 / 1.73	1.51 / 1.79	1.57 / 1.89	1.63 / 1.98	1.68 / 2.06	1.75 / 2.19	1.79 / 2.26	1.85 / 2.36	1.88 / 2.43	1.92 / 2.51	1.97 / 2.59	2.03 / 2.69	2.10 / 2.82	2.19 / 2.99	2.30 / 3.20	2.46 / 3.51	2.70 / 3.98	3.09 / 4.82	3.94 / 6.90
125	1.25 / 1.37	1.27 / 1.40	1.31 / 1.46	1.36 / 1.54	1.39 / 1.59	1.45 / 1.68	1.49 / 1.75	1.55 / 1.85	1.60 / 1.94	1.65 / 2.03	1.72 / 2.15	1.77 / 2.23	1.83 / 2.33	1.86 / 2.40	1.90 / 2.47	1.95 / 2.56	2.01 / 2.65	2.08 / 2.79	2.17 / 2.95	2.29 / 3.17	2.44 / 3.47	2.68 / 3.94	3.07 / 4.78	3.92 / 6.84
150	1.22 / 1.33	1.25 / 1.37	1.29 / 1.43	1.34 / 1.51	1.37 / 1.56	1.44 / 1.66	1.47 / 1.72	1.54 / 1.83	1.59 / 1.91	1.64 / 2.00	1.71 / 2.12	1.76 / 2.20	1.82 / 2.30	1.85 / 2.37	1.89 / 2.44	1.94 / 2.53	2.00 / 2.62	2.07 / 2.76	2.16 / 2.92	2.27 / 3.14	2.43 / 3.44	2.67 / 3.91	3.06 / 4.75	3.91 / 6.81
200	1.19 / 1.28	1.22 / 1.33	1.26 / 1.39	1.32 / 1.48	1.35 / 1.53	1.42 / 1.62	1.45 / 1.69	1.52 / 1.79	1.57 / 1.88	1.62 / 1.97	1.69 / 2.09	1.74 / 2.17	1.80 / 2.28	1.83 / 2.34	1.87 / 2.41	1.92 / 2.50	1.98 / 2.60	2.05 / 2.73	2.14 / 2.90	2.26 / 3.11	2.41 / 3.41	2.65 / 3.88	3.04 / 4.71	3.89 / 6.76
400	1.13 / 1.19	1.16 / 1.24	1.22 / 1.32	1.28 / 1.42	1.32 / 1.47	1.38 / 1.57	1.42 / 1.64	1.49 / 1.74	1.54 / 1.84	1.60 / 1.92	1.67 / 2.04	1.72 / 2.12	1.78 / 2.23	1.81 / 2.29	1.85 / 2.37	1.90 / 2.46	1.96 / 2.55	2.03 / 2.69	2.12 / 2.85	2.23 / 3.06	2.39 / 3.36	2.62 / 3.83	3.02 / 4.66	3.86 / 6.70
1000	1.08 / 1.11	1.13 / 1.19	1.19 / 1.28	1.26 / 1.38	1.30 / 1.44	1.36 / 1.54	1.41 / 1.61	1.47 / 1.71	1.53 / 1.81	1.58 / 1.89	1.65 / 2.01	1.70 / 2.09	1.76 / 2.20	1.80 / 2.26	1.84 / 2.34	1.89 / 2.43	1.95 / 2.53	2.02 / 2.66	2.10 / 2.82	2.22 / 3.04	2.38 / 3.34	2.61 / 3.80	3.00 / 4.62	3.85 / 6.66
∞	1.00 / 1.00	1.11 / 1.15	1.17 / 1.25	1.24 / 1.36	1.28 / 1.41	1.35 / 1.52	1.40 / 1.59	1.46 / 1.69	1.52 / 1.79	1.57 / 1.87	1.64 / 1.99	1.69 / 2.07	1.75 / 2.18	1.79 / 2.24	1.83 / 2.32	1.88 / 2.41	1.94 / 2.51	2.01 / 2.64	2.09 / 2.80	2.21 / 3.02	2.37 / 3.32	2.60 / 3.78	2.99 / 4.60	3.84 / 6.64

TABLE E
Critical values of chi square °

df						Probability under H_0 that $\chi^2 \geq$ chi square								
	.99	.98	.95	.90	.80	.70	.50	.30	.20	.10	.05	.02	.01	.001
1	.00016	.00063	.0039	.016	.064	.15	.46	1.07	1.64	2.71	3.84	5.41	6.64	10.83
2	.02	.04	.10	.21	.45	.71	1.39	2.41	3.22	4.60	5.99	7.82	9.21	13.82
3	.12	.18	.35	.58	1.00	1.42	2.37	3.66	4.64	6.25	7.82	9.84	11.34	16.27
4	.30	.43	.71	1.06	1.65	2.20	3.36	4.88	5.99	7.78	9.49	11.67	13.28	18.46
5	.55	.75	1.14	1.61	2.34	3.00	4.35	6.06	7.29	9.24	11.07	13.39	15.09	20.52
6	.87	1.13	1.64	2.20	3.07	3.83	5.35	7.23	8.56	10.64	12.59	15.03	16.81	22.46
7	1.24	1.56	2.17	2.83	3.82	4.67	6.35	8.38	9.80	12.02	14.07	16.62	18.48	24.32
8	1.65	2.03	2.73	3.49	4.59	5.53	7.34	9.52	11.03	13.36	15.51	18.17	20.09	26.12
9	2.09	2.53	3.32	4.17	5.38	6.39	8.34	10.66	12.24	14.68	16.92	19.68	21.67	27.88
10	2.56	3.06	3.94	4.86	6.18	7.27	9.34	11.78	13.44	15.99	18.31	21.16	23.21	29.59
11	3.05	3.61	4.58	5.58	6.99	8.15	10.34	12.90	14.63	17.28	19.68	22.62	24.72	31.26
12	3.57	4.18	5.23	6.30	7.81	9.03	11.34	14.01	15.81	18.55	21.03	24.05	26.22	32.91
13	4.11	4.76	5.89	7.04	8.63	9.93	12.34	15.12	16.98	19.81	22.36	25.47	27.69	34.53
14	4.66	5.37	6.57	7.79	9.47	10.82	13.34	16.22	18.15	21.06	23.68	26.87	29.14	36.12
15	5.23	5.98	7.26	8.55	10.31	11.72	14.34	17.32	19.31	22.31	25.00	28.26	30.58	37.70
16	5.81	6.61	7.96	9.31	11.15	12.62	15.34	18.42	20.46	23.54	26.30	29.63	32.00	39.29
17	6.41	7.26	8.67	10.08	12.00	13.53	16.34	19.51	21.62	24.77	27.59	31.00	33.41	40.75
18	7.02	7.91	9.39	10.86	12.86	14.44	17.34	20.60	22.76	25.99	28.87	32.35	34.80	42.31
19	7.63	8.57	10.12	11.65	13.72	15.35	18.34	21.69	23.90	27.20	30.14	33.69	36.19	43.82
20	8.26	9.24	10.85	12.44	14.58	16.27	19.34	22.78	25.04	28.41	31.41	35.02	37.57	45.32
21	8.90	9.92	11.59	13.24	15.44	17.18	20.34	23.86	26.17	29.62	32.67	36.34	38.93	46.80
22	9.54	10.60	12.34	14.04	16.31	18.10	21.24	24.94	27.30	30.81	33.92	37.66	40.29	48.27
23	10.20	11.29	13.09	14.85	17.19	19.02	22.34	26.02	28.43	32.01	35.17	38.97	41.64	49.73
24	10.86	11.99	13.85	15.66	18.06	19.94	23.34	27.10	29.55	33.20	36.42	40.27	42.98	51.18
25	11.52	12.70	14.61	16.47	18.94	20.87	24.34	28.17	30.68	34.38	37.65	41.57	44.31	52.62
26	12.20	13.41	15.38	17.29	19.82	21.79	25.34	29.25	31.80	35.56	38.88	42.86	45.64	54.05
27	12.88	14.12	16.15	18.11	20.70	22.72	26.34	30.32	32.91	36.74	40.11	44.14	46.96	55.48
28	13.56	14.85	16.93	18.94	21.59	23.65	27.34	31.39	34.03	37.92	41.34	45.42	48.28	56.89
29	14.26	15.57	17.71	19.77	22.48	24.58	28.34	32.46	35.14	39.09	42.56	46.69	49.59	58.30
30	14.95	16.31	18.49	20.60	23.36	25.51	29.34	33.53	36.25	40.26	43.77	47.96	50.89	59.70

° Abridged from Table IV of R. A. Fisher and F. Yates, *Statistical Tables for Biological, Agricultural, and Medical Research*, published by Oliver & Boyd, Ltd., Edinburgh, by permission of the authors and publishers.

TABLE F
Critical values of the Pearson-product
moment correlation coefficient °

	Level of significance for one-tailed test			
	.05	.025	.01	.005
df	Level of significance for two-tailed test			
	.10	.05	.02	.01
1	.988	.997	.9995	.9999
2	.900	.950	.980	.990
3	.805	.878	.934	.959
4	.729	.811	.882	.917
5	.669	.754	.833	.874
6	.622	.707	.789	.834
7	.582	.666	.750	.798
8	.549	.632	.716	.765
9	.521	.602	.685	.735
10	.497	.576	.658	.708
11	.476	.553	.634	.684
12	.458	.532	.612	.661
13	.441	.514	.592	.641
14	.426	.497	.574	.623
15	.412	.482	.558	.606
16	.400	.468	.542	.590
17	.389	.456	.528	.575
18	.378	.444	.516	.561
19	.369	.433	.503	.549
20	.360	.423	.492	.537
21	.352	.413	.482	.526
22	.344	.404	.472	.515
23	.337	.396	.462	.505
24	.330	.388	.453	.496
25	.323	.381	.445	.487
26	.317	.374	.437	.479
27	.311	.367	.430	.471
28	.306	.361	.423	.463
29	.301	.355	.416	.456
30	.296	.349	.409	.449
35	.275	.325	.381	.418
40	.257	.304	.358	.393
45	.243	.288	.338	.372
50	.231	.273	.322	.354
60	.211	.250	.295	.325
70	.195	.232	.274	.303
80	.183	.217	.256	.283
90	.173	.205	.242	.267
100	.164	.195	.230	.254

° Abridged from R. A. Fisher and F. Yates, *Statistical Tables for Biological, Agricultural, and Medical Research,* published by Oliver and Boyd, Ltd., Edinburgh, by permission of the authors and publishers.

Glossary of Research Methods Terms

Analysis of Covariance: A method of statistical control through which scores on the dependent variable are adjusted according to scores on a related, often antecedent, variable.

Analysis of Variance: A statistical technique by which it is possible to partition the variance in a distribution of scores according to separate sources or factors; although variance is partitioned, the statistical test tests for differences between means.

Applied Research: Research whose goal orientation is toward the solution of an immediate, specific, practical problem.

Aptitude: The potential for achievement.

Attitude: A tendency to possess certain feelings toward a specified class of stimuli.

Basic Research: Research whose goal orientation is directed toward goals such as theory building and contributing to the existing body of knowledge rather than the solution of an immediate problem.

Central Limit Theorem: A theorem which states that given any population with a mean and finite variance, as sample sized increases, the distribution of the sample means approaches a normal distribution with mean equal to the population mean and variance equal to the population variance divided by sample size.

Cluster Sampling: The selection of groups of elements called clusters rather than single elements; all elements of a cluster are included in the sample and the clusters are usually selected randomly from the larger population of clusters.

Coding: The translation of raw or observed data into categories or classifications in preparation for analysis.

Coefficient of Equivalence: A measure of test reliability based on the correlation between parallel forms of a test administered at approximately the same time to a single group of individuals.

Coefficient of Internal Consistency: A measure of test reliability computed on an internal analysis of the data secured from a single administration of the test.

Coefficient of Stability: A measure of test reliability based on the correlation between a specific test and a retest (usually a parallel form) given at a later time to the same group of individuals.

Common Factor Variance (in validity of measurement):   The co-variation or the variance that the observed test scores have in common with the scores of the criterion measure.

Concurrent Validity of a Test: The extent to which scores on the test match performance on contemporary criterion measures.

Confidence Interval: An interval estimate of a parameter constructed in such a way that the interval has a pre-determined probability of spanning the parameter.

Confounded Variables: Variables operating in a specific situation such that their effects cannot be separated.

Constant: A characteristic that has the same value for all observed units of a research study.

Construct Validity of a Test: The extent to which a test measures one or more dimensions of a theory or trait.

Contamination of Data: The presence of sampling biases, uncontrolled variables, or other factors which tend to make the data unusable for the purposes of the research.

Content Validity of a Test: The extent to which the content of the test items reflect the academic discipline, behavior, or whatever is under study.

Contingency Table: The array into which a set of enumeration data may be grouped according to two or more classification variables.

Continuous Variable: A variable that can take on any value within an interval(s) on the scale of measurement.

Control Group (in the context of an experiment): A group of subjects that does not receive any experimental treatment, and which is included for comparison purposes.

Correction for Continuity: A correction applied when certain techniques are used with small samples and the underlying distribution of the statistic is discrete but a continuous distribution from tabled values is used as an approximation for the underlying distribution.

Correlation: The extent of relationship between two variables; in statistical analysis the relationship must be quantifiable.

Correlation Coefficient: The measure of the extent of relationship between two variables.

Correlation Matrix: An array consisting of the correlation coefficients between several (three or more but usually considerably more) variables; if a square array is reported, the diagonal values are one and the coefficients below the diagonal are symmetric to those above, hence those below are usually not reported.

Covariate: The measure used in an analysis of covariance for adjusting the scores of the dependent variable.

Degrees of Freedom: The number of ways in which the data are free to vary; the number of observations minus the number of restrictions placed on the data.

Dependent Variable: The consequent (assumed to be) of the independent variable.

Directional Hypothesis: A hypothesis stated in such a manner that a direction, usually indicated by greater than or less than, is hypothesized for the results.

Discrete Variable: A variable that can take on only a limited, finite number of values.

Distribution: The total observations or a set of data on a variable; when observations are tabulated according to frequency for each possible score, we have a frequency distribution.

Experiment (in educational research): A research situation in which one or more factors are systematically varied according to a pre-conceived plan, in order to determine the effects of this variation.

Experimental Mortality: The dropout of subjects in terms of participation in the experiment; the lack of certain subjects to continue in the experiment until its conclusion.

Experimental Validity (two types): Internal: basic minimum necessary in terms of control, measurement, analysis, and procedures to make the results of the experiment interpretable. External: the extent and appropriateness of the generalizability of the experimental results.

Ex Post Facto Research: Research in which the independent variable(s) have already occurred and in which the researcher begins with the observations on a dependent variable, followed by a retrospective study of possible relationships and effects.

F-Ratio: A ratio of two variances or estimates of two variances computed to test the homogeneity of two variances; the underlying distribution is the F-distribution and when the statistical test is applied it is referred to as an F-test.

Fixed Effects Model: A term usually associated with analysis of variance; an analysis in which the levels of the independent variables are determined or "fixed" by the researcher rather than selecting the levels randomly from a larger population of possible levels.

Histogram: A graphical representation of the scores in a distribution, consisting of rectangles, the areas of the rectangles being proportional to the frequencies of the scores.

Homogeneity of Regression: The situation of equal or approximately equal regression coefficients within two or more groups, i.e., "the same regression."

Homoscedasticity: In the context of correlation, the condition that for all values of one variable the distributions of the values of the other variable have approximately the same variability.

Hypothesis: In general, a conjecture about a situation; in the context of inferential statistics, a statement about a parameter.

Independent Variable: In experimental research, the variables deliberately manipulated by the researcher; in non-experimental research, variables that classify or identify the participants.

Interaction (in context of analysis of variance): The effect of one independent variable upon another; the lack of the effect of one independent variable to remain constant over the levels of another.

Interval Scale: A measurement scale which in addition to ordering scores also establishes an equal unit in the scale so that distances between any two scores is of a known magnitude; also called equal-unit scale.

Kruskal-Wallis One-Way Analysis of Variance: A nonparametric technique which tests the ranks for two or more independent samples; the null hypothesis tested is that the sum of ranks and hence the averages of the populations from which the samples were selected, are equal.

Kuder-Richardson Methods: Procedures for determining the reliability of a test from a single form and administration of the test without splitting the test.

Latin Square: An $n \times n$ square array, including n different letters or symbols so arranged that each symbol appears once and once only in each row and column.

Level of Confidence: The probability associated with a confidence interval of the interval spanning the corresponding parameter; commonly used confidence levels in educational research are .95 and .99.

Level of Significance: A probability associated with the test of a hypothesis by statistical techniques which determines whether or not the hypothesis is rejected; commonly used levels in educational research are .05 and .01: also called the alpha level.

Likert-Type Scale: A scaling procedure commonly associated with measuring attitudes which requires a graded response to each item or statement. In scoring, the alternate responses to items are assigned numerical values and the individual's score is the sum of the numerical values corresponding to his response.

Linear Relationship: A relationship between two variables such that a straight line can be fitted satisfactorily to the points of the scattergram; the scatter of points will cluster elliptically around a straight line rather than some type of curve.

Longitudinal Studies: Studies which involve measuring the same subjects two or more times during a period of time (usually of considerable length such as several months or years); e.g., measuring the mathematics performance of the same students at yearly intervals as they progress from the fourth grade through senior high.

Maturation: Psychological and biological processes operating and causing systematic variation within individuals with the passing of time.

Mean: The sum of the scores in a distribution divided by the number of scores in the distribution.

Measurement: The assignment of numerals to objects or events according to specific rules.

Measures of Central Tendency: Points in a distribution that locate the distribution in terms of the measurement scale; points within the distribution about which the scores tend to group themselves.

Measures of Variability: Interval measures of a distribution that indicate the amount of dispersion or spread in the distribution.

Median: The point in a distribution below which 50 per cent of the scores lie.

Median Test: A nonparametric technique for testing whether or not two or more independent samples have been selected from populations with a common median.

Mode: The point or score of greatest frequency in a distribution.

Multiple Correlation: The relationship between a single variable and a combination of two or more other variables.

Multiple-Treatment Interference: Carry-over or delayed effects of prior experimental treatments that may affect the results of subsequent treatments when individual subjects receive two or more experimental treatments in succession.

Nominal Scale: A measurement scale that simply classifies elements into two or more categories indicating that elements are different, but not according to order or magnitude.

Normal Distribution: A family of bell-shaped, symmetrical distributions whose curve is described mathematically by a general equation sometimes called the Laplace-Gaussian normal probability function.

Norms: Descriptive statistics which summarize the test performance of a reference group of individuals.

Null Hypothesis (context of inferential statistics): A hypothesis stated so that no difference or no relationship is hypothesized; a nondirectional hypothesis.

Objectivity in Test Scoring: The extent to which equally competent scorers get the same results when scoring test performance.

One-Tailed Statistical Test: A directional test of a statistical hypothesis so constructed that the rejection region for the null hypothesis is located entirely in one tail.

Operational Definition: A definition expressed in terms of the processes or operations that are going to be used to measure the characteristic under study.

Optimum Allocation in Stratified Random Sampling: Selecting the sample in such a manner that the strata contributions to the sample are proportional to the strata populations and the strata variances.

Ordinal Scale: A measurement scale that classifies and ranks elements or scores.

Parallel Forms of a Test: Two (or more) forms of a test that are equivalent in terms of factors such as difficulty.

Parameter: A characteristic or measure of a population; e.g., the population mean.

Parsimony, Law of: Explanations of phenomena should be kept as simple as possible and consistent with the data.

Periodicity (in Systematic Sampling): A periodic characteristic that follows the listing of the elements and the selection interval so that a bias is introduced into the systematic sample.

Personality: In general, the sum total of an individual's mental and emotional characteristics; in the context of psychological testing, personality inventories usually are designed to measure characteristics such as emotional and social adjustment.

Pilot Study: A study conducted prior to the major research study which in some way is a small-scale model of the major study, conducted for the purpose of gaining additional information by which the major study can be improved; e.g., an exploratory use of the measurement instrument with a small group of subjects for the purpose of refining the instrument.

Population: The totality of all elements, subjects, or members that possess a specified set of one or more common characteristics which define it; in inferential statistics, the group to which inferences are made.

Post-Mortem Test: A statistical test conducted to locate the specific sources of significance when differences between three or more sample means are tested and the null hypothesis rejected.

Power of a Statistical Test: The probability of rejecting the null hypothesis when an alternate hypothesis is true; this probability is equal to one minus the probability of making a Type II or beta error.

Prediction: The estimation of scores on one variable from the information of one or more other variables.

Predictive Validity of a Test: The extent to which predictions made from the test are confirmed by subsequent data.

Projective Technique: A situation in which the individual responds to stimuli in such a way that he projects into his responses his feelings, traits, and the like; commonly associated with personality measurement.

Proportional Allocation in Stratified Random Sampling: Selecting the sample in a manner such that the sample size is divided among the strata proportional to population sizes of the strata.

Random Sample: A sample selected in such a way that the selection of one member of the population in no way affects the probability of selection of any other member.

Range: One plus the difference between the two extreme scores of a distribution.

Ratio Scale: A measurement scale which in addition to containing an equal unit also establishes an absolute zero in the scale.

Regression (as a threat to experimental validity): A tendency for groups, especially those selected on the basis of extreme scores, to regress toward a more average score on subsequent measurements, regardless of the experimental treatment.

Regression Equation: The equation of the regression line for a set of bivariate data.

Regression Line: The straight line of best fit (usually according to the least squares criterion) for a set of bivariate data.

Reliability Coefficient: A measure of the consistency of a test.

There are several methods of computing a reliability coefficient, depending upon the test and the test situation.

Reliability of Measurement: The consistency or accuracy of the measurement.

Response Set: The tendency for an individual to respond to items or other stimuli in a consistent manner, regardless of the content or context of the stimuli.

Sample: A subset of the population under study.

Sampling Ratio: The ratio of sample size to population size; also called the sampling fraction.

Scattergram: The plot of points determined by the cross tabulation of a set of bivariate data.

Significant Statistic: A statistic whose appearance by chance in the light of the hypothesis is less than the probability as designated by the significance level; e.g., a significant difference: a difference too large to be attributed to chance (random sampling fluctuation) in the light of the hypothesis.

Sign Test: A nonparametric technique for testing differences between two related samples in terms of direction rather than in terms of magnitude of the differences between pairs of observations. It derives its name from the plus and minus signs assigned to the directions of differences.

Simple Random Sample: A sample selected in such a way that all members of the population have an equal probability of selection; in the case of sampling without replacement from a finite population, every possible sample of a given size has an equal chance of being selected.

Skewed Distribution: A distribution whose shape is not symmetrical.

Split-Half Method: A procedure for determining the reliability of a test by which a single form of the test is divided into comparable halves, the scores on the halves correlated, and the reliability coefficient computed by applying a special formula known as the Spearman-Brown Step-Up Formula.

Standard Deviation: A measure of variability which is the positive square root of the variance.

Standard Error of a Statistic: The standard deviation of the underlying distribution of the statistic.

Standard Error of the Mean: The standard deviation of the underlying distribution of the mean.

Standard Normal Distribution: The normal distribution with a mean of zero and a standard deviation of one.

Standard Score: A score given in terms of standard deviation units from the mean of the distribution; a negative score indicates below the mean and a positive score above the mean.

Statistics: In the context of descriptive statistics, measures taken on a distribution; in the context of inferential statistics, measures or characteristics of a sample; in a more general sense, the theory, procedures and methods by which we analyze data.

Stratified Random Sampling: A sampling procedure through which the population is divided into two or more subpopulations, called strata, and elements for the sample are then randomly selected from the strata.

Subjects (used in the context of experiments): The individual participants in an experiment that are measured on the dependent variable; i.e., the observable units of an experiment.

Systematic Sampling: A selection procedure through which all sample elements are determined after the selection of the first element, since each element on a selection list is separated from the first element by a multiple of the selection interval.

Thurstone-Type Attitude Scale: A procedure that requires the individual to check all statements or items with which he agrees; all items have a scale value as determined by a panel of judges prior to use, and the individual's score is the median scale value of all the statements checked.

Trait: A tendency to respond in a certain way to situations.

Transformation: A systematic alteration in a set of observations through which specific characteristics of the set are changed.

Two-Tailed Statistical Test: A test so constructed that when testing the null hypothesis, the rejection region of the underlying distribution is contained in both tails of the distribution; a nondirectional test of a hypothesis.

Type I or Alpha Error: In inferential statistics, the error of rejecting a true hypothesis.

Type II or Beta Error: In inferential statistics, the error of failing to reject a false hypothesis.

Unbiased Statistic: A statistic computed in a manner such that the mean of its underlying distribution is the parameter that the statistic estimates.

Underlying Sampling Distribution of a Statistic: The distribution (usually theoretical) of all possible values of the statistic from all possible samples of a given size selected from the population.

Uniform Distribution: A distribution of scores such that all possible scores have equal frequency; also called the rectangular distribution.

Validity Coefficient: A coefficient based on the correlation of the scores of the test with scores on a criterion measure.

Validity of Measurement: The extent to which a measurement instrument measures what it is supposed to measure.

Variable: A characteristic that takes on different values for different observed units of a research study.

Variance: A measure of variability which is the average value of the squares of the deviations from the mean of the scores in a distribution.

Index